1985: Interindustry Forecasts of the American Economy

1985: Interindustry Forecasts of the American Economy

Clopper Almon, Jr.
Margaret B. Buckler
Lawrence M. Horwitz
Thomas C. Reimbold
University of Maryland

Lexington Books
D.C. Heath and Company
Lexington, Massachusetts
Toronto   London

Library of Congress Cataloging in Publication Data

Main entry under title:

1985: Interindustry forecasts of the American economy.

1. United States—Economic conditions—Mathematical models. 2. Inter-
industry economics. 3. Economic forecasting. I. Almon, Clopper. II. Title:
Interindustry forecasts of the American economy.
HC106.6.N56   330.9'73'092   73-21608
ISBN 0-669-92494-6

Published simultaneously in Canada.

Printed in the United States of America.

International Standard Book Number: 0-669-92494-6

Library of Congress Catalog Card Number: 73-21608

Contents

List of Figures

List of Tables

Acknowledgments

The research reported in this volume has been conducted by INFORUM, the Interindustry Economic Research Project of the University of Maryland. It has been made possible by contributions to the University by the Interindustry Economic Research Fund, the General Electric Foundation, and the Arthur D. Little Foundation. In addition, the interest and support through subscription by a number of firms is gratefully acknowledged. These firms include Rockwell International; National Distillers and Chemical Company; Scudder, Stevens and Clark; Wood, Struthers, and Winthrop; International Business Machines; Champion International; Xerox; Midland Ross; The Conference Board; Ernst and Ernst; Donaldson, Lufkin, and Jenrette; Babcock & Wilcox; Consad Research Corporation; Chase Econometric Associates; Stanford Research Institute; Business Week; C&O-B&O Railroad; Dow Chemical Corporation; Celanese Corporation; Foxboro Company; Bethlehem Steel Company; National Association of Machine Tool Builders; and Gulf and Western. Their help, prodding, and corrections have added greatly to the accuracy and readability of the work. Their interest and encouragement has kept us going when the mountain of work threatened to weigh us down.

Numerous graduate students at the University of Maryland have contributed to this work. Douglas Nyhus made the machine-tool and paper-industry applications described in Chapter 10. Dwight Porter contributed the appendix to Chapter 2 and developed some of the programs used in estimating the equations of that chapter. I. Gordon Odell contributed the section "Search for a Merger Partner" in Chapter 10. David Belzer, David Gilmartin, Edgar Carlyle, David Curry, Robert Kurz, Richard Froyen, Frederick Peacock, Benjamin Matta, and Charles Bausell made significant contributions to the work over the past seven years. Professor Thomas Mayor estimated an earlier set of investment equations for the model; his cost-of-capital variable survives in the present model. Professor Lloyd Atkinson was instrumental in helping us to estimate consumption directly from product shipment data.

All computations were performed at the University of Maryland Computer Science Center; its support is gratefully acknowledged.

Kay Miller, Gloria Jackson, and Patricia Drake, three excellent secretaries, have successively "managed" our research project and contributed to the preparation of the manuscript. Clopper Almon, father of the first author, read, corrected, and clarified the manuscript.

1   Overview

1985 stands twelve years ahead of us as this book is finished. Twelve years ago, America planned confidently for its future, and that future held what no one planned. Today, with less confidence and better techniques, in a society doubtful of its leadership but awakening to its problems, in a world of floating currencies and new alliances, business still must plan. It must decide what plants to build, what products to develop, what ventures to launch, and what hopes to abandon. It must move capital to the growing industries and avoid its waste on products whose days are numbered. It must find ways to satisfy our economic needs without destroying the earth, water, air, and fire around us. It is our hope that the work reported in this book can help with the decisions which these tasks impose.

However broad our hopes, this book is quite specific. It does not offer direct advice on the problems just raised, nor does it spin a web of social-science-fiction speculations about the future. Instead, it offers to those who must make decisions a tool, a model, to explore the future of the economy. And it contains forecasts to 1985 made with the aid of that model.

This tool was built to explore the future, but its makers hammered and shaped it upon the last of the past. We know that no past relationship can be relied upon to continue into the future, yet we know of nothing more reliable. Therefore, while we based the forecasts presented in this book on these past-shaped parts, at the same time we designed the tool so that those who have the wit to foresee changes in these relationships can easily fit new parts into it and explore their effect on the forecasts which the model then generates.

Do not expect, therefore, to find startling, incredible prophecies of the future here. The forecasts offered here are our seriously considered best judgment of the most probable forecast. Yet they are no mere straight-line extrapolation past trends, for the forces are already discernible which will make those lines bend—and sometimes break.

Our model is designed to give a comprehensive yet detailed year-by-year forecast of the American economy over the next twelve years. It is comprehensive, covering the entire economy, so that it can cover all uses of a resource such as labor or savings, all markets for a product such as copper, and all sources of pollutant such as smoke. It is detailed so that it can speak directly to the needs of business planners who must decide upon strategies for capital investment, diversification, product development, sales management, and provision of adequate supplies of materials. The forecast for one year contains over 15,000 numbers. These include:

1

- Sales of the products of 185 industries which cover the entire economy
- Consumer purchases, exports, imports, and inventory change of each of these products
- Capital equipment expenditure by 90 industries (combinations of the 185) which cover the whole economy
- Employment by these 90 industries
- Construction by 28 types

But the bulk of the 15,000 numbers come in the items which tie all the pieces together, which make the model a closely-knit, *consistent* whole, namely, the distribution of the sales of each of the 185 products to:

- Material used by each of the other 184 industries
- Capital investment by each of the 90 groups of industries
- Material used by each of the 28 types of construction
- Government purchases by 9 categories
- Inventory change
- Exports less imports (each shown separately)
- Personal consumption

Consistency is indeed the keynote of the model. An industry's investment is consistent with the growth in its output. Its employment is consistent with both its investment and its output. Its output is consistent with the demands from all the industries which use its products and with consumer and government demands. And these consumer and government demands are consistent—via the outputs, investment, and employment which they generate—with the labor force of the future years.

The total output of the model can be conveniently thought of as a table such as that shown in Figure 1-1. The 185 products sold are listed down the left side as sellers, and each row of the table shows the distribution of sales of a product among buyers. The sum of all entries to the right of the heavy vertical line equals gross national product. The model produces a table such as this for each year of the next twelve.

This sort of detail means that it is no longer necessary or appropriate for a maker of printing presses to relate his sales projections crudely to GNP. The model provides him projections of equipment purchases by newspapers and by commercial printing, which are already part of a carefully worked-out model of the whole economy. Nor need the refiner of railroad fuel look to GNP forecasts, for the model provides a forecast of railroad traffic based on the output of everything hauled by railroads. And so on for many another product; *this model bridges the gap between aggregate GNP projections and the specific markets in which the product is sold.*

In this introductory chapter, we shall describe in a brief and simple fashion

Figure 1-1. Distribution of Sales of 185 Products to Type of Buyer

Buyer / Seller	185 — Products Bought for Use in Production	90 — Capital Equipment Buyers	28 — Types of Structure Purchased	9 — Government Categories	4 — Other Final Demand Categories			
					Plus Exports	Less Imports	Inventory Change	Personal Consumption
185 Products Produced and Sold	A Matrix / Sales to Intermediate Use	B Matrix / Sales to Capital Equipment Investment	C Matrix / Sales to Construction Investment	G Matrix / Sales to Federal and State & Local Government				
	Employment (90 Industries)							

GNP — COMPONENTS

how the whole forecasting model works, explain how to read the forecasts, and then look at the picture which they paint of the future of the American economy. The next eight chapters describe the individual parts of the basic model and frequently raise and partially answer the question we are most commonly asked: "If you had built a model like this five years ago, how well would it have forecast where we are today?" The tenth chapter recounts a number of applications to problems of business forecasting.

How the Forecasts Are Made

Any one forecast is the result of three steps: make structural forecasts, project outside factors, and combine by calculation. More explicitly, we take first:

Step (1). Specify *structural relationships* in the economy, such as:

— How much plastic will be used per automobile in 1985? Or more generally,
— How much input will a unit of each product require from each other product in 1985 and how much in each intervening year?
— How will consumers divide each dollar of additional income among the various consumer goods?
— What fraction of the increase in demand will be supplied by imports?
— How much investment will each industry need for each million dollars of expansion in its output? How rapidly will it install the new capacity after the need is felt?
— How rapidly will productivity change in each industry?

Note that the answers to these questions do not determine the size of the economy, but only its proportions, its shape, or structure. To determine the absolute size, we go on to take:

Step (2). Project outside factors such as population, labor force, employment, number of households, defense spending by product, and other government spending by category. This step also includes projections of interest rates, depreciation rates, and relative international prices.

The first two steps involve a great deal of both discretion and econometric analysis, but judgment has the last word before proceeding to the final step, which is done entirely inside the computer, namely:

Step (3). Calculate the forecasts by combining the overall controls provided by the outside factors with the structure. The basic logic here is *to determine the course of after-tax consumer income which, together with the specified government demand, yields the specified level of employment.* Note carefully this logic. In the basic model, we do *not* calculate income, apply assumed tax rates, and drive consumption with the after-tax income so generated. That procedure could give employment far out of line with the labor force if the tax rates were badly set. Implicitly, we assume that Congress will adjust tax rates so that by 1980 or 1985 we will be near full employment.

Work on prices, wages, and income, which will be the subject of a subsequent book, will enable us to check whether present tax rates would give full employment. But that check is not crucial to the logic of the basic model, which, to repeat, assumes that after-tax income will be such as to give us some specified level of employment.

Let us now examine a little more closely how each of the three steps has been taken.

Structural Forecasts

Consumption expenditures per capita by product have been related to income per capita, rate of change of this income, relative prices, time, and, in some cases, the proportions of the population in specific age groups. In finding this relationship, we used a comparison of households of different incomes to determine the long-term response, or elasticity, of expenditures on various products to changes in income levels. Then we impose this income elasticity in a time-series study which uses income and other variables mentioned above to explain the actual growth of consumption expenditure. This analysis was done for each of the 133 (out of 185) products which consumers buy. Since there are no published historical series for personal consumption expenditures in this much detail, we have had to make our own series from five-digit product shipments, exports, imports, and the allocation factors used in making "benchmark" national accounts. Simulation testing of the equations—estimating through 1963 and forecasting through 1971—has led to some revisions in the assumed income elasticities. Chapter 2 describes this work in detail.

Equipment investment equations—the subject of Chapter 3—were derived from an analysis of the postwar investment behavior of the 90 industries into which the 185 products were grouped. (The grouping was necessary because investment data are not available in the 185 product detail.) The basic assumption of the equations is that the capital an industry desires, K^*, depends on the gross output, Q, of that industry and the cost of capital, r, to the industry. The equation used is simply $K^* = aQr^\sigma$, where a is a constant and σ shows the percentage by which the desired capital output ratio goes down when the price of capital goes up 1 percent. Actual capital stock, however, is not always—indeed, is scarcely ever—equal to desired stock. Only gradually do firms invest to bring the stock up to the desired level when output has risen. Our equations allow for the spreading, over up to six years, of the spending necessary to bring capital up to the desired level. How much of the total needed is spent in the first year in which it is needed, and how much in the second, and so on, is determined separately for each of the industries. (The technique used is the polynomial interpolation or "Almon" distributed lag). Into the calculation of r, the real cost of capital, go the real interest rate (the nominal rate minus the rate of inflation), the physical depreciation rate, the depreciation rate for tax purposes, the tax rate, and the investment tax credit, trends in equipment costs, and trends in the price of the product produced.

In the selection of the forecasting equation, we combine *a priori* expectations with the desire for a good fit to historical data. We expect that the life of capital is about what is legally allowed and that an increase in output should eventually lead to an equal percentage increase in capital, provided that r does not change. We have found that if we ignore these expectations in the process of curve fitting, we shall often find them violated in the results. But on the other hand, we can often make the equations conform closely to them at very little cost to the closeness of the fit to the historical data. Thus our equations are not just the outcome of a curve fitting exercise, but they have some economic sensibility built into them.

Again it must be noted that there are no published historical series on equipment investment by industry which add up to the total in the national accounts. We have had to make up our own series from a variety of sources.

Our work on *construction* builds on a broad foundation of data and ideas inherited from previous architects of residential construction equations, but it clears new land in all the other categories. For residential construction, we use total consumption, the number of households, the housing stock, and the relative cost of buying and renting to explain fundamental demand. Cyclical fluctuations in credit availability are reflected by the difference between long-term and short-term interest rates. General industrial construction and that for particular industries such as stores or telephone lines or railroads, are related to the output of the appropriate industry or industries and to its stock of buildings. Chapter 4 gives the full picture.

Inventory change is not a major factor in growth, but it absorbs part of the productive power of the economy and must be accounted for. Moreover, the inventory equations must give reasonable results in the first few years of the forecast or when the model is run to simulate cycles, so these equations also get a chapter, the fifth, to themselves.

Imports are related to the domestic demand for the product, and *exports*, to that demand in the previous year. They also consider relative international prices and are influenced by changes in the exchange rate. Chapter 6 describes this part of the model, which has been much exercised of late.

Government demands have been divided into nine categories, five Federal:

1. Defense
2. Atomic Energy Commission
3. National Aeronautics and Space Administration
4. Commodity Credit Corporation
5. Other Federal

and four state and local:

6. Education
7. Health, Welfare and Sanitation
8. Public Safety
9. General

The state and local categories are related to consumer income and to the school-aged population; the federal categories are all specified independently of the model. Finding the past composition and totals for these items, fitting equations to them or simply projecting them into the future, as the case may be, is the business of Chapter 7.

A never-ending pursuit is the projection of the *input-output coefficients* such as the dollars of steel used in automobiles per dollar of automobile output, or in general, the use per unit of output of each of the ingredients. It is these coefficients which link the GNP components discussed so far with product outputs and industry employment. They make it possible to fill in the parts of Figure 1-1 labeled "A Matrix," "B Matrix," "C Matrix," and "G Matrix." The sales in these matrices for the year 1963 are shown in a table prepared by the Commerce Department. Before forecasting into the future, we had first to bring that table up to date. We, therefore, first brought the Commerce Department table up to 1967, the year of the most recent economic censuses, and then brought this 1967 table forward, by a balancing procedure, to be consistent with all the 1971 data which we could find, especially the 1971 *Annual Survey of Manufactures*.

We have gathered historical data on trends in a number of the input-output coefficients. In particular, the rows for paper, petroleum refining, steel, nonferrous metals, and machine-tools have been studied in some detail. Logistic curves have been estimated and are applied to forecast the individual coefficients in these rows. These curves either rise toward a finite ceiling or decline to a floor at or above zero. For other rows, where we have not yet analyzed the coefficients in detail, we change all coefficients in the row by the same percentage. This percentage is also obtained from a logistic curve. In this case, it is estimated by comparing the history of actual intermediate use—including use by construction—with what it would have been had the input-output coefficients remained constant. Similar but separate curves are estimated for each row of the B matrix, which distributes equipment investment by buyers to the various types of equipment. Although this sort of "across-the-row" coefficient change leaves much to be desired, it insures that no broad and pervasive movements are left out of consideration. All this work is the matter of Chapter 8.

Employment, the subject of Chapter 9, is calculated by dividing output by labor productivity. Productivity forecasts in turn involve a cyclical variable such as output or its rate of change, and a trend variable, either time or the average installation date of the capital equipment in the industry. The use of this last variable is the outcome of many attempts to try to make labor productivity depend on capital investment. Productivity may move along at an exponential rate relative to the trend variable, or it may accelerate or slow down relative to that variable. In many industries it slows down.

The parts described in Chapters 2 through 9 form a basic model. Although the precise form of these parts is recent, a basic model with essentially these parts has been operating for some seven years. A number of applications have been made to such diverse problems as evaluating diversification possibilities for an aerospace company, detailed analysis of the products and markets of the paper industry, projection of pollution costs of alternative growth patterns, and search for a minimum-risk way to enter the machine tool business. These and other applications are discussed in Chapter 10.

The basic model, as described in this book, avoids consideration of any financial flows. Three further parts, to be the subject of a subsequent volume, extend and complete the model by adding wages, prices, and income flows. Wage equations will relate changes in wages in each industry to labor-supply factors such as the level of unemployment and the Consumer Price Index, and to demand factors such as the level of output, its rate of change, and labor productivity. Price equations will use previous changes in unit labor and material costs as supply factors and changes in output as demand factors. These equations work with a monthly period, so that the wages of, say January, can go into the prices of February, while the prices of December went into the wages of January. Actually, the lag between changes in prices and wages or between costs and prices is not just one month, but is spread over a number of months. The precise shape of those lags is one of the principal subjects of study. Finally, from the wages and prices, a final link calculates personal income, taxes, and disposable income. In the process, it develops corporate profits, dividends, the distribution of income by size class, social security and unemployment payments, other transfers, and the income of the federal, state, and local governments. A working version of the price, wage, and income sections is nearing completion as this volume goes to press.

Forecasts of the Overall Controls

Once the structural forecasts are completed, and the equations are selected and set to go, we have to take a few forecasts from outside the model to guide it. We use the Census Bureau's projection of population (Series E) and household formation, and the Bureau of Labor Statistics' projection of the labor force. These projections assume a 2.1-child family as the norm. Interest rates and the real cost of capital must be set by assumption. The exchange rate was introduced after the devaluation of the dollar in 1971, but by 1973 it was no longer clear what "the" exchange rate was. We have used a weighted average of recent rates but have assumed that the effects of the changes will be spread over a number of years. The rate is manually adjusted so that by 1980 and afterwards the current-plus-long-term-capital account will be in balance.

Calculations

The course of the calculation is summarized in Figure 1-2. Connections shown in solid lines are in the basic, real model; dotted lines show financial links developed in the subsequent volume. The boxes shown on the left side are all exogenous, specified from outside the model, except that as the forecast moves into the future, the "outputs of previous years" become the forecasts for those years. We begin with a trial value of disposable income (and relative prices), and calculate personal consumption expenditure (PCE). The total PCE, along with household and interest rate forecasts, determine residential and certain other types of construction such as private hospitals and schools. Construction by type is converted to a bill of materials by putting it through the C matrix. Likewise, the exogenous government demands by program are converted to bills of materials by the G matrix. Equipment spending is then forecast from outputs of previous years and exogenous assumptions about the cost of capital. Industry-related construction is handled similarly. These two can then be converted from purchases by buyers to purchases by types of machinery bought or to construction materials by the B and C matrixes, respectively. By adding Consumption + Exports + Government + Investment, we get the list of total final demands by industry. By use of the A matrix of input-output coefficients, these final demands are converted to product outputs. Final demand for cars is converted into demand for steel, paint, tires, upholstery. The demand so generated for steel is converted into demands for iron ore, coal, oil, electricity, and so on. At the same time, imports and inventory change are calculated. From changes in output and capital investment, labor productivity is determined. Divided by it, product outputs yield employment, which, subtracted from the labor force, leaves unemployment. If the unemployment so attained is not close to that previously specified, we change the assumed disposable income, and recalculate the whole model.

The portions connected by dotted lines show how wages, prices, profits, taxes, and disposable income can then be calculated. We will use this portion of the model to ask whether the present tax functions leave a disposable income equal to that required to achieve the specified level of employment.

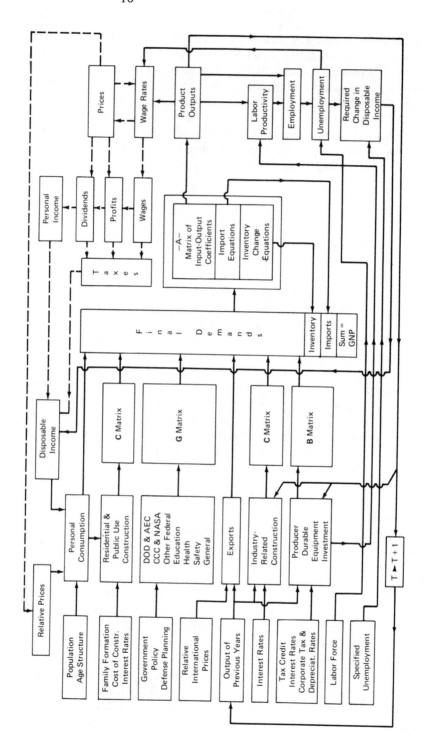

Figure 1-2. Flow Diagram of the Inforum Model with Solution Procedure

How the Forecasts Are Presented

Figure 1-1 is a convenient way to *think* about the forecasts; but if printed, it would measure about four feet by thirty feet, so it is hardly convenient as a way to *look* at them. We have devised several ways to present them to make them easy to read. These are shown, for the real parts of the model, in the End Tables at the end of this volume. These End Tables summarize all of the forecast and illustrate all of the types of tables. Inclusion of all tables and graphs of all types would make this volume too heavy to read easily. Instead, a separate *Supplement*, photo-offset from computer pages, is available to provide the full detail.

The first four pages of the End Tables gives the precise description of the sectors of our model in terms of the Standard Industrial Classification (SIC). The last of these pages also notes some peculiarities of the statistical definitions of consumption, exports and imports. Anyone perplexed, for example, by the negative export of "margins" should consult those notes. A summary of the GNP accounts in familiar form appears on E6. Here all dollar amounts are in 1971 constant dollars. Total employment, the unemployment rate, and the key assumptions appear on E7. Next, on pages E8 and E9, come growth rates between selected pairs of years for the items shown on the previous two pages. These and all the growth rates in the model are expressed in percent per year, abbreviated hereafter to "%py," and are based on *continuous*, not annual, compounding.

Personal consumption expenditure (PCE) on the 55 largest items in the consumer's budget are presented on page E10; page E11 shows growth rates for the PCE items.

This pattern of values followed by growth rates extends through pages for exports, imports, producer durable equipment investment by the 90 investing industries, 28 types of construction, employment by industry, sales by product, and labor productivity in 90 industries.

A more vivid way of looking at this same data is illustrated on E38. There we bring together and plot the forecasts of output, personal consumption, export and import for one of the 185 industries, in this case, sector 7, Fruits and vegetables. Besides the plot, each series is listed with historical and forecast values. The 1971 value of output is taken as 100 for these plots. Such pages have been made and studied for all 185 products.

Still another sort of plot gives output, investment, employment, and labor productivity for one of the 90 investment industries. Page E39 gives the one for sector 1, Agriculture. The *Supplement* has such pages for all 90 of the investment-employment industries.

None of the presentations so far show the thousands of intermediate flows which fill the **A**, **B**, **C**, and **G** matrixes of of Figure 1-1. These appear in the pages we refer to as the "matrix listing." Page E40 presents a sample for one row of the table, namely, sector 110, Pumps, compressors, and blowers. Here the *buyers* are listed down the left side and their purchases in 1971, 1973, 1975, 1980, and 1985 shown to the right on the same line. The growth rates of the purchases between selected pairs of these years are shown further to the right. On these pages, note the four-way division of sales; the model distinguishes between (1) intermediate use of materials components or spare parts, (2) capital equipment investment, (3) construction materials and components and (4) personal consumption, government, exports and imports. Because of this detail by buyer, the model actually specifies more than 185 different products, for "Pumps, compressors, and blowers" sold to capital investment by petroleum extraction are different from the "Pumps, compressors, and blowers" which go into airplanes. Matrix listing pages for all products are found in the *Supplement*. All sales amounting to more than 0.4 percent of total sales in a row are listed there.

At this point, we urge the reader to get acquainted with the End Tables and the *Supplement*. If, as we describe in the following section what the forecasts say, he will check our statements with end tables or the *Supplement*, then he will learn his way around in them and doubtless discover interesting paths on which we have not commented. He may also—though we hope he won't—find some error. If so, we would like to know about it.

A Picture of the Economy: 1973-85

The Great Slowdown

In the decade ahead, the growth of the American economy will steadily slacken. Percentagewise, each year will bring a smaller and smaller increase in the labor force, labor will grow more productive at a slower and slower rate; gross national product will creep up ever more modestly. The sedate seventies and the aging eighties follow the soaring sixties. U.S. economic growth tapers off. This theme pervades our whole forecast; the growth rates in Table 1-1 show it in broad outline.

Table 1-1
Aggregate Growth Rates In Percent per Year—%py

	1961-69	1969-73	1973-75	1975-80	1980-85
GNP (Real)	4.6	3.7	3.1	2.8	2.2
Labor Force	2.1	1.8	1.7	1.6	1.1
GNP/employed person	2.2	1.9	1.1	1.2	1.0

Between 1980 and 1985, the labor force, labor productivity, and GNP will be growing less than half as fast as they grew from 1963 to 1969. This is not a prophecy of gloom nor of depression, but of prosperous maturity. It entails no swelling of the ranks of the unemployed and no disastrous declines in the outputs of any major industry. It *does* involve substantial shifts in the composition of GNP and significant changes in the growth rates of some industries. Firms which expect prosperity to mean a return to growth rates of the 1960s could be sharply disappointed. Governments which have counted on the rapid growth of revenue from sales and income taxes to cover soaring welfare and medical costs will find that they must raise tax rates or cut programs. Exuberant youth has energy for all sorts of projects; maturity demands discretion in its use. As the economy matures, we shall, as a nation, have to consider more and more carefully how we spend our resources.

The sources of this retardation are three:

1. A slowdown in the growth rate of the labor force
2. A shift of more and more employment into sectors with low rates of productivity growth
3. A decline in the growth rates of productivity in individual sectors

The first of these factors is well known and common to all long-run forecasts of the U.S. economy. The rate of growth of the labor force declines because it was abnormally high during the late 1960s, which saw not only the entry of the children of the postwar baby-boom into the labor force but also an influx of women released from maternal care of infants by the "baby-bust" of the early 1960s. By 1980, that same baby-bust will begin to erode the number of new workers.

Our second factor, the shift to industries with slowly growing productivity, is ignored by the many long-run forecasts which begin from a projection of GNP. But it should be clear that there can be no such thing as a correct aggregate projection of GNP, for the rate of growth of GNP depends upon the rate of growth of labor productivity, and that differs widely among industries. Only when we know what the industrial composition of GNP will be can we venture a guess of what its growth will be.

Our forecasts, as we have said, show a shift toward sectors with low rates of productivity increase. Employment in the sector Finance and services (including financial, medical, and business services, but excluding transport, trade, and utilities) will swell from 21.6 percent of all employment in 1971 to 25.5 percent by 1985. But the rate of growth of labor productivity in this sector will average only 0.65 percent per year. Wholesale and retail trade employed 21.7 percent of all workers in 1971; by 1985, that share will rise to 22.7 percent. Productivity gains in this sector will average only 1.6%py over the period. All sectors averaging less than 1.6%py in productivity gains engaged 56.6 percent of privately employed workers in 1971; by 1985, they will be up to 61.6 percent. At the other end of the spectrum, sectors with rapidly growing productivity such as agriculture and railroads have shrinking employment. Forecasts which neglect these shifts will miss on the high side, and all the aggregate forecasts of which we know are higher than is ours.

"Output" is, of course, difficult to measure in the service industries, and part of our slowdown in GNP may conceivably stem from inadequate measures of output. If one is of the opinion that productivity per worker has been rising more than 0.65 percent per year in the medical, legal, teaching, ministerial, advertising, or engineering professions, then one should revise upward our GNP figures and declare all of the addition to be in a revaluation of services. Personally, we find that the 0.65 percent per year productivity increase derived from official sources is rather generous for what we see going on in hospitals, courts, classrooms, pulpits, and ad agencies.

The third factor behind the slowdown ahead, the retardation in the rate of increase in productivity in individual industries, is discernible in nearly two-thirds of the industries. Some notable examples are shown in Table 1-2. In all these major industries, the drop between 1971-75 and the 1980-85 period is 0.8 percentage points per year or more.

Naturally, we expect the productivity rise to slacken in the future only because we have seen it slowing down in the past. We conducted a contest among various forms of productivity equations and picked the slowing-down kind only if it out-performed the constant or speeding-up kinds in explaining past, historical changes in productivity. Perusal of the productivity plots in the *Supplement* reveals, besides the ten sectors in Table 1-2, a number of other clear cases of slowdown.

What has caused this slowdown? We have only our untested speculations. One

Table 1-2
The Slowdown in Labor Productivity

Industry	Productivity Growth Rate in %py		
	1971-75	1975-80	1980-85
Agriculture	6.2	5.7	5.3
Mining	3.7	2.1	1.2
Industrial Chemicals	6.6	4.8	4.6
Petroleum Refining	9.0	5.1	4.3
Steel	1.7	.6	.4
Non-Ferrous Metals	1.8	1.4	1.0
Household Appliances	4.1	2.9	2.6
Motor Vehicles	2.0	.9	.4
Airlines	4.8	3.2	2.5
Communication	3.6	3.0	2.7

line of explanation sees the cause in investment. During the depression, World War II, and the Korean War, know-how accumulated; but shortage of funds or of material kept it from being implemented. From the mid-fifties to the mid-sixties, many previously pent-up ideas were incarnated into productive machinery. Often the innovations were simple, perhaps replacing push carts by conveyors— but they required funds, engineering time, and the incentive of high wage rates. After a glorious decade of productivity gains, the well of ideas began to run dry in the late sixties and early seventies. We merely extend that drying-up of opportunities for large productivity gains at low cost.

An entirely different possible explanation hinges on the structure of the labor force. Since 1965, when the productivity slowdown became noticeable, youths, women, and blacks have been entering the labor force in unprecedented numbers. It may seem the most benighted prejudice to blame these groups for the slowdown, but their common complaint is that they are paid less than middle-aged white men. Now if wages reflect productivity, then when workers of less than average pay are employed, productivity falls, or at least rises more slowly than it would otherwise. If this explanation is right, the slowdown should pass over into a new burst of productivity in a few years when the youth component of the labor force wanes, the women's share stabilizes, and the black-white differential closes. Since we project the slowdown to persist, we implicitly reject this labor force explanation. It is a better argument for explaining an overall slowdown in productivity—involving a shift of the labor force among industries—than for explaining the industry-by-industry slowdown which we observe. It just seems irrelevant to the slowdown in Agriculture or Steel, seems incapable of explaining so sharp a turn as occurs in, say, Tires and tubes,[a] and seems inapplicable in Communication, where productivity slowed down while the percentage of women remained steady. The labor force explanation might make a good topic for research, but until it is better established, we shall stick with our bearish expectations.

Because our aggregate GNP projection *is* low by comparison with all others we have seen, we must stress that none of the others have been based on so careful an analysis of productivity gains industry-by-industry. We urge the reader to look at each and every productivity plot in the *Supplement*, as we have done. In comparison with history, none of the projections seems too low to us. A number of them, indeed, look rather on the high side of plausible. A few, such as the one for Communication equipment (67), may look low at first glance, but if one also observes the flattening out of that industry's output and employment, it seems reasonable. Higher rates of productivity increase would cut back employment, and these cuts would stiffen union opposition to changes which eliminate jobs.

[a]Throughout this book, we capitalize the first and only the first letter of a sector name. Thus, "Tires and tubes" refers to one sector; "Construction, mining, and oil-well machinery" is also one sector, but "Construction, Mining, and Oil-well machinery" would be three sectors.

Because our forecasts are lower than the others we have seen, we have, where in doubt, tried to err on the high side. This desire explains our choice of the 4.0 percent unemployment target. The increase of youths, women, and blacks in the labor force means that to get down to 4.0 percent unemployment, the age-sex-race-specific unemployment rates must be lower than they were when an overall 4.0 percent rate was achieved in the mid-1960s. Four-percent unemployment today means a tighter, more inflation-prone labor market than it did in 1965. The percentage of young workers, however, will decline; and unemployment rates for blacks and for women should gradually approach those for white men. To follow our maxim, "If in doubt, shoot high," we have therefore held to the 4-percent target for 1975 and later years, despite recent experience with rapid inflation at higher unemployment rates.

The Composition of GNP

With a bit of luck, the private sector will grow faster than the public sector in the decade ahead. The luck needed is to avoid war or heavy armament expenditures and to hold the birth rate to the two-child norm. With those conditions, we expect government purchases of goods and services will average only 1.8%py from 1973 to 1983 while total GNP averages 2.7%py and personal consumption climbs at a 3.1%py rate. These rates and all that follow refer to constant-dollar amounts; inflation will make the current-dollar values grow more rapidly. Gross private capital formation climbs more slowly than consumption, 1.8%py, but the sluggishness is mostly in residential construction, which barely regains its high 1973 level by 1983. Producer durable equipment (PDE), on the contrary, steps along at 3.3%py. But PDE starts with a dash—10.5%py between 1971 and 1975—and ends at a crawl—2.6%py from 1980 to 1985.

In government, the laggards are defense, education, and highway construction. Defense, by assumption, declines to 1975 and then rises slowly at about 1.0%py. Nondefense federal expenditure for goods and services (excluding transfers and subsidies) grows faster than defense and averages 2.9%py from 1973 to 1983. That growth is a continuation of this past trend for this item. Education and educational construction will level out as the number of school-aged children levels out. Highway construction tapers off as the interstate program nears completion.

In foreign trade, both exports and imports will grow faster than GNP. Exports will outpace imports from 1973 to 1978, averaging 6.8%py compared to only 2.8%py for imports. This improvement in the balance of payments reflects our assumption that exchange rates will not change significantly until the long-term effects of recent devaluations and float have been worked out. That will take until 1978. Our equations seem to think that the devaluation was excessive and that by 1978 the balance of payments will be some $8.2 billion in surplus. A few years of such surpluses would be welcome enough; but, after foreign dollar holdings have been drawn down, such surpluses will necessitate an appreciation of the dollar. We introduce an appreciation of about 0.3 percent per year, beginning in 1979, to bring the balance of payments back to equilibrium by 1985. From 1978 to 1985, imports will therefore outstrip exports and grow at 4.6%py, by comparison with exports' pace of 3.2%py. The timing in this scenario could prove far wrong. The dollar may begin to recover long before 1979. We adopted this timing to show the full effects of present changes before bringing the balance of payments back to equilibrium by the end of the forecast. How the float will work with huge foreign dollar holdings we do not pretend to know. The timing we have adopted seems not altogether implausible.

The Forecasts by Industry

Food industries will show steady, if moderate, growth. Canned and frozen foods lead the list with a 3.7%py growth from 1971 to 1985, while Dairy products are the cow's tail with only 1.3%py. Even this much growth is good news for Dairy products, which have remained almost constant since 1958. The equations of the model attribute the slight rise to the increase in the number of babies as the girls of the postwar baby-boom become young mothers. The Dairy recovery will be good news for the Dairy machinery industry, which should see its sales shoot up 48 percent in the next five years. Soft drinks and flavorings also grow faster than total consumption at 3.4%py. Little leaven raises the old staff-of-life, Bakery products (1.7%py); and the once-luxury, Meat, simmers along at 2.6%py. Poultry and eggs come to roost at only 1.0%py. Fruit and vegetable raising grows 2.5%py, but it is the input into Canned and frozen foods and into Fats and oil that sprout fast; consumer purchases of fresh fruits and vegetables are stunted to 0.8%py. Grain growing maintains 1.4%py with help of a 3.0%py growth in its exports; domestic use averages 1.3%py. Perhaps we have underrated the strength of the natural foods movement, but our forecasts show the basic meat-bread-eggs-milk-vegetable menu to expand only about 1.4%py faster than population's 0.9%py. The rapid growth in the food sectors is confined to the instant, indigestible, or intoxicating.

The *Apparel* industry, excluding the knits, sagged sadly after 1967. Sales slackened partly because the rest of the industry had to make room for the knits and also because the fashion world ran into consumer opposition. In the long run, we expect that clothes will exert their old pull on the consumer's dollar and that the apparel industry will parade off at 5.9%py from 1971 to 1975. The general slowdown then sets in, and Apparel's growth rate drops to 2.7%py from 1975 to 1980 and creeps along at 1.3% py from 1980 to 1985. The popularity of knits, however, is much a matter of fashion, and our equations are not much good at predicting it. The total demand for clothes, however, should be about right.

The basic *Textile* industry, which makes natural yarns and woven fabrics, is in for a slow future. The inroads of knit fabric trims the growth of its sales to Apparel to 1.7% per year. Its best customers are the knitting industry itself, for natural yarns, and the Floor covering industry, also for yarns. That textile Floor covering industry is a puzzler. It doubled its sales between 1963 and 1970, and is still looking around very much in bewilderment. It has little knowledge of who buys how much of which of its products, or of how nearly its markets are saturated. We expect that its industrial markets are much less saturated than its home markets, and will therefore almost double, during 1971 to 1975, while home purchases average only 4.8%py. By the last five years of the forecast, however, the rates will have dropped to 3.7%py and 2.8%py, respectively.

Most of the *fiber* input to all textile industries will come from the noncellulosics. Their 1971-85 growth rate of 6.5%py leaves only the remnants to cellulosic fibers (1.4%py) or cotton (1.7%py) or wool (2.5%py). The energy crisis may, of course, make air-conditioning so expensive that people rediscover the virtues of cotton; but barring such a denoument, the nonabsorbents will absorb most of the growth.

Besides floor coverings, other fast-growing, consumer-oriented industries include Hotels and lodging places (4.2%py 1971-85), Airlines (4.3%py), Telephone (5.3%py), Cleaning and toilet goods (4.6%py), Toys, sporting goods and musical instruments (3.9%py), Drugs (4.5%py), and Radio and TV sets (6.0%py). This high rate on Radio and TV sets should be interpreted carefully. Like all the others, it is in constant dollars; but a major stimulus to it is the expected decline in the price of color TV sets. Thus the revenues of the TV-set industry will grow less than the volume of its output. Its growth nevertheless keeps well ahead of more active or demanding sources of information, culture, or entertainment, such as Books (3.5%py), Periodicals (3.0%py), Schools, churches, and charities (3.9%py), Newspapers (2.7%py), or Movies and live entertainment (1.0%py). Work-saving Household appliances cook along at 4.2%py, faster than total spending, while Furniture relaxes at 3.0%py. Medical services stay at 3.3%py.

The *Automobile*, the king of consumer goods, will wear its crown but wearily. After clocking 5.0%py, from 1971 to 1975, sales brake down to 3.8%py from 1975 to 1980, and to 2.6%py for the following five years. One might suspect that we have been excessively swayed by the horrors of driving the Capital Beltway or by hopes of the Washington Metro or by the recent high prices of gasoline. Perhaps these factors induced us to consider the forecast reasonable in the face of booming sales in 1972, but the factor that generated the forecast is simply the drop in the rate of growth of income. Past experience shows that an income increase causes people to splurge on cars. A $1,000 increase in annual income eventually leads to a sustained increase of about $33 in automobile purchases each year, but in the year of the rise, auto purchases shoot up some $220 as people buy on their recently improved credit. The slowdown in income growth in the 1980s, therefore, will press hard on the automobile industry, quite apart from what congestion, competition, and cost of fuel may do to it.

Steel, which is already battling aluminum and plastics for its largest market, the auto, will see the growth in that market decline from 2.1%py between 1973 and 1975 to only 0.2%py from 1980 to 1985. Steel will fare better in its sales to Service industry machinery, where, less liable than in autos to the corrosive influence of plastics and aluminum, it will grow at 4.5%py from 1973 to 1985. Overall, however, steel production will grow at only 0.4%py from 1973 to 1985. Copper faces much the same future as steel. Aluminum and plastics reap the markets lost by steel and copper. Aluminum expands 4.5%py 1971-85 (vs Steel's 1.7 and Copper's 1.5), while Plastic materials and resins run away at 7.5%py. Lumber lags behind GNP at 2.2%py. At 3.1%py Paper keeps pace with GNP, but falls short of plastics, for indeed it yields some of the ground the plastics gain.

In the energy sectors, *Fuel oil* burns ahead at 4.7%py.[b] This rapid growth is due almost entirely to two factors: (1) the 11%py growth in sales to electric utilities, brought about by the substitution of oil for coal and gas in electrical generation; and (2) the 7.6%py growth in the sales to Trucking, resulting from substitution of diesel fuel (which is classified as fuel oil) for gasoline (which is not so classified).

Other industrial use rises only slightly, that by Paper, for example, averaging only 0.9%py from 1971 to 1985. Overall, Petroleum refining runs only 3.6%py, with household gasoline use growing only 3.1%py.

Electric utilities, with 4.3%py growth, run a close second to Fuel oil. The major fast growing markets are in Communication, Services, Trade, and Banks. The growth in trade and banking use is largely air-conditioning. Growth in industrial use is lower and in Aluminum is only 2.0%py. Our growth rates for electricity look low to people accustomed to kilowatt-hour growth rates; our rates refer to the total dollar value of sales deflated by a price index. This measure grows more slowly than the kwh measure simply because much of the kwh growth is on the lowest step of the price scale. A glance at the plot for Electric utilities (sector 160) in the supplement shows that there is no sudden break with past growth rates.

What happens to *Gas utility* depends on what its regulators do. Our growth rate of 3.1%py reflects some of the problems of recent years but essentially assumes that the industry's historical growth can be continued. *Coal*, which is besmudged by charges of pollution, will share but little in the growth of its customers. We find 1.5%py for 1971-85, but an economical way to remove

---

[b]Oil price increases in December 1973 changed this picture considerably. Their effects have been spelled out in detail in forecasts made by INFORUM after this book was in production.

sulfur from stack gas or a relaxation on pollution standards in view of the high costs they impose on energy users could bring coal crackling back.

Investment goods generally will, despite the slowdown, fare about the same as do consumer goods. Producer durable equipment (PDE) rises rapidly from 1971 to 1975 at 10.5%py, then slows to 3.2%py from 1975 to 1980 and cools on down to 2.6%py from 1980 to 1985. A pattern seen in many industries is a boom in investment until 1975 or 1976, then a stabilizing or even dropping for a few years to about 1978-80, and then a modest recovery. With variations, this pattern fits all the major manufacturing industries. But the variations are considerable, and we urge the reader to peruse now the investment plots of the *Supplement.* Some industries such as Floor coverings (17)[c] have only a 1977-78 hiccup in the growth of their investment. Others, such as Plumbing and heating (49) reach a peak in 1975 or 1976 which they never again approach. Motor vehicles (70) hits a high in 1974 and then grows at about 2.5%py to 1985. Just to keep up its present volume, Steel (46) will have to more than double its 1972 investment in the next few years. Industrial chemicals needs some 50 percent increase in investment spending from 1972 to 1975 and then a 25 percent growth over the following ten years. Investment by Agriculture increases at 1.3%py in the decade ahead. Communication (85) and Electric utilities (87), continue the soaring growth of investment in recent years. Although the percentage growth of sales of the Airlines (83) slackens, it continues to be one of the fastest growing investors. To accommodate the swelling traffic it will simply have to invest much faster than in 1971 and 1972, when spending averaged only about 70 percent of the Jumbo year of 1970. Our projection shows 1985 investment as almost double the average of four good years, 1967-70. That prospect, of course, looks good to the Aircraft industry (71), which in turn revives its investment.

It would be easy to continue to write with loving care about a thousand more series in the model. We have scarcely touched on exports, imports, employment, or the shifting structure of the sales of most of the 185 industries. Yet perhaps enough has been said both to illustrate what sorts of things can be read from the End Tables and the *Supplement* and to show how closely all parts of the model are knit together. The use of fuel oil by Electricity, for example, depends on the sale of electricity to Aluminum; Aluminum's growth depends on Aircraft's growth, and Aircraft's growth depends on investment by Airlines, and Airline's investment depends on consumer spending on airfares, and consumer spending on airfares depends on disposable income and disposable income is so adjusted that the jobs in refining fuel oil, together with jobs in all other industries, employ the labor force.

With this much guidance, we hope the reader will now undertake to explore for himself the vast chambers of the *Supplement.* We had best turn our efforts to explaining and justifying in detail how those chambers were constructed. The

[c]Numbers following industry names refer to the investment plot number.

reader who prefers not to be bothered by the technicalities of their construction but wants to find out how they have been used may turn immediately to the applications of Chapter 10.

2 Personal Consumption Expenditure

In 1952, personal consumption expenditure (PCE) absorbed 62.7 percent of the gross national product. After two decades of growing prosperity and growing welfare rolls, of swings in taste from tail fins to subcompacts, from mini-skirts to blue jeans, from TV dinners to nature foods, in 1972 PCE still claimed 62.7 percent of GNP. Yet within this overall stability, consumers have much changed their spending patterns. Services took only 34 percent of their budget in 1952. Twenty years later, over 42 percent went for services—yet service, as everyone knows, is the one thing you can scarcely find anymore.[a] In 1952, consumers spent half again as much (52.6 percent) on nondurables—mostly food and clothing—as on services. By 1972 these necessary items accounted for less than did services—only about 41.5 percent of PCE. Durable goods—automobiles, dishwashers, TV sets, and the like—increased their relative share from 13 percent to 16 percent of PCE in these twenty years.

Industries upon which the consumer has smiled, such as trailer coaches, have soared. Those on which he has turned his back, such as pottery, have cracked. Even an industry such as printing presses, which does not sell directly to the consumer, nevertheless depends upon whether he decides to read more or, say, to eat more. If to read, it prospers, if to eat, it starves. No other component of final demand approaches PCE in magnitude. The whole industrial composition of our forecasted economy, therefore, rests upon our forecasts of what consumers will spend on the products of each industry. No part of the model is more crucial than its consumption equations.

In the following sections, we explain the sources of data, the types of equations we have used, and the successes and difficulties we have met. Throughout the chapter, on pages facing the text, graphs show these successes and difficulties more vividly than do our words. In these graphs, the solid lines give the actual course of constant-dollar spending on an item. The dashed line shows the spending "predicted" by our equation when fit through 1971 and forecast both over the past and out to 1985. The dotted line from 1965 to 1971 shows the "forecast" for those years made by our equation when estimated only through 1964 and then "forecast" with actual income, price, and population numbers through 1971. Comparison of the solid line and the dotted line shows how well an equation using our specification and fitting methods would have forecast the next seven years had they been applied in 1964.

---

[a]About 35 percent of these "services," however, are from houses, both rented and owner-occupied.

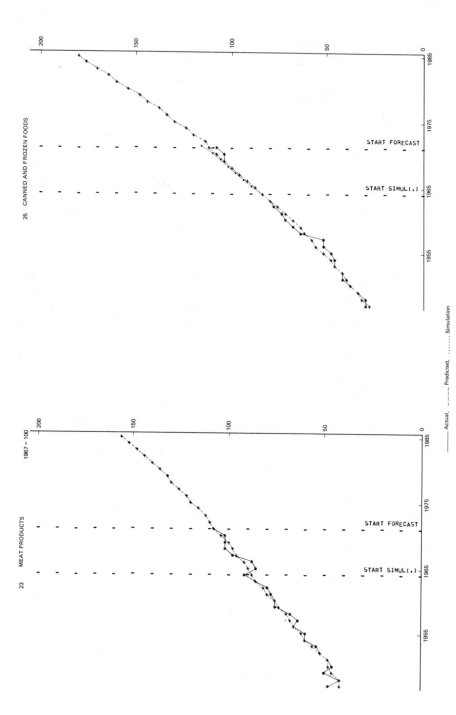

25 CANNED AND FROZEN FOODS

23 MEAT PRODUCTS

1967 = 100

START FORECAST

START SIMUL(.)

—— Actual, — — — Predicted, ... Simulation

What Do We Consume?

To make these forecasts, we naturally had to begin by asking, What have consumers spent in the past on the products of our industries? That may seem a simple question, but month upon month of labor went into answering it. There are, to be sure, tables of "Personal Consumption Expenditure by Type of Product" in the national accounts; but, though they are based on production statistics in certain "benchmark" years, they rely on less firm sources, such as sales of various types of stores, in other years. These series may, therefore, creep relative to production statistics. Moreover, they group items from many different industries under a single head. The rather specific category, "China, glassware, tableware and utensils" covers products from at least four of our industries. To use these categories would only shift the problem to determining the industrial composition of each of them. The assumption that the composition had remained constant was inconsistent with statistics on product shipments.[b] We therefore decided to discard the national accounts series and to use these shipments to determine the course of sales to PCE by each industry.

From the Department of Commerce, we obtained the amount of each 5-digit[c] product which it allocated to PCE in the 1963 input-output table.[d] We then constructed historical time series on 5-digit product shipments from 1958 to 1971, added imports and subtracted exports[e] to get domestic use. Next, PCE as a fraction of domestic use in 1963 was computed. We then assumed that this fraction remained constant in earlier and later years and computed the implied PCE at the 5-digit level. The 5-digit PCE was then aggregated to the 185-sector level.

For most products, the assumption of a constant PCE proportion is fairly realistic at the 5-digit level, as the following example illustrates.

SIC Number	Product Name	% Allocated to PCE
24991	Picture & mirror frames	85
24992	Pallets and skids	0

The first of these items, picture frames, is a consumer good and will always be purchased chiefly by consumers. The second, pallets and skids, is virtually never purchased by consumers. At the 5-digit level, therefore, the PCE share will be

[b]This assumption was used in Almon's earlier book, *The American Economy to 1975;* the smaller number of sectors made it slightly less offensive there.

[c]"5-digit" refers to the 5-digit level of detail of the Standard Industrial Classification. There are some 1100 5-digit products.

[d]Unfortunately, these allocations included retail-sales taxes and other excise taxes. Our PCE estimates, like those in the official input-output table, are therefore in the somewhat peculiar unit of "producer prices plus the value of excise taxes."

[e]We had consistent export and import series only at the 185-sector level. Within each sector, these exports and imports were prorated to the 5-digit level in proportion to domestic shipments. All of this 5-digit work is described by Thomas Reimbold in Inforum RM#37.

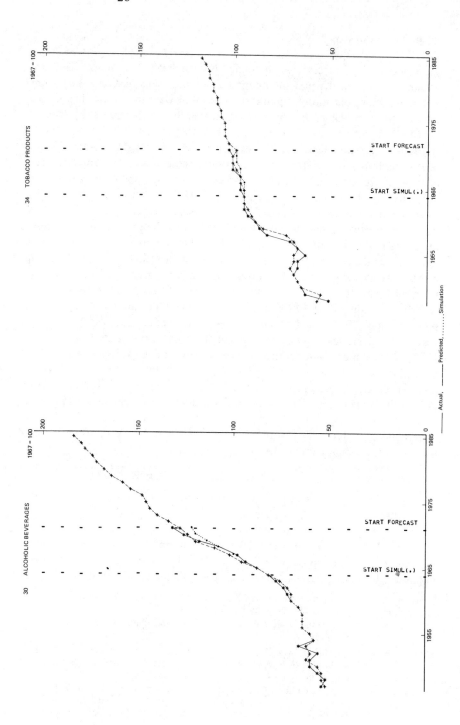

fairly constant for each of them. But both products are in the same 4-digit product class, 2499. The PCE share of the 4-digit product will shift if the product mix shifts. The assumption of constant PCE shares is therefore much sounder at the 5-digit than at the 4-digit level. We had to abandon the constant-PCE-share assumption and just use our judgment, however, for three products:

1. Small arms, for they are not divided between military and civilian at the 5-digit level; the Vietnam War played havoc with the PCE share.
2. Carpets, once principally PCE items, have found new markets as investment and construction goods.
3. Household furniture, which has found increasing use in offices.

To estimate consumption spending prior to 1958 by the same method required, to put it plainly, more work than it was worth, for the change in the SIC numbers in that year affected a great many 5-digit numbers. Moreover, as we shall see, early years carry less weight than recent years in determining the forecast. We therefore took a short cut. At the 185-sector level, we regressed PCE on total sector output over the years 1958-70. We then used these equations to "backcast" PCE from 1957 to 1947, years for which we had estimates of output, but not PCE.

The 5-digit approach could be used, of course, only on manufactured commodities. An entirely similar approach was applied to the few agricultural commodities such as eggs, which sell directly to the consumer, and to retail deliveries of coal. For the service sectors, we used the PCE tables of the national accounts in constant dollars and a table of the percentage distribution of each category among the input-output industries, both kindly given to us in full detail by the Commerce Department. In the service sectors, there is very little problem in going from the national accounts categories to our sectors.

Our forecasting equations, to be explained in the next section, use consumption in constant dollars and the trend of the price of each product relative to the overall price level (more precisely, relative to the PCE deflator). To get these from what we have, we need price indexes for each product. In the process of preparing the "Gross Product Originating by Industry," the Commerce Department has prepared constant-dollar output series for each 4-digit industry. In this work, it has used the maximum detail of the Wholesale Price Index to deflate, in as much detail as possible, the current-dollar output of the various industries. These unpublished series, an intermediate product from the point of view of the Commerce Department, have been kindly made available to us. The 4-digit price deflator is used to convert the current-dollar 5-digit PCE into constant dollars before aggregation to our 185 sectors. The ratio of the current-dollar to the constant-dollar PCE of an industry we take as its price index. We divide this price index by the overall PCE deflator to obtain the relative price term used in the equations.

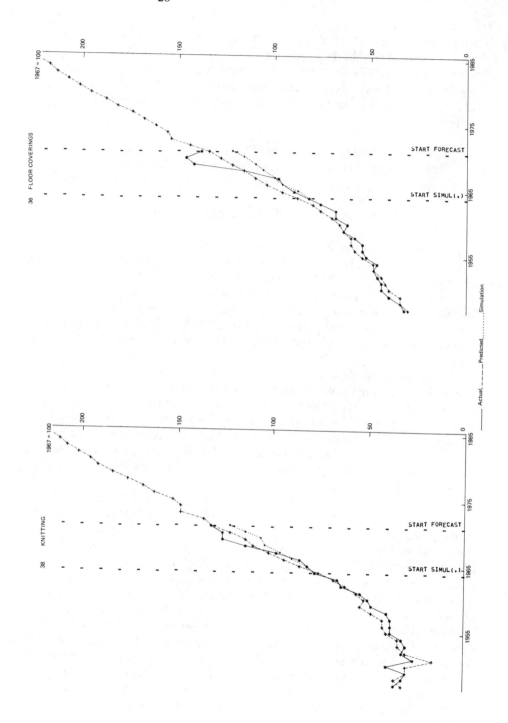

The final, constant-dollar series for consumption are shown on the output-consumption-export-import plots in the *Supplement.*

The Forecasting Equations

For forecasting, our basic plan was to relate consumption per capita of each item to per capita disposable income, its increase during the past year, the relative price of the item, and a time trend.

We have used two types of equations, which we may name

$$\text{Impulse: } c_t = b_1 + b_2\,y_t + b_3\,(y_t - y_{t-1}) + b_4\,p_t + b_5 t$$

and

$$\text{Habit: } c_t = b_1 + b_2\,y_t + b_3\,(y_t - y_{t-1}) + b_4\,p_t + b_5\,c_{t-1},$$

Here y is disposable income per capita in constant dollars, and c and p are the constant-dollar per capita consumption and the relative price, respectively, of a particular good or service, and t is time in years.

Impulse and Habit look much alike, but note carefully the last terms, t in Impulse and c_{t-1} in Habit. They make all the difference. To see how differently the two work, let us take a simple example ignoring prices, and see how each responds to a once-and-for-all upward step in income. Let us take as samples:

Impulse

$$c_t = 0.1 y_t + 0.2(y_t - y_{t-1})$$

Habit

$$c_t = 0.04 y_t - 0.01(y_t - y_{t-1}) + 0.6 c_{t-1}$$

If, since time immemorial prior to $t = 0$, income has been $1000, then by both equations $c_0 = $100. Now in year 1, let us increase income by 10 percent to $1100 and leave it there indefinitely. What will then happen to consumption? As Figure 2-1 shows, both Impulse and Habit eventually produce a 10 percent, $10 rise in spending. But Impulse has reached its destination by year 2; Habit takes forever to get there. In this case, Impulse actually overshoots the mark in year 1. That behavior is characteristic of durables such as automobiles or appliances, where credit lets buyers splurge when their income first goes up. Impulse *can* make *less* than the whole change in the first year if it puts a negative b_3 on the change in income. It uses that ploy to handle items with habits which adjust within a year. Alcoholic beverages are a typical example. ("Next time you buy a case of wine, I wish you'd get a little better one.") But for real laggards such as insurance, electric and gas utilities, cigarettes, and coffee, there is no substitute for Habit, as we shall see.

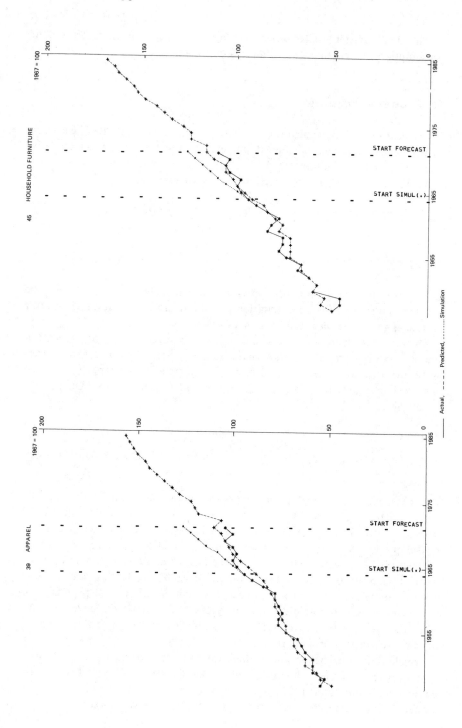

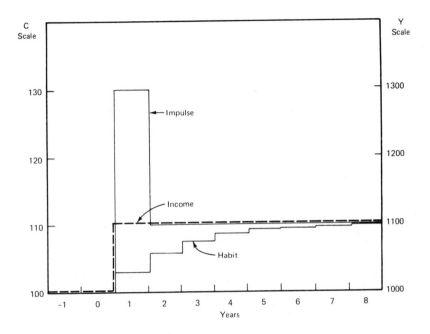

Figure 2-1. Impulse and Habit

If the two equations work about equally well, we prefer Impulse because its time term offers a convenient handle by which we may crank in, if we like, a break from the past trend. We could use it to pose questions such as, What happens if the trend to knit garments is reversed? or What changes if Amtrak stops the downward trend in rail travel? Habit on the other hand, is rigid; it recognizes no influence outside income and price. The addition of a time trend to it would only exacerbate the statistical problems which we must now examine.

Tests of Ways of Estimating the Equations

Both Impulse and Habit can be fit by ordinary least-squares methods to our historical data. But how reliably will equations so fit forecast the future? Only time will answer that question, but if we shift to the past and ask how well would these equations have forecast 1964-70, had we fit them to the data for 1947-63, then we can tackle the question. The columns of Table 2-1 show the

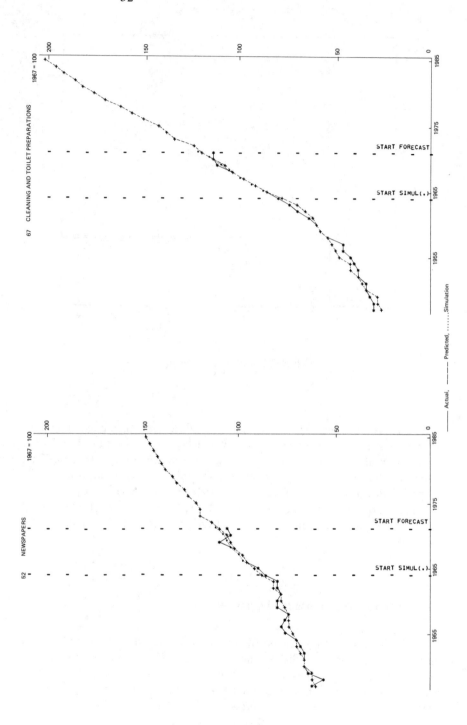

Table 2-1
PCE Simulation Comparison (1964-71)

SEC# OUTPUT DEFINITION   MEAN ABSOLUTE ERROR (1964-71) IN PERCENT OF ACTUAL PERSONAL CONSUMPTION EXPENDITURES

SEC# OUTPUT DEFINITION	TMP-TS	TMP-CS	TMP-CSAGF	HAR-TS	HAR-CS	TMP-CHOTC	TMP-CHAGF	HAR-CHOTC	HAR-CHOTC	FTNSEL	BFST
2 POULTRY AND EGGS	7.0	7.0	2.0	2.0	6.0	2.0	1.2	76.0	2.0	2.0	7
7 FRUITS, VEGETABLES, AND	7.0	7.0	2.0	2.0	18.0	11.0	11.0	11.0	2.0	2.0	3
21 MEAT PRODUCTS	11.0	6.0	5.0	17.0	5.0	2.0	4.0	10.0	4.0	2.0	6
24 DAIRY PRODUCTS	6.0	12.0	12.0	6.0	12.0	8.0	4.0	4.0	6.0	5.0	8
25 CANNED AND FROZEN FOODS	8.0	7.0	7.0	20.0	6.0	4.0	4.0	3.0	4.0	3.0	6
26 GRAIN MILL PRODUCTS	7.0	8.0	9.0	25.0	17.0	5.0	4.0	18.0	5.0	5.0	8
27 BAKERY PRODUCTS	7.0	12.0	11.0	15.0	7.0	4.0	4.0	7.0	7.0	3.0	9
28 SUGAR	17.0	9.0	9.0	19.0	17.0	9.0	9.0	7.0	9.0	7.0	7
29 CONFECTIONERY PRODUCTS	10.0	11.0	12.0	9.0	7.0	7.0	9.0	3.0	2.0	3.0	6
30 ALCOHOLIC BEVERAGES	3.0	3.0	4.0	24.0	10.0	3.0	9.0	10.0	4.0	3.0	5
31 SOFT DRINKS AND FLAVORT	11.0	4.0	4.0	24.0	19.0	3.0	9.0	3.0	3.0	3.0	6
32 FATS AND OILS	5.0	5.0	6.0	6.0	17.0	9.0	9.1	8.0	9.0	4.0	7
33 MISC FOOD PRODUCTS	13.0	12.0	12.0	18.0	10.0	8.0	9.1	8.0	8.0	1.0	8
34 TOBACCO PRODUCTS	28.0	15.0	14.0	27.0	6.0	10.0	10.0	1.0	10.0	5.0	7
35 BROAD AND NARROW FABRIC	8.0	8.0	6.0	7.0	6.0	6.0	5.0	6.0	6.0	5.0	8
36 FLOOR COVERINGS	8.0	4.0	5.0	7.0	7.0	9.0	10.0	7.0	9.0	7.0	6
38 KNITTING	17.0	2.0	10.0	11.0	17.0	11.0	12.3	13.0	11.0	11.0	6
39 APPAREL	23.0	13.0	15.0	11.0	15.0	12.0	11.0	10.0	12.0	10.0	8
48 HOUSEHOLD TEXTILES	11.0	4.0	4.0	4.0	5.0	4.0	1.0	4.0	4.0	4.0	7
65 HOUSEHOLD FURNITURE	8.0	12.0	14.0	15.0	10.0	11.0	10.0	7.0	7.0	7.0	8
49 PAPER PRODUCTS, NEC	8.0	8.0	6.0	27.0	5.0	5.0	4.1	3.0	5.0	3.0	8
52 NEWSPAPERS	8.0	4.0	5.0	6.0	3.0	3.0	7.0	4.0	3.0	2.0	7
53 BOOKS, PERIODICALS, AND	73.0	2.0	2.0	4.0	18.0	2.0	2.3	18.0	2.0	2.0	4
66 DRUGS	9.0	14.0	15.0	6.0	17.0	2.0	3.0	12.0	2.0	2.0	6
67 CLEANING AND TOILET PRE	7.0	6.0	9.0	3.0	3.0	8.0	4.1	6.0	8.0	5.0	5
69 PETROLEUM REFINING AND	18.0	6.0	6.0	13.0	6.0	8.0	8.0	7.0	6.0	5.0	4
72 TIRES AND INNER TUBES	4.0	4.0	5.0	5.0	13.0	6.0	6.1	7.0	6.0	5.0	8
73 RUBBER PRODUCTS	33.0	10.0	10.0	13.0	10.0	2.0	2.0	2.0	2.0	2.0	7
76 LEATHER FOOTWEAR	25.0	3.0	3.0	7.0	10.0	3.0	3.1	10.0	3.0	3.0	7
77 OTHER LEATHER PRODUCTS	25.0	6.0	6.0	4.0	6.0	5.0	5.1	5.0	5.0	5.0	8
123 HOUSEHOLD APPLIANCES	21.0	12.0	12.0	4.0	6.0	2.0	2.1	2.0	2.0	2.0	6
125 RADIO AND TV RECEIVING	32.0	19.0	19.0	11.0	10.0	13.0	13.1	12.0	13.0	10.0	5
133 MOTOR VEHICLES AND PART	70.0	10.0	10.0	9.0	17.0	10.0	10.0	11.0	10.0	9.0	4
140 TRAILER COACHES	16.0	33.0	34.0	19.0	19.0	33.0	34.0	19.0	33.0	16.0	1
147 JEWELRY AND SILVERWARE	26.0	11.0	11.0	11.0	11.0	8.0	8.0	16.0	8.0	8.0	7
148 TOYS, SPORTING GOODS, M	10.0	9.0	10.0	27.0	7.0	8.0	7.3	7.0	8.0	7.0	6
152 BUSSES	7.0	20.0	20.0	9.0	11.0	14.0	12.0	6.0	14.0	3.0	1
155 AIRLINES	16.0	17.0	18.0	6.0	26.0	16.0	17.3	27.0	16.0	6.0	4
158 TELEPHONE AND TELEGRAPH	9.0	5.0	4.0	3.0	4.0	3.0	3.0	20.0	3.0	3.0	7
160 ELECTRIC UTILITIES	9.0	5.0	4.0	2.0	5.0	2.3	2.3	11.0	2.0	2.0	5
161 NATURAL GAS	8.0	17.0	16.0	18.0	5.0	17.0	16.0	5.0	17.0	5.0	5
162 WATER AND SEWER SERVICE	8.0	10.0	9.0	11.0	1.0	10.0	10.3	2.0	10.0	1.0	6
164 RETAIL TRADE	6.0	6.0	6.0	19.0	25.0	4.0	4.3	20.0	4.0	2.0	7
165 CREDIT AGENCIES AND BRO	9.0	4.0	4.0	4.0	6.0	9.0	8.3	5.0	9.0	4.0	8
166 INSURANCE AND BROKER'S	12.0	14.0	13.0	17.0	9.0	9.0	8.3	4.0	9.0	8.0	1
167 OWNER-OCCUPIED DWELLING	1.0	15.0	13.0	5.0	5.0	2.0	2.0	6.0	2.0	1.0	7
168 REAL ESTATE	4.0	2.0	1.0	24.0	4.0	4.0	1.3	4.0	4.0	4.0	5
169 HOTEL AND LODGING PLACE	4.0	13.0	12.0	15.0	4.0	7.0	7.3	2.0	7.0	2.0	5
170 PERSONAL AND REPAIR SER	5.0	13.0	12.0	10.0	2.0	4.0	4.0	26.0	4.0	2.0	8
171 BUSINESS SERVICES	18.0	4.0	4.0	7.0	2.0	4.0	5.3	4.0	4.0	2.0	5
173 AUTO REPAIR	7.0	18.0	13.0	9.0	10.0	7.0	6.0	2.0	7.0	2.0	8
175 MOTION PICTURES AND AMU	7.0	11.0	11.0	9.0	5.0	3.0	3.3	16.0	3.0	1.0	6
175 MEDICAL SERVICES	7.0	3.0	3.0	6.0	1.0	12.0	12.1	8.0	8.0	1.0	8
177 PRIVATE SCHOOLS AND NON	9.0	18.0	17.0	4.0	8.0	12.0	12.0	3.0	12.0	3.0	8
177 POST OFFICE	8.0	4.0	3.0	6.0	3.0	3.0	4.0	3.0	3.0	3.0	8
TOTAL WEIGHTED ERROR	9.2	9.9	9.3	10.9	8.3	5.8	4.5	5.8	8.1	3.5	

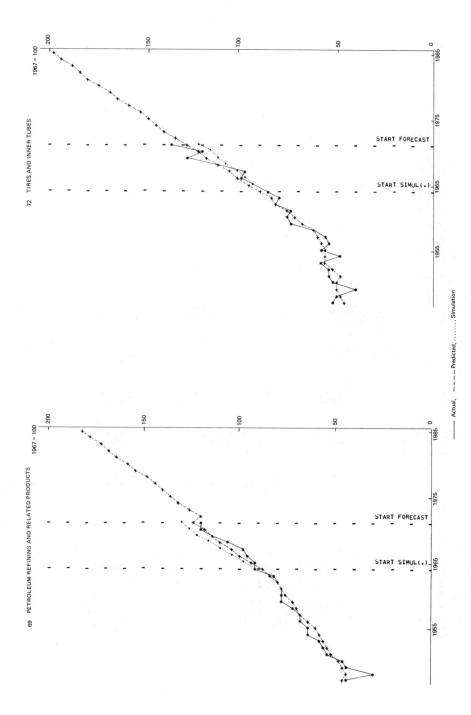

72 TIRES AND INNER TUBES

69 PETROLEUM REFINING AND RELATED PRODUCTS

—— Actual, — — — Predicted, ...Simulation

average percentage error[f] for the forecast period 1964-70 for various ways of fitting these equations to the 1947-63 data for the fifty-five industries largest in the consumer's budget.

In these tests, actual disposable income and price data for the forecast period were used. Any equation which made demand increase when price increases was kicked out as nonsense and one with no price effect was used in its place. The results for Impulse are shown in the first column, "IMP-TS" for "Impulse-time-series"; those for Habit are shown in column 4, labeled "HAB-TS" for "Habit-time series."

In this test, Habit outperformed Impulse 37 to 18, and neither performed very well. Impulse especially seems to have had difficulty separating the effects of income increases from changes in tastes, styles, products or priorities, which are all represented in it by the time trend. From 1964 to 1970, the average annual growth in income was three times what it had been over the preceding decade. Moreover, during that decade, the growth in income had been very steady. Statistically Impulse could not tell the difference between time and income. Habit, not obliged to make that distinction, fared better in the forecast.

But is it necessary to limit ourselves to time-series data in the estimation of Impulse? Can we not learn something about the effects of income from family surveys, from comparing expenditures of families with different incomes? In particular, can we learn the "income elasticity" of a product—the percentage by which the demand for the product expands when income goes up 1 percent? If so, then we can determine b_2 by imposing that elasticity on the Impulse equation[g], the coefficient of income, and then find only the other constants by curve fitting. From the 1960 Survey of Consumer Expenditures conducted by the Bureau of Labor Statistics, we calculated these elasticities by assuming that a 1 percent increase in income would be used by families of a given size and income to move toward the spending patterns of the same size family in the next higher income bracket. (Details are given in Chapter 2 of *The American Economy to 1975*. The next survey was conducted in 1972; its results are not available at the time of writing.) These elasticities are shown in the third column of Table 2-2, labeled "IMP-SURV." The results of imposing these elasticities on Impulse are shown in column 2 of Table 2-1, labeled "IMP-CS" for "Cross-Section." In 32 of 55 cases, the use of the cross-section data improved the forecast. It even cut the error by a factor of three or more in such important sectors as Apparel, Household textiles, Furniture, Books and periodicals, Rubber

---

[f]To be precise, Table 2-1 shows the root mean square percentage error defined by

$$RMSPE = \left[\sum_{t=1964}^{1970} (e_t/c_t)^2/7 \right]^{1/2}$$

where e_t is the error in year t.

[g]By the formula $b_2 = n\,c_t/y_t$, where n is the elasticity and t is the year of the survey.

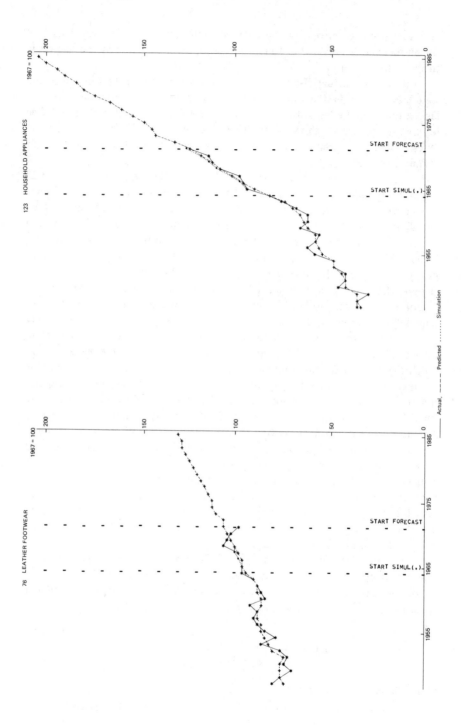

Table 2-2

PCE Income Elasticities with Price Elasticities and %-Time of Choice Equation

SEC#	TITLE	HAB-TS	IMP-TS	IMP-SURV	SEARCH	CHOICE	PRI-ELAS	%-TIME
2	POULTRY AND EGGS	-.5070	.3420	.1950	.1950	.2000	.0151	-1.7551
7	FRUITS, VEGETABLES, AND OTHER CROPS	-.2940	.2410	.4800	.2800	.3000	-.3068	-1.3568
23	MEAT PRODUCTS	-.5960	-.2230	.4500	.0508	.0500	-.1656	1.4149
24	DAIRY PRODUCTS	-.1500	-.5180	.2900	.0900	.0500	.6614	-.3653
25	CANNED AND FROZEN FOODS	.6910	-.1660	.6050	.0050	.2500	.0000	2.2914
26	GRAIN MILL PRODUCTS	1.9120	-.8250	.0100	.8100	.4500	.0000	2.1905
27	BAKERY PRODUCTS	-.0111	-.5480	.3300	.0300	.1000	-.6644	-.1425
28	SUGAR	-.9770	.6800	.0900	.6900	.1000	-.3621	.8118
29	CONFECTIONERY PRODUCTS	.9240	.9780	.0900	.9900	1.0000	-.9024	-.3343
30	ALCOHOLIC BEVERAGES	.2630	1.4570	.1400	1.6000	1.4000	-3.2524	-2.6608
31	SOFT DRINKS AND FLAVORINGS	1.5150	.2140	.4000	.4600	.5000	-.0839	.2129
32	FATS AND OILS	.6400	-.5380	.1600	.1000	.1000	-.0222	.6800
33	MISC FOOD PRODUCTS	1.2140	-.5110	.4000	.5600	1.0000	-.1844	.0000
34	TOBACCO PRODUCTS	.9510	-.7460	.3500	.5500	.0500	.0000	.0000
35	BROAD AND NARROW FABRICS	.2040	-.2070	.4900	.0900	.2500	.0000	.0000
36	FLOOR COVERINGS	.9630	-.6240	.1600	.7900	.9000	.0472	-1.0112
38	KNITTING	2.2300	3.0300	1.8500	2.3900	1.8500	-1.2148	-.4939
39	APPAREL	.1280	-.0420	1.1900	.0900	1.5000	-.9087	-.6372
40	HOUSEHOLD TEXTILES	1.3610	1.0310	1.1600	1.3600	1.0000	-.1332	-1.8618
45	HOUSEHOLD FURNITURE	2.4450	1.0000	.9800	.0800	.7000	-.6714	-.0877
49	PAPER PRODUCTS, NEC	.8510	-1.0000	.4900	.0900	.2500	-.0711	-.0807
52	NEWSPAPERS	.5270	-.2070	1.0000	.7900	1.0000	.0000	.0000
53	PERIODICALS	.9630	-.7840	1.0000	.7900	1.0000	.0000	-.5896
66	DRUGS	1.2800	1.2300	1.1900	1.1000	.8500	-.5776	-.0312
67	CLEANING AND TOILET PREPARATIONS	2.4350	1.2960	.5400	1.3200	1.5000	-.1772	-1.1145
69	PETROLEUM REFINING AND RELATED PRODUCTS	14.9850	1.2430	.3200	.2800	2.0000	-.0000	-.6639
72	TIRES AND INNER TUBES	3.8800	.3260	.6800	.0900	.8000	-.0794	.7536
73	RUBBER PRODUCTS	1.2630	1.5470	.6500	1.3500	1.0000	-.5361	.6484
76	LEATHER FOOTWEAR	-.0820	-.0830	.7400	.0400	1.0000	-.1534	.2400
77	OTHER LEATHER PRODUCTS	-.1790	.6060	.7800	.6800	.7000	-.5497	.5320
123	HOUSEHOLD APPLIANCES	1.6540	-.4060	1.1900	.8900	.9000	-.2805	-1.4715
125	RADIO AND TV RECEIVING	4.6030	1.6990	.5100	.5100	1.7000	.0000	-.3152
133	MOTOR VEHICLES AND PARTS	1.5630	3.3610	.6100	4.0100	1.7000	-1.9780	.0463
140	TRAILER COACHES	89.4550	1.0930	1.3000	1.5300	1.0000	.0000	1.3057
147	JEWELRY AND SILVERWARE	.8280	12.7690	1.8000	11.2000	1.8000	-8.2098	1.3028
148	TOYS, SPORTING GOODS, MUSICAL INSTRUMENTS	1.0790	2.5040	4.6800	2.6800	2.0000	.0000	2.1665
152	BUSSES	.2610	-.2670	.8300	.0300	.6000	.0000	-2.4626
155	AIRLINES	2.4770	-1.1580	.2000	1.1000	.5000	-.9563	2.9971
158	TELEPHONE AND TELEGRAPH	1.5700	4.3920	.9000	4.6000	2.0000	-1.1254	.0000
160	ELECTRIC UTILITIES	2.5660	1.6020	.8100	9.1000	1.5000	-.7139	1.7653
161	NATURAL GAS	.3700	6.0200	1.0000	.6000	1.7000	-.1825	.7849
162	WATER AND SEWER SERVICES	.9380	-.8170	.7500	.0500	.7500	-.0037	.8972
164	RETAIL TRADE	.5210	.1320	.7200	.0200	.7500	.0185	.0000
165	CREDIT AGENCIES AND BROKERS	1.0640	1.3110	1.2500	2.2200	1.3500	-1.1479	-2.0780
166	INSURANCE AND BROKER'S AGENTS	.8530	1.2400	1.4100	5.5000	1.4500	-.7682	.1973
167	OWNER-OCCUPIED DWELLINGS	1.4400	.2620	1.4100	2.1100	1.0000	-.3696	.7032
168	REAL ESTATE	.3860	1.6900	1.4100	.1100	.4500	.0000	1.8908
169	HOTEL AND LODGING PLACES	2.9400	.4900	2.0000	5.1100	1.4000	.0000	-.4859
170	PERSONAL AND REPAIR SERVICES	.5440	.6230	1.1900	9.0000	1.5000	-.8275	.6183
171	BUSINESS SERVICES	-.5380	.1590	1.0400	1.9000	.5000	.0000	-.2231
173	AUTO REPAIR	-.1950	-.0390	1.0400	.0400	.7000	-1.2839	2.6538
174	MOTION PICTURES AND AMUSEMENTS	1.6900	-.9520	1.6400	.8400	.5000	.0000	-2.5032
175	MEDICAL SERVICES		.8660	5.9000	.8400	.6500	.0000	.7868
176	PRIVATE SCHOOLS AND NONPROFIT ORGANIZATIO	-5.1100	.6510	2.3600	.6600	.8000	-2.9505	1.4445

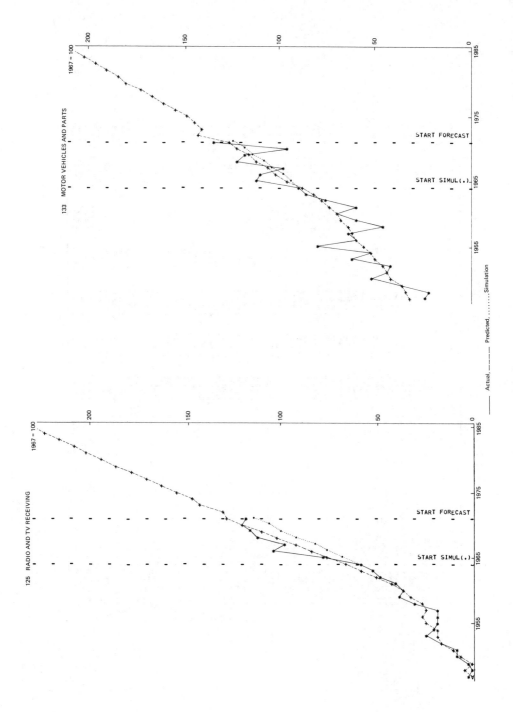

products, Shoes, Other leather products, Automobiles, Jewelry and silverware, Credit agencies, Real estate (including rent on dwelling), Business services, and Legal services. In only Drugs, Trailer coaches, Busses, Electric utilities, Owner-occupied dwellings, and Auto repair did the survey data lead to forecasts poorer by so wide a margin. Most of these sectors have peculiarities[h] which might make one skeptical of any equation which forecasted them *well*.

These results leave no doubt about the value of using cross-section income elasticities in conjunction with time series. They do leave some question, however, about whether, in every instance, we have found the appropriate elasticities. Our calculations may have erred either because the commodity group in the survey did not match well an industry of our model or because reporting was faulty or because low-income families differ from high-income families in ways other than income—to wit, in education, age, race, sex of head, region, size of community, and so on. We examine in detail the effects of such demographic variables on the demand for several types of electrical appliances in this chapter's Appendix 2A. There the demographic variables prove quite significant without affecting the income elasticities. But appliances are probably not typical of the problem items, for the use of the survey data improved their forecasts.

In the cases which were *not* improved, the imposed elasticities were apparently incorrect. When the great income boom of the sixties came, they predicted too much or too little response. This boom may, in fact, reveal more about elasticities than had the whole previous postwar period. We asked ourselves, therefore, What elasticity, had it been specified in 1963 and the other constants of Impulse estimated over the years 1947-63, would have given the best forecasts for 1964-70? This elasticity, dubbed "search," is shown in column 4 of Table 2-2. In a number of cases, the search elasticity differed little from the survey elasticity and could be adopted. In other cases, some compromise had to be struck. Six of us sat around a table and came up with our "choice" elasticity. The choice value should be reasonable, consistent with values for competing products, and should result in less, not more, reliance on the time trend. Table 2-2 shows them in the fifth column. The elasticity implied by the pure time-series estimation of Impulse is in column 2, and by the long-term elasticity of Habit-time series in column 1. A glance at columns 1 and 2 should be sufficient to convince any who still doubt the necessity of imposing elasticities on time-series data. A sixth of the elasticities estimated from time series only

---

[h]Drugs were stimulated by medicare and medicaid; trailer coaches, mostly mobile homes, evolved considerably while the price of conventional housing soared; electric utilities had a guessed elasticity because the practice of including it with the rent made it impossible to estimate its elasticity from the family survey data; the owner-occupied housing, supposed to represent what homeowners would have had to pay to rent their homes, is made up by the Commerce Department. This imputed series implies practically a zero income elasticity for owner-occupied houses, while the observed data on rental housing are consistent with the elasticity of 1.5 found from the family survey. Since it is difficult to imagine such a discrepancy, we harbor some reservations about the validity of the imputed series.

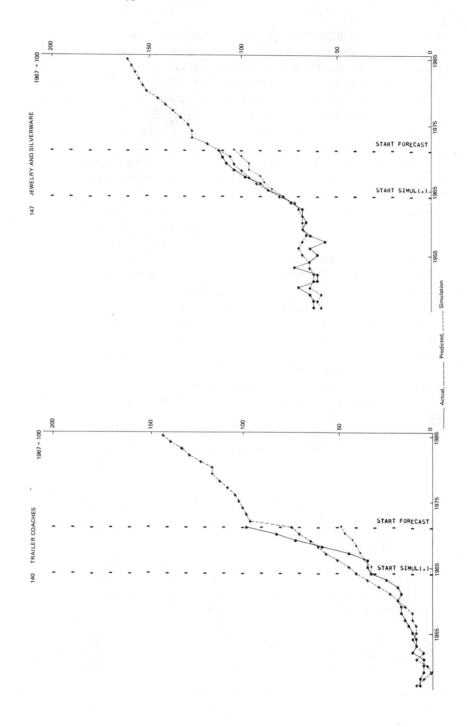

come out negative. Habit gives a 0.26 to Alcoholic beverages but a 1.51 to Soft drinks; the survey indicated just the opposite relative sizes. Somehow Habit gets a 14.9 for Cleaning and toilet preparations but only 0.8 for Jewelry and silverware!

As was to be expected, the "choice" equations forecast substantially better than the "survey" equations and out-perform the "time-series" version of Impulse 46 to 9. They also forecast better than Habit-time series 42 to 13. Obviously, Habit deserves to know about the choice elasticities. We have therefore imposed them on Habit as long-term elasticities[i] and show the errors of the resulting forecasts in column 8, labeled "HAB-CHOIC," of Table 2-1. The imposition improved Habit's forecast in 35 out of 55 cases. But even the improved Habit equations were less accurate than the Impulse-choice equations in all but 19 cases.[j] The difference in most of the 19 was slight; but in 7 of the 19, Habit was decisively the best, namely: Miscellaneous food products (mostly coffee), Tobacco, Busses, Gas utility, Electric utility, Insurance, and Automobile repair. In all of these items, we are indeed creatures of habit or bound by the equipment we own—or don't own—for cooking, heating, cooling, or riding.

For our forecasts we use Habit for these 7 items and Impulse for all the rest. In all cases we impose the choice elasticity and estimate the rest of the equation over the years 1947-70.

The last two columns of Table 2-2 show the price elasticity in 1971 and the time trend term of the Impulse equations. The time-trend term, labeled "%-TIME," shows, as a percentage of 1971 consumption, the annual change in per capita consumption which would occur if income and price remained constant. Thus for sector 7, fruits and vegetables, we find that a 1 percent increase in price cuts back consumption by 0.3 percent and that, if income and price both remained constant, per capita consumption would fall by 1.36 percent of its 1971 value each year. Spending on Alcoholic beverages is quite sensitive to price, and there has been a 2.2 percent per year independent drift away from alcohol. Much of the rise in carpet demand is attributable to lower prices, as is the boom in TV sales, trailer or mobile home sales, and air travel. Conversely, the lack of growth in private schools stems from the higher prices they have had to charge, for not only is the income elasticity high (choice = 1.80), but the time term adds 1.4 percent per year as more parents despair of the state schools. Other symptomatic time terms include the 2.3 percent yearly taste shift toward Canned and frozen foods and the 2.2 percent shift towards boxed mixes and cereals (Grain mill products) despite the 1.3 percent shift toward radio and TV receivers which could be used to watch Julia Child. Less and less

---

[i]We estimate the equation subject to the constraint that $b_2/(1-b_4) = nc_t/y_t$, where n is the choice elasticity and $t = 1960$.

[j]Habit might have looked better had we done our search on it instead of on Impulse. But, as explained, we prefer Impulse if the two are about equally good, so its needs were given greater weight in the selection of the choice elasticities.

home sewing shows up in the 1 percent yearly autonomous decline in Broad and narrow fabrics. New uses for paper products stimulate a 2.6 percent shift upwards in their consumption. Newspapers continue to suffer from the competition with television. Trailer sales also enjoy an upward boost of 2.2 percent from the time term. Poor jewelry and silverware, however, despite its phenomenal revival when income began to grow in the mid-seventies, still loses 2.5 percent to an ever more informal lifestyle. These time effects seem generally reasonable and encourage use to believe that our choice income elasticities are appropriate.

Because our method of selecting this choice elasticity is somewhat unconventional in today's econometrics, a word of justification may be said in its defense. We want our forecasts to be as reliable as possible. Experience shows the folly of ignoring a priori ideas about elasticity and abandoning ourselves to the oracle of least squares. When we have considered all the information at our disposal—the survey, the response of consumers to the boom in income during the sixties, and our own observation of ourselves and our friends—these values are our best guesses of the elasticities. Honesty therefore requires that we use them. We regret that they make our method not quite reproducable as strict science would have it. But we are willing to admit that forecasting is as much art as science and that judgment must play an important role. We hope that ours has been good judgment.

Minor Problems—Jumps, Out-of-Date Data, Prosperity Backlash, and an Aging Population

Besides the major problem of selecting the right form for the equation and the right income elasticities, there were a number of minor problems of method, which we now mention briefly.

The Jump Problem. If the fitted equation misses on the high side in one year, it is likely to miss on the high side again in the next year. In technical language, the errors are usually autocorrelated; if the error is e in one year, the expected miss in the next is not zero but ρe, where ρ, called the first order autocorrelation coefficient, is between -1 and $+1$. Now the equation seldom fits perfectly in the last year of historical data, but misses by an amount we may call e_o. If we use without modification the forecast produced by the equation, there will often appear in the first year of the forecast, a jump back "onto the equation" and then steady growth thereafter. We use the autocorrelation to eliminate these jumps by adding ρe_o to the forecast for the first year, $\rho^2 e_o$ to that for the second, and so on. Because ρ is between -1 and 1, this adjustment approaches zero as we go further out into the future. The ρ-adjustment was used in all the forecasts reported in Table 2-1. Tests in forecasting 1964-70 from 1963 show that this ρ-adjustment improves the forecast of most products and never makes the forecast of any product worse.

The Out-dated Problem. By hook or crook, we have produced historical PCE data back to 1947. But is the 1947 information really as relevant for forecasting 1985 as in the 1965-70 data? We think not. We wanted to be sure that the equations fit well in recent years, but we were less concerned about how well they fit in early years. We therefore decided to attach weights to the various years. We gave a weight of 1.0 to the most recent year's information and let the weights decline a constant percent per year over the preceeding years. We experimented with the rate of decline by forecasting 1964-70 from the pre-1964 data. Of the 55 major consumer items, 14 did best with no decline; 2, with 2 percent per year; 9, with 4 percent; 7, with 6 percent; 3, with 8 percent; and 20, with 10 percent or more. Some of the error reductions were quite substantial. For Household furniture, the declining weights cut the average error 50 percent; for Jewelry and silverware, 42 percent; for Soft drinks, 34 percent; for Fats and oils, 34 percent; for Bakery products, 25 percent; for Busses, 24 percent; and for Newspapers, 23 percent. Apparel, Electric appliances, Radio and TV receivers, Automobiles, and Airlines, however, benefited not at all from the declining weights and, in fact, had a slight preference for no decline in the weights. Only three sectors, however—Water and sewer services, Hotels, and the Post office— had their record impaired as much as 20 percent by going from 0 to 6 percent decline in weights.

It is not exactly easy to draw conclusions from this test for our forecasting practice. One can hardly say that the beneficiaries of the declining weights have been the dynamic industries with strikingly new products which made earlier data obsolete. Indeed, the reverse might describe the situation more closely. (Perhaps the income sensitivity of static products declines over the years.) No generalization however, seemed really valid, so we did not feel that the preferred rate of decline was a permanent characteristic of an item. Therefore, we have *not* used the decline which proved best for forecasting 1964-70 for forecasting 1973-85. Rather, we have simply noted that more than half of the items preferred a decline of 6 percent or more per year, while only three were significantly hurt by such a decline. Therefore, we have used 6 percent on *all* items. The tests shown in Table 2-1 were all performed with 5 percent declining weights. It should also be noted that the declining weights make the last error, e_0, small. The ρ-adjustment, therefore, has less effect when declining weights are used than it would without them.

The Prosperity Backlash Problem. In comparing Impulse and Habit, we mentioned that a negative coefficient on Impulse's change-in-income term allowed it to delay for one year all or part of the response to an increase in income. Left to its own devices, least-squares sometimes gives us change-in-income coefficients that are not merely negative, but more negative than the income coefficient is positive. Where that occurs, fast growth in income leads to a drop in forecasted spending. Such behavior seems highly unlikely, so we constrain the change-in-income coefficient to be no more negative than the income coefficient is positive.

The Aging Population Problem. The equations, as stated, take no account of the changing age structure of the population. Yet the recent decline in the birth rate makes such changes inevitable. We have introduced a simple device to take some account of these age changes. For each of 32 fairly broad classes of consumer goods, we prepared an index of what might be called the "age-adjusted population" for the product, as follows:

$$D^*_t \doteq D_0 \frac{\sum\limits_{i=1}^{5} E_i D_{it}}{\sum\limits_{i=1}^{5} E_i D_{io}} \qquad (2.1)$$

where E_i is average expenditures on the good by households whose head is in age interval i in the 1960-61 Survey of Consumer Expenditures.

D_{it} is the number of households in age interval i in year t

D^*_t = age-adjusted population

t = time (0 in 1961)

If expenditures of households with a given age of head did not change—but the number of households of each age did change—then total spending would increase at the same rate as does D^*. D^* is therefore sort of a measure of the effective buying population, adjusted for changes in the age structure, or "age-adjusted population" for short. All of our equations have been estimated on a per capita basis. We have tried using, instead of the ordinary population, the age-adjusted population as the number of capita. The results of the test forecasts made in this way with Impulse are shown in Table 2-1, column 3 (with survey elasticities) and column 7 (with choice elasticities). About half the equations are improved by use of age; its consideration reduced the percentage error by a point or more in Paper products, Toys and sporting goods, Busses, Electric utility and Gas utility, Insurance, and Owner-occupied housing, all likely candidates for influence by age. For all categories improved by consideration of age when the choice elasticity is used, we have forecasted on the basis of the age-adjusted population.

Our data allowed us to consider only the age of the head of household. When the 1972 Survey of Consumer Expenditures becomes available, we hope to ascertain age-specific factors for all members of the population.

Appendix 2A: Cross-Section
Elasticities for Appliances

One of the major inputs to the estimation of the consumption functions is an income elasticity for each category calculated from the 1960-61 Bureau of Labor Statistics cross-section consumer survey. Because the calculations were based on printed data, only family size was held constant when calculating the income elasticities. Clearly, many other demographic variables may vary with income and bias such estimates of income elasticity.

For the appliances, television sets, and phonograph categories, we have been able to derive elasticities holding a great many more variables constant. Our data for this study comes from a national survey of the appliance market, begun by General Electric in 1967. The survey called for three-thousand families to be interviewed each quarter. We used a total of 11,000 interviews.

Each household was queried on the makeup of the household, the income levels of its occupants and a range of other questions so that the demographic characteristics of the household could be clearly identified. Then the interview continued with a series of questions designed to identify the household's stock of forty appliances. If any item in that stock had been acquired within twelve months, its purchase price was obtained by the interviewer. The combination of information on appliance consumption and the identification of a wide range of demographic variables for each household lends itself ideally to an econometric study of consumer buying patterns. We selected for a study a group of eleven listed in Table 2A-1.

The dependent variable for our study was the purchase price of the appliance; a zero indicated that there had been no purchase of the appliance within the past twelve months. The independent variables were created largely as "class" variables: the variable has a value of one if the household falls in a certain class; otherwise, it is zero. Income was divided into nine classes; family size, into three; age of head of household, into four; his education, into five; type of dwelling, into seven; race, into two; region, into four; urbanization, into four; length of marriage, into eight; time at current address, into two; and homeownership, into two. When all the factors were considered, the "refined" income elasticities differed only slightly from the raw ones calculated without consideration of any demographic variables, as is shown in Table 2A-1.

Some of the demographic effects, however, are quite striking. Couples married less than a year spend about $150 more on TV sets than do similarly situated couples married longer. Fortunately, living in a two-family house holds down TV purchases. Nonwhite families spend some fifty percent more on console phonographs and fifty percent less on portable phonographs than do white families, who are otherwise equivalent. Nonwhites also spend less than half as much as whites on washing machines, but families with four or more children spend an equal amount more than

Table 2A-1
Income Elasticities for Appliances

Appliance	Raw Elasticity	Refined Elasticity
All TV	0.54	0.64
Color TV	0.13	0.20
B & W TV	0.05	0.26
Tape Recorders	0.74	0.57
Console Phonographs	0.48	0.64
Portable Phonographs	0.41	0.29
Washing Machines	0.30	0.23
Dryers	0.54	0.57
Refrigerators	0.30	0.45
Freezers	−0.18	−0.19
Disposals	1.46	1.26
Blenders	0.83	0.80
Room Air Conditioners	0.27	0.23

average. Families in the South spend twice as much on freezers as do similar families elsewhere. These and other insights are graphically illustrated in the complete report on the results of this study, which is available upon request.[k]

[k]Dwight Porter, "Cross-section Analysis of Appliance Demand," INFORUM Research Memorandum No. 25. 1969.

3

Investment in Capital Equipment

At the heart of growth lies investment, and at the heart of a serious growth model must lie its investment sector. Short-term aggregate models can give investment short shrift, for it is fairly well determined by previous decisions within their time horizon, and its composition hardly matters to their broad definition of industries. For our work, the opposite is true. Beyond a year's horizon, investment is almost wholly dependent on decisions yet to be made, and those decisions will determine both the capacity and labor productivity of the investing industry and the sales of the industries which supply the investment goods. Moreover, the industrial composition of investment is of the essence in our work. Because of the detail of our industrial structure, it makes a great deal of difference whether a billion dollars of investment is made by Airlines on Aircraft or by Railroads on Locomotives and railroad equipment or by Trucking on Automobiles or by Water transport on Ships. Our investment sector must have as much detail as possible by investor and must distribute each investor's spending to the appropriate suppliers, for investment plays the lead, not a bit part, in our model.

It is no small order to build such an investment sector, for investment is notoriously volatile in total; and, in small industries, swings of 50 percent and more from one year to the next are not uncommon. Even such large and such sedate old industries as Electric utilities and Telephone increased investment fifty percent from 1969 to 1972 while Steel cut back spending by a third and Automobiles expanded it by a third from 1970 to 1972. Consumption, for all its problems, is a gentle grey mare in comparison with this wild stallion. When riding Investment, we won't sit quite so comfortably in the saddle as we did on Consumption, for leaps and lunges are his normal gait.

Our first task was to put together a complete set of data on equipment spending by buyer, covering the entire economy and matching the Producer durable equipment (PDE) shown in the national accounts as one lump sum. We have, from several sources and with some imagination, produced series for 87 investing industries, aggregates of the 185. Two more "dummy" industries[a] round out the list to 89. Together these 89 cover all investment and add to the total PDE in the national accounts. To our knowledge, it is the only complete

---

[a]Computer rental (which "buys" the machines actually leased out by the computer manufacturers) and personal automobile (which buys the cars which, in the national accounts, are assumed to be bought by individuals, mostly salesmen, for use in their business). Sector numbers run from 1 to 90, but there is no 26.

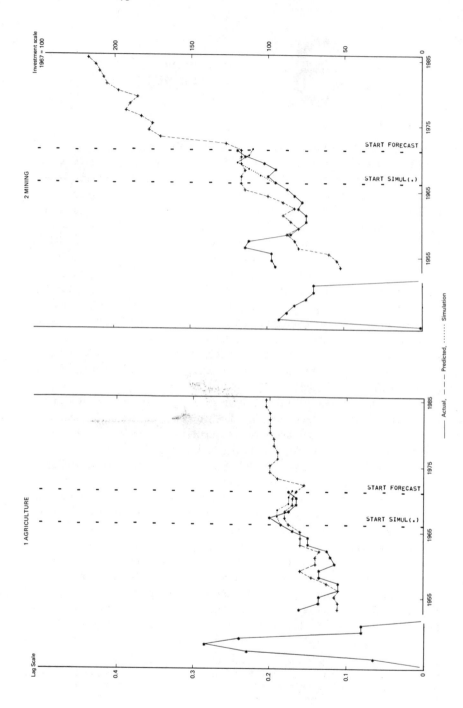

Actual, — — — Predicted, ... Simulation

set of data on PDE by buyer. The details of the sources are given in this chapter's appendix.

With this data in hand, we explored a variety of investment functions. One earlier version is reported by T.H. Mayor in [2]. Experience gradually led us to want more and more control over the economic sensibility of the equations. Otherwise, we simply could not believe the forecasts. We could not leave sensibility to chance nor, with 87 equations to estimate, could we experiment with equation after equation until we found, for each industry, the type of equation which gave a good fit, had good statistical properties, and was economically sensible. This "loving-care" approach, often applied in building small, twenty-to-forty-equation models, was simply not feasible for 87 wild-stallion equations. Instead, we have gradually evolved the "firm-hand" approach which this chapter explains.

The first section gives a simplified account of the equations and a guide to the graphs facing the text and to a summary of the results. The hurried reader can proceed straight from the introduction to the pictures. Connoisseurs of investment functions, however, may wish to savor the other sections of the text. The second section explains the theory of the investment function; the third section adapts the theoretical equation for statistical fitting with quadratic programming and explains how our "firm-hand" used the "subjective objective function" to force the statistical estimates to be sensible. The appendix, as we have said, documents the sources of the data.

Investment in Brief

The basic assumption behind the equations is that the capital desired by an industry, K^*, depends on the output, Q of that industry and the cost of capital, r, as follows:

$$K^* = a Q r^{-\sigma}.$$

Here a and σ are constants. When the cost of capital goes up by one percent, the desired capital will go down by σ percent. Actual capital stock, however, is not always—indeed, is scarcely ever—equal to desired stock. Firms invest to bring the stock up to the desired level and to replace worn out or obsolete machines. Our equations allow for the spreading, over up to six years, of the spending necessary to bring capital up to this desired level. How much of the total needed is spent in the first year in which it is needed, and how much in the second, and so on, is determined separately for each of the industries. (The technique used is the polynomial interpolation or "Almon" distributed lag.) Into the calculation of r, the real cost of capital, go to the real interest rate (the nominal rate minus the rate of inflation), the physical depreciation rate, the depreciation rate for tax

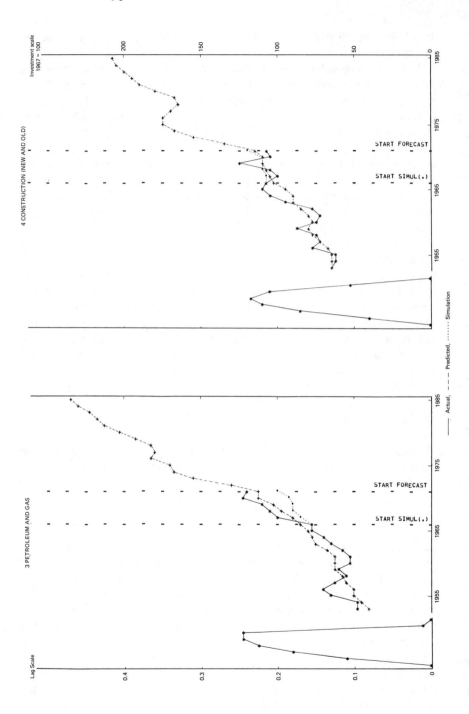

purposes, the tax purposes, the tax rate, and the investment tax credit. In selection of the forecasting equation, we combine a priori expectations about the parameters with the desire for a good fit to historical data. We expect, for example, that the life of capital is about equal to the life for tax purposes and that a one percent increase in output should eventually lead to a one percent increase in capital, provided that r does not change. If we ignore these expectations in the process of curve fitting, we find them violated in the outcome. We find, however, that we can often apply a firm hand to make the equations conform closely to our expectations at very little cost in terms of the closeness of the fit to the historical data. The equations which then result have economic sense built into them.

The plots in this chapter show the fits and forecasts of these equations for 32 of the most important of the 87 industries. On these plots, the solid line represents actual investment for the years up to 1971. The dashed line represents predicted investment, both in the past and in the future from the equation fit through 1971. The dotted line for 1967-71 shows the investment which would have been predicted for those years by an equation estimated with data only through 1966. Table 3-1 summarizes the properties of these equations. The items in it are as follows.

TEST	is the average absolute percentage error in forecasting 1967-71 investment from an equation estimated only through 1966. More precisely, it is the sum of the absolute values of the errors in these five years divided by the total investment over the five years.
CUM	is the cumulative error, the error in the total investment forecasted for the five years divided by the actual total investment over those years. If all the errors are in the same direction, *CUM* and *TEST* have the same magnitude. A minus sign indicates that the actual was below the forecast.
FIT	is the average absolute percentage error of the equation fit over the entire period 1953-71. This is the equation used in the forecasts to 1985. Its properties are described in the following columns of Table 3-1.
RHO	is the autocorrelation coefficient of the equation's misses. The best value would be 0 and the worst, 1 or −1.
SIGMA	This is σ from the basic equation. It shows the percentage change in the desired capital when the cost of capital changes by one percent.
CONSTN	The constant term from the regression equation. Our theory says it should be small relative to investment.

Table 3-1
Investment Equations (Estimated thru 1971)

SEC#	TITLE	TEST	ERRORS CUM	FIT	RHO	SIGMA	CONSTN	CUWT-1	CUWT-2	CUWT-3	CUWT-4	CUWT-5	CUWT-6	OPGLIFF	ADJLIFF
1	AGRICULTURE	5.4	-2.5	9.8	.766	.450	56.6	.065	.296	.585	.825	.908	.991	11.0	9.0
2	MINING	10.2	-5.2	19.5	.909	.400	52.8	.189	.367	.533	.688	.832	.976	10.0	8.0
3	PETROLEUM AND GAS	17.2	17.2	10.8	.751	.000	44.0	.110	.291	.518	.768	1.017	1.029	10.0	8.5
4	CONSTRUCTION	8.5	-3.5	6.9	.281	.050	129.1	.081	.252	.475	.712	.925	1.034	10.0	9.5
5	ORDNANCE	27.7	24.9	35.9	.747	2.300	-216.0	-.216	.312	.414	.480	.510	.540	12.0	7.0
6	MEAT	11.9	11.9	12.0	.754	.050	6.9	.018	.221	.516	.809	1.008	1.014	15.0	14.0
7	DAIRY	35.1	-29.1	18.8	.577	.400	25.0	.094	.510	.381	.567	.947	1.013	15.0	15.0
8	CANNED AND FROZEN	16.7	13.2	18.7	.523	-.350	6.9	.082	.231	.460	.692	.923	1.033	17.0	16.0
9	GRAIN MILL PRODUCT	7.8	-8.8	6.4	.529	-.050	3.0	.110	.241	.460	.818	.902	1.014	15.0	14.5
10	BAKERY	9.4	-6.4	8.4	.657	.350	15.1	.217	.465	.760	.956	.957	1.033	15.0	14.5
11	SUGAR	22.8	-10.9	21.2	.490	.600	3.0	.168	.383	.608	.806	.818	.941	15.0	14.5
12	CANDY	12.9	3.1	9.8	.657	.600	7.7	.122	.376	.663	.884	.940	.996	15.0	14.5
13	BEVERAGES	7.0	-7.0	5.0	.002	.300	20.1	.208	.399	.573	.729	.868	1.002	15.0	14.5
14	MISC. FOOD PRODUCT	18.1	18.1	10.8	.320	.200	6.4	.119	.313	.543	.768	.949	1.012	13.0	12.5
15	TOBACCO	20.0	-20.0	10.8	.550	.550	16.7	.230	.473	.696	.866	.949	1.019	13.0	13.0
16	FABRICS AND YARNS	8.9	1.2	10.2	.456	.200	-4.8	.066	.205	.386	.578	.750	.922	9.0	9.0
17	FLOOR COVERINGS	57.4	57.4	30.9	.709	.550	7.4	.045	.197	.419	.674	.926	1.028	13.0	13.0
18	MISC. TEXTILES	21.1	21.1	15.5	.548	.300	6.5	.074	.197	.369	.590	.860	1.008	9.0	9.0
19	KNIT FABRIC AND AP	32.4	25.3	20.4	.747	1.000	1.3	.191	.376	.553	.721	.878	.995	9.0	9.0
20	APPAREL	15.9	6.8	11.6	.275	.400	6.5	.000	.072	.217	.434	.724	1.014	9.0	9.0
21	HOUSEHOLD TEXTILES	39.9	39.9	27.0	.809	.200	25.8	.313	.594	.817	.955	.980	1.005	10.0	8.5
22	LOGGING AND LUMBER	12.2	2.7	10.3	.005	.150	14.3	.178	.370	.575	.794	.927	1.027	10.0	10.0
23	PLYWOOD, MILLWORK,	22.9	22.9	22.2	.843	.100	1.7	.185	.366	.543	.716	.885	.993	10.0	9.5
24	WOODEN CONTAINERS	73.7	-73.7	35.3	.828	.700	-2.6	.000	.229	.550	.824	.915	1.006	10.0	10.0
25	HOUSEHOLD AND OFFI	16.4	16.4	12.3	.507	.300	136.6	.126	.303	.505	.706	.881	1.015	16.0	14.0
27	PAPER AND PRODUCTS	21.1	-16.2	14.5	.498	.350	11.5	.087	.321	.612	.869	1.002	1.021	12.0	12.0
28	PAPER CONTAINERS	15.5	-14.4	10.6	.372	.300	8.0	.207	.513	.818	1.021	1.021	1.021	11.0	11.0
29	NEWSPAPERS	5.3	3.2	8.8	.365	.200	13.5	.156	.318	.485	.658	.837	1.016	11.0	11.0
30	PRINTING AND PUBLI	11.1	10.9	5.6	.456	.300	8.3	.128	.333	.565	.774	.909	.999	11.0	11.0
31	INDUSTRIAL CHEMICA	11.6	11.0	12.7	.635	.400	14.3	.119	.280	.483	.728	1.014	1.016	11.0	11.0
32	AGRICULTURAL CHEMI	41.1	-13.8	23.4	.008	.400	-8.7	.083	.384	.744	1.003	1.003	1.003	11.0	10.5
33	GLUE, INK, AND FAT	19.7	19.7	21.7	.716	.000	-1.1	.103	.408	.763	1.017	1.017	1.017	11.0	11.0
34	PLASTICS AND SYNTH	11.2	8.4	11.7	.438	.400	-7.8	.000	.173	.430	.683	.844	1.005	11.0	11.0
35	DRUGS	23.4	23.4	13.8	.790	.300	5.2	.000	.073	.218	.436	.727	.998	11.0	11.0
36	CLEANING AND TOILE	18.0	15.3	15.8	.551	.200	-1.2	.000	.071	.214	.428	.713	1.013	11.0	11.0
37	PAINTS AND ALLIED	26.9	26.9	22.6	.312	.600	90.4	.000	.146	.375	.625	.832	1.009	11.0	11.0
38	PETROLEUM REFINING	43.6	43.6	31.7	.692	.300	20.2	.089	.234	.436	.694	.874	1.013	14.0	14.0
39	TIRE AND TUBES	18.3	-.9	14.8	-.328	.300	-1.5	.078	.204	.379	.801	.902	1.001	14.0	14.0
40	RUBBER PRODUCTS	13.4	11.6	9.6	-.033	.200	6.1	.064	.249	.409	.566	.905	1.004	14.0	14.0
41	PLASTIC PRODUCTS	10.1	10.1	15.4	.256	.000	2.4	.092	.228	.448	.901	.901	1.001	10.5	10.5
42	LEATHER TANNING AN	11.3	11.9	8.8	.279	.200	22.2	.215	.459	.697	.895	.987	1.018	11.0	10.5
43	SHOES AND OTHER LE	31.6	-31.6	19.4	.175	.200	26.1	.148	.444	.765	.683	.844	1.005	11.0	11.0
44	GLASS AND GLASS PR	5.4	-4.9	10.4	.635	.300	38.3	.300	.544	.731	.862	.937	1.012	15.0	14.5
45	STONE AND CLAY PRO	17.5	9.6	15.1	.363	.150	306.2	.135	.343	.585	.823	1.019	1.019	18.0	16.0
46	IRON AND STEEL	6.9	-6.4	11.9	.519	.200	67.6	.063	.226	.446	.680	.865	1.011	14.0	14.0
47	NON-FERROUS METALS														

SECH	TITLE	TEST	ERRORS CUM	FIT	RHO	SIGMA	CONSTN	CUWT-1	CUWT-2	CUWT-3	CUWT-4	CUWT-5	CUWT-6	OPOLIFE	ADJLIFE
48	METAL CONTAINERS	4.3	3.9	9.3	.042	.100	6.4	.294	.535	.723	.858	.940	1.022	12.0	12.0
49	PLUMBING AND HEATI	23.3	1.9	16.5	.579	.850	-.3	.002	.139	.360	.614	.850	.987	12.0	9.5
50	STRUCTURAL METAL P	16.8	9.0	7.8	.431	.200	-.7	.150	.324	.510	.697	.875	.988	12.0	12.0
51	STAMPINGS	16.8	14.1	19.0	.444	.400	10.1	.000	.156	.408	.694	.955	.997	12.0	12.0
52	HARDWARE,PLATING,	5.4	3.0	4.6	-.103	.000	16.1	.146	.353	.585	.807	.985	1.016	11.5	11.5
53	ENGINE AND TURBINE	20.5	20.3	16.7	.583	.200	7.2	.204	.428	.642	.816	.910	1.022	12.0	12.0
54	FARM MACHINERY	8.3	-7.7	9.0	.128	.300	-5.6	.158	.340	.528	.703	.846	.971	12.0	11.5
55	CONSTUCTION,MINING	13.2	12.4	9.5	.019	.200	17.3	.109	.273	.481	.722	.985	1.022	12.0	12.0
56	METALWORKING MACHI	14.8	-14.8	11.7	.237	.700	-6.4	.210	.418	.609	.770	.887	1.004	12.0	12.0
57	SPECIAL INDUSTRIAL	9.0	-2.6	10.3	.255	.300	-3.7	.168	.354	.541	.712	.850	.988	12.0	12.0
58	GENERAL INDUSTRIAL	7.6	-6.3	7.4	.127	.400	10.2	.180	.356	.528	.696	.860	1.005	12.0	12.0
59	MISC. MACHINERY AN	16.4	-3.4	20.8	.821	1.200	-11.2	.219	.407	.564	.691	.787	.883	12.0	9.5
60	OFFICE AND COMPUTI	21.8	-12.9	14.9	.293	.400	-2.0	.042	.150	.324	.563	.868	.968	12.0	12.0
61	SERVICE INDUSTRY M	14.9	14.9	18.2	.426	.600	4.3	.068	.180	.337	.539	.786	1.008	12.0	12.0
62	ELECTRIC MEASURING	9.7	-8.0	9.4	.175	.300	-4.3	.154	.316	.485	.661	.845	.967	12.0	11.5
63	ELECTRIC APPARATUS	9.5	9.2	7.5	-.198	.100	-2.1	.181	.365	.544	.711	.858	1.005	12.0	12.0
64	HOUSEHOLD APPLIANC	19.2	17.8	24.6	.661	.500	-.8	.183	.359	.528	.690	.845	1.000	12.0	12.0
65	ELECTRIC LIGHTING	6.6	1.5	9.4	.344	.200	4.3	.000	.110	.315	.602	.957	1.024	12.0	12.0
66	RADIO-,TV-SETS AN	17.5	-10.1	26.2	.415	1.000	.000	.405	.709	.913	1.002	1.013	1.013	8.0	7.5
67	COMMUNICATION EQUI	22.1	22.1	19.5	.731	1.000	13.3	.089	.212	.368	.513	.781	1.004	8.0	8.0
68	ELECTRONIC COMPONE	24.3	24.3	14.5	.562	.100	-6.9	.254	.471	.657	.794	.724	.982	8.0	8.0
69	BATTERIES, X-RAYS	19.6	19.6	16.9	.451	.100	-1.4	.208	.437	.687	.873	.968	1.014	12.0	11.5
70	MOTOR VEHICLES AND	24.4	-26.2	23.2	.728	.100	83.3	.398	.697	.896	.996	.996	.996	10.0	9.5
71	AIRCRAFT AND PARTS	34.4	-25.3	27.7	.759	.200	63.0	.091	.216	.374	.565	.796	1.015	12.0	9.5
72	SHIPS AND BOATS	3.9	3.6	16.0	.093	.200	5.4	.000	.110	.315	.565	.818	.980	12.0	9.5
73	LOCOMOTIVES,RAILR	37.5	-27.8	23.9	.629	.450	-1.0	.165	.329	.493	.728	.818	1.006	12.0	10.0
74	CYCLES,TRAILERS A	18.2	-17.8	15.9	.690	.100	-.6	.262	.563	.834	1.005	1.006	1.006	12.0	10.0
75	ENGR. AND SCIENT.	10.7	-4.2	15.6	.912	.000	.6	.440	.603	.728	.815	.902	.991	11.5	11.5
76	MECH. MEASURING DE	10.7	-1.6	12.6	.313	.100	4.2	.234	.439	.615	.762	.880	.998	12.0	9.5
77	SURGICAL AND MEDIC	7.7	-5.0	17.0	-.123	.200	3.4	.141	.296	.466	.650	.849	.991	12.0	12.0
78	OPTICAL AND PHOTOG	9.3	1.6	8.4	-.143	.100	-1.8	.078	.217	.417	.679	1.002	1.002	12.0	10.0
79	MISC. MANUFACTURED	5.2	-3.5	16.2	.780	.200	-2.8	.046	.147	.304	.565	.783	.919	12.0	7.5
80	RAILROADS	12.7	-7.5	16.8	.024	.200	43.7	.366	.665	.882	1.001	1.006	1.006	10.0	10.0
81	TRUCKING	15.7	6.2	18.0	.579	.000	-45.9	.408	.714	.918	1.020	1.020	1.020	8.0	8.0
82	OTHER TRANSPORT	97.5	-97.5	38.0	.926	.000	112.0	.000	.300	.700	1.000	1.000	1.000	16.0	16.0
83	AIRLINES	17.4	14.0	22.0	.312	.100	443.3	.104	.243	.418	.628	.874	1.020	16.5	6.0
84	WHOLESALE AND RETA	11.6	11.6	7.8	.821	.100	264.5	.411	.719	.925	1.028	1.028	1.028	6.0	6.0
85	COMMUNICATION	9.7	9.7	7.8	.770	.000	-91.1	.351	.626	.825	.948	.995	1.039	8.0	8.0
86	FINANCE, INSURANCE	8.9	-1.5	9.5	-.027	.000	159.8	.406	.710	.913	1.014	1.014	1.014	10.0	9.5
87	ELECTRIC UTILITIES	31.1	31.1	20.5	.886	.000	-25.7	.000	.297	.694	.991	.991	.991	16.5	16.5
88	NAT. GAS, WATER AN	30.0	20.6	27.0	.622	.000	349.8	.099	.235	.408	.617	.863	1.031	10.0	10.0
89	WHOLESALE TRADE	6.9	6.9	7.3	.779	.300	548.3	.111	.252	.424	.626	.859	1.039	9.5	9.5
90	RETAIL TRADE	14.3	14.3	7.3	.846	.100	-38.5	.025	.211	.477	.743	.927	1.004	8.0	8.0
91	AGRIC.,MING,ACONST	2.6	-1.4	6.0	.752	.200	748.6	.000	.209	.519	.824	1.016	1.016	10.0	10.0
92	MANUFACTURING	3.5	-3.5	5.3	.509	.150	1539.0	.115	.258	.429	.628	.855	1.038	10.5	13.2
93	TRANSP.&SERVICES	11.5	11.5	5.3	.655	.100	1472.6	.115	.258	.429	.628	.855	1.038	11.8	11.8
94	TOTAL EQUIPM. EXP.	4.9	4.1	4.3	.391	.100		.042	.195	.421	.682	.940	1.023	11.9	11.9

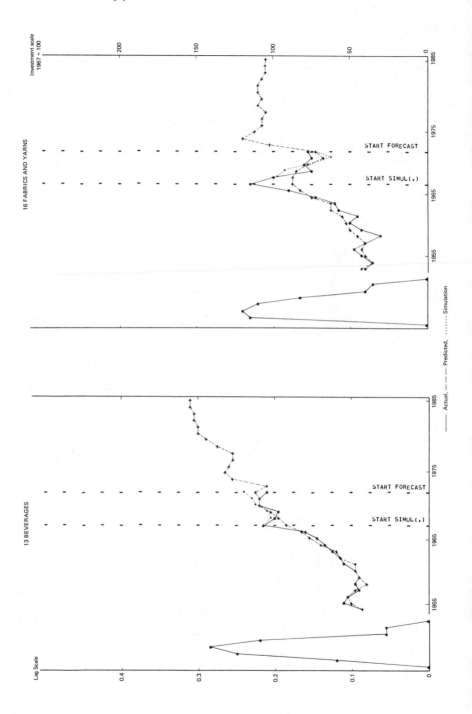

CUWT–1 thru *CUWT*–6	These six *cumulative weights* answer the questions, if output rises by one percent, by what percent will capital stock have risen in response after one year? after two years? . . . after six years? The equations assume that all response takes place in six years.
ORGLIFE *ADJLIFE*	These two columns show the average life of the capital stock in the industry. The one marked "ORG" (for "original") shows the 1960 life as we took it from the Treasury Department's *Depreciation Guidelines*. The ADJusted life shows the revised life used in our equation; the revision, if any, was made to improve the fit of the equation. The firm hand prevents any drastic revision.

The cumulative weights show which of the industries invest quickly, and which slowly, in response to an increase in output. Some twenty industries, such as Communication (85) get off to a fast start and have the greatest response in the first two years after the rise in sales. About forty more, such as Printing and publishing (30), follow a nice symmetric pattern with maximum response in the third and fourth year. Finally, some two dozen laggards, such as Household textiles (21), Paints (37), or Petroleum refining (38), can't seem to get started; they delay the peak of their response until the fifth and sixth years. The cumulative response by the end of the sixth year also indicates whether capital rises more or less, percentagewise, than does output. A priori, we expect a cumulative effect of 1.00 and have used our "firm hand" to insure that no equation wanders far from that norm. Several, such as Ordnance, Floor coverings, and Miscellaneous manufactured products fall below 0.95; their capital-output ratio declines as output increases. Most cumulative effects, however, are above 1.00 and indicate an increase in the capital-output ratio as output increases. The highest are in Trade (1.039), Construction (1.034), Petroleum and gas wells (1.029), and Communication (1.028).

How well do the equations forecast? That remains to be seen. But we can say something about how well their predecessors, estimated on data only up through 1966 would have forecasted the years 1967 to 1971. Their average error over those five years is shown in the first column of Table 3-1. Half of them are less than 15 percent; over 80 percent of them are less than 25 percent. For Agriculture, Mining, and Construction combined, the error was only one percent and the fifth-year error was less than one percent. For all manufacturing combined, the error in 1967, the first year of the test, was 4 percent; by 1968 it had fallen to only 2 percent, but it then climbed back to 8 percent in the fourth year of the forecast just before returning to 1 percent in the last year and averaged 3 percent for the five years. The cumulative errors, shown in the CUM column of Table 3-1 indicate similar accuracy. A quarter of the equations predicted total spending over the five-year test period to within 5 percent. Half of the equations came within 11 percent. Only thirteen industries missed by more than 25 percent. Total investment by all industries was underpredicted by 5 percent.

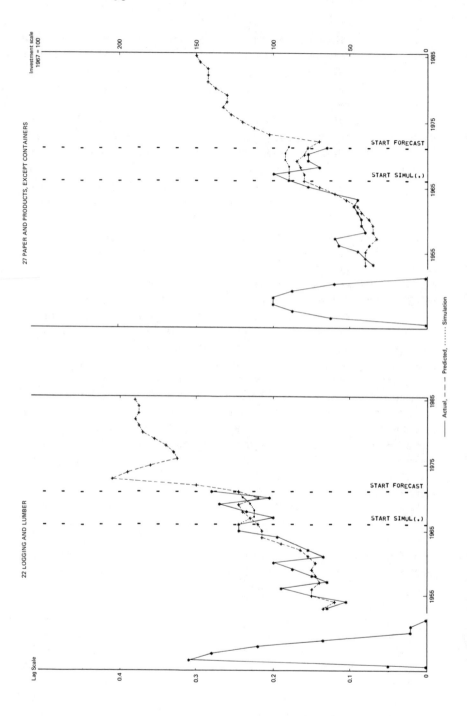

This performance requires no apology. Clearly the equations are working well in most industries. We must not fail, however, to note the industries with the big misses, for it is only from mistakes that we learn. Of the thirteen sour industries, six may be forgiven as small, volatile industries much affected by the timing of the building of a few large plants. These six are:

17 Floor covering—1969 spending was more than twice the 1966 level, but the prediction was back to within $5 million of actual by 1971.

21 Household textiles—spending doubled from 1966 to 1970.

24 Wooden containers—too small really to be a separate sector, it spent only $5 million in 1971.

37 Paint—a big plant was built in 1970, when spending doubled and then fell back in 1971 to its earlier level.

44 Glass—huge investment in 1966 made the equation think that the desired capital-output ratio had risen. In fact, it had not, and investment dropped sharply in 1967.

72 Locomotives and railroad cars—a highly volatile small industry.

Seven large investors, however, had cumulative errors of over 25 percent. Each has its own peculiarities:

7 Dairy—the problem is a bias caused by a lack of data on fluid milk plants prior to 1954. The addition of more years of data reduces that problem.

19 Knitting—the cumulative error for the first three years of the test was zero. Then in 1970 and 1971 investment exploded upward. Even the equation fit through 1971 refuses to explain this explosion. We expect a drop back from this 1971 level.

38 Petroleum refining—1968 spending was three times that of 1965, which was the highest in seven years. Many refineries were built when accelerated amortization was available during the Korean War. The industry then coasted for more than a decade. The capital-output ratio slid down 30 percent from 1958 to 1966. Apparently the industry then woke up to the fact that excess capacity was no longer its problem; and, in the next two years, invested more than in the preceding seven. The capital-output ratio moved up and by 1971 regained the 1958 level. Since we see no evidence that capacity is excessive today, our forecasts keep the capital-output ratio at about that level in the future.

70 Automobiles—a knowledge of style-change years is necessary for accurate prediction of this erratic spender. The graph shows that despite the large error, the trend was right; the 1970 forecast was squarely on the nose.

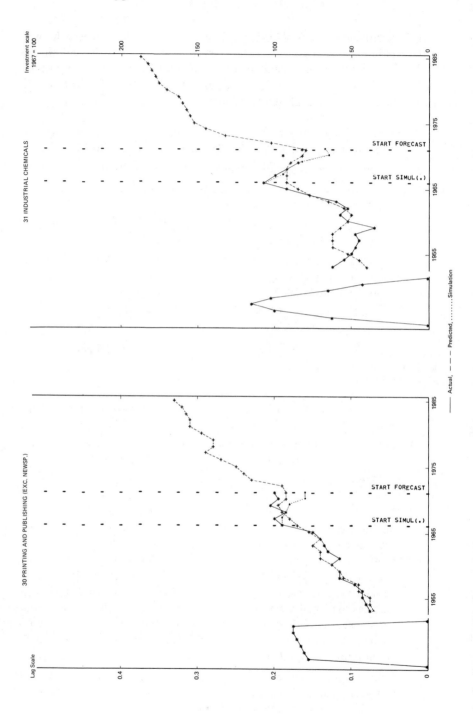

71 Aircraft—tooling up for the major plane models makes it impossible to predict investment here without knowing when the models will be introduced. The experience with the jumbo jets made the equation speed up its reaction time. The equation fit increase for the fourth and fifth year after a sales increase. The equation fit over the whole period but all the response within three years of the increase and 40 percent in the same year with it.

82 Other transportation—the "actual" data are derived as a residual and are, we fear, totally unreliable.

89 Electric utilities—in 1966, the equation overpredicted for the ninth year in a row. For nine years, it has insisted that the utilities should invest, but they wouldn't. Then came the brownouts. By 1971, investment shot up to twice the 1966 level. Various reasons for the speedup may be found—the switch from winter peaking to summer peaking or the introduction of nuclear power plants. But it is fairly clear that the utilities had let their capacity sag badly relative to demand. Their capital output ratio fell 27 percent from 1958 to 1966. Whatever rationality there may be in such behavior eluded our equation, which for the next five years found itself underpredicting. The capital-output ratio was back up to the 1961 level by 1971, and the forecasts keep it about there.

Lest this recital of difficulties leave the reader doubtful of the value of the equations, we must in all modesty call attention to the highly satisfactory performance of the equations for such major sectors as Agriculture, Mining, Construction, Fabrics and yarn, Logging and lumber, Tires and tubes, Shoes, Stone and clay products, Instruments, Airlines, and Finance, insurance, and services. All of these and a dozen others had cumulative errors of 5 percent or less over five years. Surely these equations deserve some confidence when, fortified with five years's more experience, they sally forth into the future.

Theory of the Equations

In the preceding section, we stated that the investment equations were based upon the equation

$$K^* = aQr^{-\sigma} \tag{3.1}$$

where

K^* is desired capital

Q is output

r is the cost of capital

σ is the elasticity of substitution of capital for labor.

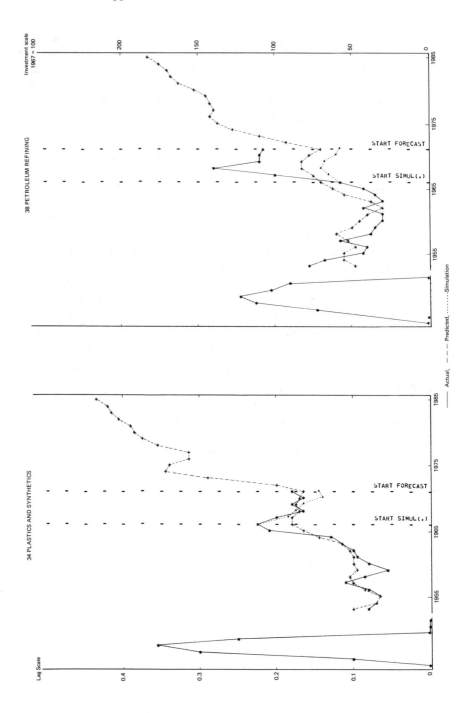

34 PLASTICS AND SYNTHETICS

38 PETROLEUM REFINING

Investment scale
1967 = 100

Lag Scale

START FORECAST

START SIMUL(.)

————— Actual, ——— Predicted, ...Simulation

This equation expresses a production function with constant returns to scale and a constant elasticity of substitution, σ, between capital and labor. That is, a 1 percent increase in r brings about a σ-percent decrease in the K^*/Q ratio, as is easily seen by differentiation (3.1) with respect to r.

Equation (3.1), however, is not really an investment equation, because it gives us desired stock, K^*, not gross investment, V. Our first task in this section is, therefore, to convert (3.1) into an investment equation which will involve net investment, N, actual capital, K, and r. We shall then have to explain these variables. What precisely is r? How do we measure K? How do we get an estimate of replacement R to take us from gross investment, V, to net investment, $N = V - R$?

An Investment Equation

The change in the desired stock during one year is the desired net investment in that year. This change may be expressed as a function of the percent changes in output and rental rate by differentiating both sides of Equation (3.1) with respect to time. The change in desired capital stock becomes

$$\dot{K}^* = a(\dot{Q}r^{-\sigma} - \sigma Q\dot{r}\,r^{-(1+\sigma)})$$

where the dot over a letter denotes a derivative with respect to time. By dividing both sides by K^* and using (3.2), we get

$$\frac{\dot{K}^*}{K^*} = \frac{\dot{Q}}{Q} - \sigma\frac{\dot{r}}{r}$$

or

$$\dot{K}^* = \left(\frac{\dot{Q}}{Q} - \sigma\frac{\dot{r}}{r}\right)K^*.$$

To obtain an equation which can be estimated, the unobservable K^* on the right must be replaced by actual capital K. Then, with the first difference approximation replacing the differential, the preceding equation becomes

$$X_t = \left(\frac{Q_t - Q_{t-1}}{Q_{t-1}} - \sigma\frac{r_t - r_{t-1}}{r_{t-1}}\right)K_{t-1} \tag{3.2}$$

where X_t denotes the approximation to the change in desired capital, between time $t-1$ and t.

In fact, the actual net investment called forth by changes in output and rental rate is not spent immediately but is spread over several years. We let w_i be the

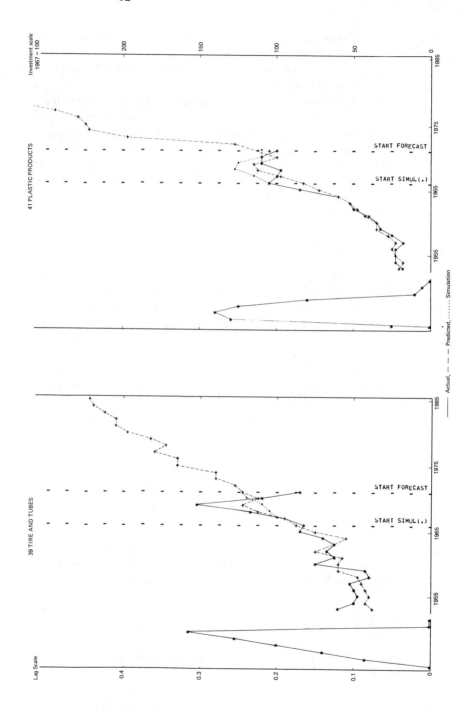

fraction of this spending which occurs in the ith year after the capital was first desired. The observed net investment is then given by

$$N_t = \sum_{i=0}^{n} w_i X_{t-i} + \epsilon_t \qquad (3.3)$$

where n is the length of the lag distribution. We expect the w's to be positive and their sum to be one. Equation (3.3), with X_t defined by (3.2) is our desired investment equation. An adjustment for cases in which X_t is negative will be described at the end of this section.

For a large number of industries the RHO statistic in Table 3-1 indicates significant autocorrelation in the errors. If we missed on the high side in one year, we are apt to err on the same side again the next year. It is therefore possible to improve the predictive power of the equation by making an autocorrelation adjustment just as we did in the consumption equations. The SIM*ERR column in Table 3-1 was calculated from forecasts with this ρ-adjustment.

The Rental Rate

The rental rate, r, is, in theory, the marginal product of capital. A profit maximizing firm sets the cost of one additional unit of capital, S_c, equal to its after-tax return S_r. This return is the marginal physical product of capital, r, times the value-added per unit, P_v, less the corporate profit tax-at-rate T:

$$S_r = r P_v (1-T)$$

and the cost of the additional unit is

$$S_c = P_e (r_r + d) (1 - Tz - C)$$

where P_e = price of the capital equipment

r_r = real rate of interest

d = physical depreciation rate

C = rate of investment tax credit

z = present value of the stream of depreciation generated by a one dollar investment.

By collecting terms and solving for the rental rate, r, we get[b]

[b]The derivation of Equation (3.4) is taken from [3]. The actual calculations draw heavily on the work of Thomas Mayor reported in [2].

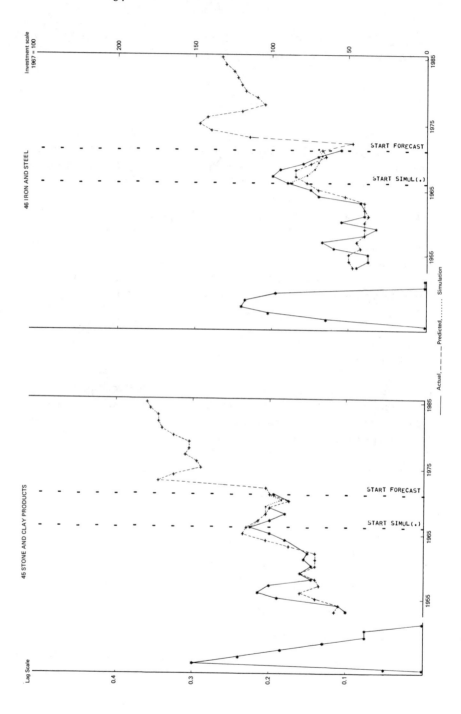

$$r = \frac{P_e\,(r_r + d)\,(1 - Tz - C)}{P_v\,(1 - T)} \qquad (3.4)$$

The *price indices* of capital equipment and value-added are found by making use of the industry sales coefficient matrix and capital flow matrix of the input-output system.

$$p_e^j = \sum_{i=1}^{n} b_{ij} p_q^i$$

$$p_v^j = p_q^j - \sum_{i=1}^{n} a_{ij} p_q^i$$

where p_q^i = price of the ith product

b_{ij} = the share of the ith product in a dollar's worth of capital bought by sector j,

a_{ij} = input of product i per unit of product j produced,

n = number of sectors

The *real rate of interest* is calculated as the difference between the nominal rate of interest (given to us by Moody's bond rates) and the expected rate of inflation. The expected inflation is taken to be a sum of past inflation levels. (See [4].)

$$r_{rt} = r_{nt} - \sum_{i=0}^{n} w_i (\Delta p_{t-i} / p_{t-i-1})$$

where r_n = nominal rate of interest (Moody's AAA bond rates)

p_t = PDE average prices in year t

$w_0 = 0.4, w_1 = 0.3, w_2 = 0.2, w_3 = 0.1$

so that the sum of the w's is 1.0.

The physical depreciation rate, d, is a function of the reciprocal of equipment's average tax life. We have adopted Mayor's estimate of d for the period of 1947 to 1960. We extended the series beyond 1960 by letting it rise in proportion to the reciprocal of the average life of equipment, L_t, for which we used the formula:

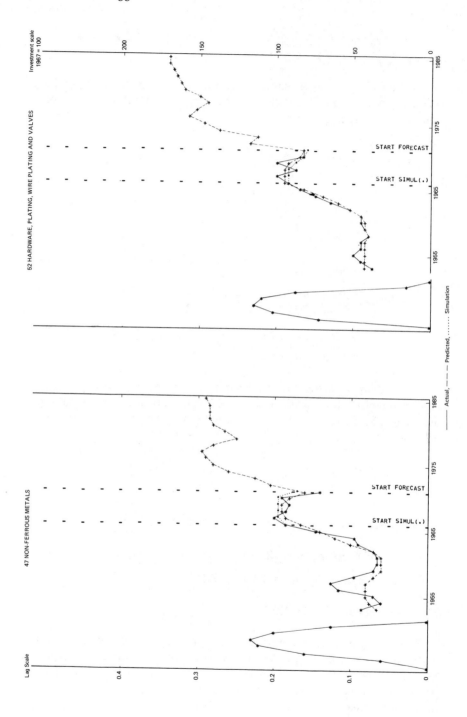

$$L_t = \begin{cases} [0.8e^{0.008\,(1980-t)^{1.1}}]\,L_{1960} & t \leqslant 1980 \\ 0.8\,L_{1960} & t > 1980. \end{cases} \qquad (3.5)$$

The term in brackets on the right of (3.5) has the value of 1.5 in 1930, 1.0 in 1960, and 0.8 in 1980. We project, in other words, a gradual shortening of equipment service lives.

For L_{1960}, we initially used the *Depreciation Guidelines* life for the appropriate industry, but L_{1960} was subject to change in the course of fitting the regression equations, as will be explained in the next section. The *tax life*, L^*, is the same as the initial guess of the physical depreciation life, L. The difference between them is that L is subject to change during the estimating procedure, but L^* is not.

The present value, z, of the stream of depreciation generated by a one dollar investment is calculated in [3, page 85] by

$$z = \frac{2}{r_r L^*}\left[1 - \frac{1}{r_r L^*}(1 - e^{-r_r L^*})\right]$$

From all these components, r for each year can then be calculated from Equation (3.4).

The Capital Stock

The capital stock in Equation (3.3) is calculated by a method that approximates the productive capacity rather than the book value of the stock. We distinguish two classes of capital: the first is that which has not yet been written off while the second has been written off but is still in service. The first-class stock, K_1, grows by the gross investment, V_t, and falls by a percentage "spilled" s_t:

$$K_{1t} = K_{1t-1} + V_t - s_t K_{1t-1}. \qquad (3.6a)$$

The second-class stock grows by the depreciation out of the first-class stock and falls by the same percent depreciation:

$$K_{2t} = K_{2t-1} + s_t K_{1t-1} - s_t K_{2t-1} \qquad (3.6b)$$

The total stock of capital is then the sum of the two classes

$$K_t = K_{1t} + K_{2t} \qquad (3.7)$$

In the above equation, s is the double-declining-balance rate of depreciation, determined from the physical life of capital given by Equation (3.5). That is,

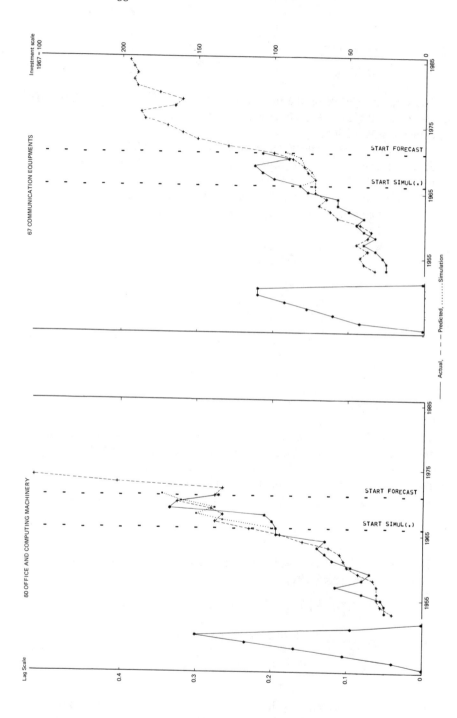

$$s_t = \frac{2}{L_t}.$$

Finally, the net investment or dependent variable of the regression, is the difference between gross investment V_t and replacement R_t, where R_t is the depreciation on the second-class stock $s_t K_{2\,t-1}$. Therefore,

$$N_t = V_t - s_t K_{2\,t-1}. \tag{3.8}$$

There is a natural analogy between this scheme and a two-bucket reservoir system. We may imagine two buckets, one above the other with water flowing into the top bucket. The water runs out of a hole in the bottom of the top bucket, into the lower bucket, and then out of a hole in the lower bucket. The flow into the top bucket corresponds to investment; the spill out of the top bucket, to depreciation; the spill out of the bottom bucket, to the replacement investment. The water in the top bucket corresponds to the book value of capital; the water in the bottom bucket, to capital that has been written off but is still in service. The sum of these two, the total water in the system, corresponds to the total capital stock retained in service. Figure 3-1 shows the implied retention curve. The dotted curve in this figure shows a one-bucket curve with the same average life as the two-bucket curve.

In comparison with the one-bucket curve, which is the usual exponential depreciation, the two-bucket curve should offer a closer approximation to the productive capacity of the capital, the capital appropriate for the production function. Yet only two words of computer memory are required to store the necessary information, K_1 and K_2, in contrast to the L words which would be required for, say, the "one-horse shay" assumption.

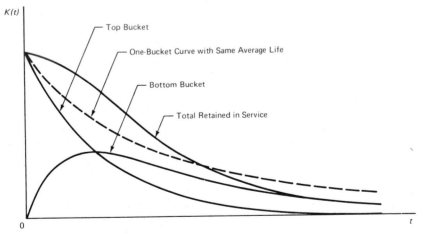

Figure 3-1. Retention Curve of Capital Stock

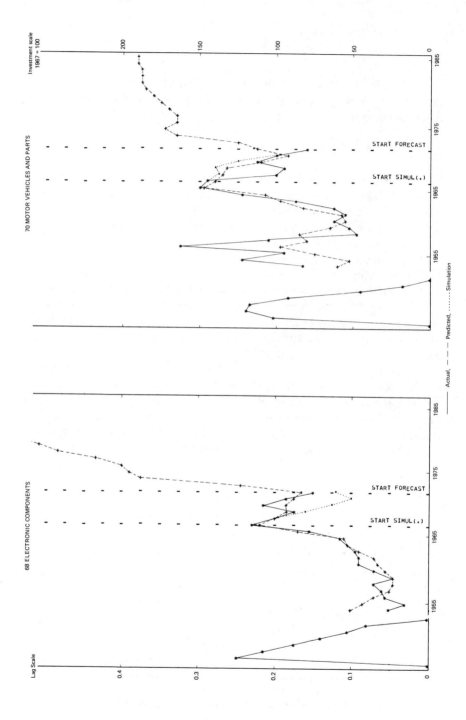

Investment scale
1967 = 100

70 MOTOR VEHICLES AND PARTS

START FORECAST

START SIMUL(.)

68 ELECTRONIC COMPONENTS

START FORECAST

START SIMUL(.)

Lag Scale

—— Actual, — — Predicted, ... Simulation

We are now in a position to describe what we do in cases in which X_t of Equation (3.2) is negative. Namely, we add that *negative* X_t to the "top bucket" capital stock and set the value of $X_t = 0$. For example, if $X_t = -30$, we conclude that the industry has in the pipeline $30 million of capital that cannot be justified by present output and capital cost levels. We assume that this $30 million will not be replaced when it wears out and therefore subtract $30 million from the capital stock.

Table 3-2 presents the total stock of capital equipment (in millions of 1969 dollars) by industry, in 1955, 1960, 1965, and 1970. For these years, it also shows the share of "top bucket" capital in the total, labeled $\% - K1/K$, and the capital-output ratio, labeled $K/Q - RT$. With capital output ratios, we find both precipitous falls, as in Floor coverings and Knitting, and dramatic rises, as in Construction, Sugar, Logging and lumber, and Glass. Most industries have, as would be expected, slightly over half of the capital still in the "top bucket."

With this method of calculating capital stock, it is also possible to calculate the average age of equipment. Table 3-3 shows the results. (The columns for 1974-80 are based on forecasts made before final 1971 data was used in the model.)

The Firm-Handed Estimation of the Investment Equation[c]

The following is the investment equation which was actually estimated:

$$N_t = a + \sum_{i=0}^{5} w_i X_{t-i} \tag{3.3a}$$

The constant term a has been added for the convenience of estimation. We were willing to change L_{1960}—in effect, to revise our view of the physical life of capital—in order to improve the fit. On the other hand, we had a variety of preconceived ideas about what results of the estimation should look like. We expected:

1. That the sum of the weights should be 1.0
2. That a, the constant term, should be zero, because it does not appear in Equation (3.3)
3. That L_{1960} should be close to L^*_{1960}

[c]This is the most mathematically demanding section of the book. The casual reader may skip it without loss of continuity, but the reader who is actually engaged in the estimation of equations may find it quite useful.

Table 3-2
Stock of Equipment, % First Class Stock and K/Q-Ratio for Selected Years

SECT#	TITLE	1955 STOCK	1955 %-K1/K	1955 K/Q-RT	1960 STOCK	1960 %-K1/K	1960 K/Q-RT	1965 STOCK	1965 %-K1/K	1965 K/Q-RT	1970 STOCK	1970 %-K1/K	1970 K/Q-RT
1	AGRICULTURE	39383.	.5139	.8020	36059.	.4810	.6700	35604.	.5079	.5840	38780.	.5062	.5770
2	MINING	7399.	.5621	.9910	9102.	.4953	1.0570	7424.	.4887	.8210	7878.	.5166	.7930
3	PETROLEUM AND GAS	2796.	.5959	.3040	3537.	.5377	.3470	3954.	.5331	.3330	5260.	.5608	.3430
4	CONSTRUCTION	11475.	.5679	.4160	14159.	.5413	.4950	16532.	.5427	.5140	18845.	.5237	.6080
5	ORDNANCE	529.	.5142	.2180	966.	.4959	.0980	546.	.5110	.0900	713.	.5007	.0890
6	MEAT	824.	.5850	.0500	986.	.4952	.0470	1150.	.5617	.0490	1438.	.5626	.0530
7	DAIRY	1108.	.6191	.1060	1598.	.5552	.1230	1917.	.5566	.1410	1947.	.5131	.1530
8	CANNED AND FROZEN FOOD	940.	.5723	.1960	1159.	.6001	.1600	1461.	.5756	.1600	1934.	.5750	.1920
9	GRAIN MILL PRODUCTS	932.	.5987	.1510	1154.	.5605	.1440	1395.	.5685	.1600	1685.	.5614	.1590
10	BAKERY	1339.	.5736	.2420	1488.	.5823	.2260	1583.	.5268	.2290	1661.	.5099	.2420
11	SUGAR	257.	.5603	.1280	343.	.5910	.1440	430.	.6146	.2130	646.	.5573	.2320
12	CANDY	351.	.5413	.1710	363.	.5248	.1540	519.	.5535	.1560	567.	.5697	.1850
13	BEVERAGES	1941.	.5574	.2320	2036.	.5251	.1490	2315.	.5430	.2000	2971.	.5651	.1850
14	MISC. FOOD PRODUCTS	1027.	.5823	.1710	1243.	.5567	.1600	1443.	.5495	.1640	1775.	.5566	.1730
15	TOBACCO	322.	.5466	.0480	407.	.5577	.0490	497.	.5533	.0580	517.	.5087	.0620
16	FABRICS AND YARNS	2704.	.5444	.2390	2691.	.4928	.2350	3079.	.5483	.2120	3764.	.5372	.2360
17	FLOOR COVERINGS	283.	.5406	.5030	276.	.5371	.3710	257.	.4826	.1940	336.	.5714	.1400
18	MISC. TEXTILES	260.	.5731	.1580	283.	.5371	.1570	362.	.5718	.1560	524.	.5859	.1990
19	KNIT FABRIC AND APPARE	753.	.4595	.3660	603.	.4561	.2470	616.	.5227	.1660	864.	.5625	.1440
20	APPAREL	869.	.5224	.0700	920.	.4978	.0640	965.	.5244	.0550	1092.	.5137	.0640
21	HOUSEHOLD TEXTILES AND	152.	.5395	.0690	175.	.5143	.0670	214.	.5701	.0590	364.	.6099	.0850
22	LOGGING AND LUMBER	1208.	.5430	.1470	1475.	.5424	.1880	1641.	.6026	.1230	1877.	.5162	.2100
23	PLYWOOD, MILLWORK, STR	390.	.5436	.1110	467.	.5525	.1130	682.	.6081	.1190	1071.	.5798	.1610
24	WOODEN CONTAINERS	67.	.6119	.1270	68.	.4853	.1310	63.	.5079	.1190	65.	.4923	.1130
25	HOUSEHOLD AND OFFICE F	649.	.5239	.1140	673.	.5022	.1130	726.	.5344	.0940	954.	.5545	.1130
26	PAPER AND PRODUCTS, EX	4781.	.6011	.4770	6243.	.5698	.5520	7473.	.5662	.5660	9686.	.5603	.5850
27	PAPER CONTAINERS	799.	.5757	.2140	1058.	.5595	.2590	1296.	.5563	.2600	1678.	.5501	.2540
28	NEWSPAPERS	865.	.5642	.1920	961.	.5255	.2000	1084.	.5341	.2020	1628.	.5450	.2820
29	PRINTING AND PUBLISHIN	1863.	.5588	.3220	2286.	.5573	.2740	2761.	.5480	.2660	3585.	.5420	.2270
30	INDUSTRIAL CHEMICALS	5106.	.6150	.7640	5925.	.5399	.6830	7404.	.5659	.5760	9635.	.5466	.5690
31	AGRICULTURAL CHEMICALS	223.	.6457	.2320	336.	.5982	.2550	540.	.5796	.2660	805.	.5443	.2820
32	GLUE, INK, AND FATTY A	661.	.5794	.2790	700.	.4986	.2710	647.	.4760	.2150	812.	.5500	.2380
33	PLASTICS AND SYNTHETIC	2439.	.5568	.8810	2798.	.5275	.7140	3694.	.5850	.5860	5022.	.5690	.3500
34	DRUGS	599.	.5593	.2860	688.	.5378	.2400	748.	.5281	.1720	1071.	.5826	.1680
35	CLEANING AND TOILET IT	331.	.5136	.1100	356.	.5281	.0840	499.	.5195	.0840	718.	.5877	.0890
36	PAINTS AND ALLIED PROD	286.	.5350	.1460	301.	.4983	.1360	308.	.5702	.1070	418.	.5813	.1410
37	PETROLEUM REFINING	2098.	.6249	.1290	2231.	.5114	.1180	2073.	.4867	.0940	3431.	.5972	.1260
38	TIRE AND TUBES	882.	.6145	.3840	1098.	.5783	.3750	1375.	.5455	.3810	1912.	.5884	.4420
39	RUBBER PRODUCTS	708.	.5805	.2870	773.	.5330	.3000	860.	.6484	.3070	1090.	.6263	.3050
40	PLASTIC PRODUCTS	505.	.6277	.3550	735.	.6166	.3370	1294.	.5948	.3570	2277.	.5505	.3320
41	LEATHER TANNING AND IN	110.	.5091	.0840	103.	.4854	.0910	97.	.5157	.0590	109.	.5138	.1170
42	SHOES AND OTHER LEATHE	212.	.5660	.0540	243.	.5910	.0630	254.	.5508	.0590	296.	.5270	.0710
43	GLASS AND GLASS PRODUC	754.	.6074	.2360	1093.	.5757	.5070	1360.	.5768	.3910	1942.	.5814	.4450
44	STONE AND CLAY PRODUCT	3358.	.6033	.4380	4445.	.5912	.4660	5089.	.5733	.4620	5675.	.5307	.5020
45	IRON AND STEEL	8655.	.6315	.2940	11437.	.5778	.2410	13449.	.5628	.4390	17678.	.5704	.6300
46	NON-FERROUS METALS	2327.	.6287	.1760	3221.	.5478	.2510	3719.	.5535	.2000	5476.	.5878	.2740
47	METAL CONTAINERS	55.	.5740	.2360	648.	.5740	.2510	766.	.5535	.2560	1003.	.5633	.2630

SECT#	TITLE	1955 STOCK	%-K1/K	K/Q-RT	1960 STOCK	%-K1/K	K/Q-RT	1965 STOCK	%-K1/K	K/Q-RT	1970 STOCK	%-K1/K	K/Q-RT
49	PLUMBING AND HEATING	420.	.4976	.3150	349.	.4413	.2490	286.	.4685	.1660	279.	.501R	.1650
50	STRUCTURAL METAL PRODU	826.	.5944	.1550	1037.	.5593	.1480	1105.	.5408	.1290	1506.	.5571	.1400
51	STAMPINGS	1368.	.5475	.2830	1410.	.5064	.2770	1504.	.5372	.2380	2077.	.5648	.3440
52	HARDWARE,PLATING, WIRE	1137.	.5875	.1480	1365.	.5480	.1740	1772.	.5745	.1570	2377.	.5557	.2030
53	ENGINE AND TURBINES	399.	.5689	.2180	508.	.5453	.2370	585.	.5521	.2090	1019.	.6202	.2370
54	FARM MACHINERY	574.	.5314	.2270	569.	.5026	.2270	604.	.5331	.1600	746.	.5362	.1900
55	CONSTRUCTION,MINING,MAT	618.	.6052	.1110	858.	.5839	.1630	1018.	.5678	.1330	1496.	.5762	.1740
56	METALWORKING MACHINERY	1605.	.6100	.2700	1769.	.5127	.3260	1753.	.5163	.2390	2111.	.5244	.2830
57	SPECIAL INDUSTRIAL MAC	684.	.5249	.2230	712.	.5070	.1860	791.	.5386	.1570	994.	.5443	.1920
58	GENERAL INDUSTRIAL MAC	911.	.5763	.2120	1118.	.5492	.2360	1305.	.5571	.1920	1702.	.5494	.2420
59	MISC. MACHINERY AND SH	458.	.5284	.3140	538.	.5242	.2780	605.	.5388	.2140	826.	.5354	.2060
60	OFFICE AND COMPUTING M	376.	.5771	.3040	584.	.5942	.2850	915.	.6077	.2280	1522.	.6196	.2000
61	SERVICE INDUSTRY MACHI	440.	.5727	.2050	453.	.5055	.1750	482.	.5228	.1170	707.	.5757	.1150
62	ELECTRIC MEASURING, TR	525.	.5752	.2030	586.	.5256	.2120	597.	.5059	.1710	758.	.5528	.1700
63	ELECTRIC APPARATUS AND	664.	.5783	.2400	732.	.5232	.2430	806.	.5434	.1810	1110.	.5622	.2260
64	HOUSEHOLD APPLIANCES	910.	.5714	.3030	819.	.4799	.2500	811.	.5179	.1710	958.	.5418	.1730
65	ELECTRIC LIGHTING AND	445.	.6067	.1930	510.	.5451	.1980	624.	.5657	.1710	861.	.5633	.2060
66	RADIO-, TV-SETS AND PH	86.	.5000	.0760	98.	.5408	.0570	172.	.6163	.0500	305.	.5344	.0760
67	COMMUNICATION EQUIPMEN	572.	.5542	.1840	773.	.5576	.1320	1076.	.5725	.1170	1698.	.5518	.1340
68	ELECTRONIC COMPONENTS	481.	.5489	.2450	682.	.5733	.2570	1066.	.5863	.1910	1760.	.5511	.2390
69	BATTERIES, X-RAYS AND	398.	.5528	.1970	401.	.4938	.2130	410.	.5146	.1530	795.	.5184	.2010
70	MOTOR VEHICLES AND PAR	4801.	.6190	.1200	5879.	.5273	.1600	6631.	.5568	.1230	2895.	.5520	.1640
71	AIRCRAFT AND PARTS	720.	.6597	.0510	1286.	.5708	.0940	1692.	.5550	.1030	424.	.5999	.1330
72	SHIPS AND BOATS	136.	.6176	.0910	228.	.6140	.1220	285.	.5649	.0700	246.	.5569	.1310
73	LOCOMOTIVES, RAILROADS	202.	.5594	.1280	187.	.4652	.1310	185.	.5297	.0500	157.	.6561	.0450
74	CYCLES, TRAILERS AND P	40.	.5000	.0730	53.	.5849	.0640	82.	.6098	.1160	124.	.5645	.0990
75	ENGR. AND SCIENT. INST	44.	.5455	.0600	67.	.6119	.0670	96.	.5729	.1310	348.	.5402	.1780
76	MECH. MEASURING DEVICE	138.	.5870	.0950	205.	.5854	.1230	281.	.5744	.1640	289.	.5813	.1520
77	SURGICAL AND MEDICAL I	120.	.5812	.2230	155.	.5742	.1740	202.	.5722	.1810	1152.	.6007	.2030
78	OPTICAL AND PHOTOGRAPH	425.	.5525	.1450	524.	.5123	.1310	681.	.5283	.1100	1010.	.5287	.1110
79	MISC. MANUFACTURED PRO	695.	.5525	1.1790	773.	.5123	1.1760	857.	.5283	.1810	2993.	.5041	.9890
80	RAILROADS	12898.	.5136	1.1790	11838.	.4725	1.1760	11816.	.5159	.9550	12993.	.5041	1.9890
81	TRUCKING	1274.	.5424	.1220	1505.	.5262	.1200	2354.	.5213	.1380	3648.	.5518	.1720
82	OTHER TRANSPORT	14783.	.6012	1.1670	15443.	.5534	1.1720	1590.	.5923	.8200	13201.	.4440	1.1920
83	AIRLINES	1502.	.5613	.6310	3144.	.6037	.6680	4802.	.5492	.1890	11682.	.5733	1.1260
84	WHOLESALE AND RETAIL T	20722.	.5560	.1860	24498.	.5346	.1930	30864.	.5862	.1290	43909.	.5539	.2250
85	COMMUNICATION	10603.	.5787	1.1080	15549.	.5688	1.1890	23516.	.5687	.2610	37693.	.5878	1.3920
86	FINANCE, INSURANCE AND	46152.	.5867	.2770	54540.	.5694	.2700	65789.	.5261	.9630	80651.	.5632	.2650
87	ELECTRIC UTILITIES	11524.	.6270	1.1590	15293.	.5538	1.1470	17125.	.5072	.2430	25120.	.5875	1.0250
88	NAT. GAS, WATER AND SE	2978.	.5695	.2910	4003.	.5538	.5250	4008.	.5492	.4910	4740.	.5534	.2350
89	WHOLESALE TRADE	20722.	.5560	.2840	24498.	.5346	.3040	30864.	.5492	.3090	43909.	.5539	.3780
90	RETAIL TRADE	20722.	.5560	.7020	68128.	.5065	.6790	70420.	.5159	.6170	77930.	.5173	.6310
91	AGRICULTURE, MINING, A	65865.	.5888	.2060	94243.	.5495	.2230	110831.	.5557	.2030	145320.	.5584	.2360
92	TOTAL MANUFACTURING	78136.	.5888	.3600	148711.	.5521	.3660	180935.	.5571	.3520	243781.	.5687	.3890
93	TRANSPORTATION AND SER	123890.	.5766	.3600									
94	TOTAL EQUIPMENT INVEST	273713.	.5746	.3350	318715.	.5423	.3430	370648.	.5480	.3150	475809.	.5559	.3480

Table 3-3

Average Age of Equipment

AVERAGE AGE OF EQUIPMENT

SEC#	INDUSTRY	1950	1955	1960	1962	1964	1966	1968	1970	1972	1974	1976	1978	1980
1	AGRICULTURE	5.4	5.2	7.1	7.2	7.0	6.6	6.2	6.1	6.0	5.5	4.9	4.4	4.2
2	MINING	4.2	4.5	5.3	5.7	5.4	5.7	5.5	5.2	5.1	4.7	4.6	4.3	4.2
3	PETROLEUM AND GAS	4.7	4.5	5.1	5.4	5.4	5.3	4.9	5.2	4.6	4.3	4.1	4.1	4.2
4	CONSTRUCTION(NEW AND OLD)	4.8	4.9	5.2	5.5	5.4	5.2	5.2	5.1	5.0	4.7	4.4	4.3	4.3
5	ORDNANCE	3.9	4.2	4.3	4.3	4.3	3.5	3.5	3.5	3.0	2.9	3.1	3.3	3.4
6	MEAT	6.8	7.3	7.9	8.0	7.9	7.5	7.4	8.3	8.4	8.1	6.6	3.3	3.4
7	DAIRY	7.2	7.3	6.6	6.8	7.0	7.4	6.9	8.3	8.4	6.7	7.5	7.0	6.4
8	CANNED AND FROZEN FOODS	7.5	8.0	8.4	8.2	8.0	7.4	6.9	6.8	6.7	6.3	5.8	5.5	5.6
9	GRAIN MILL PRODUCTS	6.5	7.5	7.9	8.0	8.1	7.2	6.9	7.9	7.7	7.7	7.6	7.3	7.1
10	BAKERY	6.7	7.9	8.3	8.2	8.8	8.0	8.0	8.5	8.4	8.0	7.6	7.3	7.2
11	SUGAR	6.8	7.9	7.3	7.1	8.1	8.6	8.6	8.6	8.4	6.3	5.9	5.8	5.8
12	CANDY	7.0	8.6	9.3	9.1	8.8	8.0	6.3	6.6	7.0	6.5	6.3	6.2	6.3
13	BEVERAGES	6.7	7.9	8.8	8.8	8.8	8.0	7.6	7.2	7.0	6.5	6.6	6.4	6.3
14	MISC. FOOD PRODUCTS	6.3	7.0	7.3	7.4	7.3	7.3	7.5	7.1	6.7	6.4	6.4	6.3	6.1
15	TOBACCO	7.7	8.4	7.9	8.2	7.9	7.7	7.9	6.8	8.0	7.6	6.9	5.5	6.3
16	FABRICS AND YARNS	5.7	7.1	8.2	8.2	8.9	6.7	6.7	8.0	8.0	6.5	5.9	5.5	3.0
17	FLOOR COVERINGS	3.3	4.2	4.9	4.9	4.8	4.1	5.8	3.1	2.9	2.3	2.7	2.9	3.0
18	MISC. TEXTILES	5.7	6.4	7.3	7.1	6.9	4.7	4.7	5.7	4.3	4.1	5.2	4.8	3.8
19	KNIT FABRIC AND APPAREL	4.5	6.4	7.1	6.7	6.4	5.2	4.7	4.4	4.3	4.1	4.0	3.8	3.8
20	APPAREL	5.1	5.1	5.8	5.9	5.6	5.2	4.5	4.9	4.8	4.6	4.1	3.9	3.8
21	HOUSEHOLD TEXTILES AND UPHOLSTERY	4.7	5.1	5.3	5.4	5.1	4.4	4.0	3.8	3.9	3.8	3.8	3.6	3.5
22	LOGGING AND LUMBER	4.8	5.2	5.2	5.4	5.3	5.0	5.3	4.7	4.6	4.2	4.0	3.9	3.8
23	PLYWOOD, MILLWORK, STRUCTURES, ETC.	5.4	5.8	5.6	5.4	4.9	4.2	4.1	4.0	3.9	3.1	3.1	3.1	3.0
24	WOODEN CONTAINERS	3.8	4.0	5.7	6.4	6.4	5.5	5.6	5.4	5.2	3.9	3.2	3.0	3.4
25	HOUSEHOLD AND OFFICE FURNITURE	5.7	5.7	6.6	6.6	6.3	5.5	5.1	5.1	5.2	3.9	4.7	4.4	4.3
27	PAPER AND PRODUCTS, EXCEPT CONTAINERS	6.3	7.1	7.5	7.8	7.9	7.2	7.2	7.2	7.3	5.3	4.8	6.2	4.3
28	PAPER CONTAINERS	6.1	6.3	6.2	6.4	6.1	5.8	5.4	5.6	5.7	5.7	6.7	6.2	6.2
29	NEWSPAPERS	4.8	5.8	6.4	6.4	6.4	5.5	5.4	5.5	5.7	5.7	5.5	5.3	5.2
30	PRINTING AND PUBLISHING (EXC. NEWSP.)	5.0	5.7	5.9	5.9	5.8	5.5	5.2	5.5	5.7	5.2	5.1	4.9	5.1
31	INDUSTRIAL CHEMICALS	5.3	5.8	5.8	5.9	5.9	5.2	5.4	5.3	5.3	5.0	4.6	4.4	4.9
32	AGRICULTURAL CHEMICALS	5.1	4.7	4.7	4.2	4.6	4.4	5.1	4.5	4.6	5.4	4.5	4.5	4.3
33	GLUE, INK, AND FATTY ACIDES	5.1	5.2	6.3	6.5	7.0	6.9	5.8	5.5	5.5	5.4	5.3	5.2	5.2
34	PLASTICS AND SYNTHETICS	5.8	5.9	5.9	6.2	6.0	6.0	5.3	5.0	5.0	4.8	4.6	4.6	4.7
35	DRUGS	5.5	5.6	6.1	6.3	6.4	6.0	5.5	5.1	5.1	4.8	4.9	4.9	4.7
36	CLEANING AND TOILET ITEMS	5.4	6.7	6.9	6.3	5.6	5.4	5.9	5.7	5.1	4.9	4.9	4.9	4.8
37	PAINTS AND ALLIED PRODUCTS	6.0	6.6	7.1	7.3	7.1	6.9	5.9	5.7	5.7	5.4	5.3	4.9	4.8
38	PETROLEUM REFINING	4.6	4.2	6.0	6.8	7.0	6.8	6.4	4.7	4.6	4.4	4.3	4.9	4.2
39	TIRE AND TUBES	5.6	5.9	6.6	6.8	6.9	6.5	6.5	5.9	5.9	5.6	5.4	5.2	5.4
40	RUBBER PRODUCTS (EXC. TIRES)	6.5	6.9	7.9	8.0	8.0	7.6	7.1	7.1	7.1	6.9	6.8	6.4	6.3

#	Industry													
41	PLASTIC PRODUCTS	6.7	5.9	5.5	5.5	4.7	5.3	4.7	4.7	4.7	4.6	4.8	5.0	5.3
42	LEATHER TANNING AND INDUSTRIAL PRODUCTS	5.2	6.7	7.4	7.5	7.5	6.7	6.0	6.2	6.0	5.5	5.2	4.7	4.9
43	SHOES AND OTHER LEATHER PRODUCTS	5.8	5.9	6.1	6.3	6.3	6.3	5.5	5.4	5.9	5.0	4.8	4.7	4.7
44	GLASS AND GLASS PRODUCTS	6.7	6.7	6.6	6.7	7.1	6.2	6.7	6.4	6.9	6.5	6.1	6.1	6.0
45	STONE AND CLAY PRODUCTS	6.7	6.6	6.7	7.0	7.1	7.2	7.3	7.2	8.0	6.4	6.4	6.0	5.9
46	IRON AND STEEL	6.9	6.6	7.4	8.0	8.2	7.5	7.8	8.0	8.0	8.5	8.2	7.8	7.7
47	NON-FERROUS METALS	6.1	5.6	6.6	7.2	7.2	6.1	6.5	5.9	6.0	5.4	5.7	5.6	5.6
48	METAL CONTAINERS	5.6	6.2	6.6	6.8	8.1	5.9	6.2	5.7	6.8	6.7	5.6	5.2	5.1
49	PLUMBING AND HEATING	5.4	5.4	7.7	8.1	8.1	7.5	7.5	6.8	6.8	5.5	5.3	5.2	4.8
50	STRUCTURAL METAL PRODUCTS	6.0	5.8	6.2	6.5	6.6	5.9	6.8	5.8	5.9	5.4	5.3	5.2	4.6
51	STAMPINGS	5.7	5.7	7.6	7.9	7.9	7.6	6.8	6.1	5.4	5.2	5.0	4.9	4.9
52	HARDWARE,PLATING, WIRE PLATING AND VALVE	6.1	6.0	6.4	6.8	6.1	5.7	6.2	5.4	4.6	4.3	4.3	4.3	4.5
53	ENGINE AND TURBINES	6.5	6.0	6.4	6.8	6.7	5.7	6.2	5.2	5.9	5.7	5.2	4.9	5.1
54	FARM MACHINERY	6.5	7.1	5.6	7.9	7.9	6.8	6.8	5.7	5.3	5.4	5.2	5.9	5.0
55	CONSTUCTION,MINING,MATER.,HANDLING MACHI	6.3	5.5	5.6	6.2	7.5	6.3	5.7	6.3	6.3	6.0	5.3	5.3	5.0
56	METALWORKING MACHINERY AND EQUIPMENT	6.1	7.2	6.6	7.5	7.6	6.8	6.8	6.4	5.9	5.8	5.3	5.9	4.9
57	SPECIAL INDUSTRIAL MACHINERY	6.2	6.1	6.3	6.6	6.6	6.4	6.4	5.6	6.0	5.1	4.9	4.5	5.4
58	GENERAL INDUSTRIAL MACHINERY	6.3	6.7	6.6	6.8	6.8	5.8	5.8	5.6	5.5	5.2	4.4	5.4	4.3
59	MISC. MACHINERY AND SHOPS	6.3	6.3	6.6	5.2	5.1	4.8	4.8	5.4	4.8	4.7	4.9	4.2	4.6
60	OFFICE AND COMPUTING MACHINERY	6.3	6.2	6.3	7.3	7.3	6.4	6.4	5.8	5.3	5.2	5.1	4.8	4.9
61	SERVICE INDUSTRY MACHINERY	6.3	6.3	7.3	7.3	7.2	6.3	6.4	5.3	5.4	5.4	5.7	4.8	4.9
62	ELECTRIC MEASURING, TRANSFORMERS AND SWI	6.0	5.9	7.0	7.3	7.3	6.4	6.4	5.9	5.9	5.1	5.0	4.8	4.9
63	ELECTRIC APPARATUS AND MOTORS	6.0	6.1	7.9	8.4	8.4	7.3	7.3	6.8	5.9	5.6	5.0	5.6	5.6
64	HOUSEHOLD APPLIANCES	6.1	6.1	7.9	6.5	6.5	8.2	8.2	7.3	6.3	6.0	6.0	4.7	4.8
65	ELECTRIC LIGHTING AND WIRING EQUIPMENT	6.0	5.6	4.6	6.6	6.6	6.5	6.5	6.4	6.3	5.3	5.0	3.3	3.4
66	RADIO-, TV-SETS AND PHONOGRAPH RECORDS	4.5	5.2	4.3	4.3	3.7	2.6	3.0	3.0	3.0	3.2	3.2	3.3	3.2
67	COMMUNICATION COMPONENTS	4.3	4.5	3.8	4.6	4.3	3.0	3.6	3.0	3.0	3.0	3.2	3.2	3.2
68	ELECTRONIC COMPONENTS	4.7	4.3	4.0	3.8	3.8	3.3	3.3	3.7	3.2	5.0	4.8	4.6	4.6
69	BATTERIES, X-RAYS AND ENGINE EL. EQUIPME	6.1	6.1	6.5	7.7	7.6	6.9	6.8	5.8	6.1	5.0	4.8	4.4	4.6
70	MOTOR VEHICLES AND PARTS	6.2	5.4	5.3	7.0	7.0	6.8	6.8	3.6	4.2	5.1	5.7	5.5	5.0
71	AIRCRAFT AND PARTS	4.5	3.4	3.0	4.3	4.3	4.0	4.0	4.4	4.2	5.1	5.1	4.8	4.8
72	SHIPS AND BOATS	5.0	5.2	4.9	5.3	5.3	5.6	5.4	6.3	5.2	5.1	4.8	4.6	4.5
73	LOCOMOTIVES, RAILROADS AND STREETCARS	6.2	6.2	7.6	8.2	7.9	7.9	6.7	6.2	6.3	4.8	2.6	2.2	2.6
74	CYCLES, TRAILERS AND PARTS	3.8	4.1	6.4	6.3	5.4	5.0	4.7	4.7	5.0	2.4	3.5	3.3	3.4
75	ENGR. AND SCIENT. INSTRUMENTS	4.7	4.9	2.9	3.0	3.0	3.3	3.1	3.1	3.6	4.0	3.5	3.3	3.4
76	MECH. MEASURING DEVICES AND THERMOSTATES	4.7	4.6	4.6	5.8	5.8	4.6	4.7	5.7	5.5	4.4	4.5	4.7	4.6
77	SURGICAL AND MEDICAL INSTRUMENTS	5.8	6.3	6.1	6.4	6.4	5.8	5.5	5.5	4.8	4.4	4.7	4.7	4.8
78	OPTICAL AND PHOTOGRAPHIC SUPPLY	4.6	4.4	4.7	4.6	4.6	4.5	4.5	4.0	4.2	3.4	3.4	3.4	3.3
79	MISC. MANUFACTURED PRODUCTS	5.8	6.1	7.0	7.4	7.4	4.7	5.7	5.4	5.6	5.7	5.2	4.8	4.8
80	RAILROADS	5.3	5.3	7.0	7.0	7.4	7.0	7.8	4.2	4.0	3.7	3.2	2.9	3.1
81	TRUCKING	5.8	4.9	4.6	4.5	4.5	4.1	3.1	3.1	3.6	12.3	12.4	11.9	11.4
82	OTHER TRANSPORT	6.2	7.1	3.8	9.2	2.7	9.5	10.6	2.2	2.4	2.9	2.9	2.7	2.7
83	AIRLINES	4.3	3.1	4.5	2.6	4.3	2.7	2.1	3.6	3.4	3.4	3.3	3.2	3.2
84	WHOLESALE AND RETAIL TRADE	4.3	4.3	4.3	4.1	4.3	4.1	3.7	4.0	3.4	3.4	3.3	3.2	3.6
85	COMMUNICATION	4.7	4.7	4.6	8.2	8.1	4.3	3.9	4.3	7.9	7.6	7.3	7.1	6.9
86	FINANCE, INSURANCE AND SERVICE	7.3	4.9	8.2	4.2	8.1	7.9	4.7	7.9	7.3	7.3	7.3	3.3	3.4
87	ELECTRIC UTILITIES	3.0	3.6	4.9	4.7	5.1	5.0	5.2	4.6	3.8	3.3	3.3	3.3	3.4
88	NAT. GAS, WATER AND SEWER SERVICE	3.4	4.3	4.7	5.2	5.4	5.5	5.5	5.5	4.9	4.7	4.6	4.4	4.3

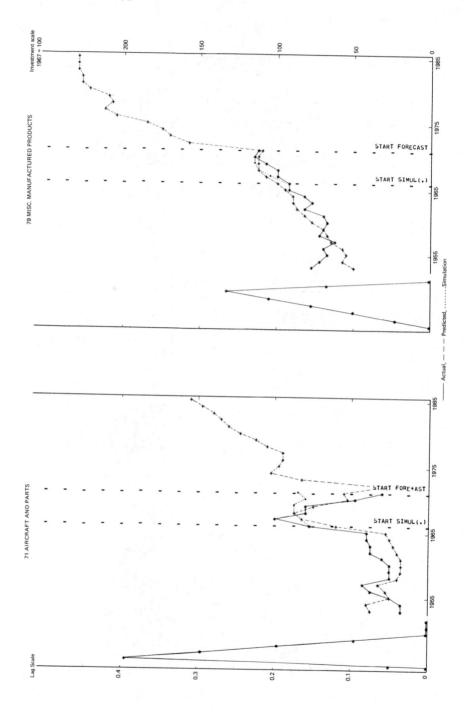

We also expected the w_i to be nonnegative and, once they began to decline, to continue declining.

Applying ordinary regression analysis yielded results which did not entirely match the preconceptions. To insure that we got nonnegative regression coefficients, we turned to quadratic programming and found that the Dantzig quadratic simplex algorithm required only a little more computing time than did ordinary least-squares analysis [5].

To express the tradeoff between our desire for a good fit and our desire to see the three above expectations realized, we devised the following objective function for the quadratic programming routine:

$$\text{Min } Z = \frac{1}{s_N^2} \sum_{t=1}^{T} (N_t - a - \sum_{i=0}^{5} w_i X_{t-i})^2 + G_2 (1 - \sum_{i=0}^{5} w_i)^2$$

$$+ G_3 \frac{a^2}{s_N^2} + G_4 (\frac{L_{1960} - L^*_{1960}}{L^*_{1960}})^2 ,$$

(3.9)

subject to $w_i \geqslant 0$ for all i, where G_2, G_3, and G_4 are constants and s_N^2 is the variance of N. The first term on the right of (3.9) is, of course, the sum of squared residuals divided by the variance of the dependent variable. The G's express our own subjective rates of tradeoff between R^2 and the three expectations. For the regressions reported here, we said that we would be indifferent between a 0.01 decrease in R^2 and:

— A 0.01 increase in the sum of the weights when the sum is 0.95
— A 0.05 decrease in the ratio of intercept over the variance in net investment, when the ratio is 0.01
— A 0.01 decrease in the ratio of L to L^* when this ratio is 1.10.

To convert these tradeoffs into values of G_2, G_3, and G_4, we rewrite (3.9) as

$$Z = (1-R)^2 + G_2 (1-S)^2 + G_3 (\frac{a}{s_N})^2 + G_4 (\frac{L}{L^*} - 1)^2 ,$$

where $S = \Sigma_i w_i$. The tradeoff rate between R^2 and S is the value of $\frac{\partial R^2}{\partial S}$ which makes $\frac{\partial Z}{\partial S} = 0$. Now

$$\frac{\partial Z}{\partial S} = -\frac{\partial R^2}{\partial S} - 2 G_2 (1-S) = 0$$

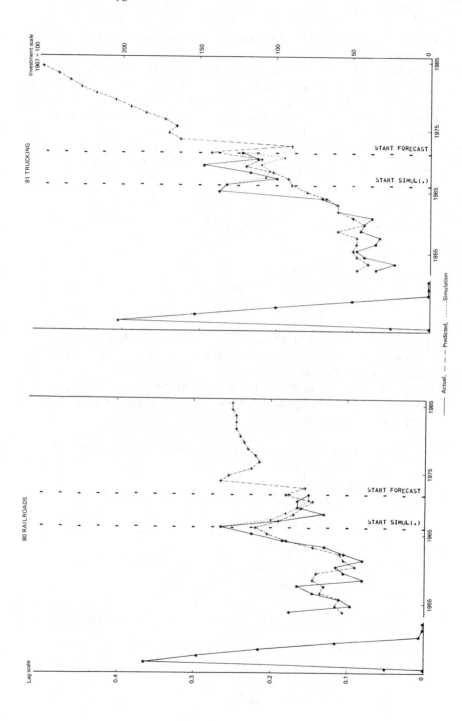

$$\text{or } G_2 = -\frac{1}{2(1-S)}\ \frac{\partial R^2}{\partial S}.$$

Since $\partial R^2/\partial S = -0.01/0.01 = -1$ and $S = 0.95$, we obtain $G_2 = -(1/0.1)(-1) = 10$; and similar calculations show that our other two assumptions imply $G_3 = 10$ and $G_4 = 5$.

Obviously, the choice of the G's is subjective. But to omit these terms from the objective function is to make G_2, G_3, and G_4 implicitly zero, and that is equally subjective. As discussed in the first section, our tradeoff function generally improved the forecasting ability.

We now proceed to express (3.9) in terms of the actual variables used in the quadratic programming routine. We shall call these variables b's. We had no prior expectation about the sign of a in Equation (3.9); to allow it to be either positive or negative, we set $a = b_1 - b_2$, where b_1 and b_2 are the first two variables of the quadratic programming problem, which must be, of course, nonnegative.

To get a smooth curve for the weights, the first five, $w_0, \ldots, w_4$, were required to lie on a second degree polynomial. By using the method of Lagrangian polynomials explained in [6], the w's may be expressed as a function of the b's. It will prove convenient to introduce $b_3 = w_0$, $b_4 = w_2$, $b_5 = w_4$, and $b_6 = w_5$. Then by using the Lagrangian polynomial formula, we may write

$$
\begin{pmatrix} b_1 \\ b_2 \\ w_0 \\ w_1 \\ w_2 \\ w_3 \\ w_4 \\ w_5 \end{pmatrix}
=
\begin{pmatrix}
1 & 0 & 0 & 0 & 0 & 0 \\
0 & 1 & 0 & 0 & 0 & 0 \\
0 & 0 & 1 & 0 & 0 & 0 \\
0 & 0 & 0.375 & 0.75 & -0.125 & 0 \\
0 & 0 & 0 & 1 & 0 & 0 \\
0 & 0 & -0.125 & 0.75 & 0.375 & 0 \\
0 & 0 & 0 & 0 & 1 & 0 \\
0 & 0 & 0 & 0 & 0 & 1
\end{pmatrix}
\begin{pmatrix} b_1 \\ b_2 \\ b_3 \\ b_4 \\ b_5 \\ b_6 \end{pmatrix}
$$

Let us denote the 8-by-6 matrix on the right by Φ.

To use the Φ matrix, we first write the first term of (3.9) in vector form as

$$\frac{1}{s_N^2} \sum_{t=1}^{T} \left(N_t - a - \sum_{i=0}^{5} w_i X_{t-i} \right)^2 =$$

$$\frac{1}{s_N^2} \left(N - (b_1 1 - b_2 1 + Xw) \right)' \left(N - (b_1 1 - b_2 1 + Xw) \right)$$

where N is a column vector of the observations on N_t, 1 is a column of 1's, and X is the matrix $(X_0, X_{-1}, X_{-2}, \ldots, X_{-6})$, where X_{-i} is a column of observations on X_{t-i}. Into this expression we then substitute

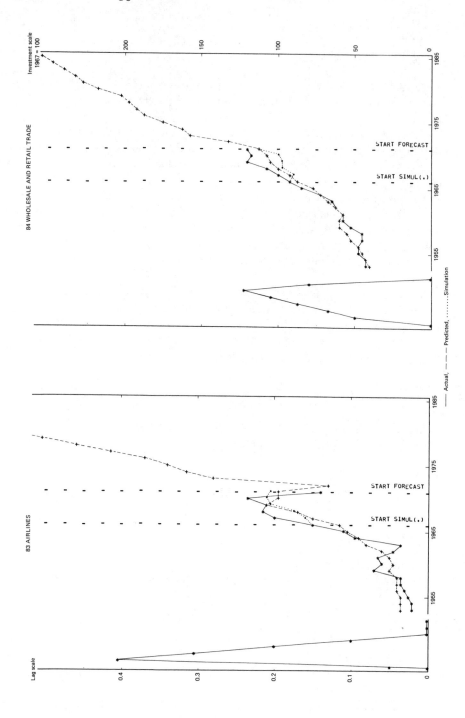

84 WHOLESALE AND RETAIL TRADE

Investment scale
1967 = 100

83 AIRLINES

Lag scale

START FORECAST

START SIMUL(.)

—— Actual, — — — Predicted, ...Simulation

$$(b_1, b_2, \mathbf{w}')' = \Phi \mathbf{b}$$

$$\mathbf{z} = (1, -1, \mathbf{X}) \, \Phi / s_N^2$$

and

$$\mathbf{n} = \mathbf{N} / s_N^2 \, .$$

The first term in (3.9) then becomes simply $(\mathbf{n} - \mathbf{zb})'(\mathbf{n} - \mathbf{zb})$. We can impose our desire that, once the weights start declining, they continue to decline, by requiring that

$$b_5 - b_4 \leqslant b_4 - b_3 \, . \tag{3.11}$$

Condition (3.11) amounts to assuming arc-concavity of the weights.

The final weight, $w_5 = b_6$, we leave free except for requiring that it be no greater than the preceding one; in terms of the b's, we require

$$b_6 \leqslant b_5 \, . \tag{3.12}$$

Finally, to prevent the sum of weights from occasionally becoming completely wild when the "subjective objective function" was not used, we required

$$0.5 \leqslant \mathbf{s}'\mathbf{b} \leqslant 1.5 \tag{3.13}$$

where $\mathbf{s}' = (0, 0, 1.25, 2.5, 1.25, 1.0)$.
We may also use this $\mathbf{s}$ vector to express the second term in (3.9):

$$1 - \sum_{i=0}^{5} w_i = 1 - \mathbf{s}'\mathbf{b} \tag{3.14}$$

To express the third term of (3.9) in terms of the $\mathbf{b}$ vector, we define

$$\mathbf{C} = \left(\frac{1}{s_N}, \frac{1}{s_N}, 0, 0, 0, 0\right), \text{ Then}$$

$$a^2 / s_N^2 = (\mathbf{Cb})'(\mathbf{Cb}). \tag{3.15}$$

The part of the objective function (3.9) which is quadratic in $\mathbf{b}$ can, with this notation, be written

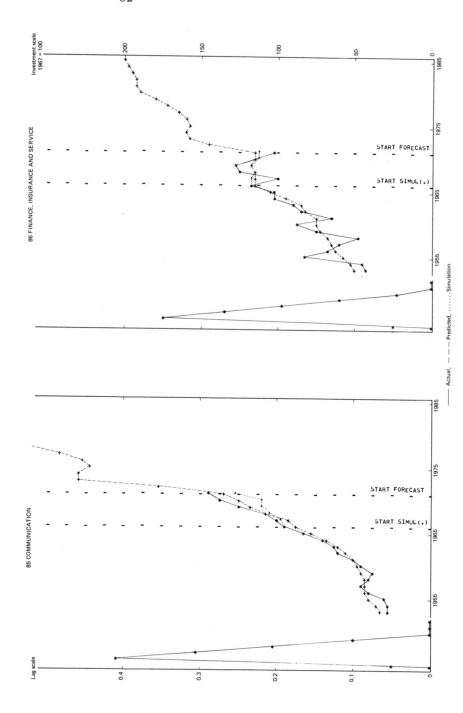

$$(\mathbf{n} - \mathbf{zb})' (\mathbf{n} - \mathbf{zb}) \quad + G_2 (1-\mathbf{Sb})' (1-\mathbf{Sb}) + G_3 (\mathbf{Cb})' (\mathbf{Cb}) \qquad (3.16)$$

$$= b' (\mathbf{z'z} + G_2 \mathbf{S'S} + G_3 \mathbf{C'C})\mathbf{b}$$

$$- 2 (\mathbf{n'z} + G_2 \mathbf{S})\mathbf{b} + \text{constant}$$

$$= b'\mathbf{Qb} - 2\mathbf{Bb} + \text{constant}$$

where the matrixes $\mathbf{Q}$ and $\mathbf{B}$ are defined by this equation. This is now in the standard form for quadratic programming. Equation (3.9) is a highly nonquadratic in L, because the capital stock and replacement depend upon it. This parameter is therefore treated separately in a manner explained below. The expression on the right of (3.16) is minimized subject to constraints (3.11), (3.12) and (3.13) which may be summarized as:

$$\mathbf{Ab} \leqslant \mathbf{k}, \qquad (3.17)$$

where

$$\mathbf{A} = \begin{bmatrix} 0 & 0 & 1 & -2 & 1 & 0 \\ 0 & 0 & 0 & 0 & -1 & 1 \\ 0 & 0 & 1.25 & 2.5 & 1.25 & 1 \\ 0 & 0 & -1.25 & -2.5 & -1.25 & -1 \end{bmatrix}, \quad \mathbf{k} = \begin{bmatrix} 0 \\ 0 \\ 1.5 \\ -0.5 \end{bmatrix}$$

Minimizing (3.16) subject to the constraints (3.17) is a standard quadratic programming problem to which we apply the Dantzig algorithm.

Since Equation (3.9) is nonquadratic in σ and L, we pick values for both variables and apply quadratic programming to the estimation of all other parameters in the equation. We then search the (σ, L) plane, as shown in Figure 3-2, to find the σ and L giving the lowest value of the total objective function, including the last term, which is not part of the objective function in the quadratic programming calculations.

We start with $\sigma = 0$ and $L = L^*$. By increasing σ and keeping L constant, point 1 is found as an initial solution. Next we change L at constant σ and find a new value for Z of the objective function (3.15). If the objective function decreases, we continue to decrease L until we reach a new optimum value, say point 2. At this point we start searching for a new optimum σ which we find at point 3. This process is continued until at point 6 we have found the optimal combination of σ and L; that is, at this point any change of either σ or L will lead to a higher value of Z.

Painful as the description of this process may be to read, the application is quick and easy. The use of quadratic programming requires only slightly more computer time than does ordinary least squares. The control which it offers over the results make it well worth the small extra cost.

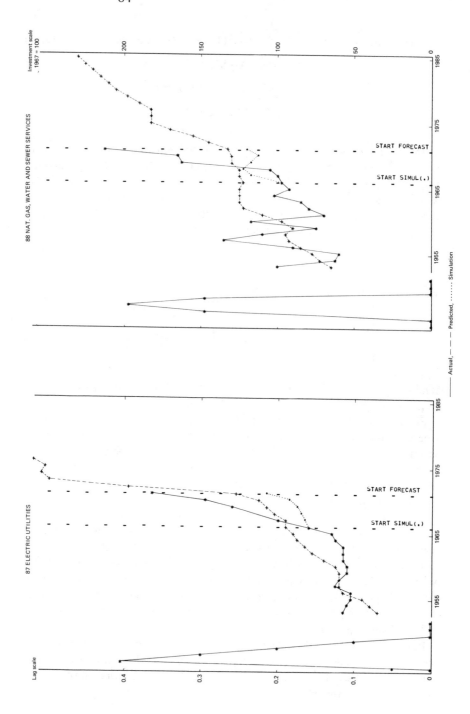

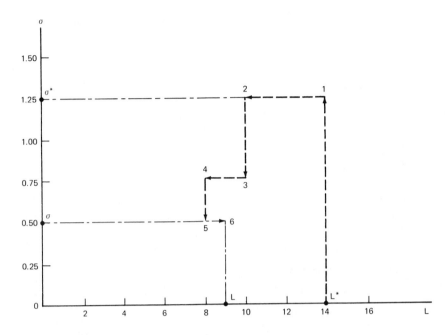

Figure 3-2. Example of Search Process

References

[1] Arrow, K.J., Chenery, H.B., Minhas, B.S., and Solow, R.M., "Capital-Labor Substitution and Economic Efficiency," *The Review of Economics and Statistics* (Cambridge, Mass.: Harvard University Press, August 1961), pp. 225-50.

[2] Mayor, T.H., "Equipment Expenditures by Input-Output Industries," *The Review of Economics and Statistics* (Cambridge, Mass.: Harvard University Press, February 1971), pp. 26-36.

[3] Hall, R. and Jorgenson, D.W., "Tax Policy and Investment Behavior," *American Economic Review* (June 1967), pp. 391-414.

[4] Feldstein, M. and Eckstein, O., "The Fundamental Determinants of the Rate of Interest," *The Review of Economics and Statistics* (Cambridge, Mass.: Harvard University Press, November 1970), pp. 363-75.

[5] Dantzig, George B., *Linear Programming and Extensions* (Princeton: Princeton University Press, 1963).

[6] Almon, S., "The Distributed Lag between Capital Appropriations and Expenditures," *Econometrica* (January 1965), pp. 173-96.

Appendix 3A: Investment Data

In the following descriptions, V_t denotes the gross equipment investment in year t in current dollars. NPE_t denotes the new plant and equipment figure for the appropriate industry in the OBE-SEC investment survey. We also use tc to denote the closest economic census year preceding year t; in the census year, $tc = t$. The census years are 1947, 1954, 1958, 1963, and 1967. In 1965, for example, $tc = 1963$.

1. Agriculture

   V_t = The sum of farm spending on motor vehicles and on other machinery and equipment.

   Source: Farm Income Situation, U.S. Department of Agriculture.

2. Mining (except oil and gas)

   Let V_{tc} = Equipment investment in the metal mining, anthracite, bituminous, and nonmetal mining industries in year tc.

   Source: *Census of Mineral Industries*

   $V_t = V_{tc} * (NPE_t$ in Mining)$/(NPE_{tc}$ in Mining)

3. Oil and Gas extraction

   V_{tc} = investment by oil and gas extraction

   Source: *Census of Mineral Industries*

   X_t = shipments of oilfield machinery

   Source: *Census and Annual Survey of Manufactures*

   $V_t = V_{tc} * (X_t/X_{tc})$

4. Construction

   The unpublished *NPE* series for construction is, beginning in 1963, 1.70, 1.93, 2.02, 2.06, 1.95, 2.18, 2.69, 2.40, 2.47P. Earlier years were obtained by moving the 1963 figure back by the output of SIC 3531, Construction Machinery. All of *NPE* was taken to be equipment.

5-79. Manufacturing

   These are taken directly from the *Census and Annual Survey of Manufactures*.

80. Railroads

   The most comprehensive figure is obtained from the formula

   $V_t = NPE_t$ (Railroad) $- C_t$ (Railroad)

   where C_t is construction from Table 1 of the U.S. Department of Commerce, Bureau of the Census, *Construction Reports*, "Value of New

Constructions Put into Place," 1946-1963 (Revised) and 1958-1970. (See also monthly supplements.) The construction expenditures of telephone and telegraph, electric utility and gas utility, used below, are from the same table.

81. Trucking

From *Transport Statistics of the U.S., Part 7*, Tables 9 and 12, one obtains the figure for Revenue Freight equipment acquired by Class I Common Carriers of General Freight (CICCGF). Besides these carriers, there are "Other Common Carriers," "Contract Carriers," and "Class II Carriers Engaged in Local Service." The depreciation on their assets totals about half of the depreciation on the assets of the CICCGF. In addition to freight equipment, the carriers buy shop equipment, office equipment, and miscellaneous equipment, totaling, according to depreciation, some 15 percent of freight equipment. We take, therefore, 1.725 (= 1.50 x 1.15) times freight equipment acquired by CICCGF as our estimates for V for this sector.

82. Miscellaneous Transportation

This sector includes mainly water transportation, buses, taxis, and oil pipelines, and travel agents. The "Other transportation" item in NP&E includes this sector plus sector 81. As a rough estimate, we assume that 25 percent of *NPE* is construction, so we set

$$V_t = 0.75 NPE_t \text{ (Other transportation)} - V_{81,t}$$

83. Airlines

$$V_t = NPE_t \text{ (Airlines)}$$

84. Trade

The 1963 figure $3757 million is moved by the index of service industry machinery, SIC 3580.

85. Communication

$$V_t = NPE_t \text{ (Communication)} - C_t \text{ (Telephone \& Telegraph)}$$

86. Finance and Service

This is a residual class classified by subtracting all other classes from total PDE.

$$V_t = PDE_t - \sum_{\substack{i=1 \\ i \neq 86}}^{90} V_{ti}$$

87. Electric Utility

$V_t = NPE_t$ (Electric Utility) $- C_t$ (Electric Utility)

88. Gas and Other Utility

$V_t = NPE_t$ (Gas and Other Utility) $- C_t$ (Gas Utility)

89. Personal Automobile

The Commerce Department allocates 15 percent of automobiles sold to individuals to *PDE* on the grounds that these cars are used by salesmen and others in their business. We continue this practice in the future, so that this *PDE* item is driven by the *PCE* equation for automobiles.

90. Computer Rental

This item represents leased computers which do not show up in the investment expenditures of the using establishment, nor in that of the manufacturing establishment. It is defined as 88.7 percent of the excess of production over exports of general purpose digital computers. Current data on production of these devices can be found in *EDP Industry Reports*, but the value found there is about twice that in the *Census of Manufactures*. For 1967, the *Census* gives $1905 million while *EDP* gives $3900. We have to adjust *EDP* data to the Census level.

4 Construction

Constuction shapes the space in which we will live in the future. Of all man's physical activities, it has the most long-lasting consequences and should be planned with a long-term view of the evolution of society and the economy. It deserves, therefore, a privileged place in a long-term model, and we treat it carefully, distinguishing no less than twenty-eight categories and relating each as closely as we can to other activities in the model. The largest and most familiar category, New residential units, is one of the most closely watched cyclical components of GNP and alone accounts for about one-third of total construction. Two of the eleven public categories, Highways and Public education, together account for about another fourth; Offices and Stores, often lumped together as "commercial," account for a sixth. Thus these five sectors by themselves form an average of 75 percent of the total each year, and usually dominate the short-run swings in the construction activity. The detail in the remaining fourteen private and nine public categories, however, makes it possible to tie construction closely to the rest of the model and to express various government policies.

This chapter describes the equations we use for each of the twenty-eight sectors. For residential construction, there is, in addition, a more detailed analysis and a comparison of our results with those of other economic investigations.

One may obtain a quick impression of the chapter by turning to Table 4-1, which contains the equations, and then by glancing at the plots facing text pages which show the history, the forecast, and the fit of the regression equations. The forecasts are shown numerically in the End Tables at the end of the book. Because last-minute adjustments may be necessary after the plots have been drawn, the summary table forecasts may differ slightly from those in the plots. The End Tables are always the latest word.

The General Form of the Equations

Because of the highly durable nature of buildings, we expect a stock-adjustment equation to be appropriate for several sectors. We assume that the *desired* stock of a certain type of buildings depends linearly upon some set of explanatory variables such as consumption, output, or interest rates. For simplicity we will here limit ourselves to one such variable and call it X, so that the desired stock at the end of the year t is $(a + bX_t)$. Let S_o denote the actual stock in the year

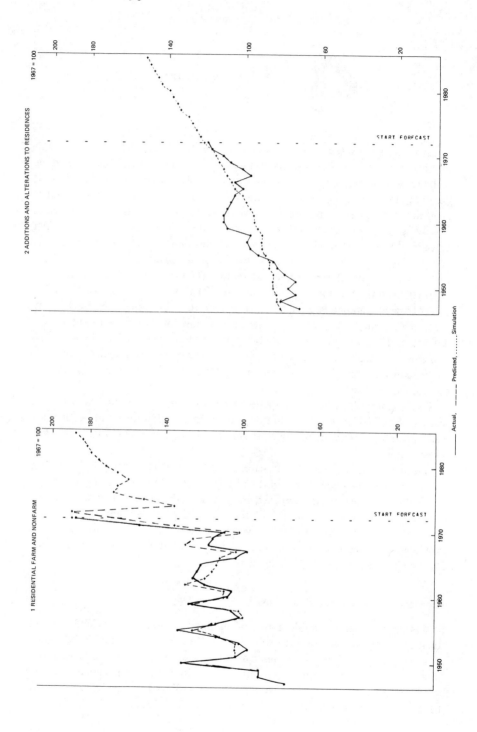

1 RESIDENTIAL FARM AND NONFARM

2 ADDITIONS AND ALTERATIONS TO RESIDENCES

1967 = 100

START FORECAST

——— Actual, – – – – Predicted, ········ Simulation

Table 4-1
Construction Forecasting Equations

In these equations the following symbols are used:

C = Consumption, in 1958 dollars (billions)
D = Interest rate differential (percent)
H = Number of households (thousands)
I = Investment in structures, in 1958 dollars (millions)
P = Builders' profit incentive (rent/cost ratio for housing)
Q = Output of the corresponding industry, in 1958 dollars (millions)
R = Real AAA interest rate (percent)
S = Stock of buildings, in 1958 dollars (millions)
SO = $(0.98)^t$
T = Time in years

Please consult the text for more complete explanations of the variables. The beginning year for each regression follows the name of the sector if it differs from 1947, and t-statistics are shown below each coefficient in parenthesis.

I. PRIVATE CONSTRUCTION

1. New Residential Units (1952)

$$I = [0.31250 + 0.05871D_{-1} + 0.39357P_{-1} + 0.05917(C/H) - 0.1140(S/H)_{-1}] \cdot H$$
$$(1.9) \quad (6.8) \qquad (2.2) \qquad (2.2) \qquad (2.5)$$

$$\bar{R}^2 = 0.79 \quad DW = 1.41$$

2. Additions and Alterations to Residential Buildings

$$I = 2200.7 + 4.470\,C$$
$$(9.5) \quad (6.7)$$

$$\bar{R}^2 = 0.64 \quad DW = 0.28$$

3. Hotels, Motels, and Dormitories

$$I = -559.1 + 3.909\,C$$
$$(3.7) \quad (9.0)$$

$$\bar{R}^2 = 0.76 \quad DW = 0.24$$

4. Industrial (1948)

$$I = 33762.6 + 2.611Q - 264.75R - 40616.6(SO) - 0.315S$$
$$(3.1) \quad (5.6) \qquad (2.0) \qquad (3.3) \qquad (4.4)$$

$$\bar{R}^2 = 0.75 \quad DW = 1.19$$

5. Offices (1948)

$$I = 10406.6 + 6.687C - 120.5R - 12243.0(SO) - 0.058S$$
$$(3.9) \quad (1.5) \qquad (1.6) \qquad (4.6) \qquad (1.6)$$

$$\bar{R}^2 = 0.97 \quad DW = 1.08$$

6. Stores, Restaurants, and Garages (1948)

$$I = 13355.6 + 0.0411Q - 97.4R - 16689.3(SO) - 0.219S$$
$$(2.5) \quad (2.9) \qquad (1.6) \qquad (2.7) \qquad (1.6)$$

$$\bar{R}^2 = 0.88 \quad DW = 1.37$$

7. Religious

(exogenous)

Table 4-1 (cont.)

8. Education (1948)

$$I = 386.4 + 0.4469C$$
$$\quad (5.1) \quad (2.1)$$

$$\bar{R}^2 = 0.74 \quad DW = 1.49$$

9. Hospital and Institutional

$$I = -729.7 + 4.502C - 3.56R$$
$$\quad (6.4) \quad (12.6) \quad (0.34)$$

$$\bar{R}^2 = 0.94 \quad DW = 0.95$$

10. Miscellaneous Nonresidential

$$I = 91.1 + 1.96C$$
$$\quad (0.81) \quad (6.0)$$

$$\bar{R}^2 = 0.58 \quad DW = 0.58$$

11. Farm Construction

$$I = 20940.1 - 10.305T - 15.81R$$
$$\quad (7.4) \quad (7.1) \quad (4.7)$$

$$\bar{R}^2 = 0.96 \quad DW = 1.26$$

12. Oil and Gas Well Drilling and Exploration
    (exogenous)

13. Railroad

$$I = 331.7 + 0.00068Q - 23.18R$$
$$\quad (2.4) \quad (0.06) \quad (5.1)$$

$$\bar{R}^2 = 0.51 \quad DW = 0.85$$

14. Telephone (1948)

$$I = 9561.4 + 0.1425Q - 71.57R - 10074.2(SO) - 0.2726S$$
$$\quad (3.8) \quad (3.5) \quad (3.2) \quad (3.6) \quad (3.1)$$

$$\bar{R}^2 = 0.93 \quad DW = 1.68$$

15. Electric Utilities

$$I = 883.0 + 0.100Q - 64.39R$$
$$\quad (5.6) \quad (8.7) \quad (2.8)$$

$$\bar{R}^2 = 0.81 \quad DW = 0.89$$

16. Gas Utilities and Pipelines (1952)

$$I = 7362.5 + 0.1626Q - 6.12R - 6995.7(SO) - 0.2242S$$
$$\quad (0.62) \quad (1.9) \quad (0.19) \quad (0.61) \quad (1.4)$$

$$\bar{R}^2 = 0.11 \quad DW = 1.91$$

17. All Other Private

$$I = -4870.6 + 21.502T - 14.12R$$
$$\quad (10.5) \quad (10.6) \quad (3.0)$$

$$\bar{R}^2 = 0.91 \quad DW = 1.58$$

Table 4-1 (cont.)

II. PUBLIC CONSTRUCTION

18. Highways
     (exogenous)

19. Military
     (exogenous)

20. Conservation
     (exogenous)

21. Sewer Systems
     $I = -41136.3 + 21.39T$
         (7.6)   (7.8)

   $\bar{R}^2 = 0.70$ $DW = 1.38$

22. Water Systems
     $I = -37644.0 + 19.521T$
         (5.1)   (5.2)

   $\bar{R}^2 = 0.51$ $DW = 0.54$

23. Residential
     $I = -17294.3 + 9.112T$
         (1.8)   (1.9)

   $\bar{R}^2 = 0.09$ $DW = 0.92$

24. Industrial
     (exogenous)

25. Education
     (exogenous)

26. Hospitals (1953)
     $I = -16532.4 + 8.637T$
         (4.9)   (5.0)

   $\bar{R}^2 = 0.56$ $DW = 0.67$

27. Other Public Structures
     $I = -127965.1 + 65.888T$
         (12.8)   (12.9)

   $\bar{R}^2 = 0.87$ $DW = 0.88$

28. Miscellaneous Public Construction
     $I = -91875.1 + 47.278T$
         (12.1)   (12.2)

   $\bar{R}^2 = 0.86$ $DW = 0.45$

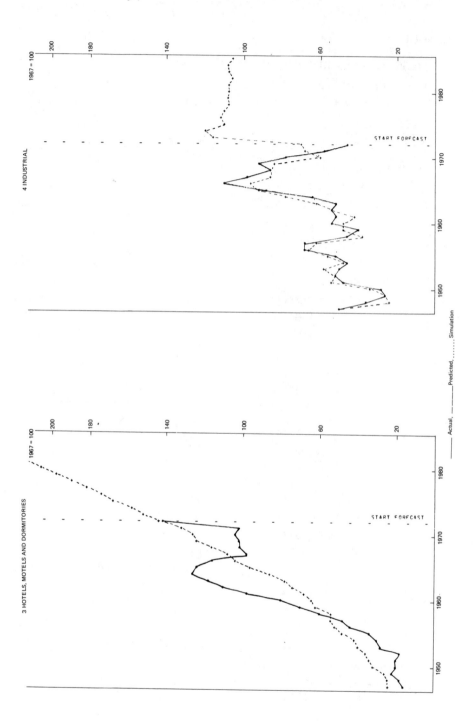

zero, I_t, the construction during year t, and d the retirement or demolition rate (assumed to be 2 percent). Then the *actual* stock at the end of the year t, S_t, is the sum of the surviving part of the initial stock, $S_O (1-d)^t$, plus the surviving part of construction since year zero, giving us:

$$S_t = \sum_{i=0}^{t-1} (0.98)^i I_{t-i} + S_0 (0.98)^t, t \geq 1. \tag{4.1}$$

Finally, we assume that construction in year $t+1$ is some fraction, λ, of the gap between desired and actual stock at the end of year t:

$$I_{t+1} = \lambda [a + bX_{t+1} - (\sum_{i=0}^{t-1} (0.98)^i I_{t-i} + S_0(0.98)^t)], t \geq 1. \tag{4.2}$$

Letting $S'_t = \sum_{i=0}^{t-1} (0.98)^i I_{t-i}$, the equation becomes:

$$I_{t+1} = \lambda a + \lambda bX_{t+1} - \lambda S'_t - \lambda S_0 (0.98)^t. \tag{4.3}$$

Note that since λ is determined uniquely as the coefficient of S'_t, the value of S_O (the initial stock) is simply obtained by dividing by λ, the regression coefficient of $(0.98)^t$. This formulation neatly sidesteps the common lack of data on stocks for most categories. Later we will discuss the actual explanatory variables used and the results of fitting this equation.

Before turning to a consideration of the various types of construction, a word must be said about some of our data. We use the historical construction series in 1958 dollars from the national accounts, Table 5.3, which in turn comes, with minor discrepancies, from the volume's summary of the Census Bureau's *Construction Reports* (*CR*). The 1970 edition of *CR* carries many of the 1967-70 figures for public utilities currently missing from the national accounts, but it does not break down the Commercial sector into our Offices and Stores sectors. These two have been lumped together since 1967, when the Census became dissatisfied with its sample in this area. We have kept the two series separate by using their 1966 ratio.

It should be noted that there is currently quite a bit of controversy among statisticians, in and out of the Census Bureau, about the accuracy of construction price deflators. The Census' deflators are currently weighted input-cost indexes with little adjustment for productivity changes. They are prepared by government agencies such as the ICC, and by private firms, notably Boekh and Handy-Whitman, and are fully documented in the *CR*. The 1970 *CR* gives explicit warnings about the accuracy of the deflators while noticeably limiting

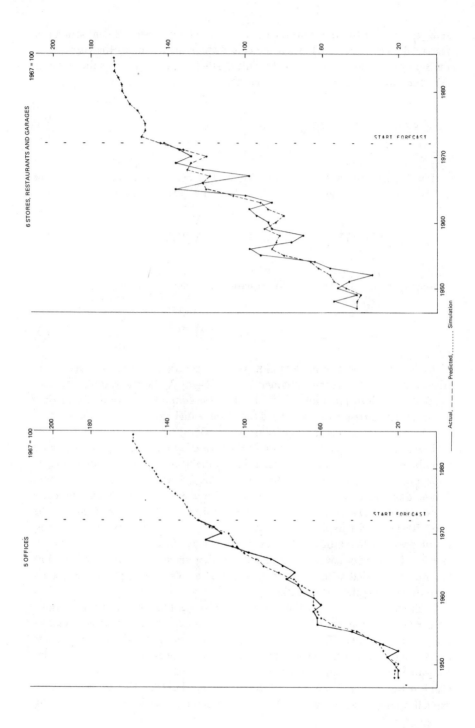

its listings of constant-dollar data. It should be obvious that especially in these times of rapidly rising construction costs, inaccurate deflators may cause large biases in the data. The problem is currently under study, and it is hoped that Census will soon settle on a set of consistent deflators for public use.

Residential Construction

This sector includes the value of new farm and nonfarm, single and multifamily dwellings, excluding the value of "additions and alterations" and "brokers' commissions." (Additions and alterations are computed as a residual and form one sector in the model. Commissions are assumed to be a constant $1 billion per year, roughly in line with recent data.)

The large volume of econometric literature dealing with residential construction can, for our purposes, be divided into four overlapping categories. In the first group, the researcher is primarily concerned with impact of income levels upon housing expenditures. Each of these studies, using either cross-section or time-series data, invariably becomes a search for the "correct" income elasticity. The second group of articles concentrates on monetary variables affecting both supply and demand for housing such as credit availability and interest rates. A third group treats homebuilding by an inventory model, and centers on vacancies and lag structures. Lastly, there are studies that emphasize no one type of explanatory variable but rather attempt to produce a reasonable equation which will forecast well. Our study falls into this last category.

Our equation for residential construction per household is:

$$\left(\frac{I}{H}\right)_t = \lambda \left[a + b \left(\frac{C}{H}\right)_t + c(D)_{t-1} + d(P)_{t-1} - \left(\frac{S}{H}\right)_{t-1} \right] \qquad (4.4)$$

where H denotes total number of households; C, total consumption expenditures; D, interest rate differential; P, builders' profit expectations (the rent/cost ratio for housing); S, the stock of housing; and λ, the adjustment rate. These variables are explained below. Note that this equation differs from (4.2) above only by having a direct estimate of S_{t-1} rather than treating S_o as a regression coefficient. All attempts to fit the data to the formulation in (4.2) resulted in incorrect (positive) signs on both stock terms. We therefore took the end-of-year 1950 net housing stock (S_o) from the Bureau of Economic Analysis series and built up a perpetual-inventory stock in the same manner as in Equation (4.1), with the 2 percent removal rate.

We will first take up the problem of choosing a set of theoretically appropriate variables that will explain housing expenditures. While we were certain that income (Y), the number of households (H), and the stock of homes (S) should all be important factors, it was equally clear that they were

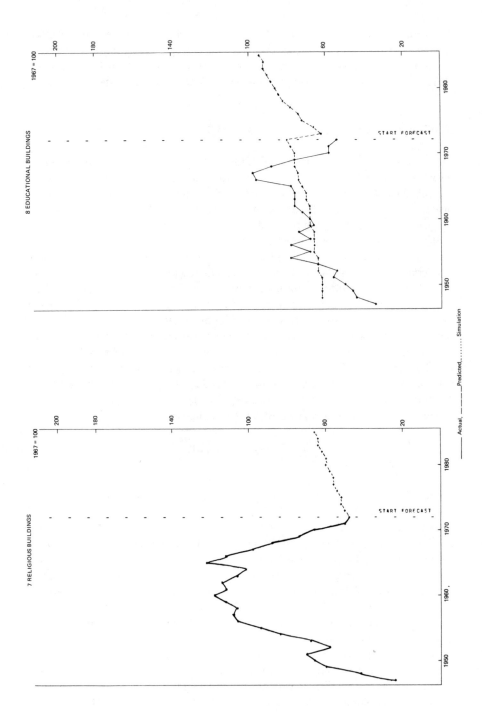

7 RELIGIOUS BUILDINGS

8 EDUCATIONAL BUILDINGS

1967 = 100

START FORECAST

————— Actual, ————— Predicted, ... Simulation

basically long-run variables and were insufficient to explain the strong short cycles in housing. At the time that these equations were developed, the model did not yet forecast internally such important short-run, monetary-type factors as interest rates, prices, and savings flows. Therefore, we might feel that we are not getting any "mileage" from, say, an interest rate that is simply forecasted as a constant. But in fact, to obtain from our historical fits the "correct" coefficients on the growth-inducing variables such as income and households, we must take account of the effects of important short-run variables. It is possible, however, to vary these assumptions when running any forecast.

Many financial-type variables were tried before we settled on those currently in the model. It was quickly discovered that interest rate levels were always insignificant and often had the wrong sign, even after subtracting the rate of change of prices so as to approximate "real" interest rates. One of the most promising rates that did *not* work was a national average of all mortgage rates (conventional and government-guaranteed) as estimated by FHA fieldworkers. We also attempted to prepare a mortgage "cost" variable by adding 2 percent for depreciation onto the rate, and taking the ratio of this sum relative to the cost of other consumption possibilities (the *PCE* deflator). Although this last attempt usually resulted in a correct (minus) sign, the coefficient never rose to be even half its standard error. From these results, it became apparent that homebuyers are not much affected by the total mortgage cost itself. One may even speculate that when mortgage rates rise, the term tends to lengthen, so as to leave monthly payments roughly the same.

The key monetary variable turned out to be credit availability, as represented by the differential (D) between long-term (AAA) and short-term (commercial paper) interest rates.[a] This approach follows Michael Evans (*Macro Economic Activity*, Harper and Row, 1969), who justifies this measure of tightness with a simple expectations theory of the term structure. For our purposes here, it is enough to notice that long-term rates may be considered to be moving averages of the more volatile short-term rates. Thus during booms, when interest rates are rising, the short-term rates tend to rise faster than do the long-term, and we see a shrinkage of the differential. Of course, during a credit shortage we would see just the opposite, where the differential becomes larger. During booms, when interest rates are rising, financial institutions shift away from homebuilders' loans and mortgages, and toward higher-yield corporate loans. Thus both supply and demand for housing are affected. In addition, because of institutional restrictions, savers will often bypass financial intermediaries in order to net higher returns in the capital markets directly, a process known as disintermedia-

---

[a]In order to represent current financial conditions, we originally used an estimated AAA-basis rate on *new* issues only, as published by the First National City Bank. Unfortunately this is no longer available, but a similar rate published by the Federal Reserve Board proved to be an excellent substitute. The two series closely overlap in 1960, so the link was made at that point.

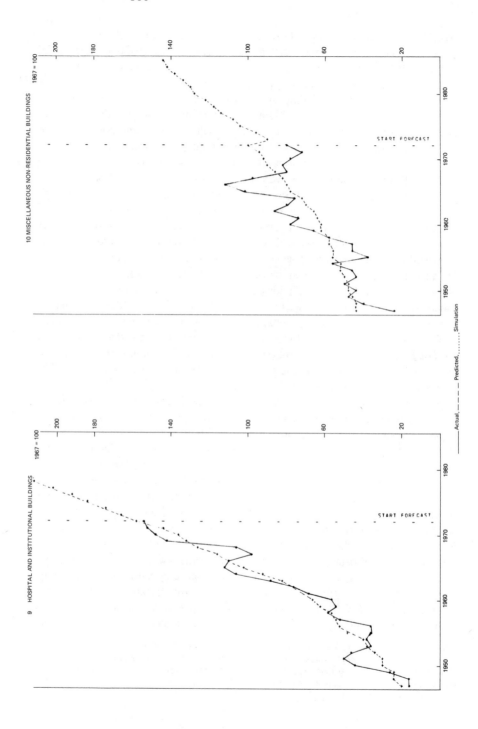

tion. This "supply of funds" concept has proved highly significant in many studies of residential construction, but for us the rate differential serves as an adequate proxy variable.

Figure 4-1 shows the average annual size of the differential over the period 1951-72. Superimposed on this graph is also the residential housing cycle. A glance at the graph suggests that there is about a one-year lag between the size of the gap (shaded) and construction, and indeed, Evans's quarterly equation shows a strong positive relation with a three-quarter lag. Note the unusually large 1971 and 1972 gaps, which help to explain the recent record levels of housing construction.

The second exogenous variable in the equation is the ratio of rent to construction costs (as measured by the CPI rent component divided by the implicit deflator for purchases of new residential units). We expect a strong positive relation to homebuilding for two reasons. First, overbuilding should be reflected in the lowering of rents relative to costs. Second, this ratio represents profit expectations by builders. Over most business cycles, construction costs rise and fall significantly relative to rents, showing the same countercyclical movements as does the rate differential.

Armed with an arsenal of appropriate variables, we began the estimation procedure with two constraints in mind. First, the adjustment rate, λ, should be

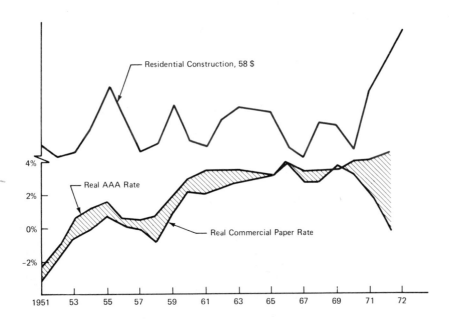

Figure 4-1. Interest Rate Differential and Residential Construction

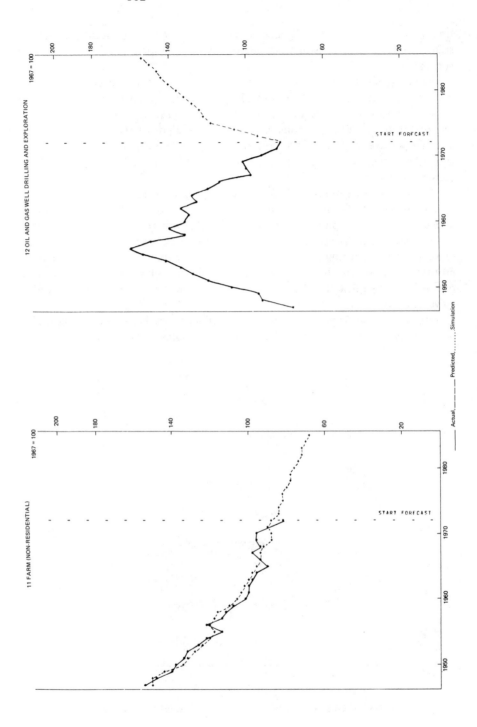

within a "reasonable" range, from approximately 0.06 to 0.25. These values represent times of 14 years to 2½ years, respectively, to close half the gap between desired and actual stock, and represents the extremes of estimates found by a large number of investigators. The second constraint requires the income elasticity[b] of housing construction to conform at least roughly to those found in other recent studies.[c] This restriction is not tight, however, since debate over income elasticities seems to be quite fashionable in the current literature. In a comprehensive survey article, de Leeuw notes that various cross-section estimates have run from about 0.4 to 2.1, that is, from very inelastic to quite elastic. After making adjustments for alleged biases in several works, he still finds a range of 0.7 up to 1.35; his own study finds 0.8. De Leeuw did not report on work by Morgan, in which a simple regression of house values on incomes using ungrouped data yielded a very low elasticity to 0.33. Further, recent work by Maisel and others criticized the use of group means in most of these studies as imparting large upward biases in the computed elasticities. Maisel's own estimate was 0.62. In sum, the evidence seems to indicate that (at least in cross-section) the income elasticity for housing is significantly lower than the often-seen approximation of unity.

A wide variety of expressions for desired stock were fitted before the current form of the equation emerged. Since the number of households always entered with an incorrect minus sign (as did household formulations), we eliminated it as an explanatory variable and instead put the equation on a per household basis. The original problem was probably caused by a downward trend in residential expenditures per household due, perhaps, to the growing importance of apartments and mobile homes, or to subsidized housing. A second alteration was the use of consumption rather than income since it gave the equation slightly more reasonable coefficients. One can argue that consumption expenditures are a proxy for permanent income, which theoretically fits better into a housing equation. The other often-used proxy, weighted values of past income, never worked as well as did consumption.

The desired stock of housing per household thus becomes

---

[b]"Income elasticity", E, is the percentage increase in, say, the desired housing stock (x) due to a 1-percent in income (y):

$$E = \frac{dx}{dy} \frac{\bar{y}}{\bar{x}}.$$

[c]In addition to the Evans text cited above, those works most closely related to our approach are: Frank de Leeuw, "The Demand for Housing: A Review of Cross-Section Evidence," *Review of Economics and Statistics (REStat)*, February 1971, pp. 1-10; Sherman Maisel, J.B. Burnham, and J.S. Austin, "The Demand for Housing: A Comment," *REStat*, November 1971, pp. 359-83; James Morgan, "Housing and Ability to Pay," *Econometrica*, April 1965; Richard Muth, "The Demand for Non-Farm Housing," in Harberger (ed.), *The Demand for Durable Goods*, University of Chicago Press, 1962; and E.H. Oksansen, "Housing Demand in Canada," *Canadian Journal of Economics and Political Science*, August 1966, pp. 302-318. Obviously this is far from an exhaustive bibliography.

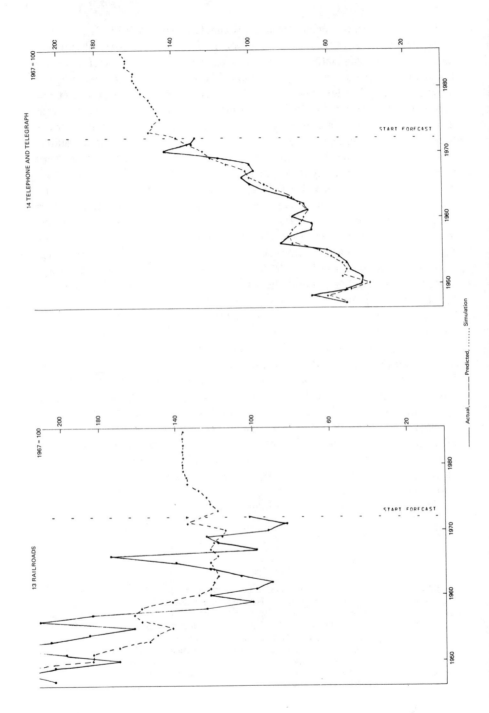

Actual, ——— Predicted, ········ Simulation

$$\left(\frac{S}{H}\right)_t^* = a + b \left(\frac{C}{H}\right)_t + c(D)_{t-1} + d(P)_{t-1}, \tag{4.5}$$

and plugging this into our stock-adjustment formulation, we obtain Equation (4.4) above. After performing the regression, we find that all coefficients are statistically significant, all with the correct sign. (See Table 4-1, sector 1.) The adjustment rate is 10 percent, which corresponds to a time of seven years to close half the gap between actual and desired stock.

The income elasticity for the desired stock (the "stock-demand elasticity") is appropriate for comparison with the cross-section studies discussed above, although not strictly so. From Equation (4.5), this elasticity is

$$\frac{dS}{dC} \frac{\overline{C}}{\overline{S}} = \frac{bC}{S^*} \text{ or } \frac{(\lambda b)C}{\lambda S^*}.$$

Here, λb is the regression coefficient on $(\frac{C}{H})$, and λS^* can be computed as mean value of the right side of Equation (4.4), excluding the stock term. The elasticity thus obtained is 0.34, a value roughly in line with Morgan's simplest regression results and Lee's lowest estimates, but lower than that obtained from other recent cross-section work. It does agree, however, with those found in a demand study of the 1947-62 Canadian housing market by E.H. Oksanen, in which corresponding time-series estimates range from 0.3 to 0.5.

Our income elasticity for housing expenditures (sometimes called the "flow-demand" elasticity) is 1.17, where here consumption is serving as a proxy for income. This seems reaaonably in line with experience. As expected, the elasticity with respect to current *income* is slightly lower, 1.08. Unfortunately, there have been surprisingly few other time-series estimates of this elasticity for the postwar period, and in fact many recent studies, including large econometric models, omit income entirely. Often they will concentrate instead on monetary flows through financial intermediaries. The only recent work following the methods used here is Oksanen's above-mentioned research. Laboring under the burden of incorrect signs on their price and rate differential variables, his equations imply a flow-demand elasticity of anywhere from 1.45 to 2.41.

Our equation itself fits better than its R^2 of 0.79 might indicate, catching every turning point since 1951 (see the first page of plots). It did not track the sustained housing boom of 1963-65 well, but accurately caught the record 1972 level. On the basis of the 1972 value of the rate differential and of the rent/cost ratio, we predict a slightly higher level of construction for 1973. Preliminary data showing a record housing year confirm the forecast and indicate that the forecast may be but a few percentage points off. For purposes of prediction after 1973, we assume that each of the two variables above will return to its average 1952-72 value; this yields a forecast which sharply drops in 1974 (due to the past year's squeeze in the financial markets), and then grows at 2.8 percent per year.

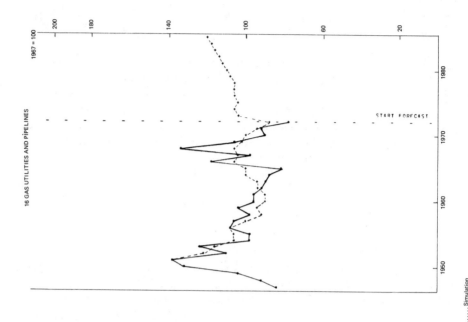

16 GAS UTILITIES AND PIPELINES

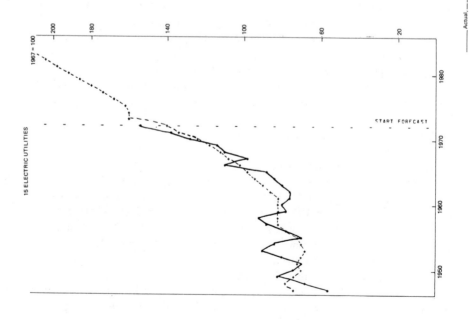

15 ELECTRIC UTILITIES

————Actual,————Predicted,........Simulation

Nonresidential Private Construction

We break down the nonresidential half of private construction into sixteen sectors, which are listed along with their respective estimated equations in Table 4-1. For six categories, the stock-adjustment equations (4.1)-(4.3) were found to work quite well: Industrial, Telephone, Offices, Gas utilities, and Petroleum pipelines, and Stores. The determinants of desired stock vary from one sector to another, although each equation includes the "real" interest rate, that is, the AAA rate, minus the average inflation rate for investment goods. The remaining explanatory variable is either consumption (used for Offices) or the output of a corresponding industry. For Telephone, Store, and Gas utility construction, these associated industries were Telephone, Trade, and Natural gas respectively. The output variable for Industrial construction is a weighted sum of the outputs for each manufacturing sector. The weights are the 1969 ratios of construction to output, that is,

$$X^t = \sum_{i=20}^{150} Q_i^t c_i^{69} / Q_i^{69}$$

where X^t is the weighted output in year t, Q_i^t is the output of industry i in year t, and c_i^{69} is the construction in industry i during 1969.

Unfortunately, for the remainder of private construction the stock-adjustment formulation had to be rejected either because it was inappropriate theoretically, or because the regression produced nonsense. Instead we use simpler functions of consumption, output, or time. Many other variations using construction costs, first differences, and logarithms were tried with little success. In cases where logarithmic formulations did work well in the regression, the forecasts tended to shoot quickly out of any reasonable range of values. Three categories in particular were troublesome to the point where we simply "eyeballed" the recent trends and assigned future values to be interpolated by the forecasting program. These were Religious construction (which since 1966 has suffered an extreme slump), Oil and gas well drilling (which is sensitive to government policies), and Gas utilities and Pipelines. This last sector should gain substantially from the recent congressional action on the Alaskan oil pipeline, although we have not attempted to estimate the exact effect.

Public Construction

All the government construction forecasts are currently made using either linear time trends or our own judgment, which ever seems more appropriate. We did regress Public education on income, and various demographic variables such as population change lagged five years, and the five-to-seventeen-year-old popula-

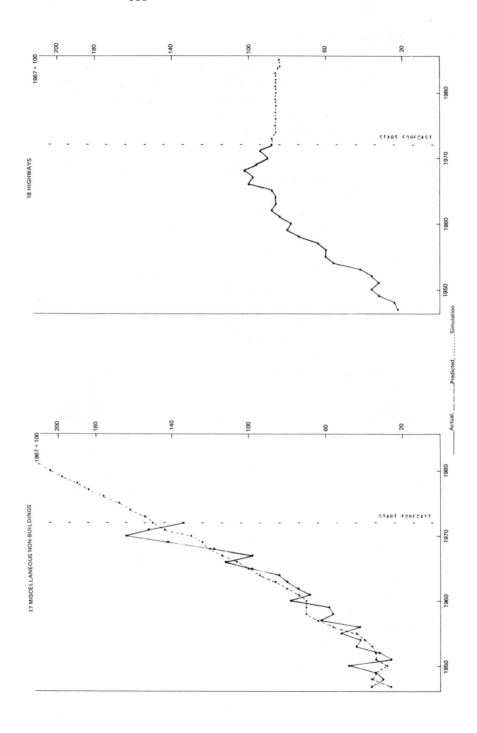

tion cohort, but all attempts resulted in incorrect algebraic signs, extremely insignificant coefficients, or unreasonable forecasts. Thus, given the slow (and currently negative) growth forecasted for the number of school-age children, we exogenously predict little growth for this important category. Highway expenditures, the largest public category, is subject to great uncertainty as the interstate program approaches completion, and as Congress contemplates revenue-sharing and a new Federal Highway Act. Therefore, we cautiously predict a slow downward trend.

Although it is possible to give only one forecast in this book, the reader should bear in mind that alternatives are easily specified, and their effects on the rest of the economy easily calculated when one has the model itself.

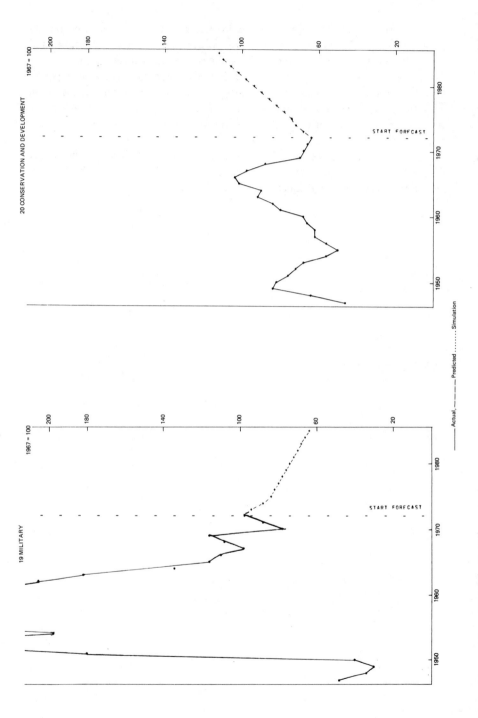

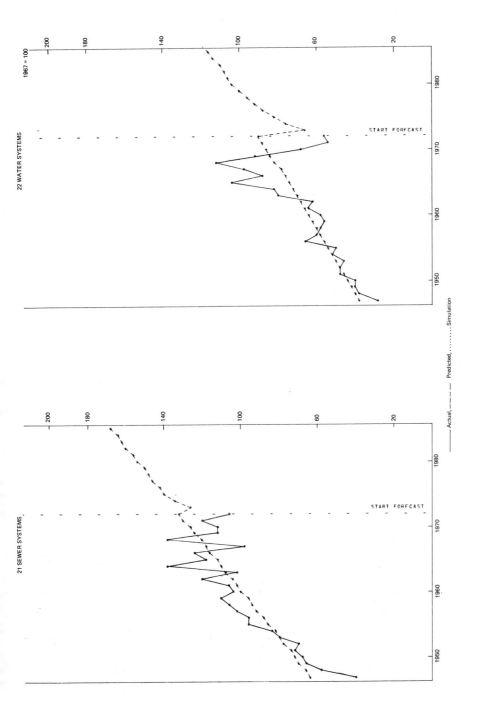

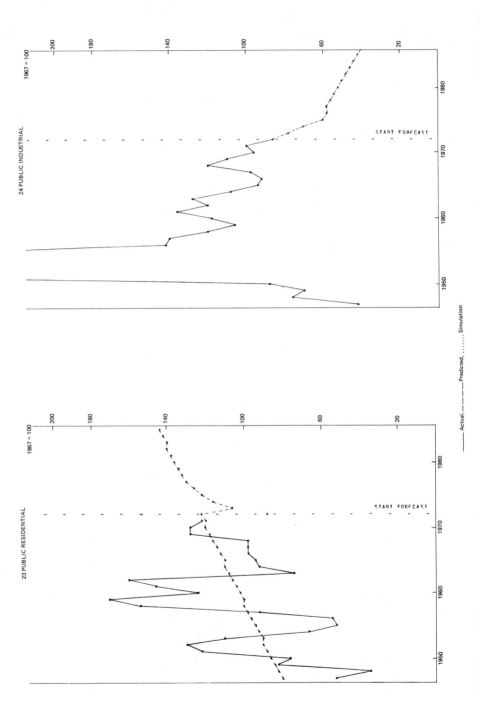

24 PUBLIC INDUSTRIAL

1967 = 100

START FORECAST

23 PUBLIC RESIDENTIAL

1967 = 100

START FORECAST

———— Actual,———— Predicted, ·········· Simulation

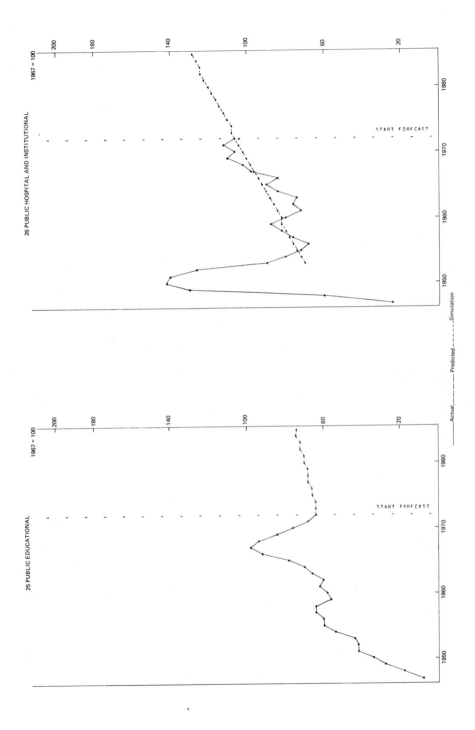

25 PUBLIC EDUCATIONAL

26 PUBLIC HOSPITAL AND INSTITUTIONAL

1967 = 100

START FORECAST

—————Actual —————Predicted —————Simulation

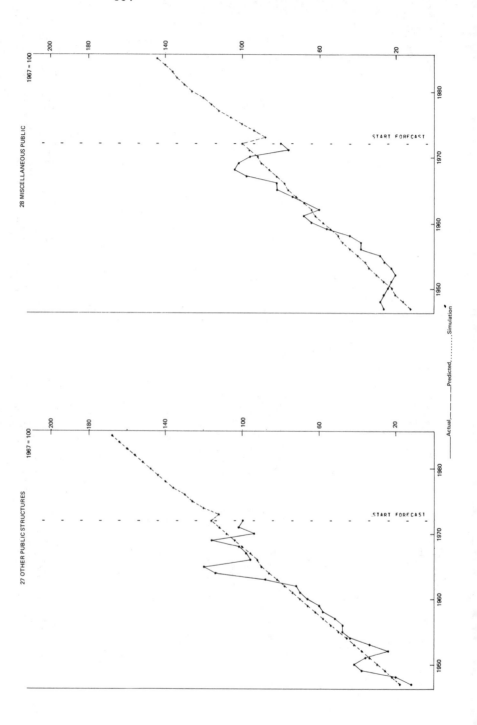

28 MISCELLANEOUS PUBLIC

1967 = 100

START FORECAST

27 OTHER PUBLIC STRUCTURES

1967 = 100

START FORECAST

Actual_____ Predicted_____ Simulation

5 Inventory Investment

Inventory investment represents a small but volatile portion of final demand. Although it generally absorbs no more than two percent of GNP, it can fluctuate so much from one year to the next that it masks the fundamental growth between them. For some products, also, it may take up five or six percent of output. For our forecasts one or two years ahead, it is therefore necessary to treat inventory change in a reasonable way, and even for the long-term, the demands on resources arising from inventory accumulation must be accounted for.

The logic of the forecasting system requires that the inventory change must be shown by the products held, not by the holder. We must know the increase in the stocks of, say, household utensils, not the increase in stocks of department stores, drug stores, hardware stores, and grocery stores, which all sell them. Many sources of data on inventories, however, are by the holder, not by the product held. We have to make a table to convert from holder to product held. As holders of inventory, we can distinguish 58 types of wholesale trade, 21 types of retail trade, and 121 manufacturing holders of raw materials. These stocks of each holder must be converted to the products held. Data on agricultural inventories, steel mill and brass mill shapes, and manufacturer's inventories of goods-in-process and finished goods come by product and require no conversion. The appendix to this chapter explains in detail how these conversions have been made.

From all these sources, we ascertain the inventory, V_i, of each product, i in a particular year. For forecasting inventory investment, we have assumed that the 1971 inventory-sales ratio was a desirable one and will, with some allowance for adjustment time, be maintained. More precisely, we set $v_i = V_i(1971)/S_i(1971)$, where S is product sales and then set inventory investment in year t equal to

$$V_i(t) - V_i(t-1) = 0.6\,[v_i S_i(t) - V_i(t-1)]. \tag{5.1}$$

The equation says, in effect, that 60 percent of the gap between this year's desired inventory and last year's actual inventory will be closed during this year. Sixty percent of the remaining gap will be closed next year, and so on. The 60 percent factor came from examination of the inventory equations in several aggregate models; with it, the equations behave reasonably in the short term and when we run the model with cyclical fluctuations. Reasonable long-term behavior is, of course, guaranteed by keeping close to the 1971 inventory-sales ratio.

115

The sales variable, S, in the above equation is not identical with the product output, Q, as it is used elsewhere in this book. Sales, S, is equal to domestic use, DU, of the product by final demand and by *other* industries plus exports, E:

$$S_i = DU_i + E_i \tag{5.2}$$

product output, Q, as used elsewhere in this book is

$$Q_i = (S_i - M_i + \Delta V_i) / (1 - a_{ii}). \tag{5.3}$$

That is, Q starts from S but *includes inventory change*, excludes imports, and includes the use by the industry of its own product. (a_{ii}, as explained in Chapter 8, is the units of product i required to produce one unit of itself). If we use Q, not S, to drive inventory investment, the model simply blows up—we speak from experience. The trouble is most evident in agriculture where several of the inventory-sales ratios are greater than one. If a \$1.00 increase in demand causes a \$1.20 increase in inventories and *if* this increase in inventories is then counted back into demand to generate a further \$1.44 of inventory accumulation, and so forth, the process clearly blows up. Hence, the exclusion of ΔV from S. Imports are not deducted from DU in S because some of the merchants' inventories will be in imported goods.

As this book is being finished, we have computed the inventory stocks by product for ten years and are fitting individual inventory-change equations for each product. It always takes a while, however, to iron out the rough spots in any new set of equations. If we are ever to complete the book, we must exclude from it some refinement which is almost but not quite complete.

Appendix 5A: Calculation
of Inventory by Product

Our object is to find a vector, **v**, of inventories by product held. Most data is on a vector, **h**, of inventories by holder. Some information, however, is directly on some elements of **v**. To bring both sources together, we create a matrix, **V**, in which the entry in the ith row and jth column is the inventory of product i held by holder j. The first step is to obtain a matrix, say **B**, such that each element, b_{ij}, shows the *share* of product i in a dollar's worth of inventory held by holder j. Then using our known vector of year-end stocks by holder, say **h**, we calculate a first estimate of **V** as

$$V = B\hat{h}$$

where $\hat{h}$ is a diagonal matrix with the elements of **h** on the diagonal.

There are 147 sectors of the model which produce goods that can be kept in inventory. Thus the V matrix has 147 rows. In the **h** vector we have tried to distinguish as many kinds of business as possible, for the kind of business tells a lot about the types of products held. Table 5A-1 shows the 349 elements currently in **h**, along with the data source for each.

Producing Sectors

Each of the first 140 columns of **B** has one 1.0 and 0's elsewhere—for we can simply assign inventories of finished goods and goods in process directly to the producing industries. Inventories of materials (the next 125 columns) are assumed to be composed of "stockable" goods held in proportion to their use as inputs. These proportions are derived from the **A** matrix of input coefficients. (See Chapter 8.) For steel and copper inventories, additional detail is available. *Current Industrial Report* (CIR) M33-3 gives, for steel, a total tonnage for holdings of all manufacturing consumers. This tonnage, multiplied by a composite price found in the *Survey of Current Business*, gives a control total for the steel row in the V matrix. The *CIR* publication also assumes that 80 percent of the stocks held by steel wholesalers consist of steel alone; this sum is placed directly into the V matrix. Detail concerning brass mill shapes is given in *CIR* M33-K. Subtotals of holdings by certain two-digit SIC groups and electric utilities are given, and there is a breakdown by shape for the total. By using this data and rough weighted averages of the appropriate BLS wholesale prices for wire and mill shapes, several control subtotals were obtained on groups of sectors within the copper row of the **B** matrix. The prices used for estimates such as this are the average of the December and the following January prices; this average is BEA's method of approximating year-end prices.

Table 5A-1
Inventory Holders and Data Sources

Cumulative Number of Columns	Number of Columns	Holder	Source of Data
1	1	Farming: Cotton	"The Balance Sheet of the Farming Sector," *Agriculture Infortion Bulletin,* USDA
2	1	Grains	Ibid.
3	1	Tobacco	Ibid.
4	1	Vegetables, other crops	Ibid.
7	3	Dairying, poultry, and eggs, meat, other livestock products	
		(Dairy inventories equal the value of milk cows)	"Livestock and Poultry Inventory, Jan. 1," USDA Crop Reporting Board, LvGnl (67)
15	8	Mining (incl. petroleum) and construction	BEA worksheets, IRS *Corporate Tax Returns* (Most recent year estimated from trend)
140	125	Manufactures (finished and in-process goods)	Census Bureau: *Annual Survey of Manufactures*
265	125	Manufactures (materials and supplies)	Ibid.
266	1	Consumers of steel mill shapes (Manufactures)	Census Bureau: *Current Industrial Report* M33-3
267	1	Consumers of brass mill shapes (Manufactures)	Ibid.
268	2	Electric Utilities (Copper Wrie and Coal)	CIR M33-K, and *Survey of Current Business*
326	58	Wholesale Trade	Census Bureau: *Current Business Report, Monthly Wholesale Trade Report,* Dec. issue, and accompanying unpublished data
347	21	Retail Trade	Census Bureau: *Current Business Report, Annual Retail Trade Report,* BR-13
349	2	Trade and Transportation (margins)	BEA, *1963 Input-Output Study*

Inventories of copper wire and coal held by electric utilities are also reported; the coal inventories, in the Survey of Current Business; the copper, in *CIR* M-33-K. The copper wire data cover only investor-owned firms, which account for 75 percent of all power sales to ultimate consumers, so an estimate of the total copper wire inventories of utilities was obtained by bringing this ratio up to 100 percent.

These known values are inserted into the **V** matrix. The steel or copper row (or part of it, in the case of copper) is then adjusted proportionately (excluding the known row element).

Wholesale and Retail Trade

Almost as much inventory is held in the trade sectors as in manufacturing, but the data are much more scarce. We try to identify as many kinds of business as are permitted by the availability of annual data. There are presently 79 kinds, 58 in wholesale trade, and 21 in retail.

The list of wholesale kinds of business comes from the *1963 Census of Business*. Annual inventory data are not carried in quite this much detail in the *Monthly Wholesale Trade Report*, but the Census Bureau has supplied us with a set of unpublished statistics. Merchant wholesalers, independent traders who hold title to the goods they sell, are the only part of wholesale trade for which annual data is published. They account for about 75 percent of all wholesale inventories. Nonpublished annual data for other wholesalers, such as manufacturers' sales branches and assemblers of farm products, were obtained from *BEA* worksheets. These were estimated by *BEA*, using detail information from the *1963 Census of Business*. No annual data is separately available for petroleum bulk stations and terminals, although in business census years, we see that they are quite important. Yearly inventories were estimated by using changes in prices and in total physical stocks (found in the *Minerals Yearbook*), then benchmarking back to 1963. Retail trade, with fewer types of business, is easier to handle, and the inventory data may simply be read out from the *Annual Retail Trade Report*.

To calculate the trade portion of the inventory coefficient matrix **B**, we would like to know the share of each product in the total inventory. On those shares there is no data at all. There is, however, data on sales by "product line." Even this information is available only in census years, so in the interim we assume that in any one kind of business there is a constant ratio of the sales of any product to the total sales. For any noncensus year, all we need do is multiply through by a vector of total sales. The derivation of these sales shares, however, is not an easy task, since the commodity lines in trade are not at all comparable to the SIC or to our own sectoring. Moreover, the 225 wholesale lines are not even comparable to the 173 in retail trade. Thus it was necessary to analyze the content of each line and assign all or part of it to one of the 139 input-output sectors. If a line had to be broken up, the product shipments from the *1963 Census of Manufactures* were used for forming ratios.

As for the inventory calculation itself, it was unreasonable to apply the same inventory-sales ratio for every product held in a certain business. Thus the basic assumption was that the *t*rade inventory-sales ratio of product i in kind-of-business j (r_{ij}^t) is proportional to that of finished product i in *m*anufacturing industry i (r_i^m). The constant of proportionality is the term that forces the total figures to add correctly:

$$r_{ij}^t = \frac{V_j}{\Sigma r_i^m S_{ij}} r_i^m,$$

where V_j is the inventory total for business j and S_{ij} is the sales of i in business j. After algebraic manipulation we see that

$$B_{ij} = \frac{V_{ij}}{V_j} = \frac{r_{ij}^t S_{ij}}{\Sigma_i r_{ij}^t S_{ij}},$$

$$\text{since } r_{ij}^t = \frac{V_{ij}}{S_{ij}}$$

So, to estimate inventories by product in trade, we need only to utilize the sales by product (from above) and the shipments for each input-output industry, in addition to the inventory data itself.

Inventory Valuation Adjustment (IVA)

In order to obtain consistent statistics for the national accounts, BEA adjusts inventory changes for differences between book value (as reported) and current replacement cost (which is desired). The calculation is complex and depends upon knowledge of reported accounting practices, but basically it is just a price adjustment. Since we know the inventories held by product and the actual IVA for trade and manufacturing in the base year, we can use the input-output deflators to estimate IVA by input-output sector. Last year's inventories by product are put into current prices and then adjusted proportionately to the correct total, in such a way that all entries, positive and negative, move in the same direction.

Ideally, year-end prices should be used for this calculation, but we used annual averages because they were readily available to us. A special problem occurs in agriculture, for which there is no IVA entry in the national accounts. This absence is due to the practice of computing agricultural inventory change as the change in quantity valued at an average price, rather than the usual subtraction of two current-dollar figures. For consistency, however, we have also applied an IVA-type adjustment to the agricultural sectors (1-8).

Trade and Transportation Margins

In the input-output model it is necessary to have all items reflect producer's prices rather than purchaser's prices. Therefore, at the retail level, we must strip off the wholesale trade margins for each product held. These margins were estimated by assuming that the vector of percentage margins for transportation and wholesale trade has remained constant since 1963 (the latest available OBE data). Retail trade stocks were then adjusted to producer prices using these ratios, and the margins placed into the transportation and trade rows. (Manufacturers' finished goods are not adjusted upward for manufacturers' profits, for these profits are not actually realized until after the good is sold.)

6 Imports and Exports

For several years our model ran happily on time trends for exports and imports. Then, to make it more realistic, we made imports of each product depend upon its domestic use. Price played no role. We excused this neglect not only by the notorious difficulties of gathering foreign price data and estimating price elasticities, but also by the argument that we could anticipate only smooth trends in prices and that such trends were already picked up by our equations. Then came the December 1971 devaluation. What effect would it have? We could not say. We had to say. We got busy. By January 1972 we had preliminary answers and by August, we had developed the system which is presented here. When the February 1973 devaluation struck, we were ready. Within hours, we had the new forecasts with the devaluation built in. Now we face the problems of floating rates, which mean, essentially, different rates for different commodities; appreciation of the deutschmark, for example, increases the cost of automobile imports but not that of coffee imports. To treat the problem adequately, we need a complete picture of trade among our major trading partners. That picture should be part of an interconnected system of national models which would also enable us to connect the exports of each country with the imports of the countries which buy its products. We hope to build such a system of models, but that hope lies beyond the confines of this book.

Exchange Rates

The foreign-trade portion of our present model contains:

1. Equations for the merchandise exports and imports of each of the 185 sectors which produce tradable merchandise
2. Equations for the other items needed to fill out the balance of goods and services
3. Exogenous specification of long-term capital flows

These items are sufficient to construct the "Balance on current account and long-term capital." When we speak of "the balance of payments," it is to this balance that we refer.

The United States kept its exchange rate constant as this balance sank from about zero in 1964 to a deficit of more than 9 billion dollars in 1971. Then, of course, we finally devalued, and not only once, but twice in just over a year. Our forecast for future exchange rates leaves them at current, 1973, levels for four or five years, just long enough to work out the effects of these rates. Then it begins to inflect them to bring the balance of payments close to zero in 1980 and 1985.

A devaluation does not make its full effect felt immediately. In a recent study [6], Junz and Rhomberg find that only 18 percent of a devaluation's effect on exports is reflected in the first year; by the second year, 28 percent; by the third year, 48 percent; by the fourth year, 82 percent; by the fifth year, 90 percent, and only in the sixth year is the full effect felt. We take 1972 as the first year of the December 1971 devaluation and consider that it averaged about 8 percent. The February 1973 devaluation, nominally 10 percent, we consider to have averaged 5 percent, for many currencies moved with the dollar. As a consequence of these two devaluations and the Junz-Rhomberg lag, the "reflected" price of the average foreign currency follows the path shown below:

	Dec. 1971 (1)	Feb. 1973 (2)	Combined (3) = (1) $\times$ (2)
1971	1.0		1.0
1972	1.0144	1.0	1.0144
1973	1.0224	1.009	1.0316
1974	1.0384	1.014	1.0529
1975	1.0656	1.024	1.0912
1976	1.0720	1.041	1.1159
1977	1.0800	1.045	1.1286
1978	1.0800	1.050	1.1340

For the forecasts of this book, we have sent the exchange rate along this "combined" path as far as 1977. After that date, we begin to inflect this reflected exchange down slightly to bring the balance of payments into approximate balance in 1980 and 1985. The exact values assumed for this index of the "reflected" price of the average foreign currency is shown with the other exogenous assumptions on Page E6 in the End Tables. This exchange rate assumption is superimposed on trends of domestic and foreign prices for individual items.

The main GNP summary tables on E5 shows the assumed course of long-term capital movements. We have assumed an excess of about $3.4 billion per year for U.S. capital exports over capital imports. This projection holds U.S. Government long-term capital flows constant at the 1971 level of $2.0 billion, and increases long-term investing by foreigners in this country *pari passu* with U.S. investing abroad.

The Components

Merchandise Imports

The merchandise trade equations have received the greatest attention, for our model concentrates on commodity production. The import equation for each product is of the form

$$M_t = (a + bD_t)p_t^{\eta} \tag{6.1}$$

where

M is imports in domestic-port prices,
D is domestic demand for the product,
  (domestic output − exports + imports)
p is the effective ratio of the foreign price to the
  domestic price,
η is the price elasticity.

The form of the equation deserves note. It is nonlinear in the parameter η. Why not use the more-easily estimated forms

$$M = aD^b p^{\eta} \quad \text{or} \quad M = a + bD + cp$$

We speak from experience on the difficulties with these two forms. The trouble with the first, the constant elasticity form, is that the elasticity with respect to domestic demand, b, frequently turns out to be much larger than 1.0, sometimes as high as 3.0. As domestic demand doubles, as it does by 1985 for some commodities, the imports with an elasticity of 3 would go up eightfold. If they already supply 30 percent of domestic demand, then they would supply 120 percent by 1985! No sector was quite that ridiculous, but some were not far from it, so we gave up this form and tried the second, the linear form. We then found, of course, that the change in the price level put the full amount of the shift in the demand immediately. A change in p which improved the balance by 8 billion in 1972 improved it by only the same 8 billion in 1980. Clearly, the price ratio had to affect the slope of the imports-domestic-demand relation, not just its intercept. Equation (6.1) is the simplest equation which provides this effect but avoids the constant elasticity with respect to domestic demand.

Of course, we have no satisfactory index of foreign prices. Where possible, we used the German and Japanese export price indexes or a weighted combination of them. In other places we had to resort to the Department of Commerce's unit value indexes for five broad commodity groups, given in *Overseas Business Reports*. For domestic price, we used the deflators for the output of the domestic industry.

The effective relative price, *p, should*, in strict logic, be a weighted average of past observed price ratios, π, with the Junz-Rhomberg weights, thus

$$p_t = 0.18\pi_t + 0.10\pi_{t-1} + 0.20\pi_{t-2} + 0.34\pi_{t-3} + 0.08\pi_{t-4} + 0.10\pi_{t-5}.$$

Unfortunately, these weights were not known to us when we estimated the equations. We realized the importance of the lag, but after some experimentation, picked a one shorter than that found by Junz and Rhomberg. Namely, we used

$$p_t = 0.25\pi_t + 0.65\pi_{t-1} + 0.10\pi_{t-2}.$$

It would be pleasant to report that we found good fits and highly reasonable estimates for all products. The fits, indeed, were not bad, especially when allowance was made for a few specific developments such as the 1965 U.S.-Canadian Automobile Agreement. But the estimates of η looked rather erratic, perhaps -8 for one type of machinery and 0 for a rather similar type. In most of these cases, however, the fit was not very sensitive to the choice of η. We, therefore, consulted other works [1, 2, 3, 4, 5] and selected what we believed to be reasonable values of η for broad import categories and some particular products; these are shown in the column labeled "a priori" in Table 6-1. We then told our computer of our preferences by asking it to maximize not just $\bar{R}^2$ but

$$\bar{R}^2 - 0.05 \left| \frac{\eta - \hat{\eta}}{\eta} \right|,$$

a "utility function" expressing our tradeoff between a good fit and conformity to our expressions. For the fifty most important imports, the resulting estimates of $\hat{\eta}$ are shown in the column labeled "estimate" in Table 6-1. The results are nearly all reasonable. In many cases, such as steel (#83), the estimated elasticity was very close to the *a priori* value, even though it may have been very different from it in a pure least-squares equation. In other sectors, however, such as rubber products (#73), the estimating process completely rejected the *a priori* value. Such a complete rejection suggests that there may be something wrong with the relative price series for that commodity.

One may object to this utility function approach that Table 6-1 does not report so much what the data says as what we thought. There is some truth in that objection, but it must be remembered that the purpose of the study was to get *reasonable* functions which do not fly in the face of the data, functions which could be used for serious forecasting. A "talking-data" study such as that of Price and Thornblade [4] can find an elasticity of *plus* 20 for imports of cars from Canada and let it go at that. But we doubt that those authors would seriously tell anyone that a 5 percent increase in the price of Canadian cars would cause their imports into the United States to double!

The U.S.-Canadian Automobile Agreement in 1965 brought a tremendous increase in motor vehicle imports from Canada. In 1965, they were $275 million; in 1970 they were $3.7 billion. Separate estimation of non-Canadian motor vehicle imports also failed to produce a satisfactory equation. Motor vehicle imports just do not relate well to domestic demand. Although domestic demand declines by 20 percent from 1969 to 1970, imports increased by 10 percent. The equation shown in Table 6-1 was fit for all motor vehicle imports. To use it in forecasting, the constant term of the equation was adjusted so that it correctly estimated 1971 automobile imports.

For one large import item, meat animals, a negative coefficient on domestic demand was found. This item was therefore related to time and price; the equation is shown at the bottom of Table 6-1.

The weighted average price elasticity, with 1970 imports as weights, was -1.97, while the weighted average of the domestic demand elasticities was 1.023, a much lower value than has been found in aggregate studies. Of course, total imports still rise faster than demand for all domestic goods, but the reason is that the fast growing industries are import intensive, not that imports are eroding domestic markets generally.

So far we have considered only imports which compete with domestic production. In addition, there are noncompetitive products such as coffee beans, diamonds, jute, and alpaca. These items are treated directly as inputs into the industries which use them. Their total appears in the End Tables at the end of this book.

Merchandise Exports

Exports should, of course, be linked to the demand of the importing countries. With considerable work, that link is possible for the past, but then one must forecast the future of those other countries. That task we are not prepared to undertake at the moment. Instead, we reasoned that the influences which we have studied in the United States—the courses of consumption, investment, and technological change—are likely to be active, though perhaps with a lag, in our major trading partners. Therefore, U.S. demand should be a good representative for foreign demand—not over the cycle of course, but over five or ten years. Therefore, we have estimated the equation

$$E_t = (a + bQ_{t-1})p_t^{\eta}$$

where E_t is exports of a product in year t, Q_{t-1} is the U.S. production of the product in the prior year, and p is the domestic-foreign price ratio. The export

Table 6-1
Summary Import Regression Results

Import = (A + B*Demand)*(Relative Price**Elasticity)
T Coefficients Are in Parentheses

Sector	Price Elasticities		Constant (A)	Demand (B)	RBARSQ	Imports—Actual and 1980 Forecasts		
	Estimate	A Priori				1970	Devalue 8%	Devalue 5%
7 Fruit, Vegetables, Oth Crops	−.27	−.27	−232.2 (−2.42)	.076 (7.70)	.929	646.	1002.	1012.
9 Forestry + Fishery Prod.	−.95	−.27	397.8 (1.71)	.125 (1.41)	.699	736.	1260.	1287.
11 Iron Ores	−.22	−.22	−53.5 (−.88)	.375 (9.26)	.873	617.	747.	737.
15 Crude Petroleum, Nat. Gas	−.22	−.22	80.3 (.53)	.109 (9.86)	.897	1937.	2720.	2742.
17 Chemical Fertilizer Mining	−.22	−.22	−91.7 (−7.34)	.444 (20.52)	.973	242.	493.	493.
23 Meat Products	−1.63	−1.63	−1222.7 (−8.41)	.094 (10.96)	.903	1251.	2025.	2124.
25 Canned and Frozen Foods	−1.10	−1.63	−103.0 (−2.95)	.052 (12.81)	.925	460.	733.	758.
29 Sugar	−.30	−1.63	350.8 (1.58)	.123 (1.75)	.191	826.	754.	761.
30 Alcoholic Beverages	−1.63	−1.63	−493.4 (−15.15)	.123 (32.68)	.981	895.	1275.	1346.
35 Broad and Narrow Fabrics	−1.10	−1.65	−429.7 (−4.43)	.077 (9.64)	.984	735.	1194.	1226.
37 Misc Textiles	−1.30	−1.65	202.0 (2.14)	.095 (2.44)	.470	380.	653.	674.
39 Apparel	−3.77	−3.77	−1082.9 (−4.33)	.115 (8.43)	.940	1554.	3322.	3700.

41 Lumber and Wood Products	−1.65	−1.65	517.2 (5.19)	.013 (1.21)	.945	665.	1027.	1070.
42 Veneer and Plywood	−1.80	−3.77	−78.3 (−7.04)	.156 (27.71)	.937	321.	405.	424.
43 Millwork and Wood Products	−1.40	−3.77	−45.7 (−1.98)	.049 (8.38)	.938	189.	338.	351.
45 Household Furniture	−6.00	−3.77	−271.2 (−5.45)	.074 (7.55)	.909	207.	648.	766.
47 Pulp Mills	.00	−1.65	50.1 (1.88)	.355 (14.83)	.947	504.	867.	856.
48 Paper and Paperboard Mills	−1.40	−3.77	362.2 (6.78)	.080 (12.03)	.939	1060.	1487.	1541.
53 Books + Periodicals	−6.00	−3.77	−6.4 (−.11)	.029 (2.77)	.694	222.	456.	535.
55 Industrial Chemicals	−1.65	−1.65	−202.5 (−2.53)	.052 (8.99)	.934	682.	1211.	1255.
59 Petroleum Refining	.00	−1.65	−522.9 (−4.10)	.092 (13.58)	.939	1793.	2730.	2739.
73 Rubber Products	−6.00	−3.77	−101.7 (−1.75)	.077 (4.34)	.777	232.	218.	255.
74 Misc Plastic Products	.00	−3.77	−49.0 (−3.96)	.041 (14.69)	.947	296.	416.	414.
76 Footwear (Exc. Rubber)	−4.00	−3.77	−1344.4 (−6.14)	.469 (7.31)	.915	509.	1435.	1579.
78 Glass	−1.60	−3.77	−65.6 (−2.57)	.068 (9.71)	.874	260.	362.	377.
80 Pottery	−4.60	−3.77	−34.7 (−1.47)	.291 (9.05)	.968	199.	284.	320.
83 Steel	−2.00	−2.00	−2013.0 (−3.65)	.136 (6.99)	.853	2396.	5886.	6116.
84 Copper	−1.10	−1.55	597.2 (4.58)	−.001 (−.03)	.939	538.	796.	820.

Table 6-1 (cont.)

Import = (A + B*Demand)*(Relative Price**Elasticity)
T Coefficients Are in Parentheses

Sector	Price Elasticities		Constant (A)	Demand (B)	RBARSQ	Imports—Actual and 1980 Forecasts		
	Estimate	A Priori				1970	Devalue 8%	Devalue 5%
87 Aluminum	.00	−1.65	−22.3 (−.51)	.055 (6.52)	.776	258.	485.	481.
88 Oth Prim Non-Fer Metals	−1.50	−1.65	302.2 (3.59)	.263 (3.33)	.941	623.	1146.	1181.
98 Cutler, Hand Tools, Hardwr	−3.80	−3.77	−101.4 (−2.61)	.079 (6.84)	.883	262.	440.	486.
103 Farm Machinery	−1.05	−1.05	−24.5 (−.65)	.096 (9.34)	.980	353.	720.	741.
106 Mach. Tools, Metal Cutting	−3.20	−5.35	−42.3 (−2.20)	.144 (11.19)	.971	160.	507.	544.
109 Special Industrial Mach	−1.05	−1.05	−487.8 (−6.73)	.193 (11.18)	.924	554.	1283.	1310.
114 Computers + Related Mach.	.00	−3.87	−64.6 (−1.88)	.042 (5.44)	.704	354.	511.	496.
115 Other Office Machinery	−3.87	−3.67	−121.7 (−4.48)	.271 (11.21)	.940	327.	647.	715.
123 Houshold Appliances	−.80	−5.42	−175.2 (−3.86)	.878 (7.57)	.803	325.	424.	435.
124 Elec Lighting + Wiring Eq.	−5.42	−5.42	−251.4 (−10.93)	.109 (16.19)	.980	231.	424.	488.
125 Radio and TV Receiving	.00	−5.42	−297.4 (−2.89)	.269 (8.78)	.884	1398.	1884.	1988.
127 Communication Equipment	−2.80	−5.42	−219.1 (−4.29)	.038 (7.56)	.799	308.	283.	305.
128 Electronic Components	.00	−5.42	−93.0 (−1.90)	.046 (5.25)	.727	349.	416.	410.

Summary of Time Equations
LN (Imports) = A + B*Time + S*Relative Price

Sector	Price Elasticities	Constant (A)	Time (B)	RBARSQ	Imports—Actual and 1980 Forecasts		
					1970	Devalue 8%	Devalue 5%
133 Motor Vehicles	-2.40	-3417.5 (-2.12)	.142 (3.60)	445	6276.	9649.	10292.
136 Aircraft Equipment, Nec	-8.00	-13.6 (-.07)	.032 (.92)	.486	249.	222.	259.
138 Cycles, Trans Equip Nec	-3.77	-62.5 (-3.52)	.435 (20.69)	.982	654.	721.	786.
143 Optical + Ophthalmic Goods	.00	-30.7 (-3.08)	.184 (13.76)	.940	183.	320.	320.
145 Photographic Equipment	.00	-15.2 (-1.19)	.062 (12.90)	.932	260.	412.	414.
146 Watches and Clocks	-1.80	-8.9 (-.71)	.212 (16.16)	.958	211.	259.	271.
147 Jewelry and Silverware	-3.77	49.4 (.94)	.064 (2.04)	.629	267.	369.	410.
148 Toys, Sport, Musical Instr.	-3.77	-528.1 (-5.59)	.301 (9.26)	.907	764.	1406.	1559.
3 Meat Animals, Oth Livestock	-1.35 (1.49)	7.5 (8.12)	-.034 (-2.54)	.273	359.	328.	340.

equations also were estimated with a "utility function" approach. The results for the fifty largest export products are shown in Table 6-2. The fits are noticeably less good than for imports; the $\bar{R}^2$ are sometimes negative as a result of the utility function. The poorer fits are due, in large part, to the fact that, although exports and domestic demand move together in the long run, they often move in opposite directions over the cycle. Slack domestic demand makes producers look hard for business abroad and offer attractive terms and delivery schedules. Because we are interested primarily in the long-term, we have retained the equations with domestic production as the driving variable wherever possible. For seven important products, however, domestic production got a negative coefficient, so a time equation was used. These are shown at the end of Table 6-2.

The weighted average price elasticity for exports was only −0.86. In other words, a 10 percent devaluation would increase the volume merchandise of exports by only 8.6 percent, so foreign currency earning from them would actually *decline*.

Other Goods and Services

To fill out the goods and services trade, the items which enter the GNP account, we needed several more items.

Passenger Fares. Both payments for and receipts from passenger fares used equations of the same form as the merchandise trade equations. The equations are:

Imports

Water Transportation $=$ $255.1 - 0.0134$ (Demand) $\bar{R}^2 = -0.069$
(7.2) (−0.48)
(Numbers in parentheses are t ratios)

Air Transportation $=$ $[-16.7 + 0.208$ (Demand)$]$ Price $^{-0.8}$
(0.8) (2.79) $\bar{R}^2 = 0.981$

Exports

Water Transportation $=$ $[-10.1 + 0.011$ (Output, lagged)$]$ Price $^{-2.2}$
(−2.1) (4.27) $\bar{R}^2 = 0.827$

Air Transportation $=$ $[65.0 + 0.120$ (Output, lagged)$]$ Price $^{-1.0}$
(4.2) (18.1) $\bar{R}^2 = 0.982$

Foreign Travel. Payments for foreign travel were related to disposable per capita income. Receipts from travel by foreigners in the United States were related to time and relative price. The relative price term is a weighted average of exchange rates, using travel receipts by country as the weights. This price term was not significant in the import equation.

Imports

Travel Payments $= [-12.53 + 0.0116 \text{ (Income)}]$ Population

$\quad\quad\quad (-6.8) \quad (13.8) \quad\quad\quad\quad\quad \bar{R}^2 = 0.940$

Exports

Travel Receipts $= 9025.6 + 133.5 \text{ (Time)} - 6697.7 \text{ (Price)}$

$\quad\quad\quad (7.9) \quad\; (23.2) \quad\quad\quad\quad\quad \bar{R}^2 = 0.978$

$\quad\quad\quad \eta = -2.9$

Trade and Transport Margins. In input-output work, exports are valued at producer prices. In balance-of-payments statistics, exports are larger by the transportation to the domestic port, and imports are smaller by the ocean or air freight and insurance margin. For reconciliation with the balance of payments, we have, therefore, estimated a series of the differences between merchandise trade in the two definitions. Their differences are related to total merchandise imports or exports respectively by:

Imports

Margins $= -7.2 + 0.147 \text{ (Total Merchandise Imports)}$

$\quad\quad\quad (0.3) \quad (160) \quad\quad\quad\quad\quad \bar{R}^2 = 0.998$

Exports

Margins $= \quad 87 \; + 0.165 \text{ (Total Merchandise Exports)}$

$\quad\quad\quad (0.4) \quad (18.2) \quad\quad\quad\quad\quad \bar{R}^2 = 0.964$

Other Transportation. Payments for or receipts from other transportation services (the movement of goods) were related to the total volume of merchandise trade as follows.

Transportation Services $= a + b$ (Trade) where Trade $= \Sigma$ Merchandise Imports plus Σ Merchandise Exports.

Imports

Water Transportation $= 633.3 + 0.019 \text{ (Trade)}$

$\quad\quad\quad\quad\quad (8.3) \quad (12.0) \quad\quad\quad\quad \bar{R}^2 = 0.998$

Table 6-2
Summary Export Regression Results

Exports = (A + B*Output, Lagged)*(Relative Price**Elasticity)
T Coefficients Are in Parentheses

Sector	Price Elasticities Estimate	A Priori	Constant (A)	Demand (B)	RBARSQ	Exports—Actual and 1980 Forecasts 1970	Devalue 8%	Devalue 5%
4 Cotton	-.22	-.22	185.2 (1.13)	.137 (1.21)	-.041	311.	386.	383.
5 Grains	-.27	-.27	-971.1 (-1.13)	.294 (3.61)	.545	2788.	5570.	5518.
11 Iron Ores	-.22	-.22	-40.7 (-.75)	.138 (2.77)	.386	202.	181.	176.
22 Other Ordnance	-1.20	-3.77	120.2 (2.03)	.078 (2.05)	.086	286.	266.	258.
23 Meat Products	-1.60	-1.63	53.4 (.58)	.812 (3.14)	.622	345.	701.	674.
25 Canned and Frozen Foods	-.80	-1.83	178.8 (6.89)	.011 (3.56)	.533	292.	397.	389.
26 Grain Mill Products	.00	-1.63	-188.3 (-1.64)	.071 (8.16)	.755	519.	897.	898.
32 Fats and Oils	.00	-1.83	-300.9 (-2.04)	.197 (5.78)	.729	793.	1289.	1255.
34 Tobacco Products	.00	-3.77	41.3 (.25)	.063 (3.34)	.459	598.	782.	784.
47 Pulp Mills	.00	-1.65	-103.3 (-1.09)	.375 (3.39)	.487	428.	943.	860.
48 Paper and Paperboard Mills	-3.77	-3.77	-484.4 (-8.99)	.118 (15.33)	.539	425.	1597.	1423.
53 Books + Periodicals	-3.77	-3.77	-278.8 (-17.37)	.080 (28.69)	.980	226	575.	515.

55 Industrial Chemicals	.00	−1.65	−615.2 (−8.31)	.123 (19.76)	.910	1497.	2150.	2120.
61 Misc Chemical Products	.00	−1.65	257.6 (5.34)	.018 (.99)	−.002	390.	386.	386.
62 Elastic Mat'ls. + Resins	−1.85	−1.85	−77.8 (−2.37)	.136 (14.43)	.928	551.	817.	773.
68 Drugs	.00	−1.65	85.9 (2.96)	.054 (10.31)	.898	457.	589.	590.
78 Glass	−.80	−3.77	−29.6 (−2.13)	.045 (10.78)	.911	163.	322.	314.
83 Steel	.00	−2.00	−128.9 (−.38)	.031 (*2.43)	.300	1260.	2017.	1939.
84 Copper	−.30	−1.65	316.5 (2.43)	.000 (.02)	−.044	335.	293.	291.
87 Aluminum	.00	−1.65	−108.0 (−3.41)	.057 (8.99)	.869	325.	393.	390.
88 Oth Prim Non-Fer Metals	.00	−1.65	28.0 (.37)	.061 (.66)	−.060	133.	98.	98.
95 Structural Metal Products	−.20	−3.77	81.3 (1.36)	.016 (2.17)	.201	277.	348.	344.
97 Metal Stampings	−1.00	−3.77	−44.1 (−1.03)	.051 (5.60)	.683	288.	446.	423.
100 Pipes, Valves, Fittings	−.80	−1.07	−135.7 (−7.24)	.118 (15.37)	.940	227.	363.	349.
102 Engines and Turbines	−1.05	−0.00	−74.5 (−1.00)	.160 (6.62)	.735	545.	1126.	1088.
103 Farm Machinery	−1.05	−1.05	−15.9 (−.18)	.107 (4.46)	.411	330.	585.	578.
105 Materials Handling Mach.	.00	−1.05	33.4 (2.55)	.050 (7.28)	.812	183.	234.	231.
106 Mach. Tools, Metal Cutting	.00	−5.35	198.7 (3.94)	.004 (.12)	−050	250.	204.	204.

Table 6-2 (cont.)

Exports = (A + B*Output, Lagged)*(Relative Price**Elasticity)
T Coefficients Are in Parentheses

Sector	Price Elasticities Estimate	A Priori	Constant (A)	Demand (B)	RBARSQ	Exports—Actual and 1980 Forecasts 1970	Devalue 8%	Devalue 5%
109 Special Industrial Mach	-1.05	-1.05	-266.5 (-2.79)	.236 (10.70)	.840	1043.	1511.	1464.
110 Pumps, Compressors, Blowers	-1.05	-1.05	-207.0 (-9.56)	.212 (21.93)	.986	365.	685.	658.
114 Computers + Related Mach.	-4.60	-3.87	-39.3 (-.61)	.203 (13.37)	.957	1217.	5538.	4539.
116 Service Industry Machinery	-1.05	-1.05	-3.7 (-.25)	.079 (20.33)	.976	422.	899.	873.
118 Electrical Measuring Instr.	.00	-5.42	-278.2 (-9.37)	.337 (13.79)	.940	249.	609.	811.
120 Motors and Generators	-1.69	-1.69	-18.4 (-1.20)	.075 (10.28)	.917	164.	441.	417.
123 Household Appliances	.00	-5.42	103.8 (15.10)	.009 (5.31)	.664	144.	176.	176.
124 Elec Lighting + Wiring Eq.	-4.20	-5.42	-265.8 (-9.11)	.126 (14.37)	.890	193.	435.	405.
127 Communication Equipment	-.40	-5.42	78.0 (2.98)	.036 (14.19)	.946	565.	817.	809.
128 Electronic Components	-5.42	-5.42	513.2 (4.25)	.047 (2.05)	.787	793.	2909.	2651.
133 Motor Vehicles	.00	-3.77	-708.8 (-1.79)	.068 (5.73)	.787	2892.	4944.	4894.
134 Aircraft	.00	-3.77	-929.4 (-3.02)	.259 (6.45)	.772	1938.	2768.	2765.
135 Aircraft Engines	.00	-3.77	80.5 (.71)	.058 (2.08)	.217	.390	349.	349.

Sector	Price Elasticities	Constant (A)	Time (B)	RBARSQ	Exports—Actual and 1980 Forecasts		
					1970	Devalue 8%	Devalue 5%
136 Aircraft Equipment, Nec	.00 −3.77	−140.2 (−.32)	.106 (1.43)	.090	746.	588.	583.
142 Mech. Measuring Devices	.00 −3.77	−179.4 (−3.79)	.221 (8.59)	.858	362.	459.	453.
144 Medical + Surgical Instr.	−2.80 −3.77	−40.3 (−6.33)	.125 (24.96)	.953	166.	401.	369.
145 Photographic Equipment	−1.40 (−3.03) −3.77 (19.14)	−45.6	.115	.985	369.	680.	664.

Summary of Time Equations

LN (Exports) = A + B*Time + S*Relative Price

Sector	Price Elasticities	Constant (A)	Time (B)	RBARSQ	Exports—Actual and 1980 Forecasts		
					1970	Devalue 8%	Devalue 5%
7 Fruit, Vegetables, Oth Crops	−.28 (−1.17)	8.1 (21.61)	.046 (9.52)	.882	326.	560.	556.
14 Coal Mining	.00 (.00)	8.3 (87.34)	.026 (2.51)	.327	603.	622.	622.
35 Broad and Narrow Fabrics	−1.28 (−1.76)	8.9 (8.90)	.004 (.52)	.199	295.	257.	253.
41 Lumber and Wood Products	−.25 (−.61)	5.4 (18.57)	.127 (14.94)	.991	511.	1692.	1670.
59 Petroleum Refining	−.63 (−1.24)	6.7 (12.10)	−.000 (−.10)	−.034	419.	340.	332.
104 Constr. Mine. Oilfield Mach	.00 (.00)	7.4 (297.42)	.045 (12.79)	.931	1783.	1678.	2678.
108 Other Metal Working Mach	−2.43 (−1.68)	8.1 (4.78)	.047 (1.55)	.045	233.	302.	281.

Air Transportation $\quad = \quad$ 111.9 + 0.009 (Trade)

$\qquad\qquad\qquad\qquad$ (−6.3)$\quad$ (24.7) $\qquad\qquad$ $\bar{R}^2 = 0.981$

Exports

Water Transportation $\quad = \quad$ 851.7 + 0.018 (Trade)

$\qquad\qquad\qquad\qquad$ (10.5)$\quad$ (10.4) $\qquad\qquad$ $\bar{R}^2 = 0.899$

Air Transportation $\quad = \quad$ 163.7 + 0.011 (Trade)

$\qquad\qquad\qquad\qquad$ (−7.3)$\quad$ (23.3) $\qquad\qquad$ $\bar{R}^2 = 0.980$

Fees, Royalties, and Other Private Services. Fees, royalties, and other private services were related to total merchandise exports and imports.

Imports

Other Services $\qquad = \qquad$ 231.7 + 0.011 (Merchandise Imports)

$\qquad\qquad\qquad\qquad$ (4.7)$\quad$ (5.8) $\qquad\qquad$ $\bar{R}^2 = 0.762$

Exports

Other Services $\qquad = \qquad$ 238.6 + 0.053 (Merchandise Exports)

$\qquad\qquad\qquad\qquad$ (−4.8)$\quad$ (27.1) $\qquad\qquad$ $\bar{R}^2 = 0.986$

Income from Foreign Investment. Receipts of income on U.S. investments abroad were made to depend upon cumulative long-term capital flows (LTCF) to foreign countries. Payments of income on foreign investments in the United States were likewise dependent on cumulative long-term capital flows to the United States. The equations were:

Imports

$\text{Payments}_t \qquad = \qquad 223.4 + 0.185 \left(\overset{t}{\Sigma} LTCF_i \right)$

$\qquad\qquad\qquad\qquad$ (2.11)$\quad$ (16.4) $i= 1947$ $\qquad$ $\bar{R}^2 = 0.957$

Exports

$\text{Receipts}_t \qquad = \qquad 226.2 + 0.161 \left(\overset{t}{\Sigma} LTCF_i \right)$

$\qquad\qquad\qquad\qquad$ (18.3)$\quad$ (51.5) $i= 1947$ $\qquad$ $\bar{R}^2 = 0.996$

The constant terms, which are both positive, may be thought of as income from investments prior to 1947. The long-term capital was not depreciated because reinvestment from retained earnings by a foreign subsidiary is not included in the balance of payments.

Remittance, Pensions, and U.S. Grants. All these items have been exogenously specified.

Long-Term Capital Flow. This quantity has become so much a tool of policy that we have also considered it exogenous.

References

[1] Ball, R.J., and Mavwah, K., "The U.S. Demand for Imports, 1948-1958," *Review of Economics and Statistics* (November 1962), 395-401.

[2] Houthakker, H.S., and Magee, S.P., "Income and Price Elasticities in World Trade," *Review of Economics and Statistics* (May 1969), 111-25.

[3] Kawahito, Kiyoshi, *The Japanese Steel Industry* (New York: Praeger Publishers, 1972), p. 162.

[4] Price, J.E., and Thornblade, J.B., "U.S. Import Demand Functions Disaggregated by Country and Commodity," *Southern Economic Journal* (July 1972), pp. 46-57.

[5] van Beek, Frits, "An Econometric Model of International Trade in Machinery and Equipment," Ph.D. thesis, University of Maryland, 1969.

[6] Junz, K., and Rhomberg, R., "Price Competitiveness in Export Trade among Industrial Countries," Paper presented to the December 1972 meeting of the American Economic Association.

7

Government

Government spending in many models is taken as "exogenous," given from outside the model, dependent upon the wisdom or whim of legislatures, or manipulated by the model's master to make it show him the "effects of alternative policies." We have taken the attitude, however, that state and local governments are subject to economic pressures not unlike those that sway firms and we should therefore be able to explain their economic behavior just as we do that of private agents. Certainly we could find no legislatures willing to budget twelve years ahead, so to get reasonable forecasts we had to do our best to anticipate how they would behave. To do so, we had recourse to our old friend, the regression equation. We have not extended that analysis to federal expenditures because Defense, AEC and NASA expenditures are dominated by noneconomic considerations, and what is left is, as far as purchases which enter the input-output table are concerned, relatively minor. It must be remembered that we follow the national accounts rules and do not consider transfer payments—welfare of social security payments, unemployment compensation and the like—as government purchases. What the recipients buy with these payments shows up as Personal Consumption Expenditure.

Although we have behavioral equations for all of state and local government purchases, we can always override them by specification from outside the model.

To develop our analysis of government spending, a nine-fold division of it proved useful:

Federal
  Defense
  1. Atomic Energy Commission (AEC)
  2. All other defense (DOD)
  Other federal
  3. National Aeronautics and Space Administration (NASA)
  4. Commodity Credit Corporation (CCC)
       Inventory Change
       Loans
  5. All other federal purchases (OND—Other nondefense)
State and Local
  6. Education (EDU)
  7. Health, Welfare, Sanitation (HWS)

141

8. Civilian Safety (SAF)
9. Other state and local (GEN)

For these nine categories, we established spending exclusive of construction and employee compensation. Public construction was dealt with in Chapter 4; employment is treated separately in this chapter.

Distribution by Product

The purchases of each of these categories of government are allocated to the 185 product sectors in the model. These distributions by product are based on the 1963 Input-Output Table prepared by the Department of Commerce and have been updated by the balancing procedure (described in Chapter 8) which makes the table consistent with more current information. The Commerce table, however, shows only two federal columns—Defense and Nondefense. We separated out AEC and NASA by using the Current Industrial Report (MA-175), "Shipments of Defense-Oriented Industries." This report was also used to update the major components of the DOD, AEC, and NASA vectors. The CCC had to be taken out of the Nondefense federal because it is so volatile. The CCC Annual Report was used to update the two CCC vectors. The AEC, NASA, and CCC vectors contain only the major spending items of these agencies which could be identified from the above sources. Other than the 1963 Table, there is no specific data available on the composition of the other government vectors. Our treatment of the CCC differs from that in the Commerce table and is explained in the appendix of this chapter.

Historical Series—Purchases by Category of Government Spending

Table 3.11 of the National Income Accounts divides government purchases into four categories—Defense, Other federal, State and local education, and Other state and local government. This table splits purchases into three components—structures, compensation of employees, and all other goods and services. By definition, this last category should provide the total for the items in a column of the table. We shall therefore call it "table purchases." These "table purchases" for Defense, Nondefense federal, and Education conform reasonably well to the 1963 Input-Output Table. However, the other state and local government category has only $6.6 billion of "table purchases" in Table 3.11 for 1963 versus the $9.8 billion in the Input-Output Table of the same year. Compensation of employees, on the other hand, is almost $2.6 billion larger in Table 3.11 than in the Input-Output Table. Structures as well as total purchases compare quite closely in the two sources. Because of these discrepancies and because this Other state and local category is an aggregate of the three categories in the model, (HWS, SAF, and GEN), we have used an alternative source to derive "table purchases" for these three. Table 3.10 of the national accounts provides total purchases (structures, compensation of employees, and other) in much greater detail by function. We aggregated the functions to the three in the model, compiled the corresponding series on total spending, and then for 1963 computed the ratio of "table purchases" to these total spending series for HWS, SAF, and GEN. Each of the three total spending series was then multiplied by the corresponding 1963 ratio to generate a series on "table purchases." The sum of the three derived table-purchases series was then compared to the corresponding series in Table 3.11 for "table purchases" by "Other state and local" functions. Our derived series ranged between 62 and 68 percent of the 3.11 series for the period 1958-65. Then the percentage gradually increased. By 1971 the two series were nearly identical. From this comparison it appears that the national accounts have gradually been brought into agreement with the 1963 Input-Output Table findings. Since most of the difference in 1963 is in compensation of employees, we adjusted that series so that the total spending (structures, compensation of employees, and other) from Table 3.11 was preserved.

Constant dollar series for federal government purchases were derived using the implicit price deflator for federal government purchases. State and local other purchases were deflated by the implicit price deflator for personal consumption spending on durable goods and services.

Forecasts of Defense-related Government Purchases and Employment

The forecasts of purchases by DOD, AEC, and NASA are exogenous assumptions. Both the level and product mix of these purchases are easily varied to study the effects of alternative types of defense spending. Both military and civilian defense employment are also exogenous assumptions.

Our "standard" assumption of defense spending for 1985 is about ten percent higher than the 1972 level. The product composition of defense purchases in 1985 is essentially that of 1972, except that spending on ships has risen slightly faster than the total.

The model is able both to scale defense spending on all products up or down or to vary the composition of the defense vector. These abilities have been extensively exercised in some applications.

Forecasts of Other Federal Purchases and Employment

CCC purchases and sales are projected to be zero. Undoubtedly, they will swing back and forth between positive and negative, but recent increases in farm prices and reductions in the maximum purchases from any one farm make it possible to hope that the net cost of the CCC will drop sharply. Major NASA hardware items decline to half the 1969 level by 1975, then remain at this level to 1985. All other federal purchases and employment are assumed to increase by 2.5 percent each year from 1971-85.

State and Local Government Forecasts

Spending and employment by state and local governments have been related to population (POP), school-aged population ($POP_{5\text{-}19}$) and per capita disposable income in 1958 dollars ($DISPC$) by the following equations:

"Table Purchases":

$$EDU / POP = -120.03 + 0.0984 \, DISPC$$
$$(18.098) \quad (0.008) \qquad \bar{R}^2 = 0.918$$

Civilian Safety

$$SAF / POP = -4.35 + 0.0044 \, DISPC$$
$$(1.10) \quad (0.0005) \qquad \bar{R}^2 = 0.856$$

Health, Welfare, Sanitation

$$HWS / POP = -29.15 + 0.0223 \, DISPC$$
$$(3.94) \quad (0.0018) \qquad \bar{R}^2 = 0.924$$

Other State and Local

$$GEN / POP = -14.54 + 0.026 \, DISPC$$
$$(3.85) \quad (0.0017) \qquad \bar{R}^2 = 0.945$$

Employment Education

$$EDU / POP_{5\text{-}9} = -19.707 + 0.041 \, DISPC$$
$$(2.49) \quad (0.001) \qquad \bar{R}^2 = 0.990$$

All Other State and Local

$$GEN / POP = 6.99 + 0.0053 \, DISPC$$
$$(0.672) \, (0.0003) \qquad \bar{R}^2 = 0.959$$

The government employment forecasts are found in sectors 92-96 of the "Persons Employed" page of the End Tables (E22). Forecasts of the sum of "table" purchases plus compensation of employees for all state and local functions and for Education can be found on the GNP summary page of the End

Tables (E5). Separate growth rates for "table" purchases by the four state and local categories can be found only in the "matrix listing" pages of the *Supplement*, for example, by looking at the sales of Office supplies (sector 183) to these categories.

Appendix 7A: Treatment of the Commodity Credit Corporation

Our treatment of the CCC necessarily differs from that of the Commerce Department. Both methods have the CCC as one of the producing industries, one of the 185 in our case, and also as a part of the Nondefense federal government expenditure, NDF_{CCC}. Let us suppose that the CCC buys or makes a loan on $100 of cotton. Both tables show this as a purchase by NDF_{CCC}. But let us now suppose further that the following year the CCC sells this cotton to yarn mills for $80, taking a loss of $20. The two alternative treatments are shown below:

	Commerce Method				Our Method		
	Yarn	CCC	NDF_{CCC}		Yarn	CCC	NDF_{CCC}
Cotton	80	20	−100	Cotton	80	0	−80
CCC	0	0	0	CCC	0	0	−20

The Yarn and NDF_{CCC} column totals are the same in both methods: The yarn mill total shows what they actually paid, and the negative NDF_{CCC} entries, the GNP components, exactly offset the purchase of the previous year. The Commerce method, however, has the inconvenience of implying infinite input-output coefficients, for the output of the CCC industry, the CCC-row sum, is always zero, but the inputs are positive. Our method has negative output with zero input, which causes no computational problem.

Statistically, the Commerce NDF_{CCC} column is equal to the change in inventories and loans outstanding while the CCC column is the loser on inventory operations by commodity. Our NDC_{CCC} column is the sum of those two columns with the negative of the CCC column total inserted into the CCC row.

8   The Input-Output Tables

In the previous chapters we have explained how the final demands—consumption, investment, exports and imports, and government spending—are forecast. In this chapter, we must show how these forecasts can be translated into demands for industries. This translation is accomplished by the tables of input-output coefficients. We shall first show how to use the coefficients for a particular year, then describe how the base-year input-output tables are made, and finally explain what we have done to forecast them into the future.

Input-Output Computations

The cornerstone of input-output is the table of "coefficients," a_{ij}, defined as the units of product i used in making one unit of product j. If i is flour measured in pounds and j is bread measured in loaves and 1.5 pounds of flour go into each loaf of bread, then $a_{ij} = 1.5$ pounds per loaf. In this book, the unit for measuring each product is one 1971 dollar's worth. If bread was 50¢ per loaf and flour 10¢ per pound in 1971, then one 1971 dollar's worth of bread is two loaves, and one 1971 dollar's worth of flour, ten pounds. In these 1971-dollar units, it takes 0.3 units of flour to make one unit of bread, so $a_{ij} = 0.3$. Although expressed in terms of a dollar's worth, these coefficients are still essentially in physical units. Future changes in the price of flour and bread do not affect them unless the physical proportions change. We shall return to that point when we discuss forecasting the a_{ij}.

Analogous to the intermediate coefficients a_{ij} are the final demand coefficients b_{ij}, c_{ij}, and g_{ij}. An equipment investment coefficient, b_{ij}, shows how many dollar's worth of product i goes into one dollar's worth of investment by investment industry j (j ranges from 1 to 90; i, from 1 to 185). A construction coefficient, c_{ij}, shows the same for construction type j; and a government coefficient, g_{ij}, shows the same for government expenditure category j.

The first step in the use of the coefficients is the calculation of final demand, F, by product:

$$F_i = \sum_{j=1}^{90} b_{ij}V_j + \sum_{j=1}^{28} c_{ij}S_j + \sum_{j=1}^{8} g_{ij}G_j + D_i + C_i + E_i \qquad (8.1)$$

147

where

V_j is equipment purchases by industry j

S_j is construction of type j

G_j is Government expenditure on category j

D_i is defense expenditure on product i

C_i is personal consumption expenditure on product i

E_i is export on item i.

Equation (8.1) says simply that the final demand for a product, say pumps, is the sum of demand for pumps as capital equipment, construction components, government or defense materials, consumer goods, and exports. The b's, c's, and g's all pertain to the future year to which the V's, S's, G's, and so forth apply. For that year, we also have forecasts, to be described below, of the a_{ij}. The output of each product, $X_1 \ldots X_n$, must satisfy the equation:

$$X_i = \sum_{j=1}^{n} a_{ij}X_j + F_i - M_i + N_i \qquad (8.2)$$

where

M_i is imports of product i

N_i is inventory change of product i.

Equation (8.2) says simply that the total output of product i must cover not only the final demand for it, F_i, but also the demand for its use as an intermediate good in other products.

This system of equations must be solved simultaneously. Both imports and inventory change, M_i and N_i, depend upon X_i, but let us ignore them for a moment and explain how the equations would be solved if we had only

$$X_i = \sum_{j=1}^{n} a_{ij}X_j + F_i. \qquad (8.2')$$

The reintroduction of M and N requires only a slight modification of the procedure. We solve equations (8.2') by successive approximations using a method known as the Seidel process. We make an initial guess—an approximation—of the solution, improve it, then improve the improved approximation, and so on. Let us denote the kth approximation X_i by X_k. If we have arrived at the kth approximation, we calculate the $(k+1)$ st approximation by the formula

$$X_i^{k+1} = (\sum_{j<i} a_{ij} X_j^{k+1} + \sum_{j>i} a_{ij} X_j^k + F_i) / (1 - a_{ii}). \tag{8.3}$$

The idea behind this formula is to take advantage of the natural sequences from a product to its ingredients. If we number the sectors so that apparel precedes textiles, which precede cotton, then equation (8.3) will calculate apparel output from apparel final demand; it will then calculate textile sales with apparel demand known, and ultimately will compute cotton sales from the known textile production. If the sectors were so numbered that each product precedes all its ingredients, then the solution of (8.2′) will be found in one iteration. If the industries were so arranged, the **A** matrix—the table with a row for each seller and a column for each buyer—would be triangular as shown in Figure 8-1a. By solving the first equation for x_1 and then using that value, solving the second equation for x_2, and so on, we quickly get the correct solution for (8.2′). Notice that this procedure is just a special case of formula (8.3). This formula, however, also works well when, as in practice, the **A** matrix is nearly, but not perfectly, triangular. The more nearly triangular we can make **A**, however, the more rapidly will the procedure converge.[a]

The standard order of the sectors does not produce a triangular matrix. For

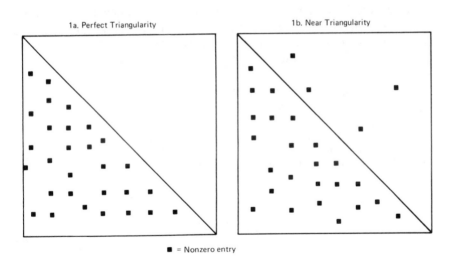

■ = Nonzero entry

Figure 8-1. Matrix Triangularity

[a]Proof of convergence, however, requires only that, under some set of prices, each product would sell for more than the cost of materials—*ex*cluding labor and capital—which go into it.

example, textiles precedes both apparel and synthetic fibers, while triangularity would require the order to be apparel-textiles-fibers. To find an order of the products which gives near triangularity, we choose as no. 1 the product for which the percentage of sales going to final demand is highest. This product happens to be in the category, Other ordnance, which sells exclusively to the government. Then we count all sales of other products to it as "final demand" for them, and pick, as no. 2 that product which, among the remaining ones, has the largest share of its sales going to this augmented final demand. This process is repeated n times to complete the list in triangular order. With the equations taken in this order,[b] the Seidel process usually converges in two or three iterations when we start it from the previous year's output.

From input-output literature, one might easily get the impression that the inverse matrix $(\mathbf{I}\text{-}\mathbf{A})^{-1}$, often called the matrix of direct-plus-indirect coefficients, should be used to solve (8.2'). Since we do *not* use this time-honored device, we perhaps owe it a word of apology. But readers not familiar with the inverse may certainly skip that word. We do not use the inverse for three reasons:

1. The inverse would occupy 185^2 = 34,225 words of computer core. By storing only the nonzero entries of the A matrix, we need only a third that much space.
2. Because all the a_{ij}'s are different in each year, we would have a different inverse in each year. But the calculation of the inverse requires about 185 times as much computer time as does the solution of (8.2') by the Seidel process. Reading in the inverse for each year would also be a time-consuming process.
3. Even if the inverse was available, the process of multiplying it by the vector of final demands would require 185^2 = 34,225 additions and

[b]Formula (8.3) would have to be rewritten with a complicated notation to express the fact that the equations are taken in a triangular order without renumbering the sectors. The alogrithm is readily described, however, by the following 8 lines of Fortran. *LIST (L)* is here the standard-order number of the product which is in the Lth place in the triangular order.

```
DO 20 L = 1, N
I = LIST (L)
SUM = 0
DO 18 J = 1, N
IF (J.EQ.I) GO TO 18
SUM = SUM + A (I,J) * X (J)
18 CONTINUE
20 X (I) = SUM / (1. − A (I,I)).
```

These lines describe one iteration. It is a simple matter to add a few more statements to calculate the maximum difference between the old and the new approximations and to iterate again if that difference is above some cutoff limit, say one million dollars.

multiplications, more than would be needed for three iterations of the Seidel process using only nonzero entries. It is therefore as much trouble to *use* the inverse as to calculate the solution directly from the nonzero a_{ij}. Clearly then, there is no point in going to all the extra trouble to find and store the inverse.

So far we have neglected the import and inventory change terms in Equation (8.2′), but this neglect must now be remedied. As explained in Chapter 5, inventory change depends linearly upon domestic use plus exports but excluding inventory change and sales of the product to itself. Imports depend linearly upon output *less* exports. The import equation, inventory change equation and Equation (8.2′) therefore form a system of three simultaneous linear equations in the three unknowns—output, imports, and inventory change. They can be solved algebraically, and the solution has been incorporated in the program for the Seidel process. The result is an efficient but far from transparent program.

Purification of the Input-Output Tables

Stampings cut in plants primarily engaged in rolling aluminum, breakfast cereals made in a plant primarily engaged in making wood pulp, or lumber sawn in a plant whose main product is furniture are all examples of secondary products. How to handle them in input-output tables has vexed many a table-maker. We have developed a method which, we believe, effectively solves the problem. It creates a product-to-product table. From looking only at that table, one would not know there was such a thing as a secondary product. The reader who is relieved to know that he doesn't need to worry about secondary products to understand our forecasts may merrily skip this section. But he who wants to know by what magic we exorcised that specter must pay attention.

Our A matrix comes from a tape prepared by the Bureau of Economic Analysis (BEA) of the Commerce Department. The tape gives a 363-order matrix for 1963 and distinguishes between "primary" and "secondary" flows. Lumber sold to furniture plants is a typical primary flow. In BEA practice, the $19 million of lumber made in plants primarily engaged in making furniture is shown as a "secondary sale" of furniture to lumber. In the printed volumes (U.S. Department of Commerce, Office of Business Economics, *Input-Output Structure of the U.S. Economy: 1963*) the two types of entries are indistinguishable. Such entries are not only confusing when looking at the table, but they can also distort the outcome of its use. If we asked what would be the impact of an increase in residential construction, the big lumber user, this furniture-to-lumber secondary entry would lead to an immediate increase in the output of the furniture industry and thereby to higher demand for textiles, wood, plastics, metal, and glue. Moreover, because the establishments in the Structural metals product sector make some furniture, which is also transferred to the Furniture sector, the demand for lumber also generates demand for structural steel to "go into" the lumber. Such distortions are probably not large, but they are disconcerting and have led to a desire to "purify" the matrix. We have been generally pleased with the results of the following purification rite.

We may postulate that each product is made by the same process, no matter what kind of establishment makes it. The vector of inputs into any establishment is therefore just a linear combination of the pure processes for the items it makes. In symbols,

$$\mathbf{f_i} = \mathbf{Mp_i} \qquad\qquad i = 1, \ldots, n. \quad (8.4)$$

where:

f_i, a column vector, is the transpose of the ith row of the *primary flow matrix*, that is, f_{ij} equals the purchases of product i by establishments in industry j. M is the product mix matrix: m_{ij} = the fraction of product j made in establishments in industry i. (The columns of $\mathbf{M}$ sum to 1.0).

p_i is the transpose of the ith row of the *pure* flow matrix; p_{ij} = inputs of product i into *product j*.

Equation (8.4) can be solved for $\mathbf{p}_i$ by

$$p_i = \mathbf{M}^{-1} f_i \qquad\qquad i = 1, \ldots, n. \quad (8.5)$$

The p_i vectors found by this formula will generally have some small negative elements and some small positive entries where the corresponding f_i vectors have zeros. The former are clearly nonsense; the latter are at best dubious and certainly inconvenient, especially because we wish to store only non-zero entries in our computer. By developing an iterative interpretation of the solution of (8.5), we shall find a way to put a stop to this nonsense.

In what follows, we shall drop the subscript i from f and p and understand that the f and p in an equation all have the same i subscript. Equation (8.4) may be then written

$$0 = -\mathbf{Mp} + \mathbf{f},$$

and by adding p to both sides we obtain

$$\mathbf{p} = (\mathbf{I} - \mathbf{M})\mathbf{p} + \mathbf{f}. \qquad\qquad (8.6)$$

The column sums of the absolute values of $\mathbf{I} - \mathbf{M}$ will be less than 1.0, save in the unlikely case in which less than half of a product is produced by establishments primarily engaged in its production. The iterative process for the solution of (8.6) will therefore converge. In this process, we take as a first approximation of p,

$$\mathbf{p}^{(0)} = \mathbf{f}$$

and then define successive approximations by

$$\mathbf{p}^{(k+1)} = (\mathbf{I} - \mathbf{M})\mathbf{p}^{(k)} + \mathbf{f}. \qquad (8.7)$$

To see the economic interpretation of (8.7), let us write out the equation for the use of a product, say electricity, in making another product, say j:

$$\mathbf{p}_j^{(k+1)} = \mathbf{f}_j - \sum_{\substack{l=1 \\ l \neq j}}^{n} m_{jl} p_l^{(k)} + (1 - m_{jj}) p_j^{(k)}. \qquad (8.8)$$

The first term on the right of (8.8) tells us to begin with the electricity purchases by the establishments in industry j. The second term directs us to remove the amounts of electricity needed for making the secondary products of those establishments, using our present estimate $[p^{(k)}]$ of the technology of those products. Finally, the last term causes us to add back the electricity used in making product j in other industries. The amount of electricity added by the third term is exactly equal to the amount stolen, via second terms, from other industries on account of their production of product j:

$$(1 - m_{jj}) p_j = \sum_{\substack{l=1 \\ l \neq j}}^{n} m_{lj} p_j$$

$$\text{Since } \sum_{l=1}^{n} m_{lj} = 1.$$

It is now clear how to keep the negative elements out of p. When the "removal" term, the second on the right of (8.8), is larger than the "primary use" term, the f, we simply scale down all components of the removal term to leave a zero balance. Then instead of adding back the "total-stolen-from-other-industries" term, $(1 - m_{jj}) p_j$ all at once, we added it back bit-by-bit as it is captured. If a plundered industry runs out of electricity with only a third of the total amount of plundering claims satisfied, we simply add only a third of each plundering product's claim into that product's cell in p.

Experience with this algorithm has shown that most of "purified" entries were quite close to the "primary" entries.[c]

Rejuvenation of the Input-Output Table

Once the 1963 was purified, it next had to be rejuvenated, for 1963 is now a decade ago and more recent data is available. We have tried to make our table consistent with much of this newer data.

The first step was to bring the table up to 1967 by using the wealth of information contained in the 1967 Census of Manufactures. This work, like the purification, was done at the 363-sector level at which the 1963 matrix was published. After updating, the matrix was aggregated to our 185 sectors. The second step was then to bring this 185-sector 1967 matrix up to 1971, which serves as the base year for these forecasts.

The plan of attack for making the 1967 matrix was to establish row and column control totals for each product, to estimate directly as many of the individual cells as possible, and then to fill in the remaining cells with flows which keep as close as possible to the 1963 coefficients while maintaining consistency with all the known 1967 data. More specifically, we subtract the directly estimated cells or "known" flows—from the corresponding row and column totals, fill in the remaining cells with the flows they would have had if the coefficients had remained constant between 1963 and 1967, and then balance this matrix to the reduced row and column totals by what is called the rAs method.[d] In this method we first scale all the elements in each row to obtain the correct row sums. Then we scale all the elements in each column to obtain the correct column sums. The rows will then be out of balance, so we again scale them so that they have the right sums, then scale the columns again, and so on until the process converges. In our experience, about ten iterations were necessary to get all the scaling factors to within 1 percent of unity.

We shall explain in a moment how we got the 1967 row and column sums and the known flows, but first we must note that the procedure did not work quite as planned. A problem arose when the supposedly "known" flows loomed large in a row but were not quite consistent with the row totals. Then the remaining small flows would have to take up all the difference between the row total and the big, "known" flows. Consequently, these small fry

---

[c]Two changes had to be made in BEA conventions, however. Advertising done by radio, TV, magazines and newspapers was considered by BEA to be a secondary product of these sectors and was "transferred"—not "sold"—to advertising. We had to change all these transfers to sales. BEA also considered many knit products to be transferred to the apparel industry. We converted these to direct sales to personal consumption.

[d]Given a starting matrix, A, the method amounts to finding diagonal matrixes $\hat{r}$ and $\hat{s}$ such that the matrix $\hat{r}A\hat{s}$ has the required row and column sums, hence the name rAs.

suffered some enormous, and highly unlikely, changes. We therefore felt it necessary to subject the large, "known" flows to some preliminary adjustment before starting the rAs process. If we let

T be the row total

K be the sum of "known" flows in the row

S be the sum of the initial values of the other flows

$\alpha = K/(K+S)$

then we found z such that

$$Sz + Kz^{\alpha} = T.$$

We then adjusted all the "known" flows by z^{α} and all the others by z. If K is large relative to S, the two kinds of flows receive almost the same adjustment; if K is small relative to S, the "known" flows will be relatively untouched by this preliminary adjustment. We then removed the adjusted "known" flows from row and column totals and proceeded to the rAs balancing, which worked much more smoothly after the preliminary adjustment than it did without it.

The preliminary adjustment may be generalized to express different degrees of confidence in various groups of "known" flows. We could then have

$$Sz + \sum_{i=1}^{k} K_i z^{\alpha_i} = T$$

where k is the number of groups of "known" flows and the α_i express the degree of confidence in the flows in the ith group. A value of $\alpha_i = 0$ means absolute confidence while $\alpha_i = 1$ expresses minimal confidence. Our choice for α was convenient and, at the same time, expressed approximately the confidence we felt in the estimates of the known flows.

We turn now to the sources of data for the 1967 updating. The row controls were found by moving forward the 1963 row totals by the index of product shipments for the manufacturing industries and by a variety of indexes for the nonmanufacturing industries (See note on data sources in the *Supplement*). Estimates of consumption, exports, and imports by product were made as described in the chapters on these subjects. Producer durable equipment expenditure by product was estimated in the same way as was consumption. These estimates were all felt to be consistent with the row controls and were removed from the row totals before even the preliminary adjustment.

Column control totals and individual known flows were calculated from the

"Materials-Consumed-by-Kind" tables of the 1967 Census of Manufactures. Unfortunately, all of this information gives the material input to an industry, *Mi*, rather than to a product, *Mp*. For example, the plastic material input into the home furniture industry is the plastic used by the plants primarily engaged in making home furniture. But those plants also make some office furniture and the plastics used in that *office* furniture is included in the plastics used by the *home* furniture industry. Conversely, some home furniture is made by plants in other industries, and the plastic used in that furniture is *not* included among the inputs to the home furniture industry. The extent of this sort of problem is indicated by the specialization and coverage ratios, *S* and *R*, respectively.[e] If *S* and *R* remained constant from one census to another, we could neglect this problem and just use the index of *Mi* in place of the index for *Mp*. But of course *S* and *R* do change, so we adjust for the change and use as the index for *Mp*

$$\frac{Mp\,(67)}{Mp\,(63)} = \frac{Mi\,(67)}{Mp\,(63)} \cdot \frac{S\,(67)}{S\,(63)} = \frac{C\,(63)}{C\,(67)}$$

This adjustment was made at the four-digit level on all the information on materials consumed by kind. The adjusted information was then aggregated to the 363-sector level and, in index form, was used to determine the column totals and "known" flows in those columns. Other "known" flows came from examining the product shipment information at its maximum level of detail. For example, glass bottle production distinguishes a number of types of bottles, such as beer bottles and soft-drink bottles. These data readily yield known flows. In all, some 1000 known flows were established.

Column controls for the nonmanufacturing sectors were established simply as the column sums after the preliminary adjustment.

With all the information marshalled together, we put it through the preliminary adjustment and rAs balancing to get the 1967 matrix. Truth to tell, we put it through those programs dozens of times, each time discovering and removing some inconsistency in the data. The final product is, we believe, fairly accurate in the large flows, but probably quite inaccurate in the small flows, some of which underwent adjustments of 20 to 40 percent. Because most major flows were "known," the economic significance of the adjustment factors is doubtful. Consequently, they are not presented here.

The balancing for 1971 was much simpler than that for 1967, for we did not have the wealth of a Census of Manufactures upon which to draw. We first moved forward all the entries in a column by the index of that product's output, or, in the case of manufacturing, by the index of cost of materials for that

---

[e]To define *S* and *R* precisely, let *T* be the total shipments, by all plants of products belonging to a 4-digit SIC number, let *P* be the shipments of those products by the establishments classified in that 4-digit industry, and let *I* be the shipments of all products by those establishments. Then $S = P/I$ and $C = P/T$.

industry. We then scaled all of the entries in each row to get the correct row total. Less than a dozen known flows were introduced other than the final demands. We did not continue the rAs method because we doubted the column controls.

Forecasts of Input-Output Coefficients

Some input-output coefficients remain constant over the years. The newsprint-to-newspaper coefficient, for example, has scarcely budged in twenty years, while others, such as plastics-to-automobiles, have risen enormously. Our model permits—and indeed compels—us to forecast specific future changes. All of these forecasts follow a logistic curve, some examples of which appear in Figure 8-2. As the figure shows, this curve, like Zeus, can appear in many forms. All of them eventually approach a floor or a ceiling—an asymptote.[f] But some approach the asymptote quickly, so that within our forecasting period the rate of change slows down sharply and the coefficient levels out at a floor or ceiling, while others remain far from the asymptote throughout our forecasting period. The one thing the logistic curve won't do is to put a U-turn in a coefficient. Such U-turns do happen; the oil-to-electric-generation coefficient declined for years prior to 1965, and then began rising sharply. There are, however, no such U-turns among our expectations for the future coefficients, so this limitation of the logistic curve has not been inconvenient. The logistic curves have been introduced in two ways:

1. Individual coefficient change

---

[f]Mathematically, the differential equation for the logistic curve is

$$\frac{1}{c} \frac{dc}{dt} = b(a-c)$$

where

c = coefficient

a = asymptote toward which the coefficient is tending

b = constant ratio of the percentage change in c to the gap between a and c.

The solution of this differential equation is

$$c(t) = a/(1+Ae^{-bat})$$

where A is a constant of integration.

The three parameters A, a, and b can be expressed in terms of the starting value of the coefficient, its initial percentage rate of change, and the initial rate of change of that rate of change. It is in this form that the curve is specified to the model. Thus we may specify simply that a coefficient will increase 10.0 percent in the first year, but 0.5 of a point less, or 9.5 percent, in the second year. From this information, and the initial value of c, the program makes up the logistic curve.

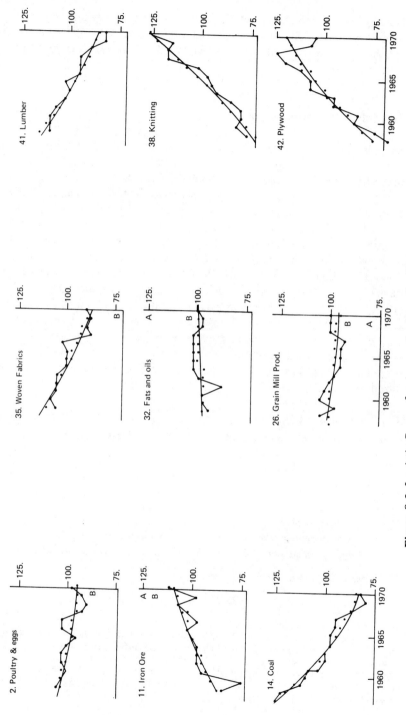

Figure 8-2. Logistic Curves for Across-the-Row Coefficient Changes.

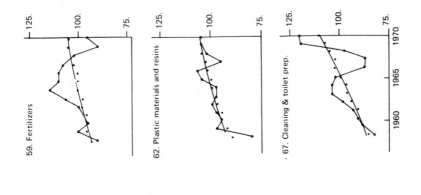

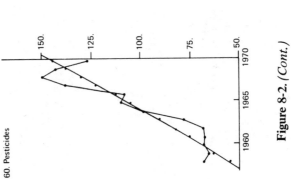

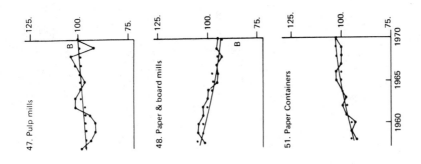

Figure 8-2. *(Cont.)*

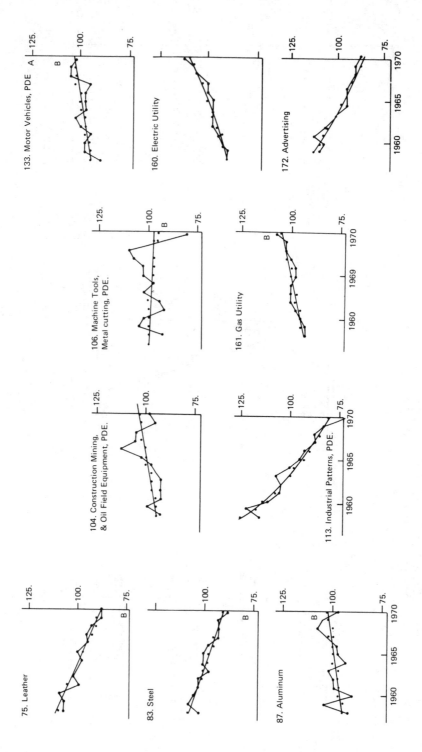

Figure 8-2. *(Cont.)*

2. Across-the-row coefficient changes: all coefficients in a row of the **A** matrix follow the same logistic curve, percentagewise. Coefficients in the row with individual changes are skipped by the across-the-row operation. Similar, but separate, across-the-row changes can be applied to rows of the **B** and **C** matrixes.

The second type, the across-the-row change has been estimated and introduced for almost all rows. To estimate them it was necessary to construct a historical series on the intermediate use of each product. We began with series on product shipments. In manufacturing, these series were made by aggregating the five-digit series mentioned in Chapter 2. On the surface it sounds simple to use the series, which are apparently, published in each *Annual Survey of Manufactures*. In fact, the numerous changes in the SIC code and the necessity to prorate the widely fluctuating "not-specified-by-kind" part of each four-digit product among its five-digit components meant that the compilation of these series absorbed over six man-months of meticulous work. The sources for the nonmanufacturing output series are described in the appendix to this chapter.

In order to get intermediate use, there must be subtracted from product shipments:

1. Personal consumption expenditure (PCE), estimated as described in Chapter 2.
2. Producer durable equipment (PDE) investment. Just as in the PCE case, we assumed that the PDE share of each five-digit product remained unchanged, except in home furniture and carpets.
3. Inventory change, as estimated in Chapter 5.
4. Exports minus imports, as estimated in Chapter 6.
5. Government demands, as estimated in Chapter 7.

The residual after these subtractions represents intermediate use by the 185 industries and by construction; let us call it simply U. We then calculate what this usage would have been had the input-output coefficients been constant at their 1969 values from 1958 to 1971. That is, we compute

$$I_i(t) = \sum_{j=1}^{185} a_{ij} x_j(t) + \sum_{j=1}^{28} c_{ij} S_j(t)$$

I stands for "Indicator," for I_i indicates how much of the product i would have been used had all the coefficients in the ith row remained constant. The ratio U/I is then treated like a single coefficient and a logistic curve is fitted to it. The various parts of Figure 8-2 show a variety of such curves. These curves show by their trend what changes have been taking place in the competition among materials. By the closeness of the scatter of points around the logistic curve, they show also how well such a uniform trend assumption would have worked in the past. For most products, such as steel, which sell largely to intermediate use, the fit is quite close. For products such as Cleaning and toilet products which go chiefly to final demands, the estimate of U has a wide margin of error, so it is not surprising that the fit is not close.

A number of the industries show little or no coefficient change, and the logistic curve fits closely. These include:

15 Crude Petroleum and Natural Gas	80 Pottery
16 Stone and Clay Mining	82 Other Stone and Clay Products
32 Fats and Oils	98 Cutlery Hand Tools
47 Pulp Mills	94 Plumbing and Heating Equipment
48 Paper and Paperboard Mills	92 Metal Cans
49 Paper Products	105 Material Handling Machinery—PDE
54 Other Printing Services	116 Service Industries Machinery—PDE
69 Petroleum Refining	120 Motors and Generators
73 Rubber Products	151 Railroads

Some of the most spectacular changes, also with close fits, are:

Going Up	% per Year Change of Logistic Curve in 1970	Going Down	% per Year Change of Logistic Curve in 1970
36 Floor Coverings—PDE	+ 4.6	14 Coal Mining	− 1.9
38 Knitting	+ 4.2	33 Miscellaneous Food Products	− 3.9
43 Millwork and Wood Products	+ 2.4	41 Lumber and Wood Products	− 2.0
60 Pesticides	+ 5.6	44 Wooden Containers	− 4.5
63 Synthetic Rubber	+ 1.2	50 Wall and Building Paper	− 1.5
65 Non-Cellulosic Fiber	+ 6.0	64 Cellulosic Fiber	− 1.6
66 Drugs	+ 2.2	73 Rubber Products—PDE	− 4.4
71 Paving and Asphalt	+ 2.4	75 Leather	− 1.5
74 Miscellaneous Plastic Products	+ 7.6	83 Steel	− 1.1
81 Cement, Concrete and Gypsum	+ 1.2	84 Copper	− .9
101 Other Fabricated Metal Products	+ 1.4	96 Screw Machine Products	− 1.6
114 Computers and Related Machinery	+ 7.9	95 Structural Metal Products— PDE	− 2.0
116 Service Industry	+ 6.3	108 Other Metal Working Machinery—PDE	− 2.3
117 Machine Shop Products	+ 4.3	109 Special Industrial Machinery—PDE	− 1.1
128 Electronic Components	+ 2.2	112 Power Transmission Equipment	− 1.3
137 Ship and Boat Building—PDE	+ 6.5	113 Industrial Patterns—PDE	− 2.8
138 Railroad Equipment—PDE	+ 2.4		
144 Medical and Surgical Instruments—PDE	+ 3.2		

	Going Up	% per Year Change of Logistic Curve in 1970	Going Down	% per Year Change of Logistic Curve in 1970
145	Photographic Equipment	+ 6.0	118 Electrical Measuring Instruments—PDE	− 5.4
145	Photographic Equipment—PDE	+ 7.9	142 Mechanical Measuring Devices—PDE	− 3.5
155	Airlines	+ 2.8	154 Water Transportation	− 4.5
156	Pipelines	+ 1.9	157 Freight Forwarding and Travel Agents	− 1.9
158	Telephone and Telegraph	+ 3.2		
160	Electric Utilities	+ 1.6	162 Water and Sewer Services	− 2.0
165	Banks and Credit Agencies	+ 3.9	166 Insurance	− 2.1
171	Business Services	+ 1.1	172 Advertising	− 1.7

We can perform similar calculations for the rows of the **B** matrix, for distribution of capital equipment investment. In this case, U is the sales of the product to *PDE*—the second item deducted above—and

$$I_i(t) = \sum_{j=1}^{90} b_{ij} V_j(t).$$

Some of the plots for these *PDE* U/I ratios are included in Figure 8-2, where they are marked by the letters *"PDE"* at the end of their title. Generally, they seem to show a wider dispersion around the trend line than do the intermediate uses. There appear to be cyclical effects on the product-composition of the investment dollar. Machine tools, for example, increase in importance during booms and decrease during recessions. We have not taken these cyclical effects into account in the overall model, but have done so rather carefully in specific application to machine tools, described in Chapter 10.

Logistic curves such as those shown in Figure 8-2 have been calculated for all products for which output estimates were available. The continuation of the logistic curves into the future has been applied to all of the coefficients in a row which do not have their own individual logistic curve. In this fashion we can be fairly certain that we do not miss any broad and pervasive coefficient changes, yet, at the same time, keep as our objective the specification of individual coefficient changes on all important coefficients.

That objective has not yet been reached, but a substantial start has been made. Individual coefficient changes have been estimated for major flows in the steel, copper, aluminum, lead, paper, paper container, fuel oil, and electricity rows. All of these have used physical volume measures of sales; except for electricity and fuel oil, the data has come from trade association sources (electrical usage comes from the *Annual Survey of Manufactures;* fuel oil usage comes principally from the *Minerals Yearbook*). The economic content of this work eludes generalization save to say that important flows generally had close fits and that there were no big surprises in the direction of movement; steel goes down and plastics go up. The final result can be read from the matrix listing in the *Supplement.*

Before leaving the subject of coefficient change, we must make two points on which we often find confusion. The first and simplest is that coefficient change is by no means the same thing as technological change. Between 1963 and 1967 computer technology made great strides from the second to the third generation machines. This step was made possible by revolutionary technological changes in the electronic components which go into computers. But between those two years the coefficient of Electronic components to Computers changed scarcely at all. On the other hand, the coefficient of Glass into Soft drinks increased 35 percent per year as bottlers shifted from returnable to nonreturnable bottles—a "technology" long known to pickle packers. It is our impression, on looking at hundreds of these logistic curves, that they reflect changes in laws, preferences, prices, and product mixes at least as much as they reflect advances in technology. We refrain, therefore, from the flashy term "technological change" and stick with the unexciting but correct expression, "coefficient change."

The second point concerns the sum of the coefficients in a column of the **A** matrix. The difference between the value of shipments and the cost of materials in industry j is called "value added" by that industry, VA_j. We may then define a value-added coefficient, $va_j = VA_j/X_j$. Because all products are measured in units of one 1971 dollar's worth, as explained in the first section, *in 1971* we shall find that

$$\sum_{i=1}^{185} a_{ij} + va_j = 1, \quad \text{for all industries,} j. \tag{8.9}$$

It has often been supposed that this relation imposes a useful restriction on projections of the future coefficients. That supposition, however, is absolutely erroneous, for this equation need not hold at all for any year except the one whose prices are used to determine the units of measurement. To illustrate that point, let us return to the bread-and-flour example of the first section. Suppose that a flour substitute, Carhyd, derived from petroleum, sold in 1971 for $5.00 per pound, but that thereafter the price falls to around 20¢ per pound while flour prices rise to 60¢ per pound. Meanwhile bakers learn to use Carhyd so that by 1984, a loaf of bread is made of one pound of Carhyd and half a pound of flour. In 1971 prices, that is $5.00 of Carhyd and $.05 of flour per loaf, and since there are two loaves in a 1971 dollar's worth of bread, the 1984 coefficients in the bread column are

Carhyd	10.00
Flour	.10

The sum of just these two coefficients is greater than 1.0, so Equation (8.9) certainly does *not* hold in 1984. The example is extreme, to be sure, but it demonstrates that there is absolutely no logical ground to expect Equation (8.9) to hold for future coefficients when the units are a 1971 dollar's worth. From the 1984 coefficients, one can produce 1984 prices. If those prices are used to define units, Equation (8.9) will hold for 1984 *by definition*; but in no case does it provide a useful restriction on the coefficients. Consequently, we don't use Equation (8.9) for that purpose; and if you know anyone who does, mark him down as a rank amateur.

Appendix 8A: Sources for Historical Output Series

The full statistical base for computing the output of an industry as done by the Department of Commerce is available only in economic census years, 1958, 1963, 1967. We have to be content with a simpler series which can be easily calculated each year. The sources of these are described below. *Each industry's 1963 output from the government 1-0 table has been moved forward and backward by the series described here.*

Agricultural Products (1-7)   *Statistical Abstract of the U.S. 1972 (SAUS)*

In the agricultural sectors, the definition of output should be production, not marketing. However, the basic source for these sectors is farm marketings. Production may be significantly larger than marketing when, for example, a farmer raises part of the feed for his livestock. For crops, we have adjusted the marketing statistics to include other production.[g]

Sector	Current Dollar Output Source	Deflator Source
1. Dairy products	*SAUS* 72 T.991—Dairy Products	Wholesale Price Index (WPI) —Fluid Milk
2. Poultry and eggs	*SAUS* 72 T.991—Eggs, Broilers, Turkeys, and other poultry	Prices received by farmers in *Survey of Current Business* (SCB)—Poultry and eggs
3. Livestock	*SAUS* 72 T.991—Hogs, Cattle, Sheep, Wool, Other Livestock products	WPI—Livestock
4. Cotton	*SAUS* 72 T.991—Cotton	Prices received by farmers— Cotton
5. Grains (see note g)	*SAUS* 72 T.991—Food grains, feed grains	WPI—Grains
6. Tobacco	*SAUS* 72 T.991—Tobacco	Prices received by farmers— Tobacco
7. Other crops (see note g)	*SAUS* 72 T.991—Oil bearing crops, Vegetables, Fruits and tree nuts, Other crops	WPI—Fruits and vegetables— fresh and dried

Agricultural Services, Forestry, Fisheries (8, 10)

8. Forestry and fishery products	Fishery—Value of catch *SAUS* 72 T.1061, "Fisheries—Quantity and Value of Catch"	Unpublished—Bureau of Economic Analysis (BEA) Gross Product Originating

---

[g]For grains (5) and other crops (7), production that was not marketed was estimated by taking the difference between farm value (*SAUS* 72-T.1010, "Principal Crops—Acreage, Production, Value") and marketings of principal crops (*SAUS* 72-T.990, "Farm Marketings by Price Support Status"). Corn, wheat, sorghums, oats, and barley were used to adjust grains; hay was used to adjust other crops.

	Forestry—Cost of Stumpage[h]	(GPO) Agr. Services, forestry, fisheries
10. Agricultural services	GPO—Agricultural services, forestry, fisheries	GPO

Mining (11-17)   *SAUS* 72 T.1083, "Mineral Production"—Value

11. Iron ore	*SAUS* 72 T.1083—Iron ore	*SAUS* 72 T.1087, "Average Price of Selected Mineral Products"—iron ore
12. Copper ore	*SAUS* 72 T.1083—Copper ore	*SAUS* 72 T.1087—Copper, electrolytic
13. Other nonferrous metals	*SAUS* 72 T.1083—Total metals, less Iron ore and less Copper ore	*Minerals Yearbook* 1969[i] T.30, "Index of Average Unit Mine Value of Minerals Produced"—Nonferrous metals[i]
14. Coal mining	*SAUS* 72 T.1083—Bituminous and lignite, Pa. anthracite	WPI—Coal
15. Crude petroleum and natural gas	*SAUS* 72 T.1083—Total mineral fuels less Coal	WPI—Crude petroleum
16. Stone and clay mining	*SAUS* 72 T.1083—Total Non-metals less chemical fertilizer mining	GPO-SIC 14
17. Chemical fertilizer mining	*SAUS* 72 T.1083—Barite, Fluorspor, Potassium salts, Borate, Phosphate rock, Rock salt, Sulfur	GPO-SIC 14

Construction (18-19)

18. New construction	*SCB* July issues. National Accounts T.5.2—"purchases of Structures by Type"	*SCB* T.5.3

The appropriate output for new construction is value added, obtained by multiplying total structures by row 18 of the construction matrix.

19. Maintenance and repair construction	GPO	GPO

Manufacturing (20-150)

The value of product shipments by 5-digit SIC are the sources for manufacturing outputs. This data, from the *Annual Survey of Manufactures,* becomes available with about a two-year lag. The deflators for 4-digit industry shipments are unpublished data supplied by BEA.

The total output includes, besides the producer's value of products shipped, the excise and retail sales taxes on those products, plus the value of contract services, plus the increase in finished product inventories.

Transportation (151-157)	*SAUS* 72 T.872 "Operating by Type of Transport"	
151. Railroads	*SAUS* 72 T.872—Railroads	GPO-SIC 40

---

[h]Cost of stumpage for any year t is estimated by

$$\text{Cost of stumpage}_t = \left(\frac{\text{Cost of stumpage}}{\text{Total Cost of Materials}}\right)_s \times \text{Cost of Materials}_t$$

The Census of Manufactures and the Annual Survey of Manufactures product cost of stumpage and/or materials for the lumber sectors—Standard Industrial Classification (SIC) 2411, 2421, 2426, 2429.

[i]Nonferrous metals price index was adjusted to exclude copper.

152. Busses and local transit	*SAUS* 72 T.872–Motor carriers of passengers	PCE-Sector 152
153. Trucking	*SAUS* 72 T.872–Motor carriers of property	GPO-SIC 42
154. Water	*SAUS* 72 T.872–Waterlines	GPO-SIC 44
155. Airlines	*SAUS* 72 T.872–Domestic scheduled air carriers	PCE-Sector 155
156. Pipelines	*SAUS* 72 T.872–Pipelines	GPO-SIC 46
157. Transportation services	GPO-SIC 47	GPO-SIC 47

Communications (158-159)

158. Telephone and telegraph	*SAUS* 72 T.793, "Telephone and Telegraph Systems"– Operating revenues, domestic telephones, and Total	GPO-Telephone and Telegraph
159. Radio and TV broadcasting	*SAUS* 72 T.800, "Commercial Broadcast Stations, Number and Revenues"–Total revenues	GPO-Radio and TV

Utilities

160. Electricity	*SAUS* 72 T.825, "Electric Utilities-Balance Sheet and Income Account of Privately Owned Companies"–Electric operating revenues	Consumer Price Index (CPI) Electricity
161. Natural gas	*SAUS* 72 T.835, "Gas Utility Industry-Summary"–Revenues	CPI-Gas
162. Water and sewer services	*SAUS* 72 T.657, "Summary of State and Local Government Finances"–Water supply revenue	CPI-Residential water and sewer services

Trade (163-164)

163. Wholesale trade	GPO	GPO
164. Retail trade	GPO	GPO

The output of trade is trade margins only. The entries in the trade rows show the trade margins on all items bought by a particular industry or type of final demand.

Finance, Insurance and Real Estate (165-168)

165. Banking	*FDIC Annual Report*, Table 113, Commercial bank noninterest income; + T.2.5 *SCB*, "Services Rendered without Payment from Financial Intermediaries."	PCE (personal consumption expenditures)–sector 165
166. Insurance	*SCB* July issues T.1.12, "National Income by Industry"	PCE-sector 166
167. Owner-occupied housing	*SCB* July issues T.2.5, "Personal Consumption Expenditures" + .75 x Rental Value of Farm Dwellings.	*SCB* T.26
168. Real Estate	*SCB* T.1.12, Income + *SCB* T.6.9, Capital Consumption Allowances	PCE-sector 168

Services (169-176)

Outputs for the following service sectors are derived by adding an estimate of intermediate use to personal consumption expenditures.

169. Hotels and Trailer
     Courts

170. Personal and Repair
     Services

173. Auto Repair

174. Movies and
     Amusements

175. Medical Services

176. Private Schools and
     Nonprofit Organiza-
     tions

The estimates of intermediate use are derived by multiplying outputs for all other sectors by the 1969 A-matrix coefficients for the service sectors. PCE deflators were used to convert series to 1969 constant dollars.

171. Business Services	*SCB*. T.1.12 Misc. business services + Legal services + Misc. professional services.	PCE-Sector 171
172. Advertising	*SAUS* 72 T.1259, "Advertising —Estimated Expenditures"	GPO-SIC 73
177. Post Office	*SAUS* 72 T.786, "U.S. Postal Service—Summary," Total Revenues	PCE-Sector 177

Government Enterprises and Dummy Sectors

Outputs for these sectors are obtained in the same manner as the service sectors; i.e., using interindustry coefficients to estimate intermediate flows. Sector 179 is not defined.

178. Federal Government
     Enterprises

180. Other State and Local
     Enterprises

182. Business Travel
     (Dummy)

183. Office Supplies
     (Dummy)

184. Unimportant Industries
     (Dummy)

185. Complete Rental

The computer rental industry in the Maryland model has only one input (Sector 114—Computers and related machinery) and its sales are the value of rentals to other industries and final demand. Our study of computer demand estimated a simple equation relating computer shipments and rental value:

$$S_t = 2.22(R_t - 0.87R_{t-1})$$

The output series prior to 1966 is scaled by a monthly rental value index reported by Chow in "Technological Change and Demand for Computers" (*American Economic Review*, December 1967). Subsequent outputs have been calculated by turning the above equation around and solving for R_t; the shipments data comes from *EDP Reports*. The deflator used is the 4-digit deflator for electronic computing equipment.

9 Employment

Newspaper accounts of month-to-month changes in unemployment and talk of hard core, structural unemployment may lead one to think that the number of jobs bears but a loose relation to the number of job seekers. But looked at over decades, the economy has done a remarkable job of matching the two. Like the car of a slightly inebriated driver, though it may wobble, it generally follows the road. If it is going 30 miles per hour and we need to predict where it will be two minutes from now, we can scarcely do better than to forecast that it will be squarely in the middle of its lane a mile down the road. If at that time it is five feet to the right, bumping along with two wheels on the shoulder, well, our forecast of the change in position was still accurate to within a tenth of a percent.

We use the same logic for long-term forecasting of the economy. The labor force, which can be relatively confidently predicted, is the road and our forecast puts the economy squarely on it. But to know whether or not a given forecast of industry outputs puts us on the road, we must know how much employment it generates. This chapter, therefore, has two parts; first, a description of the labor-force projections; second, an explanation of how we go from the output of an industry to its employment. An appendix explains the sources we use for employment statistics. (Because the Bureau of Labor Statistics publishes no reconciliation between its labor-force and unemployment statistics on the one hand and its employment-by-industry statistics on the other, we have had to make that reconciliation ourselves. It is the subject of this chapter's appendix.)

Labor Force Projections

Our labor-force projections, shown in Figure 9-1, are those released by the Bureau of Labor Statistics (BLS) in March 1973. They are based upon the Series E population projection, which presumes that the decline in fertility rates will stabilize at 2.1 children per woman, the rate which eventually produces a stable population. Over twelve years, the fertility rates affect labor force forecasts only through their effect on the number of women with children under five. The decline in the birth rate was largely responsible for the phenomenal increase in women in the labor force between 1964 and 1972. The number of women aged 25-35, for example, increased 22 percent over those years, while the number of women of that age in the labor force shot up 56 percent. The increase in the

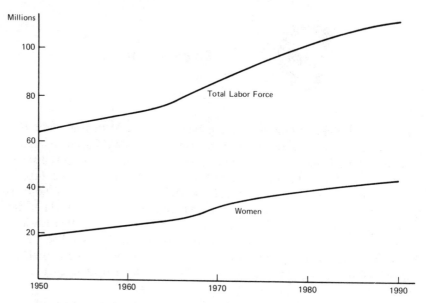

Figure 9-1. Labor Force Projections. Source: Bureau of Labor Statistics

expected participation of women implies that the labor force will grow more rapidly than population of working age—those 16 and over. Between 1972 and 1980, this working-age population will average 1.5%py growth, while the labor force climbs at 1.7%py. During the last five years of our period, however, 1980-85, the growth of the working-age population will drop to 1.0%py, though the labor force will probably climb slightly faster at 1.1%py. The excess stems from a slight increase in the age-specific participation rates for women and a shift in the distribution by age of the men over 16 so that a larger proportion of them fall in the prime working ages. Compared to the recent past, however, the next twelve years will show very slow change in the composition by sex of the labor force. Women's share shot up from 33.6 percent in 1964 to 37.4 percent in 1972; it will creep, says BLS, only to 38.5 percent by 1980 and inch up to 38.7 percent by 1985.

The radical and pervasive change which we must anticipate is not, as in the past, in the participation of women but in the abrupt, 35 percent drop in the growth of the total labor force—from 1.7 percent per year in 1972-80 to 1.1 percent per year in 1980-85. As we have already seen, this plunge ramifies through every aspect of our forecasts. The numerical values for the labor-force projections are shown on Page E6 of the End Tables.

Labor Productivity Projections

Labor productivity, as we use the term, is a very simple concept: output of an industry (in constant dollars) divided by its employment in constant-hour man years. Employment in constant-hour man years is nonproduction workers plus production workers adjusted for changes in the length of the workweek. Specifically, we use for our employment by industry i in year t (E_{it}),

$$E_{it} = \frac{H_i(t)}{H_i(1969)} P_i(t) + N_i(t)$$

where

H = average weekly hours of production workers

P = average number of production workers

N = average number of nonproduction workers

The ratio of the output Q_{it} to E_{it} is what we must project. Because it is convenient to have curves which are bounded below by zero rather than curves which grow upward without bound, we express productivity by the labor required per unit of output:

$$EOQ_{it} = E_{it}/Q_{it}$$

where

EOQ stands for "E over Q."

We have tried four approaches to forecasting EOQ:

1. An exponential time trend, i.e., a constant yearly percentage change in productivity.
2. A production function such as was used for capital investment in Chapter 3.
3. A variant of the exponential trend in which time moves forward only when investment is made. More precisely, the time variable is replaced by the average installation date (AID) of the capital stock.
4. A generalization of the exponential time trend so that the rate of change of EOQ depends upon the level of EOQ.

Each of these types was taken in conjunction with the changes in output since the previous year. This change picks up the cyclical changes in productivity. Productivity rises during booms and falls—or rises more slowly—during recessions. An alternative cyclical variable tried with the first and third approaches is the level of output. It can also pick up economies of scale in labor productivity.

The second of these formulations, the one with the production function, would be the natural, common-sense favorite. What could be plainer than that more capital per worker means more output per worker? We therefore devoted a considerable effort to making this approach work. We tried Cobb-Douglas functions, CES functions, "vintage" models and "disembodied" progress models.

The results were uniformly disappointing. Either the time trend equation of approach I out-performed the more elaborate specification or, if the time-trend equation was a special case of the more elaborate specification, the extra variables added little of significance. The basic problem lies, no doubt, in the measurement of capital. Many industries actually show decreasing capital-output ratios when the capital stock is computed as in Chapter 3. The "vintage" models mark up capital of later years to indicate that it is more effective than that of earlier years. But the mark up factor is then assumed to follow a time trend, so we are brought back to a time trend to explain productivity change. The business cycle presents an additional problem. When output declines, employment also goes down but by a smaller proportion. Capital, however, does not go down. Capital per employee therefore goes up while output per employee goes down. That movement is just the opposite of what the production function requires. Attempts to save the scheme by saying that the capital in use declines in proportion to output seem rather hypothetical and do not work better than just the change in output and a time trend, as in approach 1.

The strong performance of the time trend suggested that, if we wanted to make labor productivity depend on investment, we had best make "time" depend on investment in some way. Could we devise a time-like variable that moves forward only when an industry invests? The average installation date (AID) of the capital stock—the present date minus the average age of the stock—is indeed such a variable. Moreover, it is easily computed from the two-bucket depreciation scheme described in Chapter 3. This AID proves a respectable rival for calendar time in these equations, as we shall see, though time is better in a slight majority of cases.

Despite the strong performance of the time trend, we could see evidence in our plots of EOQ that, in some industries, the rate of change of EOQ diminishes as EOQ gets smaller. That is, that productivity changes slows down as it advances. Let us see how we can build that effect into our equation. Approach 1 can be expressed by the equation:

$$\frac{\Delta EOQ_t}{EOQ_{t-1}} = a_1 ,$$

where $\Delta EOQ_t = EOQ_t - EOQ_{t-1}$. In other words, in approach 1 the percentage rate of productivity change is constant. We simply generalize this equation to:

$$\frac{\Delta EOQ_t}{EOQ_{t-1}} = a_1 + a_2 EOQ_{t-1} \quad \text{or} \quad \Delta ln EOQ_t = a_1 + a_2 EOQ_{t-1}$$

where we have used the fact that the change in the natural logarithm approximates the percentage change. Figure 9-2 shows four typical curves which can result from this equation. The top curve shows a situation in which a_1 is

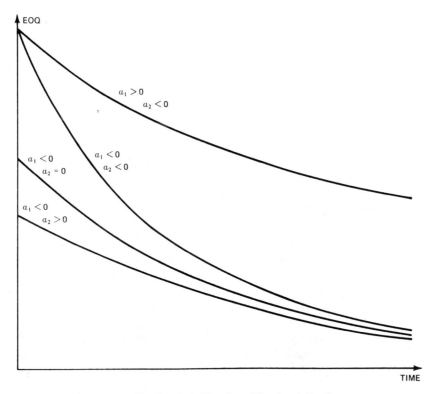

Figure 9-2. The Logistic Family of Productivity Curves

positive and a_2 negative. The curve approaches a floor above zero. The three lower lines all have a_1 negative. The middle one of the three is a pure exponential with $a_2 = 0$. The one above it has a_2 negative; its percentage rate of decline slows down and approaches that of the exponential. The lowest curve has a_2 positive; its percentage rate of decline accelerates and approaches that of the exponential.

The top curve in Figure 9-2 is a logistic curve. Because all these curves are special cases of the same general form, we shall refer to this whole family as logistic curves. By crossing the time and the *AID* approaches with the change in output (*DQ*) and level of output (*LQ*) variables, we have four types of equations, to which we add the logistic curve as a fifth:

TIME*DQ:	$\ln EOQ_t$	$= a_0 + a_1 t + a_3 \Delta \ln Q_t$
TIME*LQ:	$\ln EOQ_t$	$= a_0 + a_1 t + a_3 \ln Q_t$
AID*DQ:	$\ln EOQ_t$	$= a_0 + a_1 AID + a_3 \Delta \ln Q_t$

AID*LQ: $\qquad$ $\ln EOQ_t = a_0 + a_1 AID + a_3 \ln Q_t$

LOGIS: $\qquad$ $\Delta \ln EOQ_t = a_1 + a_2 EOQ_{t-1} + a_3 \Delta \ln Q_t$

Table 9-1 shows the results of fitting these three forms to our data. The types of equation are listed across the top. Under each type of equation are two columns:

RF – for Regression Fit–the average percentage error[a] for the equation fit up through 1966.

SF – for Simulation Fit–the average percentage error[a] when the equation fit up through 1966 was used to forecast the next five years, 1967-71.

Declining weights of 6 percent per year were used in this fitting, as in the consumption equations of Chapter 2.

The two columns labeled "WINNER" show which equation gave the best regression fit and which gave the best simulation fit. To help us choose a form for forecasting, we had the computer–IT–take an average of the RF and SF errors for each type of equation and select the type with the smallest average. After close examination of the forecasts, we wished to choose a different equation in fifteen industries. The choices are shown in the two columns labeled "CHOICE." The left column, labeled "IT," shows the ones made by it, the computer, and right column, labeled "US," shows the ones made by us. The following table summarizes the results:

	WINNER		CHOICE	
	RF	SF	IT	US
TIME*DQ	15	12	15	19
TIME*LQ	33	21	24	26
AID*DQ	3	13	14	13
AID*LQ	27	14	8	11
LOGIS	11	29	28	20
Total	89	89	89	89

The logistic curve, with its retention, took only eleven of the regression fit contests, but performed much better in the simulation tests, where with 29 wins, it was the best of the five.[b] Despite the performance in simulation, we were

[a]Strictly speaking, the root mean square percentage error.

[b]TIME*DQ is just a special case of LOGIS. LOGIS must be fit to the first difference of ln EOQ; to calculate EOQ itself, we must choose a starting value, EOQ_1, calculate EOQ_2, and from it calculate EOQ_3, and so forth. If we choose the actual EOQ_1 as the starting point, the fit is often very bad, so we choose the initial EOQ to make the errors average out to zero. In effect, EOQ_1 becomes an additional parameter, corresponding to a_0 in TIME*DQ. But in TIME*DQ, a_0 is chosen simultaneously with a_1 and a_3. Because of that difference, TIME*DQ sometimes gives better fits than does LOGIS.

somewhat suspicious of the logistic, especially when applied to industries where productivity increases had been unusually low in 1969-71. For such industries, the logistic often showed little or no further productivity change out to 1985. In these cases, we discarded the logistic and turned to the second best equation. In this way, nearly half of the logistic equations selected by *IT* were thrown out. Had we kept logistic curves everywhere *IT* chose them, we would have had substantially lower projections of GNP.

In the choice of equations, we also considered the sign and magnitude of the coefficients on the variables in the first four types of equations. The coefficient on $\Delta 1nQ$ or $1nQ$, a_3, was constrained to be negative but not more negative than $-1/2$. That limit requires, in effect, that half of the increase in employment stemming from an increase in output must come in the same year with the output increase. (Without that requirement, the model may require wide gyrations of income to match a reasonable specification of total employment.) The sign of the coefficients on time and level of output both had to be negative for the equation to be chosen by either *IT* or *US*.

For the forecasts, to 1985, of course, we have estimated equations through 1971, the most recent year for which we have reliable output data. The fitting begins in 1952 unless the sector is marked with an * on the right of Table 9-1; the * means that it begins in 1958, the earliest year of available data. The average percentage errors for the chosen equations are shown in the column of Table 9-1 labeled "*CHCE/*RF**." Just to the left, the column labeled "*TIME*" shows, for comparison, the average percentage errors for the *TIME*DQ* equation, which serves as a sort of standard of comparison. This *TIME*DQ* equation extrapolates past trends in productivity out into the future. The final column of Table 9-1, labeled "*RATIO*−85," shows the ratio of productivity predicted by the chosen equation to what would have been predicted by the *TIME*DQ* extrapolation.[c] In fifteen industries, the use of the level of output, *AID*, or an accelerating logistic led to higher 1985 productivity than the extrapolation equation would have projected. But for most industries, the opposite was the case. For nearly a third the lag behind the extrapolation is 10 percent or more by 1985. The greatest lag behind the extrapolation shows up in Communication equipment, Mining, Batteries, X-ray and engine electric equipment, Ordnance, Communication, Electric utilities, Airlines, and Agricultural chemicals. These all have 30 to 40 percent lags by 1985. Just behind them, with lags between 25 and 30 percent come Automobiles, Radio and TV sets, Tires and tubes, Canned and frozen food, and Engineering and scientific instruments.

Possible causes for this retardation in productivity are discussed in the first chapter. The forecasted productivity curves can be seen in full in the output-investment-employment-productivity plots in the *Supplement*. The growth rates are summarized on pages E35-36 in the End Tables.

---

[c]In three industries, 24, 44, and 88, a *TIME*DQ* equation was chosen but the coefficient on time was altered to give what we felt to be a more reasonable forecast. For them, *RATIO*−85 shows the ratio of this judgment productivity to that from the equation before we tampered with it.

Table 9-1
Choice Selection of Employment Equations

SECH	INDUSTRY	TIME*DJ (1) *RF*	*SF*	TIME*LG (2) *RF*	*SF*	AID*DO (3) *RF*	*SF*	AID*LG (4) *RF*	*SF*	LOGIS*TME (5) *RF*	*SF*	WINNER&CHOICE *RF*	*SF*	*IT*	*US*	TIME CHCE *RF*	*RF*	RATIO-RS	SECH
1	AGRICULTURE	4.1	3.0	2.9	1.9	2.6	1.8	2.3	1.1	3.0	7.3	4	5	4	5	4.8	2.2	1.071	1
2	MINING	3.7	19.0	4.0	19.0	4.1	23.2	4.6	23.2	4.6	12.3	1	1	4	5	7.2	8.5	.624	2
3	PETROLEUM AND GAS	6.5	2.9	6.6	2.3	7.1	3.0	7.3	3.5	4.5	13.3	4	5	2	2	8.1	4.4	1.012	3
4	CONSTRUCTION(NEW AND O	4.6	10.7	2.8	2.3	4.7	11.3	3.6	3.6	3.9	3.0	5	2	5	2	7.8	3.6	1.062	4
5	ORDINANCE	6.2	6.5	6.4	7.1	6.4	4.8	6.8	6.0	12.3	1.8	1	5	3	5	8.2	12.3	.572	5
6	MEAT	5.0	8.2	3.0	3.6	3.7	4.8	6.8	6.0	2.6	2.7	4	2	2	5	5.3	4.0	.784	6
7	DAIRY	5.0	8.2	1.8	2.5	3.7	6.0	4.1	4.1	2.6	5.6	4	5	2	5	4.2	2.2	1.018	7
8	CANNED AND FROZEN FOOD	2.6	10.1	3.2	3.3	5.7	11.1	3.1	2.1	4.4	6.5	4	2	5	5	6.1	4.5	.740	8
9	GRAIN MILL PRODUCTS	2.6	4.5	1.0	5.9	3.0	5.1	1.0	6.0	1.5	1.5	5	2	5	5	3.7	1.6	.759	9
10	BAKERY	4.1	12.8	2.5	2.5	2.5	4.2	1.3	2.4	2.8	2.2	4	1	1	5	2.2	2.2	1.012	10
11	SUGAR	2.2	5.8	4.0	7.4	4.4	13.3	4.0	8.7	6.6	21.6	4	1	1	5	7.3	7.3	1.000	11
12	CANDY	2.5	8.3	2.3	1.8	3.0	6.8	3.5	8.0	2.4	4.5	1	5	2	4	3.4	5.7	.900	12
13	BEVERAGES	2.1	2.1	.8	4.7	2.4	4.2	2.3	2.1	3.4	10.2	2	2	2	2	5.2	2.2	.951	13
14	MISC. FOOD PRODUCTS	5.1	1.3	1.5	5.5	5.0	4.2	.8	.3	1.2	3.6	4	5	2	2	1.6	.8	.936	14
15	TOBACCO	1.4	2.4	.8	4.7	2.1	4.2	1.5	4.9	4.7	4.1	1	1	2	2	5.4	3.3	1.452	15
16	FABRICS AND YARNS	2.6	1.3	3.2	5.5	5.0	7.3	2.8	1.8	1.4	5.0	1	2	2	2	1.9	1.5	.926 *	16
17	FLOOR COVERINGS	2.2	7.8	3.2	5.8	6.0	8.3	3.6	6.3	3.3	8.0	2	2	2	2	2.7	2.7	1.000 **	17
18	MISC. TEXTILES	2.1	2.4	4.4	4.9	6.1	4.4	2.5	5.3	4.5	12.5	2	1	3	1	2.6	3.9	1.000 **	18
19	KNIT FABRIC AND APPARE	4.1	12.4	1.1	12.4	2.1	2.2	1.4	2.0	1.9	14.1	4	3	3	5	2.4	3.2	.872	19
20	APPAREL	2.1	2.4	1.1	4.9	6.1	4.4	1.4	2.0	4.5	14.1	5	1	5	5	3.5	3.4	1.000 **	20
21	HOUSEHOLD TEXTILES AND	1.5	9.1	6.6	7.3	3.9	9.3	5.8	3.0	1.1	13.6	5	2	1	2	3.7	2.5	.965	21
22	LOGGING AND LUMBER	3.0	6.6	2.5	.6	4.1	8.0	3.2	1.8	2.2	4.6	2	2	4	3	2.6	2.5	.771	22
23	PLYWOOD, MILLWORK, STR	2.4	2.4	1.9	2.4	3.7	3.5	1.7	1.7	4.8	5.8	5	1	2	1	8.8	8.8	.934	23
24	WOODEN CONTAINERS	7.2	8.8	4.7	30.6	7.1	9.3	5.8	30.1	7.1	37.5	2	2	2	3	8.8	6.4	1.000 **	24
25	HOUSEHOLD AND OFFICE F	3.5	1.3	3.3	7.3	3.9	4.2	3.8	2.0	2.2	5.8	2	2	2	2	8.8	6.4	.987	25
26	PAPER AND PRODUCTS, EX	3.6	4.0	2.5	2.4	3.7	3.3	2.6	1.8	4.2	4.8	2	2	2	2	1.4	1.4	1.000	26
27	PAPER CONTAINERS	2.0	1.9	1.9	1.9	1.9	2.5	1.7	1.7	2.0	.9	2	2	2	1	2.0	2.0	.922	27
28	NEWSPAPERS	1.6	6.9	.6	.9	1.5	4.5	.8	1.5	2.3	2.3	2	2	2	2	2.3	2.3	1.064	28
29	PRINTING AND PUBLISHIN	4.3	3.3	3.1	4.0	4.0	4.7	1.8	2.4	3.8	2.0	2	2	5	3	2.3	2.8	.966 *	29
30	INDUSTRIAL CHEMICALS	2.3	2.3	1.7	2.8	3.0	10.7	1.4	2.4	2.0	5.7	2	2	3	3	2.7	2.8	.686 *	30
31	AGRICULTURAL CHEMICALS	2.4	11.8	1.0	3.3	2.8	3.3	1.0	2.1	2.0	5.9	4	1	5	1	4.8	1.6	.905	31
32	GLUE, INK, AND FATTY A	4.4	3.6	4.9	3.6	4.8	3.3	5.1	3.3	5.7	8.5	4	4	1	1	5.9	6.6	.973	32
33	PLASTICS AND SYNTHETIC	1.4	6.2	1.4	7.0	1.7	8.9	1.3	6.1	2.8	6.6	4	4	1	1	5.9	2.9	1.000	33
34	DRUGS	1.8	1.1	2.1	2.6	2.6	1.9	2.3	1.6	1.9	5.7	4	1	1	1	1.9	1.9	1.000	34
35	CLEANING AND TOILET IT	1.0	4.1	.7	1.8	1.1	3.4	.8	.8	.9	1.3	2	4	5	5	1.9	1.2	.784	35
36	PAINTS AND ALLIED PROD	2.8	8.5	1.5	3.7	3.4	8.5	1.1	4.3	2.0	5.0	4	1	5	5	4.8	3.1	.867	36
37	PETROLEUM REFINING	2.8	8.2	3.7	7.3	4.4	21.3	5.0	15.6	5.8	2.4	4	4	4	5	4.9	4.4	.914	37
38	TIRE AND TUBES	8.5	6.3	5.9	10.6	9.1	8.6	5.9	11.9	7.8	9.3	1	5	5	5	7.5	7.5	.739	38
39	RUBBER PRODUCTS (EXC.	2.7	10.2	2.7	7.5	2.5	13.2	2.4	10.2	5.0	28.7	4	2	2	2	4.8	3.5	.949	39
40	PLASTIC PRODUCTS	4.0	12.9	4.1	6.3	3.6	13.3	4.1	4.6	4.6	7.2	4	2	1	1	5.9	5.9	1.000	40
41	LEATHER TANNING AND IN	1.4	3.9	3.2	4.4	3.6	6.1	3.6	7.5	4.6	9.8	2	1	1	3	4.2	4.2	.993	41
42	SHOES AND OTHER LEATHE	2.3	2.3	1.8	2.9	2.3	1.8	1.9	2.7	2.6	9.8	2	1	1	1	2.7	2.7	1.000	42
43	GLASS AND GLASS PRODUC	3.9	5.5	2.2	3.5	3.3	5.2	2.2	3.7	3.1	2.5	5	5	5	5	4.7	4.7	.993	43
44	STONE AND CLAY PRODUCT	1.0	3.4	.9	1.3	1.0	3.6	1.0	1.2	1.2	.9	2	2	5	2	1.4	1.2	1.000 **	44
45	IRON AND STEEL	.9	5.9	1.1	4.0	.8		1.2	3.5	1.6	2.1	3	5	5	4	2.0	1.7	.988 *	45

SECH	INDUSTRY	TIME*DU (1) *RF*	*SF*	TIME*LO (2) *RF*	*SF*	ATM*DO (3) *RF*	*SF*	ATM*LO (4) *RF*	*SF*	LOGIS*TME (5) *RF*	*SF*	WINNER&CHOICE *RF*	*SF*	*IT**IS*	TIME CHCF *RF*	*RF*	RATIO-85	SECH
47	NON-FERROUS METALS	1.7	6.3	2.0	3.2	2.3	6.0	2.2	2.3	1.4	1.7	5	5	4	2.8	2.5	.893	*	47
48	METAL CONTAINERS	2.7	1.9	2.3	2.7	2.3	1.1	2.9	2.9	4.7	6.7	5	3	4	3.0	3.2	.978	*	48
49	PLUMBING AND HEATING	1.9	3.4	1.8	1.6	2.2	3.6	2.0	1.1	2.1	3.9	2	5	4	2.6	2.1	1.084	*	49
50	STRUCTURAL METAL PRODU	4.7	4.6	4.5	3.1	4.8	5.4	4.5	2.9	9.0	7.4	2	4	2	5.4	5.4	.824	*	50
51	STAMPINGS	.8	5.0	4.5	5.7	5.2	4.0	.7	.6	1.0	5.7	2	1	2	2.2	2.2	1.000	*	51
52	HARDWARE,PLATING, WIRE	2.0	4.7	1.5	2.9	1.0	4.0	3.0	3.0	1.6	3.0	2	4	4	2.4	2.2	.901		52
53	ENGINE AND TURBINES	2.2	3.2	1.1	3.8	1.5	2.6	2.7	4.5	1.3	5.7	5	4	4	3.8	1.7	.872		53
54	FARM MACHINERY	4.2	4.4	2.2	5.7	2.0	4.1	1.1	3.1	2.0	2.0	5	4	3	4.4	1.1	.920		54
55	CONSTUCTION,MINING+MAT	2.8	4.8	2.1	3.1	2.9	4.7	2.1	3.1	2.0	4.2	5	5	4	5.1	2.7	.933		55
56	METALWORKING MACHINERY	4.2	1.4	2.6	2.3	4.1	2.0	2.6	2.8	3.0	7.1	2	1	3	5.1	5.0	1.005		56
57	SPECIAL INDUSTRIAL MAC	5.3	1.8	4.5	2.6	4.8	2.0	4.7	4.6	7.5	11.5	2	1	3	6.2	5.5	1.038		57
58	GENERAL INDUSTRIAL MAC	2.0	1.1	3.1	4.4	1.9	1.1	1.8	5.9	2.1	4.9	4	1	3	6.2	5.5	1.012		58
59	MISC. MACHINERY AND SH	5.7	3.0	3.0	15.3	5.2	7.5	3.1	3.1	3.8	15.0	2	3	3	4.6	5.8	.954		59
60	OFFICE AND COMPUTING M	4.1	6.4	2.0	2.1	4.1	7.5	3.0	3.2	3.3	9.0	2	5	5	2.0	2.1	.885		60
61	SERVICE INDUSTRY MACHI	2.3	2.3	1.8	2.7	3.1	2.5	3.0	3.0	1.6	3.5	2	5	2	2.0	2.1	.765		61
62	ELECTRIC MEASURING, TR	3.6	4.8	2.8	2.0	3.6	6.5	2.4	2.7	2.8	5.5	2	4	2	2.0	7.2	.945		62
63	ELECTRIC APPARATUS AND	1.5	1.6	2.0	2.8	1.6	2.5	2.3	2.7	2.3	4.9	2	2	1	1.7	7.2	.912		63
64	HOUSEHOLD APPLIANCES	2.0	4.7	4.3	2.5	2.5	4.1	2.3	4.0	1.0	10.3	4	1	4	5.1	3.5	.903		64
65	ELECTRIC LIGHTING AND	2.9	15.2	2.0	10.8	1.2	8.3	5.9	5.9	1.0	12.6	1	2	1	5.1	2.0	1.000		65
66	RADIO-TV-SET, AND PH	4.4	7.4	2.0	11.3	1.2	4.2	2.3	5.9	2.8	3.5	2	2	4	7.2	2.9	.735		66
67	COMMUNICATION COMPONEN	6.1	7.4	4.6	11.3	6.1	4.2	4.6	11.4	5.7	11.5	5	5	3	6.8	7.1	.597		67
68	ELECTRONIC COMPONENTS	6.8	10.5	7.3	7.8	5.7	10.1	4.7	4.9	8.4	14.2	5	5	5	7.2	5.8	.929		68
69	BATTERIES, X-RAYS AND	3.7	11.0	4.0	11.2	4.4	11.3	10.9	10.9	5.6	2.6	2	2	5	5.8	6.0	.640		69
70	MOTOR VEHICLES AND PAR	15.8	9.7	7.3	7.8	13.5	12.5	7.7	8.4	8.4	14.2	5	3	3	16.5	8.0	.724		70
71	AIRCRAFT AND PARTS	4.2	3.1	3.7	3.4	4.2	2.8	3.7	3.3	7.0	14.2	2	2	3	4.7	4.1	.800		71
72	SHIPS AND BOATS	9.8	12.7	6.4	14.0	9.3	16.4	7.8	17.7	10.5	19.2	2	2	4	12.6	9.0	.958		72
73	LOCOMOTIVES, RAILROADS	3.2	10.3	6.8	2.7	7.7	8.4	6.7	3.0	11.7	24.4	2	4	4	12.2	9.0	1.407		73
74	CYCLES, TRAILERS AND P	5.6	36.3	2.8	16.1	5.6	35.0	6.6	15.2	8.3	31.9	2	5	5	10.9	8.4	.853		74
75	ENGR. AND SCIENT. INST	5.2	3.7	2.8	4.0	5.2	3.6	2.8	3.9	5.7	9.8	2	3	3	5.8	5.8	.979	*	75
76	MECH. MEASURING DEVICE	3.4	5.6	2.5	8.3	3.4	5.6	2.8	8.3	2.4	4.8	2	5	3	5.1	4.2	1.000		76
77	SURGICAL AND MEDICAL I	2.7	9.7	2.5	3.1	3.4	4.2	4.1	4.1	2.1	10.8	5	1	1	2.7	3.2	.934		77
78	OPTICAL AND PHOTOGRAPH	3.9	9.7	2.5	3.9	2.7	2.7	3.5	5.0	2.8	10.9	5	1	4	7.9	4.3	1.000		78
79	MISC. MANUFACTURED PRO	6.4	1.1	4.1	3.8	5.2	4.1	5.0	7.2	2.8	9.9	2	5	2	2.5	2.0	1.000		79
80	RAILROADS	1.7	1.7	1.7	2.0	1.7	2.0	1.7	1.7	3.0	3.0	4	1	5	4.1	4.1	1.114		80
81	TRUCKING	2.7	5.8	2.4	7.6	2.6	5.8	2.4	7.4	3.0	4.3	4	3	5	2.5	2.0	.935		81
82	OTHER TRANSPORT	5.8	2.4	6.8	2.6	5.8	2.4	3.0	3.6	1.6	4.3	4	3	5	4.1	4.1	1.071		82
83	AIRLINES	5.8	1.4	5.4	6.8	5.4	2.7	8.7	8.7	3.0	3.6	3	5	5	8.2	10.0	.680		83
84	WHOLESALE AND RETAIL T	1.1	3.2	1.0	5.4	1.0	3.9	1.0	5.4	1.6	3.2	1	5	5	1.4	1.7	1.000		84
85	COMMUNICATION	2.1	9.7	2.1	9.2	2.5	10.5	2.5	10.5	2.5	5.4	1	5	5	4.8	4.7	.674		85
86	FINANCE, INSURANCE AND	.5	1.3	.4	2.6	1.8	1.6	.5	1.9	.9	1.2	2	5	1	.8	.8	1.000		86
87	ELECTRIC UTILITIES	1.3	6.0	.7	6.2	1.8	13.6	.9	6.3	1.1	3.9	2	5	1	3.0	2.5	.668		87
88	WAT. GAS, WATER AND SE	.9	7.3	.7	6.0	1.2	11.1	.8	7.4	.5	7.3	2	5	2	3.2	3.2	1.000		88
89	WHOLESALE TRADE	1.8	1.3	1.1	3.5	1.2	2.0	1.1	3.4	1.9	.9	4	3	5	1.8	1.8	1.000		89
90	RETAIL TRADE	1.1	3.9	1.0	6.2	4.4	4.4	6.2	6.2	1.6	4.4	3	1	1	2.2	2.2	1.000		90
	NUMBER OF WINS	15	12	33	21	3	13	27	14	11	29								
		15		24		14		8		28									

Over the entire period 1971-85, the fastest productivity growth comes in Railroads (6.2%py), Knit fabric (6.2%py), Agriculture (5.8%py), Electronic components (5.4%py), Industrial chemicals (5.0%py), Floor coverings (4.8%py), Optical and photographic equipment (4.7%py), Drugs (4.5%py), Petroleum and gas extraction (4.4%py), Office and computing equipment (4.4%py), Radio TV sets, and phonograph (4.2%py), and Railroad equipment (4.1%py). At the low end come Metal working machinery (−1.0%py), Glue, ink, and fatty acids (−.6%py), Batteries, X-ray, etc. (−0.1%py), Electric lighting and wiring equipment (0.1%py), Other transport (largely water transport and travel agents) (0.2%py), Stampings (0.2%py), Finance and services (0.4%py), Ordnance (0.4%py), and Iron and Steel (0.5%py). When we find two old cronies like Railroads and Steel at the opposite ends of the spectrum, we must remember that these productivities are *labor* productivity only in the crudest sense. They completely ignore capital's contribution. Moreover, they do not measure the present level of even that crude labor productivity, but only its rate of change. Productivity can grow so fast in Railroads because it has such a long way to go. In Finance and services, which includes a lot of economic forecasters, productivity can scarcely—or does scarcely—grow at all. Either we're so good we can't get better, or we're hopeless.

Appendix 9A: Labor Force Statistics and Labor Balance

Unfortunately, there is no single set of statistics on employment by industry in which the industry employment adds up to the total employment reported in the labor force statistics. Ideally, we would like to have for each industry all employees, all self-employed, and all unpaid family workers, for all these are counted as "employed" in the labor force. But we have to settle for less and to use different sources for different industries. The sources are three:

1. *Employment and Earnings and Monthly Report on the Labor Force* (U.S. Department of Labor). The labor force table shows total employment in *agriculture*. This total is exactly what we are looking for, because it fits perfectly with the labor force estimates.

2. National Income Accounts, Tables 6.3, 6.4, and 6.6 (July issues of the *Survey of Current Business*). This source permits us to include self-employed. It is therefore used where self-employment is important, namely, construction, transportation, communication, trade, and all of the service industries (agricultural services, forestry and fishery included in employment sector 1). It is also the most convenient source for government enterprises and the government industry. It does not provide sufficient industry detail in manufacturing and does not permit adjustments for the length of the work week in productivity calculations.

   By definition, Table 6.6, "Number of persons engaged in production by industry," is derived from Table 6.4, "Number of full-time equivalent employees by industry," by adding estimates of self-employment by industry. Therefore, we subtract the figures in Table 6.4 from those in Table 6.6 to estimate the number of self-employed by industry. To this estimate, we add the figures in Table 6.3, "Average number of full-time and part-time employees by industry." The reason for counting the part-time employees on the same basis as full-time employees is that they are so counted in the labor force statistics.

3. The same document used for source 1 also provides, in the Establishment Data section, the most detailed information by industry. It was therefore used for all of the manufacturing industries. A useful historical compilation is found in *Employment and Earning Statistics for the United States, 1909-1967* (U.S. Department of Labor: October, 1967). We put employment for SIC 138 under the petroleum extraction industry rather than under the construction industry as specified by the sectoring plan of the I-O table.)

Table 9A-1
Labor Balance: 1960, 1965-71 (in 1000's)

Source[a]	1960	1965	1966	1967	1968	1969	1970	1971
1 Agriculture	5,458	4,361	3,979	3,844	3,817	3,606	3,462	3,387
2 Agricultural Services, Forestry & Fisheries	305	325	325	330	334	345	351	357
2 Mining	737	670	667	650	646	659	665	654
2 Construction	3,596	3,990	4,079	4,012	4.114	4,323	4,227	4,305
3 Manufacturing	16,796	18,062	19,186	19,447	19,781	20,167	19,349	18,529
2 Transportation	3,045	2,713	2,797	2,834	2,878	2,907	2,880	2,833
2 Communication	844	885	933	972	983	1,055	1,128	1,130
2 Utilities	628	638	647	658	669	685	702	710
2 Trade	13,818	15,021	15,550	15,925	16,441	17,076	17,425	17,761
2 Finance and Insurance	2,977	3,348	3,436	3,537	3,689	3,875	3,999	4,099
2 Services	11,580	13,485	14,013	14,360	14,791	15,231	15,575	15,733
2 Government	11,276	13,211	14,451	15,234	15,976	16,106	16,139	16,119
Total Jobs in Model	71,060	76,709	80,063	81,812	84,119	86,035	85,902	85,617
2 Persons Employed	68,294	73,820	76,051	77,104	79,437	81,365	81,723	81,858
Reconciliation Adjustment	2,766	2,889	4,012	4,708	4,862	4,670	4,179	3,759
1 Unpaid Family Workers (outside agriculture)	529	591	500	506	485	517	502	521
2 Self-Employed in Manufacturing	375	349	340	323	325	315	331	327
Multiple Job Adjustment	3,670	3,829	4,852	5,537	5,672	5,502	5,012	4,607

[a]For explanation of source numbers, see text.

The total employment from these sources for the years 1960, 1965-71 are shown in the line "Total Jobs in Model" in Table 9A-1. Below this line appears the number of persons employed as reported in the labor force statistics (more correctly, this line shows total civilian employment plus military employment derived from source 2). Notice that the total jobs exceed the total employed. The reason naturally lies in the fact that many people hold more than one job. In the labor force, they are counted as one employed person, but in our jobs-by-industry statistics, they necessarily turn up once for each job. To convert our reconciliation adjustment into a true "multiple job adjustment," we add self-employed in manufacturing and unpaid family workers[d] in nonagricultural industries. The result appears in the bottom line of Table 9A-1.

[d]From source 1 (January issue), "Employed persons by class of worker, sex, and age."

10 Applications

There is a certain aesthetic pleasure in building a model such as this one, but the greatest excitement always comes when someone puts it to use to answer questions which matter to him. We have recently had that pleasure on a number of occasions. We do not know of all the applications. Some are very informal: a researcher who needs a forecast of the demand for newspaper presses pulls out our printed forecast and uses it. Others involve large amounts of supplemental data and much computation. Because we are apt to know about this second kind, we will describe some of them; but the first, informal type of application is certainly more frequent and may be the more important.

The formal applications include search for merger possibilities, portfolio selection, investment decisions, analysis of the sensitivity of profits to various government policies, and analysis of the environmental impacts of various rates of growth.

Search for a Merger Partner

Before it included interindustry forecasting as a technique for locating a merger partner, the corporate planning staff of North American Aviation (NAA) had proposed a number of possible merger candidates to management. But each proposal met the same fate. The management was consistently able to find some shortcoming as a basis for rejecting the candidate company. Back the staff would go to look for a better prospect. After a number of such encounters, they realized that they would remain on a treadmill until they devised a foolproof system for future merger recommendations.

The system that the staff eventually devised included the interindustry forecasting model and a computer system for sorting several thousand domestic manufacturing concerns. Virtually every company with published financial information was included in the data bank. The key company information which was accumulated on tape included sales, profits, market value of equity, and product diversity. It was a relatively easy task, once the data was in the computer, to sort through a large number of companies and select only those that met the criteria for size, profitability, and certain tests for merger feasibility. For example, the computer could eliminate companies with high price/earnings ratios which would cause unacceptable earnings dilution or companies which were too expensive in terms of total market value.

In a matter of a few weeks, the staff was able to reduce the total prospect list to about 100 companies. Working with this relatively small list, they then made a product breakdown of the sales of each company and connected the growth of each product line to the growth of one or more cells of the input-output table. The model used for forecasting the table was an ancestor of the one described in this book. With these connections it was then easy to compare the growth prospects of the various companies with one another against *a common economic background* and to test their sensibility to the swings in defense and space spending to which NAA was itself sensitive. The companies were then ranked by growth rate, and after a careful consideration of numerous factors, a list of twenty was drawn up and presented to management. An effort was made to show the extent to which each candidate company might benefit from North American's technological resources.

This system provided management with a logical means for determining the priority of each candidate and for deciding which candidates to recommend to the board of directors for merger talks. The system worked, and a diversification strategy and a list of five candidate companies was presented to the board at its next meeting. The board, which had reacted somewhat unenthusiastically to all previous diversification schemes, responded favorably to management's proposal to start contacting candidates. A program of company contacts commenced immediately.

Within a few months, discussions were started with all of the top priority candidates. Various factors, however, prevented an eventual merger with any of these top few prospects. In one case, North American was outbid and the prospect merged with another. In other cases the prospective brides could not be wooed. Along the way, the president of NAA described his search for a merger partner in a speech to the business community. His remarks were later incorporated in a news story on the company which was read by Willard F. Rockwell, Jr., the president of Rockwell-Standard. Mr. Rockwell contacted the North American's president, who called the director of corporate planning, who recommended that the overture by Rockwell be pursued. It seems that Rockwell-Standard had been high on the priority list of twenty candidate companies, but for financial reasons had not been among the top five. It was not much of a trick for the planning staff to lay out the facts on Rockwell-Standard, including a forecast of the company's probable long-term sales growth based on interindustry projections.

In due course, a merger between the two companies occurred. The newly created company became North American Rockwell, later to be transformed into Rockwell International. It is a little known fact that two companies later acquired by Rockwell, Miehle-Goss-Dexter and Rockwell Manufacturing, were high-priority candidates on the original North American list. This continuity in diversification planning suggests that the relatively complex original project was worth the effort.

Profit in an Uncertain Environment

The Good Try Corporation, under a different name long a sponsor of this forecasting model, has independently developed a rather elaborate model of profit potential on each of a large number of products which it makes. One of the crucial variables, or course, is the level of sales of the product. Good Try, of course, wants not just one, fixed projection of sales, but rather it wants to know how its profits will be affected by possible variations in those sales. What would happen to profits if:

Defense expenditures were drastically cut or sharply stepped up?

NASA purchases soared or collapsed?

Import quotas were established along the lines of bills presently in Congress? Or if the dollar were devalued? (That was before it was.)

Labor productivity and GNP grew more rapidly or less rapidly than Good Try expects?

Investment in Agriculture, Communication, Electric utilities or other sectors grew faster or slower than expected?

Spending on schooling does *not* slow down as the number of students drops?

To relate these broad developments to the manifold widgets which GT makes requires just such a model as we have constructed. We can fairly easily run this model under all the above assumptions and translate them into their implications for each of the 185 products in the model. The next step then is to translate from the model's products to the widgets. One could of course simply assume that GT's sales of product g moved in proportion to the sales of our product class i of which g is a part. But the GT people go two steps beyond that assumption. In the first place, they know the distribution of the sales of g by customer industry. That is, they know g_j, the sales of g to our industry j. As a first step, therefore, they can set

$$g_j = \bar{g}_j(x_{ij}/\bar{x}_{ij}),$$

where x_{ij} is the use of our product i in making our product j, a letter with a bar stands for a value in a standard forecast, and a letter without a bar, for a value in a variant. GT, however, is a major factor in many markets and has found that, where one market for a product grows while others lag behind, GT's smallfry competition get in and take more than their share of the growth. If on the other hand, all markets for a product are growing well, GT's broad advertising and wide product lines help it to pick up sales in the slowest growing part of the market. GT finds therefore that the preceding equation is better replaced by

$$g_j = \bar{g}_j \left(\frac{x_{ij}}{x_{ij}} \right)^{1/2} \left(\frac{X_i}{\bar{X}_i} \right)^{1/2} \quad ,$$

where X_i is the total output of product i. If the industry's output grows by 10 percent and sales to market j also grow by 10 percent, then the sales of GT's product g to that market grow by 10 percent. But if the particular market (X_{ij}) increases 10 percent with no increase in the total sales of product i, GT will get only a 4.9 percent increase in that market. Conversely, if the industry grows by 10 percent without, however, an increase in market j, GT nonetheless can expect to pick up market shares and show a 4.9 percent increase in that market.

The sales-by-market that come from this analysis are then summed and put into the profit model. What the profit model then says about GT's profits, GT pretty much keeps to itself. We do know that import quotas with concomitant reductions in exports to keep international trade in balance turned out to be bad news indeed for GT. Like many other progressive companies, it has a greater stake in good export potential than in having its home markets artificially shielded.

The Paper Skirt

The five-fold division of the paper industry in our 185 industries once seemed adequately detailed to us; and to our academic colleagues, no doubt, it seemed altogether needless and burdensome hairsplitting. But when Champion Paper joined our group of sponsors, we were soon informed that such gross, broad, nondescript paper sectors as we had were of little interest to a paper maker. Most of Champion's interest lay in one part of one of our sectors, namely in writing and printing papers (excluding newsprint), part of sector 48, Paper and paperboard mills. Moreover, separating out printing and writing paper would not help the Champion people much; they needed to distinguish some forty types of paper and to produce separate forecasts for such items as "Printing paper, Coated 2 sides, No. 1," "No. 2," and so on. Clearly there was no possibility of expanding the model to this sort of detail in the paper industry. Not only would the cost of operating the model increase rapidly, but other industries would demand equal treatment, and we would soon find ourselves with a totally unmanageable beast.

What then could the model offer the Champion people?—detailed projections of the industries which buy paper. That, it seems, is often the case; the model seems hopelessly aggregated in a firm's own product area but wonderfully detailed for its customer industries.

Now it so happens that the paper industry has fairly good data on the tons of paper of each of some forty grades of printing and writing paper sold to various markets, which translate into eight of our sectors, including the office supply dummy[a] sector. One can think of this data arrayed in additional rows across the bottom of the input-output table as shown in Figure 1-1 (Chapter 1). If it reaches all the way across the table, it looks like sort of a "skirt" tacked to the table. A skirt such as this differs from a disaggregation in that it does not require columns for the separate products and, consequently, does not automatically feed back into the model.

We set out, therefore to use the paper data to make a "paper skirt" forty rows deep and to sew it to the model. Now a grade of paper sold to a sector of our model defines what we shall call a "market," and the quotient of the tons of paper sold in that market divided by the output of the sector (in constant dollars) is what we shall call the "market quotient." Our approach has been to calculate each market quotient for each year 1959-71, fit a logistic curve to the series, extrapolate the quotient according to the logistic curve, and finally to multiply the projected quotient for a future year by the future year's output of the paper-using industry. Figures 10-1 and 10-2 show this process for one market, coated 2 sides, no. 4 printing paper sold to Book printing. Figure 10-1 shows the market quotient; from 1961 to 1966 it rose rapidly, then sagged, and in 1970 and 1971 regained the peak. The logistic curve, fit by least-squares and untouched by human hands, views the 1966 high as premature, the 1970 and 1971 return as timely, but sees no great future growth. It approaches a ceiling about 13 percent above the 1971 value, and, by 1980, will have essentially reached that ceiling. To get total sales in tons to this market in some future year, we simply multiply the market quotient for that year, projected by the logistic curve, by the output of book printing for the same year. Figure 10-2 shows such a projection. As the market quotient flattens out towards 1980, the market relies for its growth more and more heavily on the growth in the purchasing industry, book printing. The percentage growth rate slows down steadily, and, after 1975, the absolute tonnage increment gets smaller each year.

A total of 126 paper markets were analyzed in this way. (Not all grades of paper are sold to all eight buyers.) The fit shown in Figure 10-1 is typical. Some big markets have closer fits; some very small ones, much worse fits. About two-thirds of the quotients are falling, one-third rising. People in the industry often understand why a quotient is going up or down and can compare their own hunches about the future with the logistic curve's prognostication. And if they don't know why a market quotient has moved as it has, they want to find out why.

Table 10-1 shows several ways of bringing the forecasts together. The first

---

[a]Instead of having a dozen tiny entries in each column for stationery, pens, ink, paper clips, typewriter ribbons, mimeograph masters, and so on, these items are all considered to be "sold" to a hypothetical, "dummy" industry which then sells a single product called "office supplies" to all industries. There is no employment and no value-added in the dummy sector. Business travel expenses are handled in the same way.

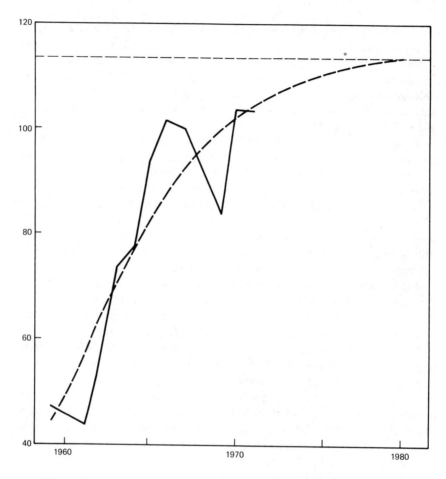

Figure 10-1. Market Quotient: Coated 2 Sides No. 4 to Book Printing

panel is an excerpt from a five-page "product manager's" table showing sales of a grade by user. The totals and subtotals by market (e.g., Total printing papers to Magazine publishing) may either be taken as the sum of its individual parts, as here, or it may be derived independently from its own market quotient and logistic curve. Comparison of the two serves as a check on the reasonableness of the forecasts. The second panel of Table 10-1, an excerpt from a four-page "market manager's" table, brings together sales of different grades to a single

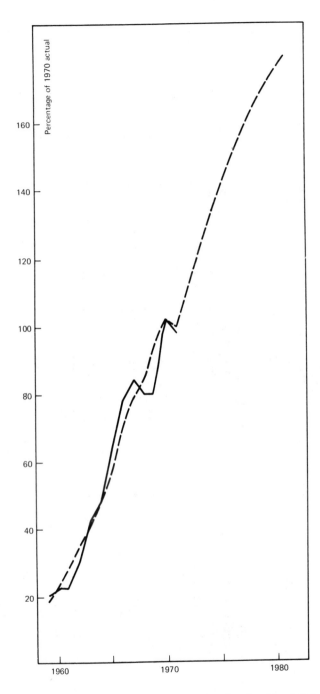

Figure 10-2. Total Sales: Coated 2 Sides No. 4 to Book Printing

Table 10-1
Five Ways to Look at the Paper Skirt

		1962	1967	1969	1971	1972	1973	1974	1975	1976	1977	1982
							Grade by User					
10000	Total Printing Papers	4938.1	6659.9	7372.8	7422.5	8131.9	8553.6	9026.5	9559.8	10098.3	10576.7	12774.8
10001	Magazine Publishing	1593.2	1893.4	1937.8	1777.8	1976.2	2033.9	2114.6	2211.8	2310.7	2390.9	2711.5
10002	Oth. Periodical Publish.	500.6	718.5	766.3	814.1	873.5	919.1	976.5	1042.8	1112.1	1174.2	1467.3
10003	Book Publishing	415.0	652.8	784.7	762.6	868.0	938.7	1011.1	1090.9	1164.6	1226.8	1478.0
10004	Commercial Printing	1323.4	2051.2	2461.0	2543.1	2804.6	2972.2	3153.7	3349.8	3547.5	3732.4	4626.2
10005	Labels and Wraps	214.5	264.5	256.6	279.2	276.5	282.5	289.5	297.3	305.3	311.7	339.7
10006	Converting	891.4	1079.5	1166.4	1245.7	1333.1	1407.2	1481.1	1567.2	1658.1	1740.7	2152.1
11000	Total Uncoated Groundwood	942.0	1305.6	1405.1	1371.1	1539.7	1618.2	1710.7	1816.5	1923.9	2019.4	2460.5
11001	Magazine Publishing	253.4	207.6	198.1	150.8	168.9	166.6	166.4	167.5	168.6	168.5	164.0
11002	Oth. Periodical Publish.	358.9	562.7	642.1	691.0	742.0	785.1	838.5	900.0	964.2	1022.5	1302.1
11003	Book Publishing	74.4	139.7	160.2	127.5	175.7	190.6	206.1	223.3	239.3	253.2	311.6
11004	Commercial Printing	79.1	218.0	233.2	268.7	298.9	319.7	341.6	364.7	387.6	408.9	508.2
11005	Labels and Wraps	2.8	1.3	1.4	1.4	1.2	1.2	1.2	1.2	1.2	1.2	1.1
11006	Converting	173.4	176.3	170.1	131.7	153.0	155.0	156.9	159.8	163.0	165.1	173.5
12000	Total Uncoated Book	1751.9	2316.1	2691.1	2873.0	3073.2	3263.3	3461.9	3683.6	3907.4	4111.8	5088.4
12001	Magazine Publishing	37.4	20.5	23.7	17.7	22.8	24.3	25.9	28.0	30.1	32.0	40.7
12002	Oth. Periodical Publish.	16.4	12.0	8.4	3.0	7.8	8.3	8.8	9.4	10.0	10.6	13.2
12003	Book Publishing	281.9	373.8	470.0	462.9	503.0	541.1	579.8	622.6	661.6	694.0	820.3
12004	Commercial Printing	737.8	1044.9	1225.0	1291.4	1394.3	1473.6	1560.5	1655.2	1751.3	1841.6	2283.9
12005	Labels and Wraps	20.2	24.3	21.5	22.9	19.5	20.0	20.6	21.1	21.8	22.3	25.0
12006	Converting	658.2	840.6	942.5	1075.1	1125.8	1196.0	1266.3	1347.3	1432.6	1511.3	1905.3

Grade by User (Cont.)

Code	User	1982	1977	1976	1975	1974	1973	1972	1971	1969	1967	1962
12110	Offset	2938.4	2367.1	2244.2	2110.1	1974.5	1849.8	1733.1	1600.6	1483.3	1209.1	776.1
12111	Magazine Publishing	34.8	26.0	24.1	22.0	20.0	18.3	16.7	12.5	11.2	7.6	5.6
12112	Oth. Periodical Publish.	11.2	9.0	8.5	8.0	7.5	7.0	6.7	2.3	5.7	7.7	3.3
12113	Book Publishing	705.5	575.4	543.1	505.3	464.5	427.1	390.4	364.8	329.0	232.0	126.0
12114	Commercial Printing	2137.3	1718.1	1632.2	1540.8	1450.6	1367.5	1291.3	1192.1	1117.3	942.9	627.4
12115	Labels and Wraps	7.7	6.0	5.6	5.2	4.9	4.5	4.1	.9	4.3	3.3	.9
12116	Converting	41.9	32.6	30.7	28.8	27.0	25.4	23.9	28.0	15.8	15.6	12.9

User by Grade

Code	Grade	1982	1977	1976	1975	1974	1973	1972	1971	1969	1967	1962
1	Magazine Publishing	2711.5	2390.9	2310.7	2211.8	2114.6	2033.9	1976.2	1777.8	1937.8	1893.4	1593.2
11	Total Printing and Fine Paper	2711.5	2390.9	2310.7	2211.8	2114.6	2033.9	1976.2	1777.8	1937.8	1893.4	1593.2
10001	Total Printing Papers	2711.5	2390.9	2310.7	2211.8	2114.6	2033.9	1976.2	1777.8	1937.8	1893.4	1593.2
11001	Total Uncoated Groundwood	164.0	168.5	168.6	167.5	166.4	166.6	168.9	150.8	198.1	207.6	253.4
12001	Total Uncoated Book	40.7	32.0	30.1	28.0	25.9	24.3	22.8	17.7	23.7	20.5	37.4
12101	MF, EF, Etc., Supercal	4.9	5.2	5.2	5.2	5.3	5.4	5.5	4.8	12.0	12.0	31.3
12111	Offset	34.8	26.0	24.1	22.0	20.0	18.3	16.7	12.5	11.2	7.6	5.6
12121	Envelope	.7	.5	.5	.5	.4	.4	.4	.2	.1	.6	.1
12131	Tablet	.2	.2	.2	.2	.1	.1	.1	.1	.2	.2	.1
12141	Other Uncoated Book	.1	.1	.1	.1	.1	.1	.1	.1	.2	.1	.3
13001	Total Coated	2506.8	2190.4	2112.0	2016.3	1922.3	1843.0	1784.5	1609.3	1716.0	1665.3	1302.4
13101	Total Coated 1 Side	6.6	4.7	4.3	3.8	3.4	3.1	2.8	.4	3.0	1.3	.6
13201	Total Coated 2 Sides	2500.2	2185.7	2107.7	2012.5	1918.9	1839.9	1781.7	1608.9	1713.0	1664.0	1301.8
13211	Coated 2 Sides No. 1	1.1	1.0	1.0	1.0	.9	.9	.9	.5	1.0	2.1	.7
13221	Coated 2 Sides No. 2	6.9	6.1	6.0	5.7	5.5	5.3	5.2	4.5	5.9	5.3	5.3
13231	Coated 2 Sides No. 3	31.4	32.5	32.6	32.5	32.3	32.5	33.0	19.1	63.8	61.0	47.3
13241	Coated 2 Sides No. 4	321.8	220.3	199.5	177.9	157.6	139.6	124.2	131.5	67.1	50.9	36.3

Percentage Composition of Grade by User

		1962	1967	1969	1971	1972	1973	1974	1975	1976	1977	1982
13221	Magazine Publishing	.039	.037	.041	.040	.041	.042	.043	.044	.045	.045	.049
13222	Oth. Periodical Publish.	.074	.057	.072	.005	.016	.015	.015	.015	.014	.014	.012
13223	Book Publishing	.045	.048	.038	.049	.051	.053	.054	.056	.057	.059	.062
13224	Commercial Printing	.791	.795	.818	.897	.880	.878	.876	.875	.872	.871	.866
13225	Labels and Wraps	.007	.001	.005	.004	.002	.002	.002	.002	.002	.001	.001
13226	Converting	.043	.062	.026	.004	.010	.010	.010	.010	.010	.010	.009
13220	Coated 2 Sides No. 2	1.000	1.000	1.000	1.000	1.000	1.000	1.000	1.000	1.000	1.000	1.000

		1962	1967	1969	1971	1972	1973	1974	1975	1976	1977	1982
13231	Magazine Publishing	.280	.229	.205	.080	.110	.102	.095	.090	.085	.080	.063
13232	Oth. Periodical Publish.	.090	.045	.046	.003	.009	.008	.007	.007	.006	.006	.005
13233	Book Publishing	.061	.137	.092	.093	.156	.164	.171	.178	.184	.188	.199
13234	Commercial Printing	.546	.583	.656	.819	.720	.721	.721	.720	.720	.721	.728
13235	Labels and Wraps	.001	.002	.001	.002	.003	.003	.003	.003	.003	.003	.004
13236	Converting	.021	.005	.001	.003	.002	.002	.002	.002	.002	.002	.001
13230	Coated 2 Sides No. 3	1.000	1.000	1.000	1.000	1.000	1.000	1.000	1.000	1.000	1.000	1.000

Percentage Composition of User by Grade

		1962	1967	1969	1971	1972	1973	1974	1975	1976	1977	1982
11004	Total Uncoated Groundwood	.046	.085	.078	.087	.089	.090	.091	.092	.093	.093	.095
12004	Total Uncoated Book	.426	.408	4.07	.417	.413	.414	.415	.417	.418	.420	.426
13104	Total Coated 1 Side	.025	.026	.031	.027	.028	.029	.030	.030	.031	.032	.035
13204	Total Coated 2 Sides	.267	.283	.302	.291	.301	.302	.304	.305	.305	.306	.307
21004	Total Chemical Wood Writing	.065	.052	.051	.051	.047	.046	.045	.044	.044	.043	.041
22004	Total Cotton Fiber Writing	.006	.005	.004	.004	.004	.004	.004	.004	.004	.004	.003
23104	Total Cover	.023	.016	.015	.014	.013	.013	.012	.012	.011	.011	.010
23204	Total Text	.056	.051	.045	.039	.042	.041	.041	.040	.040	.039	.037
24004	Total Thin Papers	.004	.002	.002	.003	.002	.002	.002	.002	.002	.002	.002
25004	Total Bleached Bristols	.083	.072	.065	.066	.061	.059	.056	.054	.053	.051	.045
4	Commercial Printing	1.000	1.000	1.000	1.000	1.000	1.000	1.000	1.000	1.000	1.000	1.000

Percentage Composition of Generic Grade by Detailed Grade

		1962	1967	1969	1971	1972	1973	1974	1975	1976	1977	1982
21100	Bond and Writing	.326	.313	.307	.306	.295	.291	.287	.284	.281	.278	.266
21110	Form Bond	.246	.305	.337	.367	.374	.384	.394	.403	.411	.419	.451
21120	Ledger	.033	.024	.022	.021	.020	.019	.018	.017	.017	.016	.014
21130	Mimeograph	.081	.063	.049	.045	.045	.042	.041	.039	.037	.036	.030
21140	Duplicating	.080	.072	.078	.074	.073	.072	.072	.071	.070	.070	.068
21150	Papeterie	.035	.026	.026	.022	.021	.020	.019	.019	.018	.018	.015
21160	Comm., Copy and Oth. Tech.	.096	.103	.101	.094	.100	.100	.099	.098	.098	.098	.095
21170	Manifold	.016	.009	.005	.005	.004	.004	.004	.004	.003	.003	.002
21180	Opaque Circular	.019	.013	.011	.011	.009	.008	.008	.007	.007	.007	.005
21190	All Other	.068	.072	.064	.055	.060	.060	.059	.058	.057	.057	.054
21000	Total Chemical Wood Writing	1.000	1.000	1.000	1.000	1.000	1.000	1.000	1.000	1.000	1.000	1.000

user. Each of these two tables may then be converted into percentages, as shown in the next two panels. From the first of these, it readily appears that Magazine publishing, once a major market for Coated 2 sides, no. 3, is dwindling in relative importance, while Book publishing and Commercial printing both expand. From the second percentage panel the market manager for Commercial printing can see substantial stability in his product mix. The final percentage panel gives a production manager's view about the detailed product composition of the generic product, Chemical wood writing papers. The spectacular rise in Form bond within that generic product is simply explained: that's what computer paper is.

The forecasts can readily be made under a variety of assumptions, such as the Good Try Corporation used. The figures shown here, in fact, are based on a run of the model which is by no means our best-judgment forecast. These figures, therefore, definitely do *not* represent the thinking of Champion Paper management.

Other Skirts and Skirt-making

Once one has the program for making skirts, it is fairly simple to make them out of different materials. Besides our paper skirt, we have made a steel skirt with eleven types of steel and an oil skirt with sixteen petroleum products.[b] A plastics skirt and partial aluminum and copper skirts, have been basted together. Advertising and railroads are on the skirt-maker's agenda. Not to be left out of the environmental movement we have helped Resources for the Future make a pollution skirt with particulates, hydrocarbons, sulfur oxides, carbon monoxide, and nitrogen oxides as air pollutant lines and chemical oxygen demand, biological oxygen demand, refractory organics, suspended solids, dissolved solids, nitrogen and phosphate compounds as water pollutant lines.[c]

The paper skirt is the most perfect in that every market has its own logistic curve. In the other skirts, there are products for which we know the sales by market in only one year although we know the total output in every year. In the oil skirt, for example, residual fuel oil use by each industry in 1967 is known to us from the Census of Manufactures for that year, but for other years we have only an estimate of total residual fuel oil used by industry, excluding utilities and transportation. We proceed much as we did with the across-the-row coefficient changes described in Chapter 8. From the one year's distribution we make up an index of what use would have been had all market quotients remained constant. The ratio of actual use to this index is then treated like a

[b]C. Almon, "Use of the Maryland Interindustry Forecasting Model to Project Petroleum Demand" in M. Searl, ed., *Energy Modeling*, Resources for the Future (Washington, 1973).

[c]See *Population, Resources and the Environment*, U.S. Commission on Population Growth and the American Future (GPO, 1972).

market quotient itself: a logistic curve is fitted to it and extrapolated. The fit is shown in Figure 10-3. The model's forecasts then drive the constant quotient index, which, multiplied by the logistic curve's extrapolations, gives the total industrial use of residual fuel oil in future years. This technique, which is an automatic option in our skirt-maker program, considerably expands its applicability. It was used, for example, for certain types of plastics used in "packaging." Since we did not know the distribution of this packaging by user industry at all, we used the distribution of fiberboard boxes, which we did know.

We wish to apply much the same technique to forecasting company sales and perhaps earnings, as an aid in the management of portfolios of stocks. We intend to identify as best we can the product composition of the sales of a company such as, say, Union Carbide. It is our experience that data on the division of sales by product is hard for the outsider to find and may not be comparable from one year to the next. As a first cut, therefore, we try to guess at it for one year, and then ask what would have been the sales of the company had it maintained a constant share of the sales of each of its product lines. The ratio of actual sales to these would-have-been sales is then treated just like a market quotient and fit by a logistic curve. To forecast future sales the logistic curve is extrapolated and multiplied by what sales would be in the future years if the company held onto its base-year market shares. Such an analysis can show how a company has fared relative to the markets it serves, how its future sales may grow, and how it would be affected by the alternative assumptions Good Try has used. It will also be possible to put these forecasts through a portfolio selection program such as that described in the next section.

How to Stay Out of Trouble in a Risky Business

Several years ago, we constructed a machine-tool skirt showing the sales of ten types of tools[d] to investment by thirty-five of our ninety equipment investment sectors. We did not have the sales distribution for even one year, but from the *American Machinist Inventory of Metal Working Equipment* we knew the stocks of a number of different types of tools bought in the ten years 1959-68. We assigned values to each type of tool and summed to get something like a distribution of a decade's sales. This distribution we then used to make up a constant-market-quotient index (CMQI) much as we did with fuel oil. The ratio of actual machine tool domestic demand (DD) to this CMQI could be treated essentially as a market quotient and a logistic curve fitted to it. Inspection of the plot of this ratio for any of the ten tool types, however, shows it to have highly

[d]The ten-way division of the industry was: Lathes, Boring machines, Drilling machines, Milling machines, Grinding and polishing machines, Gear cutting machines, Other cutting machines, Presses, Punch and shear, and Other forming.

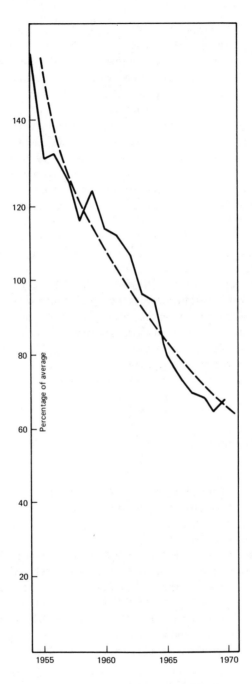

Figure 10-3. Composite Market Quotient for Industrial Use of Residual Fuel Oil

cyclical. Machine tool's share of a dollar of investment rises during booms and sinks during recessions. The solid line in Figure 10-4 illustrates this cyclical variation in the case of drilling machines. Machine tool sales swing up and down so violently because not only do they depend on the volatile investment of other companies, but even their share in that investment swings up in booms and down in recessions. Clearly, a simple logistic curve such as has been used for the market quotients in other skirts is inappropriate here. To get in the cyclical variation, we expressed the logistic curve in a form similar to that used in the employment chapter:

$$\Delta ln \left(\frac{DD}{CMQI}\right)_t = a_0 + a_1 \left(\frac{DD}{CMQI}\right)_{t-1} + a_2 \Delta CMQI_t + a_3 \Delta CMQI_{t-1}$$

$$+ a_4 \Delta CMQI_{t+1}$$

The resulting cyclical logistic curve is illustrated by the dotted line in Figure 10-4. The forecast of the DD/CMQI ratio now depends upon the forecast of the model. But given this forecast, first the ratio and then the tool demand (DD) can be quickly calculated. Moreover, we may make bold to presume that sales-by-buyer in a future year will be proportional to the buyers' contributions to the $CMQI$ for that year. In this way, we obtain sales forecasts of tools by type by buyer, a total of 340 numbers for each year.

One of the sponsors of our work, not presently in the machine tool business, found it in some ways an attractive area for diversification. But the sponsor's planners were concerned about the extreme cyclical swings in the machine tool business. They could see the risks of real trouble on that roller coaster. Is there any way, they wanted to know, to pick out certain tool types selling to certain markets in such a way as to get a minimum variance for the whole mix? To be more precise, they wanted to pick out a mix of products and markets with sales totaling at least $50 million in 1969 with minimum variance for its growth rate. Realistically, they also admitted, it would probably not be possible to get more than a quarter of the sales in any one market.

This problem seemed to us ideal for application of quadratic programming. We put the buyers into ten groups and calculated the variances and covariances, over the years 1955 to 1980, of each of the 100 markets so defined with each other. (The variances and covariances were those of the deviations around a time trend fitted to each market.) We would then specify a growth rate and find the minimum-variance entry which would achieve that growth rate. In this way we could trace out a "menu" of strategies.

The first results were not surprising. They said, "Get into Other cutting," the catchall category for new, fast-growing multipurpose machinery and machining centers, or transfer machines. That, however, is not a market one can enter

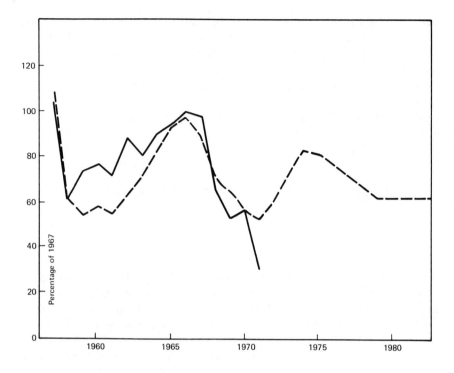

Figure 10-4. Composite Market Quotient for Boring Machines

without a firm base in conventional machines, so for our analysis (but not for the sponsor's planning) we struck it from the list. The absolute minimum-variance strategy then found is shown in the top panel of Table 10-2. It had a standard deviation of only $6.4 million in its sales, but its growth rate was only 2.4%py. At the opposite end, the maximum growth entry, shown by the bottom panel of Figure 10-2, gets the growth rate up 4.7%py but with a standard deviation of $11.3 million. Generally, there is a shift from a heavy emphasis on forming tools at the slow-and-safe end toward lathes and boring machines at the fast-and-risky end.

Table 10-2
Optimal Product Mixes for a $50-Million Entry into Conventional Machine Tools

Minimum Variance Entry

Sales (Millions of Dollars)	Of
8.05	Presses to electronic and lighting equipment
4.15	Presses to electrical apparatus and appliances
3.76	Punch and shear to metal products
3.05	Punch and shear to instruments, ships, trains, misc. mfg.
1.98	Punch and shear to electronic and lighting equipment
3.46	Other forming to electronic and lighting equipment
1.88	Other forming to instruments, ships, trains, misc. mfg.
5.76	Lathes to electronic and lighting equipment
2.42	Lathes to engines and turbines
5.18	Grinding and polishing to electronic and lighting equipment
2.00	Grinding and polishing to engines and turbines
4.73	Gear cutting machinery to automobiles
3.58	Gear cutting machinery to industrial, office, & service mach.
50.00	

Maximum Growth Entry

12.69	Lathes to Metal products
5.76	Lathes to Electronic and lighting equipment
4.46	Lathes for Farm, construction, mining machinery
4.05	Lathes to Motor Vehicles
1.55	Lathes to Engines and turbines
7.72	Boring machines to Instruments, ships, trains, misc. mfg.
4.73	Gear cutting machinery to Motor vehicles
4.87	Presses to Motor vehicles
50.00	

This quadratic programming study did just what was desired of it. It selected the relevant markets from a confusing mass of numbers. The planners weren't elated by the prospects it showed, but they set to work to see exactly how an "optimal" acquisition might in fact be made.

One morning as they were working away, our bill for the computer time for the quadratic programing arrived, and its recipient, John, took it into his boss for payment. "John," said the boss, as John came in, bill in hand, "remember that machine tool project? Well, forget it."

"Forget it? What do you mean forget it?"

"I mean I saw the president yesterday. He was just back from a meeting of the board of that tool company he's a director of, and he said to me, 'If there is one business we don't want to get mixed up with, it's those machine tools. In that business, you're going full blast one month and the bottom drops out the next.' "

"Okay," said John, "just pay this bill, and I'll forget it. That's the only sure way to stay out of trouble with machine tools anyway."

Not all business risks can be avoided so simply. In particular, the problem of portfolio selection must be faced by many companies. The combination of the company analysis suggested at the end of the last section with the risk-versus-growth analysis of this section invites investigation.

Each application invariably requires us to look closely at some part of the model which has not previously been scrutinized. Scrutiny turns up short-comings, and shortcomings lead to refinements, which, guided by sponsors who know the area, steadily improve the model. The work on each of the skirts is reflected in the forecasts in this book. Every company and every government agency that needs forecasts in greater detail than a dozen or so broad aggregates has a potential application. Many of these may be along the lines of those discussed here, but none is so routine as to be uninteresting to us. We welcome the opportunity to discuss them.

Some of the newest possible applications, however, reach beyond the scope of the basic model. Inflation has been one of our most persistent problems, and income distribution is always a matter of concern. A subsequent volume will extend the model to reach into these areas. At the same time, these extensions will enable us to check whether present tax policies are consistent with the growth shown by the basic model.

End Tables

DEFINITIONS FOR THE 185 SECTORS IN THE I*N*F*O*R*U*M FORECASTING MODEL
(THE 90-SECTOR NUMBERS OF INVEST AND EMPLOY FOLLOW AFTER TITLES)

SECTOR TITLES	IO-90	STD. INDUSTRIAL CLASSIFICATION
1 DAIRY FARM PRODUCTS	(1)	132
2 POULTRY AND EGGS	(1)	133
3 MEAT, ANIMALS AND MISC LIVESTOCK PR	(1)	135 136 139 193
4 COTTON	(1)	112
5 GRAINS	(1)	113
6 TOBACCO	(1)	114
7 FRUITS, VEGETABLES, AND OTHER CROPS	(1)	122 123 119 192 842
8 FORESTRY AND FISHERY PRODUCTS	(1)	741 811 822 823 843 861 912 913 914 919
9 NO DEF'N	(0)	0
10 AGRICULTURAL, FORESTRY AND FISHERY	(1)	710 723 729 731
11 IRON ORES	(2)	1011 1062 1064 1069 989
12 COPPER ORE	(2)	1021
13 OTHER NON-FERROUS METAL ORES	(2)	1031 1051 1092 1093 1094 1099
14 COAL MINING	(2)	1111 1211
15 CRUDE PETROLEUM AND NATURAL GAS	(3)	1311 1312 1313 1321
16 STONE AND CLAY MINING	(2)	1441 1442 1452 1453 1454 1455 1459 1493 1494 1495 1496 1497 1498 1499 1500
17 CHEMICAL FERTILIZER MINING	(2)	1473 1474 1475 1476 1477 1479 1500 1500 1500 1500 1500
18 NEW CONSTRUCTION	(4)	1500
19 MAINTENANCE AND REPAIR CONSTRUCTION	(0)	1500
20 COMPLETE GUIDED MISSILES	(5)	1925
21 AMMUNITION	(5)	1929
22 OTHER ORDNANCE	(5)	1931 1941 1951 1911 1999
23 MEAT PRODUCTS	(6)	2010
24 DAIRY PRODUCTS	(7)	2021 2022 2023 2024 2026 2036 2031 2032 2033 2034 2035
25 CANNED AND FROZEN FOODS	(8)	2037 2041 2043 2045 2042 2044 2046
26 GRAIN MILL PRODUCTS	(9)	2041
27 BAKERY PRODUCTS	(10)	2050
28 SUGAR	(11)	2060
29 CONFECTIONERY PRODUCTS	(12)	2070
30 ALCOHOLIC BEVERAGES	(13)	2082 2083 2084 2085
31 SOFT DRINKS AND FLAVORINGS	(13)	2086 2087
32 FATS AND OILS	(14)	2091 2092 2093 2094 2096
33 MISC FOOD PRODUCTS	(14)	2095 2097 2098 2099
34 TOBACCO PRODUCTS	(15)	2111 2121 2131 2141
35 BROAD AND NARROW FABRICS	(16)	2211 2221 2231 2261 2262 2201 2241 2269 2281 2282 2283 2284
36 FLOOR COVERINGS	(17)	2270
37 MISC TEXTILES	(18)	2291 2292 2293 2294 2295 2296 2297 2298 2299
38 KNITTING	(19)	2251 2252 2253 2254 2259 2256
39 APPAREL	(20)	2310 2320 2330 2340 2350 2360
40 HOUSEHOLD TEXTILES	(21)	2370 2380 2392 2394 2395 2396 2391 2393 2393 2394 2395 2397 2398 2399
41 LUMBER AND WOOD PRODUCTS	(22)	2411 2421 2426 2429
42 VENEER AND PLYWOOD	(23)	2432

DEFINITIONS FOR THE 185 SECTORS IN THE INFORUM FORECASTING MODEL
(THE 90-SECTOR NUMBERS OF INVEST AND EMPLOY FOLLOW AFTER TITLES)

SECTOR TITLES	IO-90	STD. INDUSTRIAL CLASSIFICATION					
43 MILLWORK AND WOOD PRODUCTS	(23)	2431	2433	2491	2499		
44 WOODEN CONTAINERS	(24)	2440					
45 HOUSEHOLD FURNITURE	(25)	2511	2512	2514	2515		
46 OTHER FURNITURE	(25)	2521	2522	2531	2541	2542	2591
		2599					
47 PULP MILLS	(27)	2611					
48 PAPER AND PAPERBOARD MILLS	(27)	2621	2631				
49 PAPER PRODUCTS, NEC	(27)	2642	2641	2643	2645	2646	
		2647					
50 WALL AND BUILDING PAPER	(27)	2649	2661				
51 PAPERBOARD CONTAINERS	(28)	2650					
52 NEWSPAPERS	(29)	2711					
53 PERIODICALS	(30)	2721					
		2730					
54 BOOKS	(30)	2731					
55 INDUSTRIAL CHEMICALS	(31)	2810					
56 BUSINESS FORMS, BLANK BOOKS	(30)	2761	2782				
57 COMMERCIAL PRINTING	(30)	2751	2752				
58 MISC. PRINTING & PUBL., INCL. GREET	(30)	2741	2771	2753	2789	2790	
59 FERTILIZERS	(32)	2871	2872				
60 PESTICIDES AND OTHER AGRICULTURAL C	(32)	2879					
61 MISC CHEMICAL PRODUCTS	(33)	2861	2890				
62 PLASTIC MATERIALS AND RESINS	(34)	2821					
63 SYNTHETIC RUBBER	(34)	2822					
64 CELLULOSIC FIBERS	(34)	2823					
65 NON-CELLULOSIC FIBERS	(34)	2824					
66 DRUGS	(35)	2830					
67 CLEANING AND TOILET PREPARATIONS	(36)	2840	2844	2844			
68 PAINTS	(37)	2851					
69 GASOLINE	(38)	2911	2990				
70 HEATING OIL	(38)	2915					
71 PAVING AND ASPHALT	(38)	2951	2952				
72 TIRES AND INNER TUBES	(39)	3011					
73 RUBBER PRODUCTS	(40)	3021	3031	3069			
74 MISC PLASTIC PRODUCTS	(41)	3079					
75 LEATHER TANNING AND INDUSTRIAL LEAT	(42)	3111	3121				
76 LEATHER FOOTWEAR	(43)	3131	3140				
77 OTHER LEATHER PRODUCTS	(43)	3151	3161				
78 GLASS	(44)	3211	3221	3229			
79 STRUCTURAL CLAY PRODUCTS	(45)	3251	3253	3255	3259		
80 POTTERY	(45)	3261	3262	3264	3269		
81 CEMENT, CONCRETE, AND GYPSUM	(45)	3241	3273	3274	3275		
82 OTHER STONE AND CLAY PRODUCTS	(45)	3281	3291	3292	3293	3295	3296
		3297					
		3299					
83 STEEL	(46)	3310	3320	3391	3399		
84 COPPER	(47)	3331	3341	3351	3362		
85 LEAD	(47)	3332					
86 ZINC	(47)	3333					
87 ALUMINUM	(47)	3334	3352	3361			
88 PRIMARY NON-FERROUS METALS, NEC	(47)	3339					
89 NON-FERROUS ROLLING AND DRAWING, NE	(47)	3356					

DEFINITIONS FOR THE 185 SECTORS IN THE I*N*F*O*R*U*M FORECASTING MODEL
(THE 90-SECTOR NUMBERS OF INVEST AND EMPLOY FOLLOW AFTER TITLES)

	SECTOR TITLES	IO-90	STD. INDUSTRIAL CLASSIFICATION
90	NON-FERROUS WIRE DRAWING AND INSULA	(47)	3357
91	NON-FERROUS CASTINGS AND FORGINGS	(47)	3369
92	METAL CANS	(48)	3411 3392
93	METAL BARRELS, DRUMS AND PAILS	(48)	3491
94	PLUMBING AND HEATING EQUIPMENT	(49)	3431 3432 3433
95	STRUCTURAL METAL PRODUCTS	(50)	3441 3442 3443 3444 3446 3449
96	SCREW MACHINE PRODUCTS	(51)	3450
97	METAL STAMPINGS	(51)	3461
98	CUTLERY, HAND TOOLS AND HARDWARE	(52)	3421 3423 3425 3429
99	MISC FABRICATED WIRE PRODUCTS	(52)	3341 3498
100	VALVES, PIPE FITTINGS, AND FABRICAT	(52)	3492 3493 3494 3496
101	OTHER FABRICATED METAL PRODUCTS, NE	(52)	3471 3479 3497 3499
102	ENGINES AND TURBINES	(53)	3511 3519
103	FARM MACHINERY	(54)	3522
104	CONSTRUCTION, MINING, AND OIL FIELD	(55)	3531 3532 3533
105	MATERIALS HANDLING MACHINERY	(55)	3534 3535 3536 3537
106	MACHINE TOOLS, METAL CUTTING	(56)	3541
107	MACHINE TOOLS, METAL FORMING	(56)	3542
108	OTHER METAL WORKING MACHINERY	(57)	3544 3545 3548
109	SPECIAL INDUSTRIAL MACHINERY	(58)	3551 3552 3553 3554 3555 3559
110	PUMPS, COMPRESSORS, BLOWERS AND FAN	(58)	3561 3562 3564
111	BALL AND ROLLER BEARINGS	(58)	3562
112	POWER TRANSMISSION EQUIPMENT	(58)	3566
113	INDUSTRIAL PATTERNS	(60)	3565 3567 3569
114	COMPUTERS AND RELATED MACHINES	(60)	3571 3573 3574
115	OTHER OFFICE MACHINERY	(61)	3572 3576 3579
116	SERVICE INDUSTRY MACHINERY	(59)	3581 3582 3585 3586 3589
117	MACHINE SHOP PRODUCTS	(62)	3590
118	ELECTRICAL MEASURING INSTRUMENTS	(62)	3611 3612 3613
119	TRANSFORMERS AND SWITCHGEAR	(63)	3621
120	MOTORS AND GENERATORS	(63)	3622 3624 3629
121	INDUSTRIAL CONTROLS	(63)	3623 3632 3633
122	WELDING APPARATUS AND GRAPHITE PROD	(63)	3631 3634 3635 3636
123	HOUSEHOLD APPLIANCES	(64)	3639
124	ELECTRIC LIGHTING AND WIRING EQUIPM	(65)	3641 3642 3643 3644
125	RADIO AND TV RECEIVING	(66)	3651
126	PHONOGRAPH RECORDS	(66)	3652
127	COMMUNICATION EQUIPMENT	(67)	3661 3662
128	ELECTRONIC COMPONENTS	(68)	3671 3672 3673 3674 3679
129	BATTERIES	(69)	3691 3692
130	ENGINE ELECTRICAL EQUIPMENT	(69)	3693 3694
131	X-RAY EQUIPMENT AND ELECTRICAL EQUI	(70)	3693 3699
132	TRUCK, BUS, AND TRAILER BODIES	(70)	3713 3715 3717
133	MOTOR VEHICLES AND PARTS	(70)	3711 3714
134	AIRCRAFT	(71)	3721
135	AIRCRAFT ENGINES AND PARTS	(71)	3722 3723
136	AIRCRAFT EQUIPMENT, NEC	(71)	3729
137	SHIP AND BOAT BUILDING AND REPAIR	(72)	3731 3732

DEFINITIONS FOR THE 185 SECTORS IN THE I*N*F*O*R*U*M FORECASTING MODEL
(THE 90-SECTOR NUMBERS OF INVEST AND EMPLOY FOLLOW AFTER TITLES)

SECTOR TITLES	IO-90	STD. INDUSTRIAL CLASSIFICATION
138 RAILROAD EQUIPMENT	(73)	3741 3742
139 CYCLES AND PARTS, TRANSPORTATION EQ	(74)	3751
140 TRAILER COACHES	(74)	3791 3799
141 ENGINEERING AND SCIENTIFIC INSTRUME	(75)	3811
142 MECHANICAL MEASURING DEVICES	(76)	3821 3822
143 OPTICAL AND OPHTHALMIC GOODS	(76)	3831 3851
144 MEDICAL AND SURGICAL INSTRUMENTS	(77)	3841 3842 3843
145 PHOTOGRAPHIC EQUIPMENT	(78)	3861
146 WATCHES, CLOCKS, AND PARTS	(78)	3870
147 JEWELRY AND SILVERWARE	(79)	3910
148 TOYS, SPORTING GOODS, MUSICAL INSTR	(79)	3931 3942 3943 3949
149 OFFICE SUPPLIES	(79)	3950 3955
150 MISC MANUFACTURING, NEC	(79)	3961 3962 3963 3964 3981 3982 3983 3984 3987 3988 3991 3994 3995 3999
151 RAILROADS	(80)	4000
152 BUSSES	(82)	4100
153 TRUCKING	(81)	4200 4730
154 WATER TRANSPORTATION	(82)	4400
155 AIRLINES	(83)	4500
156 PIPELINES	(82)	4600
157 TRAVEL AGTS, OTH TRANS SER.	(82)	4700 4701 4702 4705 4706 4707 4708 4709
158 TELEPHONE AND TELEGRAPH	(85)	4800 4801 4802 4804 4805 4806 4807 4809
159 RADIO AND TV BROADCASTING	(85)	4830
160 ELECTRIC UTILITIES	(87)	4910
161 NATURAL GAS	(88)	4920 4930
162 WATER AND SEWER SERVICES	(88)	4940 4950 4960 4970 4930
163 WHOLESALE TRADE	(84)	5000
164 RETAIL TRADE	(84)	5200 5300 5400 5500 5600 5700 5800 5900
165 CREDIT AGENCIES AND BROKERS	(86)	6000 6100 6200
166 INSURANCE AND BROKER'S AGENTS	(86)	6300 6400
167 OWNER-OCCUPIED DWELLINGS	(0)	
168 REAL ESTATE	(86)	6500 -6561 6600
169 HOTEL AND LODGING PLACES	(86)	7000
170 PERSONAL AND REPAIR SERVICES	(86)	7200 -7230 -7240 7600 7694 7699 -7694 -7699
171 BUSINESS SERVICES	(86)	7300 -7230 -7240 -7310 -7396 8900
172 ADVERTISING	(86)	7310
173 AUTO REPAIR	(86)	7500
174 MOTION PICTURES AND AMUSEMENTS	(86)	7800 7900 7220
175 MEDICAL SERVICES	(86)	8010 8020 8030 8040 8060 8061 8070 8090
176 PRIVATE SCHOOLS AND NONPROFIT ORGAN	(86)	8200 8600 8921
177 POST OFFICE	(0)	0
178 FEDERAL GOV. ENTERPRISES	(0)	0
179 LOCAL GOV. PASSENGER TRANSIT	(0)	0

DEFINITIONS FOR THE 185 SECTORS IN THE I*N*F*o*R*U*M FORECASTING MODEL
(THE 90-SECTOR NUMBERS OF INVEST AND EMPLOY FOLLOW AFTER TITLES)

SECTOR TITLES	IO-90	STD. INDUSTRIAL CLASSIFICATION
180 STATE AND LOCAL ELECTRIC UTILITIES	(0)	0
181 DIRECTLY ALLOCATED IMPORTS	(0)	0
182 BUSINESS TRAVEL	(0)	0
183 OFFICE SUPPLIES	(0)	0
184 UNIMPORTANT INDUSTRY	(0)	0
185 COMPUTER RENTAL	(0)	0
186 PERSONAL CONSUMPTION EXPENDITURES	(0)	0
187 DEFENSE EXPENDITURES	(0)	0
188 NON-DEFENSE FEDERAL EXPENDITURES	(0)	0
189 EDUCATION	(0)	0
190 HEALTH, WELFARE, AND SANITATION	(0)	0
191 POLICE, FIRE, AND SAFETY	(0)	0
192 GENERAL STATE AND LOCAL GOV. EXPEND	(0)	0
193 CHANGE IN INVENTORIES	(0)	0
194 EXPORTS	(0)	0
195 IMPORTS	(0)	0

STATISTICAL DEFINITIONS

Personal Consumption Expenditures (PCE) are in producer prices plus excise
taxes--not consumer prices. Entries in Wholesale and Retail Trade
(sectors 163 and 164) are trade margins--i.e., the difference between
what the stores pay for the goods and what they sell them for. Likewise, a total transportation margin has been computed, but it is not
entered into the transportation rows because these rows are on a by-
product-hauled basis rather than on a margin basis. The sum of PCE
in producer-plus-excise prices plus trade margins plus transportation
equals PCE in consumer prices.

Exports are in producer prices. Census Bureau and balance-of-payments export
figures are in domestic port prices. The difference is the transportation cost from farm or factory to port, and, for some products, a wholesale trade margin. This cost appears in the line labeled "Margins and
Scrap" under "Exports" on E5.

Imports, to be comparable with domestic production, are expressed in domestic
port prices. Census and balance-of-payments practice is to show them
in foreign port prices. We have added the cost of ocean and air transportation to each product. In the GNP summary on E3, the Merchandise
Import lines are in domestic prot prices; the "Margins and Scrap" line
is a catch-all line defined so that, when added to the two merchandise
lines the total equals "merchandise" by balance-of-payments definition.

Outputs are defined as product shipments plus contract receipts plus changes
in inventories of finished goods and goods in process, plus excise taxes.

NOVEMBER 1973 FORECAST GNP SUMMARY (BILLIONS OF 1971$)

	1971	1972	1973	1974	1975	1976	1978	1980	1983	1985
GROSS NATIONAL PRODUCT	1050.36	1104.02	1181.37	1206.59	1255.88	1289.84	1366.30	1445.46	1548.22	1609.64
PERSONAL CONSUMPTION EXPENDITURES	664.90	692.72	726.34	750.88	782.60	802.37	860.08	916.31	993.06	1039.36
DURABLE GOODS	103.48	109.94	113.23	117.23	123.52	126.36	137.26	147.19	161.05	169.52
NONDURABLE GOODS	278.12	286.68	300.80	310.59	321.89	329.97	350.60	371.02	399.05	416.16
SERVICES	283.30	296.22	311.55	322.59	336.60	345.62	371.13	396.26	430.25	450.51
GROSS PRIVATE DOMESTIC INVESTMENT	151.97	170.73	207.38	198.24	206.01	212.64	217.71	232.54	247.13	255.45
STRUCTURES	80.94	89.61	99.37	88.37	92.01	96.59	97.18	102.29	107.46	110.08
RESIDENTIAL	42.58	51.19	51.93	40.08	43.67	47.15	46.02	49.17	52.11	53.58
PRODUCERS' DURABLE EQUIPMENT	67.41	75.98	94.05	99.07	102.72	106.34	111.58	120.64	131.10	137.38
AGRICULTURE	5.37	4.84	5.86	6.31	6.33	6.29	6.38	6.51	6.67	6.85
MINING	2.40	2.55	3.18	3.33	3.38	3.62	3.72	3.97	4.28	4.47
CONSTRUCTION	2.53	3.17	3.64	3.90	4.18	4.41	4.38	4.71	5.07	5.28
NONDURABLE GOODS	7.80	8.56	10.65	11.53	12.17	12.59	13.13	13.98	14.98	15.71
DURABLE GOODS	7.81	9.33	12.78	14.21	14.66	15.53	14.67	15.34	16.58	17.23
TRANSPORTATION	4.29	3.98	6.98	7.39	7.30	7.28	7.77	8.36	9.10	9.48
COMMUNICATION	7.76	9.51	12.09	12.28	12.43	12.87	14.27	16.10	18.01	19.20
UTILITIES	7.24	7.39	9.10	9.36	9.62	10.02	11.05	12.18	13.62	14.43
TRADE	8.53	9.32	10.81	11.24	12.07	12.91	13.89	15.24	16.85	17.85
FINANCE AND SERVICES	6.64	9.34	10.02	10.47	11.03	10.96	13.52	12.45	12.97	13.20
INVENTORY CHANGE	3.60	5.11	13.94	10.72	11.20	9.62	8.84	9.48	8.40	7.81
EXPORTS OF GOODS AND SERVICES	66.13	63.45	68.18	76.14	81.51	87.15	95.69	102.40	113.01	119.57
MERCHANDISE	36.88	33.41	35.91	40.90	43.79	46.94	51.19	54.02	58.51	60.99
MARGINS AND SCRAP	5.90	5.43	5.83	6.63	7.10	7.60	8.28	8.73	9.45	9.85
TRAVEL	2.46	2.85	3.11	3.39	3.77	4.06	4.44	4.69	5.05	5.30
PASSENGER FARES, OTH TRANSPORT	3.71	3.94	4.20	4.43	4.61	4.78	5.07	5.34	5.73	5.98
OTHER PRIVATE SERVICES	1.97	2.01	2.18	2.53	2.72	2.94	3.23	3.43	3.73	3.90
INVESTMENT INCOME	12.01	12.90	14.07	15.29	16.58	17.91	20.67	23.58	28.22	31.44
GOVERNMENT	3.21	3.24	3.24	3.24	3.24	3.24	3.24	3.24	3.24	3.24
IMPORTS OF GOODS AND SERVICES	-65.41	-63.16	-68.10	-69.21	-70.55	-72.25	-78.50	-86.96	-99.57	-108.20
MERCHANDISE	-47.77	-45.71	-50.08	-50.30	-50.60	-50.96	-54.39	-60.19	-68.65	-74.42
NON-COMPETITIVE MERCHANDISE	-3.10	-3.26	-3.44	-3.51	-3.63	-3.72	-3.91	-4.10	-4.35	-4.50
MARGINS AND SCRAP	-5.32	-5.45	-5.98	-6.01	-6.05	-6.09	-6.51	-7.23	-8.28	-9.00
TRAVEL	-4.29	-4.44	-4.82	-5.02	-5.38	-5.50	-6.08	-6.60	-7.23	-7.58
PASSENGER FARES, OTH TRANSPORT	-4.30	-4.46	-4.46	-4.67	-4.80	-4.92	-5.31	-5.74	-6.39	-6.82
OTHER PRIVATE SERVICES	-0.87	-0.85	-0.93	-0.91	-0.91	-0.92	-1.03	-1.05	-1.14	-1.22
INVESTMENT INCOME	-3.06	-3.86	-4.53	-5.25	-6.01	-6.83	-8.53	-10.36	-13.33	-15.46
GOVERNMENT	-7.42	-7.42	-6.92	-6.22	-5.62	-5.62	-5.62	-5.62	-5.62	-5.62
FOREIGN LONG-TERM CAPITAL TO U.S.	2.27	2.31	2.50	2.69	2.88	3.00	3.23	3.46	3.81	4.04
U.S. LONG-TERM CAPITAL ABROAD	-6.35	-6.59	-6.96	-7.32	-7.69	-7.91	-8.35	-8.79	-9.45	-9.89
U.S. GOVT. LONG-TERM CAPITAL FLOWS	-2.19	-3.84	-3.82	-3.80	-3.79	-3.79	-3.79	-3.79	-3.79	-3.79
GOVERNMENT PURCHASES	232.76	238.68	245.53	248.70	254.33	257.90	269.40	279.28	292.92	301.97
PUBLIC CONSTRUCTION	30.10	28.59	29.86	30.72	31.38	32.04	33.20	34.25	35.75	36.72
NATIONAL DEFENSE	69.71	71.08	69.12	67.16	65.20	65.90	67.31	68.71	70.82	72.23
NON-DEFENSE FEDERAL	24.10	25.12	26.49	27.87	29.24	29.98	31.46	32.95	35.34	36.93
STATE AND LOCAL	108.85	113.92	119.99	122.81	128.30	129.75	137.16	143.07	150.67	155.71
EDUCATION	52.54	55.22	58.10	59.18	61.65	61.94	64.33	65.67	67.49	69.23
PRODUCTIVITY($1000 PER EMPLOYEE)	12.68	12.97	13.50	13.51	13.79	13.92	14.27	14.62	15.08	15.39
PRIVATE SECTOR	13.94	14.30	14.34	14.94	15.27	15.43	15.86	16.29	16.87	17.27

NOVEMBER 1973 FORECAST   GNP SUMMARY   (BILLIONS OF 1971$)

	1971	1972	1973	1974	1975	1976	1978	1980	1983	1985
EMPLOYED PERSONS (MILLIONS)	81.94	84.24	86.60	88.34	90.12	91.67	94.77	97.84	101.56	103.51
PRIVATE INDUSTRY	65.60	67.41	69.48	71.17	72.69	74.09	76.57	79.14	82.18	83.64
CIVILIAN GOVERNMENT	13.52	13.76	14.22	14.43	14.84	14.98	15.60	16.09	16.77	17.25
DEFENSE	1.13	1.09	1.03	.97	.91	.91	.91	.91	.91	.91
MILITARY	2.81	3.06	2.90	2.74	2.59	2.59	2.60	2.60	2.61	2.62

EXOGENOUS ASSUMPTIONS

	1971	1972	1973	1974	1975	1976	1978	1980	1983	1985
CONSUMPTION										
DISPOSABLE PER CAPITA INCOME 58$	2679.00	2770.00	2900.00	2960.00	3077.00	3104.00	3277.00	3418.00	3566.00	3636.00
POPULATION - SERIES E (MILLIONS)	207.05	208.80	210.50	212.16	213.92	215.79	219.79	224.13	231.04	235.70
SCHOOL AGE POPULATION	59.91	59.61	59.18	58.75	58.32	57.97	56.32	54.62	53.35	53.46
PLANT AND EQUIPMENT INVESTMENT										
LONG-TERM INTEREST RATE	.02	.03	.02	.02	.03	.03	.02	.02	.02	.02
SHORT-TERM INTEREST RATE	-.00	-.00	.02	.02	.02	.02	.02	.01	.01	.01
RENT/CONSTRUCTION COST INDEX	-.79	.76	.75	.77	.80	.80	.80	.80	.80	.80
HOUSEHOLDS (MILLIONS)	64.37	66.67	67.64	68.87	70.08	71.54	74.44	77.30	81.45	84.21
INVESTMENT TAX CREDIT	.00	.07	.07	.07	.07	.07	.07	.07	.07	.07
FOREIGN TRADE										
AVERAGE FOREIGN CURRENCY PRICE	1.00	1.01	1.03	1.05	1.09	1.12	1.13	1.13	1.12	1.11
EMPLOYMENT										
LABOR FORCE (THOUSANDS)	86929.00	88991.00	90576.00	92171.00	93376.00	95391.00	98621.00	101809.00	105684.00	107716.00
CIVILIAN UNEMPLOYMENT RATE	5.93	5.53	4.53	4.26	4.01	4.01	4.01	4.00	4.00	4.00

NUMBERS HAVE BEEN SCALED TO 1971 PUBLISHED LEVELS AND MAY NOT ADD TO TOTALS

NOVEMBER 1973 FORECAST

SUMMARY OF ANNUAL GROWTH RATES

	71-85	71-75	75-80	80-85	71-73	73-83	73-75	73-78	75-78	78-83
GROSS NATIONAL PRODUCT	3.05	4.47	2.81	2.15	5.88	2.70	3.06	2.91	2.81	2.50
PERSONAL CONSUMPTION EXPENDITURES	3.19	4.07	3.15	2.52	4.42	3.13	3.73	3.38	3.15	2.8A
DURABLE GOODS	3.53	4.42	3.51	2.58	4.54	3.52	4.31	3.83	3.52	3.20
NONDURABLE GOODS	2.88	3.65	2.84	2.30	3.92	2.83	3.39	3.06	2.85	2.59
SERVICES	3.31	4.31	3.26	2.57	4.75	3.23	3.87	3.50	3.26	2.96
GROSS PRIVATE DOMESTIC INVESTMENT	3.71	7.61	2.42	1.86	15.54	1.75	-.33	.97	1.84	2.53
STRUCTURES	2.20	3.20	2.12	1.47	10.26	.76	-3.85	-.45	1.82	2.01
RESIDENTIAL	1.64	.63	2.38	1.72	9.92	.04	-8.66	-2.42	1.75	2.49
PRODUCERS' DURABLE EQUIPMENT	5.09	10.53	3.22	2.60	10.65	3.32	4.40	3.42	2.76	3.22
AGRICULTURE	1.74	4.13	.54	1.04	4.42	1.29	3.83	1.70	.28	.8A
MINING	4.44	8.54	3.23	2.34	14.11	2.97	3.06	3.16	3.22	2.7A
CONSTRUCTION	5.06	12.12	2.78	2.30	18.16	3.32	6.93	3.70	1.55	2.93
NONDURABLE GOODS	5.00	11.12	2.77	2.34	20.58	2.61	6.67	4.19	2.53	2.64
DURABLE GOODS	5.66	15.76	2.90	2.33	24.84	2.60	6.89	3.70	2.01	2.44
TRANSPORTATION	5.65	13.28	2.70	2.50	22.28	2.60	2.28	2.16	2.15	3.16
COMMUNICATION	6.47	11.76	5.17	3.52	22.15	3.98	1.38	3.31	2.06	4.65
UTILITIES	4.93	7.11	4.73	3.36	11.40	4.03	2.75	3.88	4.63	4.18
TRADE	5.27	8.68	4.66	3.16	11.85	4.44	5.51	5.02	4.69	3.86
FINANCE AND SERVICES	4.91	12.70	2.42	1.17	20.61	2.56	4.79	2.79	1.45	2.37
INVENTORY CHANGE	5.53	28.38	-3.33	-3.88	67.69	-5.06	-10.93	-9.10	-7.88	-1.02
EXPORTS OF GOODS AND SERVICES	4.23	5.23	4.56	3.10	1.53	5.05	8.92	6.78	5.35	3.33
MERCHANDISE	3.59	4.29	4.20	2.43	-1.34	4.88	9.92	7.09	5.20	2.67
MARGINS AND SCRAP	3.66	4.61	4.16	2.41	-.58	4.83	.80	7.01	5.15	2.65
TRAVEL	5.48	10.68	4.35	2.45	11.76	4.85	9.61	7.12	5.46	2.5A
PASSENGER FARES, OTH TRANSPORT	3.41	5.41	2.97	2.25	6.18	3.12	4.63	3.78	3.22	2.46
OTHER PRIVATE SERVICES	4.88	8.10	4.58	2.61	5.12	5.37	11.07	7.85	5.70	2.89
INVESTMENT INCOME	6.89	8.27	7.04	5.79	7.90	6.90	8.23	7.70	7.34	6.23
GOVERNMENT	.07	.24	.00	.00	.48	.00	.00	.00	-.00	.00
IMPORTS OF GOODS AND SERVICES	3.59	1.89	4.18	4.37	2.01	3.80	1.77	2.84	3.56	4.75
MERCHANDISE	3.17	1.44	3.47	4.24	2.76	3.15	.52	1.65	2.41	4.66
NON-COMPETITIVE MERCHANDISE	2.66	3.98	2.39	1.87	5.15	2.35	2.81	2.58	2.43	2.12
MARGINS AND SCRAP	3.76	3.19	3.58	4.38	6.86	3.25	.53	1.70	2.47	4.81
TRAVEL	4.07	5.65	4.09	2.79	5.86	4.05	5.45	4.63	4.08	3.47
PASSENGER FARES, OTH TRANSPORT	3.29	2.76	3.57	3.43	1.84	3.60	3.68	3.49	3.37	3.71
OTHER PRIVATE SERVICES	2.41	1.17	2.54	3.27	1.97	2.34	.37	1.18	1.73	3.51
INVESTMENT INCOME	11.57	16.95	10.83	8.01	19.64	10.79	14.26	12.66	11.59	8.92
GOVERNMENT	-1.93	-6.96	.00	.00	-4.24	-1.93	-9.67	-3.87	-.00	.00
FOREIGN LONG-TERM CAPITAL TO U.S.	4.12	5.99	3.65	3.08	4.83	4.21	7.16	5.13	3.78	3.29
U.S. LONG-TERM CAPITAL ABROAD	3.16	4.78	2.67	2.36	4.56	3.06	5.00	3.65	2.74	2.47
U.S. GOVT. LONG-TERM CAPITAL FLOWS	3.91	13.68	.00	.00	27.46	-.10	-.50	-.20	-.00	-.00
GOVERNMENT PURCHASES	1.86	2.22	1.97	1.56	2.67	1.77	1.76	1.86	1.92	1.67
PUBLIC CONSTRUCTION	1.42	1.04	1.75	1.39	-.39	1.80	2.47	2.12	1.88	1.4A
NATIONAL DEFENSE	.25	-1.67	1.95	1.00	-.43	.24	-2.92	-.53	1.06	1.02
NON-DEFENSE FEDERAL	3.05	4.83	2.39	2.2E	4.74	2.88	4.93	3.44	2.44	1.88
STATE AND LOCAL	2.56	4.11	2.18	1.69	4.87	2.28	3.35	2.68	2.23	1.88
EDUCATION	1.97	4.00	1.26	1.06	5.03	1.50	2.97	2.04	1.42	.96
PRODUCTIVITY($1000 PER EMPLOYEE)	1.38	2.09	1.17	1.03	3.11	1.11	1.07	1.11	1.13	1.12
PRIVATE SECTOR	1.53	2.29	1.29	1.17	3.48	1.21	1.09	1.19	1.25	1.24

NOVEMBER 1973 FORECAST

SUMMARY OF ANNUAL GROWTH RATES

	71-85	71-75	75-80	80-85	71-73	73-83	73-75	73-78	75-78	78-85
EMPLOYED PERSONS (MILLIONS)	1.67	2.38	1.64	1.13	2.77	1.59	1.99	1.80	1.68	1.38
PRIVATE INDUSTRY	1.74	2.56	1.70	1.11	2.87	1.68	2.26	1.95	1.73	1.41
CIVILIAN GOVERNMENT	1.74	2.32	1.63	1.38	2.52	1.64	2.11	1.85	1.67	1.44
DEFENSE	-1.57	-5.54	.01	.01	-4.82	-1.24	-6.27	-2.50	.01	.01
MILITARY	-.51	-2.09	.13	.11	1.55	-1.05	-5.72	-2.21	.12	.12

EXOGENOUS ASSUMPTIONS

	71-85	71-75	75-80	80-85	71-73	73-83	73-75	73-78	75-78	78-85
CONSUMPTION										
DISPOSABLE PER CAPITA INCOME 58%	2.18	3.46	2.10	1.24	3.90	2.07	2.96	2.44	2.10	1.69
POPULATION - SERIES E (MILLIONS)	.93	.82	.93	1.01	.83	.93	.81	.86	.90	1.00
SCHOOL AGE POPULATION	-.81	-.67	-1.31	-.43	-.61	-1.04	-.73	-.99	-1.16	-1.08
PLANT AND EQUIPMENT INVESTMENT										
LONG-TERM INTEREST RATE	-.13	4.97	-4.33	.00	3.46	-.87	6.47	-1.75	-7.22	.00
SHORT-TERM INTEREST RATE	.12	.41	.00	.00	-2.41	.65	3.23	1.29	.00	.00
RENT/CONSTRUCTION COST INDEX										
HOUSEHOLDS (MILLIONS)	1.92	2.12	1.96	1.71	2.47	1.86	1.77	1.92	2.01	1.80
INVESTMENT TAX CREDIT										
FOREIGN TRADE										
AVERAGE FOREIGN CURRENCY PRICE	.75	2.18	.65	-.31	1.56	.79	2.81	1.89	1.28	-.30
EMPLOYMENT										
LABOR FORCE (THOUSANDS)	1.53	1.90	1.64	1.13	2.05	1.54	1.74	1.70	1.68	1.38
CIVILIAN UNEMPLOYMENT RATE	-2.81	-9.77	-.06	.02	-13.42	-1.25	-6.12	-2.45	-.01	-.04

NOVEMBER 1973 FORECAST PERSONAL CONSUMPTION EXPENDITURES MILLIONS OF 1971$

		1971	1972	1973	1974	1975	1976	1978	1980	1983	1985	
2	POULTRY AND EGGS	1424.	1415.	1417.	1409.	1412.	1401.	1402.	1399.	1387.	1373.	2
7	FRUIT,VEGETABLES,OTH CROPS	4265.	4305.	4382.	4388.	4460.	4447.	4555.	4636.	4735.	4781.	7
23	MEAT PRODUCTS	21628.	22063.	22678.	23320.	23947.	24621.	25974.	27410.	29656.	31185.	23
24	DAIRY PRODUCTS	10211.	10377.	10626.	10842.	11012.	11193.	11500.	11829.	12294.	12596.	24
25	CANNED AND FROZEN FOODS	9837.	10416.	10971.	11411.	11891.	12287.	13214.	14147.	15594.	16570.	25
26	GRAIN MILL PRODUCTS	3427.	3494.	3641.	3770.	3939.	4065.	4394.	4722.	5204.	5521.	27
27	BAKERY PRODUCTS	7188.	7501.	7699.	7849.	7946.	8068.	8265.	8480.	8841.	9068.	28
28	SUGAR	1108.	1087.	1075.	1071.	1071.	1073.	1080.	1090.	1104.	1110.	29
29	CONFECTIONERY PRODUCTS	2867.	3029.	3188.	3346.	3456.	3585.	3792.	4015.	4285.	4416.	30
30	ALCOHOLIC BEVERAGES	10359.	10454.	10922.	11272.	11747.	12007.	12823.	13597.	14510.	14970.	31
31	SOFT DRINK AND FLAVORINGS	4507.	4653.	4909.	5122.	5346.	5527.	5947.	6370.	6934.	7262.	32
32	FATS AND OILS	5430.	5486.	5545.	5488.	5355.	5370.	5456.	5541.	5668.	5747.	33
33	MISC FOOD PRODUCTS	6793.	6858.	6897.	6932.	6972.	7023.	7138.	7268.	7511.	7677.	34
34	TOBACCO PRODUCTS	844.	892.	946.	972.	1014.	1027.	1092.	1149.	1222.	1263.	35
35	BROAD AND NARROW FABRICS	1549.	1598.	1735.	1766.	1909.	1909.	2124.	2296.	2512.	2645.	36
36	FLOOR COVERINGS	3055.	3199.	3405.	3523.	3727.	3813.	4165.	4489.	4912.	5162.	38
38	KNITTING	15837.	16229.	16081.	16674.	19707.	19988.	21516.	22839.	24275.	25035.	39
39	APPAREL	2217.	2296.	2424.	2555.	2665.	2781.	2997.	3225.	3521.	3684.	40
40	HOUSEHOLD TEXTILES	4592.	4834.	5190.	5259.	5602.	5579.	6066.	6439.	6894.	7186.	45
45	HOUSEHOLD FURNITURE	2037.	2216.	2346.	2443.	2548.	2636.	2844.	3056.	3388.	3613.	49
49	PAPER PRODUCTS, NEC	1924.	2062.	2172.	2219.	2310.	2331.	2473.	2596.	2736.	2807.	52
52	NEWSPAPERS	980.	1018.	1075.	1118.	1170.	1205.	1300.	1394.	1521.	1597.	53
53	PERIODICALS	3826.	4025.	4304.	4552.	4811.	5027.	5520.	6017.	6673.	7050.	66
66	DRUGS	6018.	6481.	7021.	7339.	7814.	7914.	8803.	9514.	10420.	10954.	67
67	CLEANING + TOILET PROD.	10394.	10326.	10118.	11403.	11770.	12230.	13116.	14016.	15266.	15991.	69
69	PETROLEUM REFINING	2635.	2601.	2788.	3011.	3098.	3184.	3350.	3542.	3786.	3954.	70
70	FUEL OIL	2302.	2257.	2358.	2446.	2453.	2484.	2684.	2884.	3274.	3425.	72
72	TIRES AND INNER TUBES	3387.	3628.	3783.	3866.	3953.	4015.	4183.	4461.	4651.	4751.	76
76	FOOTWEAR(EXC. RUBBER)	956.	1048.	1135.	1200.	1261.	1309.	1411.	1510.	1552.	1751.	77
77	OTHER LEATHER PRODUCTS	4848.	5138.	5511.	5710.	6060.	6185.	6761.	7279.	7922.	8285.	123
123	HOUSEHOLD APPLIANCES	4413.	4819.	5279.	5528.	5927.	6096.	6765.	7376.	8227.	8776.	125
125	RADIO AND TV RECEIVING	29058.	31016.	30561.	31662.	33238.	34167.	37066.	39852.	43804.	46302.	133
133	MOTOR VEHICLES	2873.	2805.	2838.	2913.	2974.	3081.	3284.	3445.	3903.	4199.	140
140	TRAILER COACHES	1995.	2085.	2236.	2292.	2432.	2442.	2645.	2809.	2968.	3030.	147
147	JEWELRY AND SILVERWARE	2771.	3071.	3324.	3501.	3701.	3847.	4217.	4583.	5137.	5505.	148
148	TOYS,SPORT,MUSICAL INSTR.	2967.	2954.	2914.	2933.	2874.	2887.	2769.	2684.	2499.	2316.	152
152	BUSSES AND LOCAL TRANSIT	3664.	3924.	4151.	4405.	4603.	4845.	5267.	5666.	6335.	6734.	155
155	AIRLINES	10860.	11364.	12037.	12654.	13273.	13827.	15037.	16277.	17963.	18952.	158
158	TELEPHONE AND TELEGRAPH	11121.	11563.	12068.	12649.	13125.	13719.	14784.	15927.	17714.	18848.	160
160	ELECTRIC UTILITIES	5761.	5776.	5743.	5839.	5846.	6021.	6185.	6438.	6990.	7418.	161
161	NATURAL GAS	2705.	2809.	2835.	2635.	2638.	2692.	2754.	2850.	3056.	3209.	162
162	WATER AND SEWER SERVICES	3766.	39310.	41300.	42782.	44599.	45090.	47392.	51710.	57345.	60182.	163
163	WHOLESALE TRADE	112782.	123398.	129584.	127827.	135591.	137090.	147392.	157410.	173749.	180182.	164
164	RETAIL TRADE	19837.	21146.	22958.	24052.	24510.	26154.	28445.	30572.	33209.	34621.	165
165	BANKS,CREDIT AGEN.,BROKERS	14825.	15556.	16499.	17249.	18071.	18706.	20225.	21837.	23828.	24996.	166
166	INSURANCE	67076.	69450.	72508.	74825.	77840.	80075.	86097.	92045.	101663.	108023.	167
167	OWNER-OCCUPIED DWELLINGS	28789.	30158.	32315.	33511.	35599.	36305.	39636.	42655.	45945.	47736.	168
168	REAL ESTATE	4091.	4355.	4719.	4993.	5304.	5517.	6061.	6623.	7280.	7655.	169
169	HOTEL AND LODGING PLACES	14781.	15344.	16070.	16520.	17178.	17505.	18609.	19946.	21154.	21866.	170
170	PERSONAL + REPAIR SERVICES	5755.	6297.	6486.	6612.	6794.	6893.	7230.	7542.	7971.	8198.	171
171	BUSINESS SERVICES	11497.	11628.	11878.	12122.	12426.	12698.	13338.	14006.	14978.	15566.	173
173	AUTO REPAIR	7430.	7486.	7665.	7666.	7820.	7751.	7942.	8040.	8095.	8040.	174
174	MOVIES + AMUSEMENTS	41967.	43683.	45948.	47376.	49578.	50691.	54576.	58235.	63160.	68112.	175
175	MEDICAL SERVICES	22915.	25186.	26897.	28152.	29450.	30372.	32609.	34746.	37444.	38712.	176
176	PRIVATE SCHOOLS + NPO	1626.	1794.	1909.	1981.	2065.	2117.	2263.	2404.	2593.	2701.	177
177	POST OFFICE											

NOVEMBER 1973 FORECAST

PERSONAL CONSUMPTION EXPENDITURES   ANNUAL GROWTH RATES

	71-85	71-75	75-80	80-85	71-73	73-83	73-75	73-78	75-78	78-83	
POULTRY AND EGGS	-.26	-.22	-.19	-.37	-.25	-.21	-.19	-.21	-.23	-.21	2
FRUIT,VEGETABLES,OTH CROPS	.81	1.12	.77	.62	1.35	.78	.88	.77	.70	.78	7
MEAT PRODUCTS	2.61	2.55	2.70	2.58	2.37	2.68	2.72	2.71	2.71	2.65	23
DAIRY PRODUCTS	1.50	1.89	1.43	1.26	1.99	1.46	1.79	1.58	1.44	1.34	24
CANNED AND FROZEN FOODS	3.72	4.74	3.63	3.16	5.46	3.57	4.03	3.76	3.52	3.31	25
GRAIN MILL PRODUCTS	3.41	3.48	3.47	3.13	3.02	3.57	3.93	3.72	3.65	3.35	26
BAKERY PRODUCTS	1.66	2.51	1.30	1.34	3.43	1.38	1.58	1.42	1.31	1.35	27
SUGAR	-.01	-.85	-.36	.36	-1.50	.26	-.21	.09	.29	.43	28
CONFECTIONERY PRODUCTS	3.08	4.66	3.00	1.90	5.30	2.96	4.03	3.47	3.09	2.45	29
ALCOHOLIC BEVERAGES	2.62	3.12	2.92	1.92	2.60	2.84	3.64	3.21	2.92	2.47	30
SOFT DRINKS AND FLAVORINGS	3.41	4.27	3.50	2.62	6.31	2.93	4.26	3.84	3.55	2.71	31
FATS AND OILS	3.32	4.91	2.86	2.51	6.31	2.93	4.26	3.14	2.88	2.71	32
MISC FOOD PRODUCTS	1.81	1.38	1.89	2.08	1.15	1.69	1.61	1.77	1.88	2.01	33
TOBACCO PRODUCTS	.87	.65	.83	1.08	-.75	.85	.54	.69	.78	1.01	34
BROAD AND NARROW FABRICS	2.88	4.59	2.50	1.90	5.72	2.57	3.46	2.87	2.48	2.26	35
FLOOR COVERINGS	3.82	5.22	3.70	2.83	5.67	3.70	4.78	4.05	3.57	3.35	36
KNITTING	3.75	4.97	3.72	2.79	5.42	3.67	4.52	4.03	3.70	3.30	38
APPAREL	3.27	5.47	2.95	1.84	6.63	2.95	4.31	3.48	2.93	2.41	39
HOUSEHOLD TEXTILES	3.63	4.61	3.81	2.67	4.47	3.73	4.74	4.24	3.91	3.22	40
HOUSEHOLD FURNITURE	3.20	4.97	2.78	2.20	6.12	2.84	3.82	3.12	2.65	2.56	45
PAPER PRODUCTS, NEC	2.27	5.60	3.64	3.35	7.07	3.67	4.52	3.85	3.66	3.50	49
NEWSPAPERS	2.27	4.56	2.33	1.57	6.06	3.07	3.07	2.59	2.27	2.02	52
PERIODICALS	3.49	4.44	3.50	2.72	6.06	3.47	4.22	3.80	3.51	3.14	53
DRUGS	3.49	5.72	4.47	3.17	5.88	4.39	5.57	4.98	4.58	3.40	66
CLEANING + TOILET PROD.	4.28	6.53	3.49	3.11	2.71	3.95	5.35	4.52	3.97	3.37	67
PETROLEUM REFINING	3.10	3.18	3.49	2.82	2.14	3.44	4.22	3.85	3.61	3.04	69
FUEL OIL	2.90	4.05	2.68	2.64	1.10	2.60	2.99	2.76	2.60	2.45	70
TIRES AND INNER TUBES	2.84	2.59	2.66	2.20	1.53	3.28	3.98	3.61	2.80	2.96	72
FOOTWEAR(EXC. RUBBER)	2.27	2.91	1.84	1.37	-.89	1.85	2.29	2.01	1.83	1.69	76
OTHER LEATHER PRODUCTS	4.22	3.91	3.61	3.37	6.24	3.72	5.27	4.36	3.75	3.08	77
HOUSEHOLD APPLIANCES	3.83	6.91	3.67	2.59	8.54	3.63	4.75	4.09	3.65	3.17	123
RADIO AND TV RECEIVING	4.91	5.58	4.37	3.47	6.40	4.44	5.79	4.96	4.41	3.91	125
MOTOR VEHICLES	4.91	7.37	2.94	3.00	8.96	3.60	4.20	3.86	3.63	3.46	133
TRAILER COACHES	2.71	3.36	2.88	2.96	2.52	3.19	2.35	2.92	3.31	2.30	140
JEWELRY AND SILVERWARE	2.98	-.86	4.27	1.51	-.63	2.82	4.16	3.35	2.80	3.95	147
TOYS,SPORT,MUSICAL INSTR.	4.90	4.95	4.27	3.66	5.73	4.35	5.37	4.76	4.35	-2.06	148
BUSSES AND LOCAL TRANSIT	-1.77	7.24	-1.37	-2.95	9.11	-1.54	-.69	-1.02	-1.24	3.69	152
AIRLINES	4.35	-.79	4.15	3.45	-.89	4.23	5.17	4.76	4.49	3.66	155
TELEPHONE AND TELEGRAPH	3.98	5.70	4.08	3.04	6.24	4.00	4.89	4.45	4.16	3.56	158
ELECTRIC UTILITIES	3.77	5.02	3.87	3.37	5.14	3.84	4.20	4.06	3.97	2.45	160
NATURAL GAS	1.81	4.14	1.93	2.83	4.09	1.58	.85	1.08	1.88	2.08	161
WATER AND SEWER SERVICES	1.49	.32	1.55	2.37	-.16	1.28	.89	1.08	1.43	2.99	162
WHOLESALE TRADE	3.33	4.22	3.20	2.65	4.08	3.38	3.56	3.55	3.30	3.00	163
RETAIL TRADE	3.32	6.94	3.66	2.64	4.50	3.68	3.94	4.29	3.70	3.10	164
BANKS,CREDIT AGEN.,BROKERS	3.73	3.72	3.79	2.70	5.33	3.27	4.51	4.08	3.75	3.28	165
INSURANCE	3.40	5.31	3.35	3.20	3.89	3.52	5.17	3.44	3.36	3.32	166
OWNER-OCCUPIED DWELLINGS	3.61	6.49	3.62	2.90	5.78	3.38	5.84	4.08	3.58	2.95	167
REAL ESTATE	4.47	3.76	4.44	1.84	7.14	4.33	4.84	5.00	4.44	3.67	168
HOTEL AND LODGING PLACES	2.80	4.15	2.99	2.09	4.18	2.75	3.33	2.93	2.67	2.56	169
PERSONAL + REPAIR SERVICES	2.53	1.94	2.09	1.67	5.97	2.06	2.32	2.17	2.07	1.95	170
BUSINESS SERVICES	2.16	1.28	2.39	2.11	1.63	2.32	2.25	2.32	2.36	2.32	171
AUTO REPAIR	.56	1.94	.55	.00	1.56	.54	1.00	.71	.51	.38	173
MOVIES + AMUSEMENTS	3.25	4.17	3.22	2.55	4.53	3.18	3.80	3.44	3.20	2.92	174
MEDICAL SERVICES	3.75	6.27	3.31	2.16	7.99	3.31	4.55	3.86	3.40	2.92	175
PRIVATE SCHOOLS + NPO	3.62	5.98	3.03	2.33	8.01	3.06	3.94	3.40	3.04	2.72	176
POST OFFICE											177

NOVEMBER 1973 FORECAST

MERCHANDISE EXPORTS IN PRODUCER PRICES

MILLIONS OF 1971$

		1971	1972	1973	1974	1975	1976	1978	1980	1983	1985	
4	COTTON	487.	405.	408.	426.	433.	447.	462.	476.	496.	506.	4
5	GRAINS	2797.	3091.	2749.	2918.	3143.	3357.	3609.	3784.	4055.	4235.	5
7	FRUIT,VEGETABLES,OTH CROPS	367.	351.	380.	399.	402.	420.	440.	458.	485.	500.	7
11	IRON ORES	114.	135.	183.	203.	200.	357.	214.	220.	231.	235.	11
14	COAL MINING	565.	325.	320.	347.	347.	357.	380.	402.	436.	455.	14
	OTHER ORDNANCE	274.	421.	310.	323.	339.	353.	365.	365.	363.	361.	
23	MEAT PRODUCTS	358.	327.	446.	477.	561.	559.	612.	646.	691.	735.	23
25	CANNED AND FROZEN FOODS	305.	327.	341.	357.	376.	393.	413.	424.	449.	453.	25
26	GRAIN MILL PRODUCTS	456.	617.	622.	653.	676.	703.	745.	787.	849.	889.	26
32	FATS AND OILS	957.	991.	1025.	1081.	1118.	1164.	1242.	1322.	1444.	1522.	32
34	TOBACCO PRODUCTS	627.	668.	739.	723.	728.	737.	743.	736.	728.	723.	34
35	BROAD AND NARROW FABRICS	301.	305.	310.	322.	336.	346.	348.	338.	323.	313.	35
41	LUMBER AND WOOD PRODUCTS	446.	337.	659.	874.	711.	769.	913.	952.	1051.	1079.	41
47	PULP MILLS	328.	332.	343.	378.	403.	435.	485.	526.	578.	607.	47
48	PAPER AND PAPERBOARD MILLS	469.	415.	507.	605.	691.	795.	919.	980.	1050.	1079.	48
53	PERIODICALS	76.	81.	98.	104.	111.	119.	128.	131.	134.	133.	53
55	INDUSTRIAL CHEMICALS	1509.	1479.	1687.	1972.	2127.	2336.	2651.	2915.	3289.	3498.	55
61	MISC CHEMICAL PRODUCTS	393.	399.	403.	408.	409.	411.	415.	419.	424.	427.	61
62	PLASTIC MAT'LS. + RESINS	552.	607.	708.	838.	946.	1071.	1261.	1397.	1591.	1697.	62
66	DRUGS	442.	449.	472.	502.	524.	551.	594.	644.	713.	753.	66
69	PETROLEUM REFINING	379.	430.	439.	456.	470.	483.	501.	515.	537.	549.	69
78	GLASS	163.	175.	199.	218.	234.	258.	292.	320.	363.	389.	78
83	STEEL	763.	743.	837.	961.	968.	990.	1022.	1022.	1039.	1058.	83
84	COPPER	204.	294.	290.	291.	298.	290.	244.	226.	207.	203.	84
87	ALUMINUM	178.	247.	251.	321.	342.	367.	408.	445.	507.	553.	87
88	OTH PRIM NON-FER METALS	75.	120.	116.	133.	140.	149.	159.	166.	175.	178.	88
95	STRUCTURAL METAL PRODUCTS	252.	308.	322.	366.	371.	384.	407.	421.	444.	457.	95
97	METAL STAMPINGS	339.	354.	397.	429.	450.	483.	527.	565.	617.	644.	97
100	PIPES, VALVES, FITTINGS	248.	219.	247.	317.	336.	357.	388.	413.	465.	494.	100
102	ENGINES AND TURBINES	638.	749.	858.	1032.	1137.	1211.	1327.	1420.	1565.	1648.	102
103	FARM MACHINERY	334.	408.	396.	456.	479.	480.	477.	489.	506.	517.	103
104	CONSTR+MINE+OILFIELD MACH	1713.	1651.	1751.	2015.	2132.	2207.	2312.	2342.	2518.	2638.	104
105	MATERIALS HANDLING MACH.	191.	205.	210.	260.	271.	278.	292.	299.	323.	338.	105
106	MACH. TOOLS, METAL CUTTING	196.	211.	212.	213.	214.	214.	214.	214.	215.	215.	106
108	OTHER METAL WORKING MACH	262.	261.	268.	275.	267.	296.	306.	310.	316.	319.	108
110	SPECIAL INDUSTRIAL MACH	1373.	990.	984.	1214.	1332.	1402.	1452.	1444.	1504.	1520.	110
110	PUMPS+COMPRESSORS+BLOWERS	306.	390.	451.	533.	598.	632.	667.	670.	714.	733.	110
114	COMPUTERS + RELATED MACH.	1209.	934.	1457.	1623.	2109.	2450.	2894.	3114.	3345.	3923.	114
116	SERVICE INDUSTRY MACHINERY	440.	466.	540.	663.	704.	418.	294.	1065.	1266.	1594.	116
118	ELECTRICAL MEASURING INSTR	213.	215.	255.	350.	369.	401.	415.	463.	491.	515.	118
120	MOTORS AND GENERATORS	190.	180.	218.	280.	322.	362.	425.	471.	562.	623.	120
123	HOUSEHOLD APPLIANCES	151.	160.	167.	171.	171.	176.	181.	186.	194.	199.	123
124	ELEC LIGHTING + WIRING EQ.	192.	184.	224.	275.	288.	321.	364.	384.	409.	419.	124
127	COMMUNICATION EQUIPMENT	561.	581.	690.	801.	876.	939.	1056.	1165.	1328.	1433.	127
128	ELECTRONIC COMPONENTS	740.	747.	870.	990.	1115.	1236.	1413.	1541.	1738.	1866.	128
133	MOTOR VEHICLES	3508.	3360.	3618.	3794.	3969.	4289.	4734.	5134.	5704.	6035.	133
134	AIRCRAFT	2476.	1141.	889.	1366.	1602.	1695.	1849.	2003.	2249.	2387.	134
135	AIRCRAFT ENGINES	419.	288.	290.	296.	299.	301.	310.	320.	334.	342.	135
136	AIRCRAFT EQUIPMENT, NEC	911.	442.	383.	430.	457.	467.	488.	505.	529.	541.	136
137	SHIP AND BOAT BUILDING	51.	60.	58.	56.	54.	52.	48.	45.	40.	37.	137
142	MECH. MEASURING DEVICES	374.	262.	243.	302.	324.	342.	363.	375.	401.	411.	142
144	MUSICAL+SURGICAL INSTR.	185.	165.	223.	273.	329.	386.	443.	479.	513.	520.	144
145	PHOTOGRAPHIC EQUIPMENT	445.	593.	595.	640.	929.	1044.	1253.	1895.	1596.	1716.	145
154	WATER TRANSPORTATION	2246.	2232.	2416.	2540.	2529.	2644.	2787.	2942.	3176.	3325.	154
155	AIRLINES	1317.	1490.	1616.	1740.	1849.	1950.	2091.	2193.	2233.	2416.	155
163	WHOLESALE TRADE	2782.	0.	0.	0.	0.	0.	0.	0.	0.	0.	163

NOVEMBER 1973 FORECAST

	MERCHANDISE EXPORTS IN PRODUCER PRICES						ANNUAL GROWTH RATES				
	71-85	71-75	75-80	80-85	71-73	73-83	73-75	73-78	75-78	78-83	
4 COTTON	.29	-2.92	1.91	1.22	-8.85	1.96	3.01	2.52	2.19	1.40	4
5 GRAINS	2.96	2.91	3.71	2.26	-.87	3.69	6.70	5.45	4.62	2.33	5
7 FRUIT VEGETABLES,OTH CROPS	2.20	2.26	2.61	1.75	1.66	2.44	2.86	2.96	3.02	1.93	7
11 IRON ORES	5.17	14.06	1.92	1.32	23.83	2.29	4.29	3.10	2.32	1.48	11
14 COAL MINING	-1.55	-12.22	2.48	2.48	-28.50	3.10	4.06	3.48	3.09	2.73	14
22 OTHER ORDNANCE	1.97	5.35	1.48	-.23	6.13	1.60	4.06	3.30	2.46	-.10	22
23 MEAT PRODUCTS	5.13	9.38	4.28	2.59	10.85	4.51	7.91	6.37	5.35	2.64	23
25 CANNED AND FROZEN FOODS	2.82	5.24	2.38	1.31	5.61	1.60	4.57	3.78	3.06	1.35	25
26 GRAIN MILL PRODUCTS	4.76	9.85	3.02	2.44	15.49	2.57	4.87	3.60	3.20	2.62	26
32 FATS AND OILS	3.32	3.90	3.35	2.82	3.46	3.11	4.21	3.83	3.49	3.42	32
34 TOBACCO PRODUCTS	1.02	3.75	.20	-.34	8.22	-.15	4.33	3.12	.68	-.42	34
35 BROAD AND NARROW FABRICS	6.31	11.68	5.83	2.49	19.49	4.67	3.86	6.54	6.14	-1.47	35
41 LUMBER AND WOOD PRODUCTS	4.40	5.17	5.31	1.92	2.28	5.20	8.05	6.90	6.14	2.81	41
47 PULP MILLS	5.95	9.68	6.99	1.92	3.89	5.37	15.46	11.88	9.50	3.51	47
48 PAPER AND PAPERBOARD MILLS	4.02	9.47	3.40	.28	12.61	3.15	6.33	5.37	4.74	2.68	48
53 PERIODICALS	6.00	8.58	6.30	3.64	5.57	6.68	11.59	9.04	7.34	.93	53
55 INDUSTRIAL CHEMICALS	.59	.95	.61	.39	1.19	.52	.09	.61	1.70	4.32	55
61 MISC CHEMICAL PRODUCTS	8.02	13.46	7.80	3.89	12.40	8.10	14.51	11.56	9.59	.42	61
62 PLASTIC MAT'LS. + RESINS	3.81	4.27	4.12	3.13	3.32	4.12	5.22	4.58	4.16	4.64	62
66 DRUGS	2.65	5.39	1.85	1.27	7.39	2.00	3.38	2.63	2.13	3.65	66
69 PETROLEUM REFINING	6.23	9.06	6.28	3.90	7.99	6.43	10.14	8.46	7.34	1.37	69
78 GLASS	2.18	5.86	1.09	-.31	4.47	2.16	7.25	3.92	1.70	4.39	78
83 STEEL	.36	4.43	-1.06	-1.48	8.77	-.95	.09	-.78	-.78	-.39	83
84 COPPER	7.97	16.37	5.24	3.98	17.25	7.02	15.49	9.69	5.82	-1.47	84
87 ALUMINUM	6.13	15.52	3.37	1.39	21.58	4.10	9.46	6.32	4.23	4.35	87
88 OTH PRIM NON-FER METALS	4.27	9.72	2.49	1.68	12.34	3.22	7.10	4.68	3.07	1.89	88
95 STRUCTURAL METAL PRODUCTS	4.59	7.10	4.56	2.61	8.42	4.22	6.31	4.61	3.30	1.75	95
97 METAL STAMPINGS	6.78	7.54	4.12	3.90	7.88	6.32	15.39	8.73	5.30	3.13	97
100 PIPES, VALVES, FITTINGS	3.12	14.93	.45	2.11	14.79	6.01	14.08	9.03	4.79	3.61	100
102 ENGINES AND TURBINES	3.09	6.97	1.88	1.11	8.52	2.44	9.41	8.73	5.17	3.30	102
103 FARM MACHINERY	4.07	5.47	1.95	2.38	1.10	3.63	9.83	3.70	-.10	1.17	103
104 CONSTR,MINE,OILFIELD MACH	1.42	8.60	.04	2.42	7.09	3.86	10.51	5.55	2.70	1.71	104
105 MATERIAL HANDLING MACH.	2.73	2.18	1.52	.10	3.95	.14	.42	5.84	2.39	2.08	105
106 MACH.TOOLS,METAL CUTTING	4.74	2.35	1.61	.58	1.13	1.65	3.56	.22	.09	.05	106
108 OTHER METAL WORKING MACH	7.43	6.25	2.29	1.03	-2.61	4.24	15.11	2.69	2.12	.61	108
109 SPECIAL INDUSTRIAL MACH	8.23	11.48	1.79	1.79	5.77	5.77	19.93	7.77	2.88	.70	109
110 PUMPS,COMPRESSORS+BLOWERS	6.25	13.92	7.79	1.89	9.33	8.31	18.50	10.16	3.65	1.37	110
114 COMPUTERS + RELATED MACH.	8.48	15.08	7.30	5.39	10.19	8.52	15.69	13.73	10.54	2.90	114
116 SERVICE INDUSTRY MACHINERY	1.94	13.17	2.62	2.80	9.08	6.54	21.08	11.45	4.62	5.59	116
118 ELECTRICAL MEASURING INSTR	5.55	3.12	7.59	5.61	6.76	9.48	19.58	9.75	2.20	5.34	118
120 MOTORS AND GENERATORS	6.69	10.13	1.68	1.26	4.92	1.52	1.33	13.79	9.27	1.44	120
123 HOUSEHOLD APPLIANCES	6.61	11.11	5.71	1.74	10.63	6.03	12.62	1.60	1.78	2.33	123
124 ELEC LIGHTING + WIRING EQ.	3.86	9.21	6.46	4.14	8.15	.54	11.92	8.50	7.80	4.59	124
127 COMMUNICATION EQUIPMENT	-.26	-10.88	5.05	3.84	-1.55	6.91	12.39	9.69	6.23	4.13	127
128 ELECTRONIC COMPONENTS	-1.44	-8.42	4.46	3.23	-51.19	9.28	4.88	5.37	5.70	3.73	128
133 MOTOR VEHICLES	-3.73	-17.22	1.34	3.51	-18.44	1.41	29.43	14.64	4.78	3.92	133
134 AIRCRAFT ENGINES	-2.24	1.23	1.97	1.36	4.34	3.23	1.60	1.38	1.23	1.45	134
135 AIRCRAFT EQUIPMENT, NEC	.67	-3.58	-3.63	1.37	6.08	-3.63	8.90	4.84	2.13	1.62	135
136 SHIP AND BOAT BUILDING	7.38	14.37	2.93	1.80	-21.64	5.03	-3.63	-3.63	-3.63	1.99	136
137 MECH. MEASURING DEVICES	10.10	20.02	7.51	1.67	9.36	8.33	14.48	8.06	3.79	2.96	137
142 MEDICAL + SURGICAL INSTR.	2.80	3.46	8.04	4.23	22.79	8.88	19.39	13.70	9.91	4.88	142
144 PHOTOGRAPHIC EQUIPMENT	4.33	8.46	3.46	2.45	22.79	2.73	17.25	12.87	9.96	2.61	144
145 WATER TRANSPORTATION	10.10	14.37	3.42	1.93	10.22	3.68	6.74	5.16	2.58	2.19	145
154 AIRLINES	.00	.00	.00	.00	.00	.00	.00	.00	.00	.00	154
155 AIRLINES	.00	.00	.00	.00	.00	.00	.00	.00	.00	.00	155
163 WHOLESALE TRADE	.00	.00	.00	.00	.00	.00	.00	.00	.00	.00	163

NOVEMBER 1973 FORECAST

COMPETITIVE IMPORTS IN DOMESTIC PORT PRICES   MILLIONS OF 1971$

	1971	1972	1973	1974	1975	1976	1978	1980	1983	1985	
3 MEAT ANIMALS, OTH LIVESTK	-294	-442	-431	-420	-407	-396	-379	-366	-348	-336	3
7 FRUIT,VEGETABLES,OTH CROPS	-630	-676	-716	-712	-745	-761	-809	-865	-944	-992	7
8 FORESTRY + FISHERY PROD.	-819	-847	-901	-883	-904	-916	-964	-1023	-1104	-1155	8
11 IRON ORES	-576	-798	-844	-805	-811	-820	-834	-865	-891	-902	11
13 OTHER NON-FERROUS ORES	-176	-184	-187	-189	-193	-195	-199	-204	-209	-211	13
15 CRUDE PETROLEUM, NAT. GAS	-2555	-2270	-2386	-2456	-2529	-2613	-2772	-2962	-3235	-3408	15
16 STONE AND CLAY MINING	-69	-75	-83	-80	-83	-85	-90	-94	-100	-103	16
17 CHEMICAL FERTILIZER MINING	-258	-271	-304	-316	-339	-356	-390	-434	-491	-527	17
23 MEAT PRODUCTS	-1290	-1224	-1257	-1273	-1225	-1276	-1338	-1436	-1582	-1678	23
25 CANNED AND FROZEN FOODS	-505	-498	-525	-537	-544	-551	-591	-644	-728	-784	25
28 SUGAR	-864	-860	-864	-870	-860	-890	-911	-938	-970	-989	28
30 ALCOHOLIC BEVERAGES	-965	-966	-1004	-997	-963	-958	-986	-1039	-1088	-1104	30
32 FATS AND OILS	-226	-291	-313	-326	-343	-356	-387	-417	-462	-491	32
35 BROAD AND NARROW FABRICS	-798	-923	-1041	-1041	-1092	-1084	-1157	-1225	-1293	-1330	35
37 MISC TEXTILES	-404	-464	-481	-478	-474	-471	-487	-517	-559	-587	37
39 APPAREL	-1916	-1339	-1614	-1582	-1514	-1422	-1538	-1778	-2119	-2353	39
41 LUMBER AND WOOD PRODUCTS	-947	-875	-929	-867	-894	-925	-962	-1037	-1138	-1202	41
42 VENEER AND PLYWOOD	-401	-434	-468	-411	-438	-460	-476	-523	-579	-612	42
43 MILLWORK AND WOOD PRODUCTS	-193	-251	-272	-244	-267	-289	-311	-353	-413	-453	43
45 HOUSEHOLD FURNITURE	-539	-560	-297	-279	-287	-276	-324	-407	-546	-658	45
47 PULP MILLS	-502	-502	-562	-562	-566	-598	-636	-673	-721	-749	47
48 PAPER AND PAPERBOARD MILLS	-1123	-1181	-1249	-1120	-1232	-1236	-1277	-1335	-1408	-1452	48
53 PERIODICALS	-33	-21	-22	-23	-23	-26	-26	-32	-41	-48	53
55 INDUSTRIAL CHEMICALS	-799	-713	-787	-804	-823	-842	-830	-956	-1250	-1383	55
69 PETROLEUM REFINING	-588	-536	-606	-647	-692	-737	-830	-956	-1021	-1094	69
73 RUBBER PRODUCTS	-304	-263	-262	-235	-200	-178	-171	-182	-188	-226	73
74 MISC PLASTIC PRODUCTS	-276	-332	-403	-444	-506	-547	-640	-822	-1025	-1160	74
76 FOOTWEAR(EXC. RUBBER)	-604	-543	-568	-568	-550	-561	-685	-808	-1118	-1363	76
77 OTHER LEATHER PRODUCTS	-217	-278	-316	-336	-343	-353	-398	-466	-579	-663	77
78 GLASS	-265	-292	-317	-317	-324	-325	-346	-375	-413	-436	78
80 POTTERY	-198	-223	-239	-222	-217	-216	-224	-247	-276	-295	80
83 STEEL	-3190	-2926	-2975	-2923	-2898	-2910	-3032	-3373	-3655	-4180	83
84 COPPER	-449	-331	-405	-673	-672	-680	-718	-774	-868	-936	84
87 ALUMINUM	-346	-405	-423	-423	-447	-468	-505	-548	-605	-640	87
88 OTH PRIM NON-FER METALS	-239	-663	-736	-753	-781	-797	-841	-894	-961	-1001	88
98 CUTLERY,HAND TOOLS,HARDWR	-366	-652	-663	-568	-530	-520	-300	-352	-438	-503	98
103 FARM MACHINERY	-109	-148	-132	-137	-120	-116	-125	-155	-209	-252	103
106 MACH. TOOLS, METAL CUTTING	-736	-656	-769	-753	-701	-664	-672	-735	-838	-903	106
109 SPECIAL INDUSTRIAL MACH	-629	-353	-365	-446	-433	-421	-436	-463	-499	-527	109
114 COMPUTERS + RELATED MACH.	-112	-342	-401	-395	-191	-196	-197	-222	-267	-299	114
115 OTHER OFFICE MACHINERY	-387	-352	-198	-220	-221	-225	-247	-282	-312	-328	115
123 HOUSEHOLD APPLIANCES	-252	-266	-308	-374	-388	-382	-406	-411	-466	-481	123
124 ELEC LIGHTING + WIRING EQ.	-393	-299	-308	-289	-296	-286	-290	-308	-323	-330	124
125 RADIO AND TV RECEIVING	-1593	-1179	-1339	-1409	-1537	-1583	-1796	-1992	-2256	-2427	125
127 COMMUNICATION EQUIPMENT	-403	-332	-368	-387	-417	-437	-491	-545	-610	-650	127
128 ELECTRONIC COMPONENTS	-8535	-9318	-9372	-9375	-9185	-9103	-9721	-10884	-12641	-13858	128
135 MOTOR VEHICLES	-285	-100	-132	-137	-120	-116	-125	-155	-209	-252	133
136 AIRCRAFT EQUIPMENT, NEC	-928	-795	-795	-753	-701	-664	-672	-735	-838	-903	136
139 CYCLES + TRANS EQUIP NEC	-185	-136	-196	-221	-241	-251	-267	-293	-323	-342	139
143 OPTICAL + OPHTHALMIC GOODS	-290	-237	-221	-236	-241	-238	-257	-282	-312	-700	143
145 PHOTOGRAPHIC EQUIPMENT	-229	-184	-365	-365	-399	-424	-482	-548	-641	-328	145
146 WATCHES AND CLOCKS	-237	-205	-193	-193	-241	-238	-257	-282	-312	-191	146
147 JEWELRY AND SILVERWARE	-732	-743	-825	-837	-447	-793	-1131	-1147	-1334	-1549	147
148 TOYS,SPORT,MUSICAL INSTR.	-2472	-2195	-2330	-2439	-2505	-2577	-2731	-2901	-3157	-3319	148
154 WATER TRANSPORTATION	-1694	-1831	-1999	-2085	-2146	-2220	-2418	-2669	-3052	-3302	154
155 AIRLINES											155

NOVEMBER 1973 FORECAST

COMPETITIVE IMPORTS IN DOMESTIC PORT PRICES

ANNUAL GROWTH RATES

	71-85	71-75	75-80	80-85	71-73	73-83	73-75	73-78	75-78	78-83	
3 MEAT ANIMALS, OTH LIVESTK	.97	8.13	-2.09	-1.72	19.18	-2.14	-2.91	-2.57	-2.34	-1.71	3
7 FRUIT,VEGETABLES,OTH CROPS	3.25	4.18	3.00	2.74	6.39	2.76	1.98	2.45	2.74	3.08	7
8 FORESTRY + FISHERY PROD.	2.46	2.46	2.48	2.42	4.77	2.04	.16	1.35	2.76	2.42	8
11 IRON ORES	3.20	8.56	1.28	.84	19.08	1.10	-1.95	1.23	.92	1.33	11
13 OTHER NON-FERROUS ORES	1.57	3.29	1.14	.63	5.01	1.10	1.57	1.29	.10	.92	13
15 CRUDE PETROLEUM, NAT. GAS	2.06	-.25	3.16	2.81	-3.43	3.04	2.92	3.00	3.05	3.09	15
16 STONE AND CLAY MINING	2.89	4.81	2.46	1.80	9.11	1.91	.51	1.63	2.37	2.19	16
17 CHEMICAL FERTILIZER MINING	5.10	6.81	4.93	3.91	8.09	4.81	5.52	5.18	4.96	4.44	17
23 MEAT PRODUCTS	1.88	.47	2.52	1.91	-1.28	2.30	.35	1.24	1.84	3.36	23
25 CANNED AND FROZEN FOODS	3.15	1.89	3.38	3.91	1.98	3.27	1.81	2.37	2.74	4.16	25
28 SUGAR	.96	.47	1.26	1.06	-.01	1.16	.94	1.11	1.23	1.21	28
30 ALCOHOLIC BEVERAGES	.96	.46	1.12	1.20	1.96	.61	-1.05	-.35	-.11	1.96	30
32 FATS AND OILS	5.55	10.48	3.90	3.26	16.37	3.69	-.39	4.20	3.94	3.58	32
35 BROAD AND NARROW FABRICS	3.64	7.83	2.30	1.64	13.26	2.17	2.40	2.12	1.94	2.22	35
37 MISC TEXTILES	2.67	3.99	1.73	2.55	8.68	1.51	-.70	.26	.90	2.76	37
39 APPAREL	1.47	-5.90	3.22	5.60	-8.58	2.72	-3.21	-.96	.53	6.40	39
41 LUMBER AND WOOD PRODUCTS	1.70	-1.43	2.97	2.95	-.92	2.02	-1.94	-.39	.44	3.36	41
42 VENEER AND PLYWOOD	3.02	2.25	5.51	3.15	-7.78	2.12	-3.28	.52	2.71	3.93	42
43 MILLWORK AND WOOD PRODUCTS	6.11	8.18	5.59	4.97	7.78	6.08	-1.77	2.70	5.09	5.66	43
45 HOUSEHOLD FURNITURE	7.25	4.59	7.03	2.14	3.94	2.72	3.19	2.91	1.22	10.41	45
47 PULP MILLS	2.78	3.56	2.83	1.61	-3.48	1.43	-2.51	.92	2.73	2.53	47
48 PAPER AND PAPERBOARD MILLS	1.84	2.80	1.61	1.69	8.15	6.13	-9.51	3.23	5.17	1.95	48
53 PERIODICALS	3.92	-2.51	7.04	5.39	-19.33	4.62	.76	3.34	4.05	9.04	53
55 INDUSTRIAL CHEMICALS	4.43	4.08	4.98	3.86	1.46	5.22	4.08	5.97	5.49	5.91	55
69 PETROLEUM REFINING	-2.11	-10.48	5.29	3.74	-1.46	-2.18	-10.48	-8.50	-5.17	4.48	69
73 RUBBER PRODUCTS	10.26	15.17	9.69	6.89	18.99	9.33	11.35	10.59	10.08	8.07	73
74 MISC PLASTIC PRODUCTS	5.81	-2.37	7.69	10.47	-4.31	6.78	-1.61	2.38	5.04	17.48	74
76 FOOTWEAR(EXC. RUBBER)	7.98	11.43	6.14	7.06	18.75	2.07	4.11	4.85	5.01	3.54	76
77 OTHER LEATHER PRODUCTS	3.57	5.04	2.96	3.01	9.01	2.65	-1.27	1.77	2.22	4.19	77
78 GLASS	2.85	2.33	2.52	3.61	9.37	1.46	-1.27	-.38	1.50	4.81	78
80 POTTERY	1.93	-2.40	3.04	3.48	-3.48	2.59	-1.32	.92	2.20	3.79	80
83 STEEL	5.24	6.38	4.07	3.10	9.78	4.02	.67	1.59	2.03	3.62	83
84 COPPER	4.39	9.27	2.72	2.26	7.78	2.66	4.99	4.41	4.03	2.68	84
67 ALUMINUM	4.43	1.04	4.09	2.64	15.64	2.66	2.91	2.64	2.47	7.58	87
88 OTH PRIM NON-FER METALS	2.61	4.22	1.34	2.59	6.72	3.30	-4.63	-.99	1.44	2.71	88
98 CUTLERY,HAND TOOLS,HARDWR	7.24	14.16	2.94	6.01	7.81	3.42	.41	.70	.23	6.13	98
103 FARM MACHINERY	2.55	-.64	3.45	4.21	2.59	3.57	7.90	4.29	.89	4.86	103
106 SPECIAL METAL CUTTING	-.42	-10.00	4.49	2.34	27.90	3.49	2.49	3.49	1.88	3.49	106
109 SPECIAL INDUSTRIAL MACH.	10.58	16.87	6.85	9.28	6.01	7.36	5.34	4.49	4.16	10.23	109
114 COMPUTERS + RELATED MACH.	1.55	.01	2.41	1.93	22.49	1.90	-.09	.98	3.92	2.81	114
115 OTHER OFFICE MACHINERY	5.18	2.76	5.23	5.07	-28.39	3.92	-6.48	5.87	1.57	7.85	115
123 HOUSEHOLD APPLIANCES	3.01	-7.13	5.19	3.95	-.08	5.31	-5.88	-2.74	-2.20	4.56	123
124 ELEC LIGHTING + WIRING EQ.	-1.25	-.87	.80	1.40	10.00	5.30	-5.86	-1.66	5.45	2.15	124
125 RADIO AND TV RECEIVING	3.42	1.84	5.36	3.82	-8.69	5.04	6.17	5.74	5.45	4.34	125
127 COMMUNICATION EQUIPMENT	3.46	-21.69	5.39	9.72	-8.40	2.99	-1.00	-.73	1.89	5.25	127
128 ELECTRONIC COMPONENTS	-.20	-7.02	.94	4.13	4.67	4.58	-4.90	-1.07	1.48	10.24	128
133 MOTOR VEHICLES	4.40	-7.02	3.85	3.13	-38.47	.53	-6.28	-3.35	-1.39	4.41	133
136 AIRCRAFT EQUIPMENT, NEC	5.90	6.68	6.35	3.01	-7.77	4.99	8.49	7.17	3.36	3.82	136
139 CYCLES, TRANS EQUIP, NEC	2.56	1.20	5.21	3.01	2.98	6.44	3.74	2.78	6.29	5.70	139
143 OPTICAL,OPHTHALMIC GOODS	-1.53	-11.86	.02	5.19	4.66	-1.06	-13.39	-7.68	2.14	3.95	143
145 PHOTOGRAPHIC EQUIPMENT	5.35	2.61	5.15	5.73	-1.34	3.04	-1.73	1.30	-4.88	8.30	145
146 WATCHES AND CLOCKS	2.10	.33	2.94	2.69	10.34	3.62	3.62	3.14	2.66	2.89	146
147 JEWELRY AND SILVERWARE	4.77	5.92	4.36	4.26	5.96	3.04	3.80	3.90	2.89	4.65	147
148 TOYS,SPORT,MUSICAL INSTR.	2.56	5.92	5.15	5.73	-2.97	-1.06	2.61	1.30	-3.88	8.30	148
154 WATER TRANSPORTATION	2.10	.33	2.94	2.69	8.04	3.04	.33	3.14	2.20	2.89	154
155 AIRLINES	4.77	5.92	4.36	4.26	8.04	4.28	3.80	3.90	3.98	4.65	155

NOVEMBER 1973 FORECAST

PRODUCERS' DURABLE EQUIPMENT INVESTMENT   MILLIONS OF 1971$

#	Industry	1971	1972	1973	1974	1975	1976	1978	1980	1983	1985
1	AGRICULTURE	5368.	4839.	5464.	6315.	6332.	6285.	6385.	6506.	6673.	6853.
2	MINING	1473.	1548.	1985.	2055.	2061.	2196.	2274.	2380.	2523.	2620.
3	PETROLEUM AND GAS	9925.	1001.	1195.	1277.	1299.	1426.	1449.	1593.	1756.	1847.
4	CONSTRUCTION(NEW AND OLD)	2530.	3174.	3638.	3896.	4179.	4407.	4376.	4707.	5069.	5282.
5	ORDNANCE	96.	169.	131.	105.	89.	85.	75.	66.	53.	44.
6	MEAT	182.	167.	192.	194.	206.	212.	225.	240.	257.	269.
7	DAIRY	165.	214.	236.	242.	250.	259.	270.	282.	297.	307.
8	CANNED AND FROZEN FOODS	228.	229.	250.	256.	282.	301.	279.	299.	317.	337.
9	GRAIN MILL PRODUCTS	193.	176.	182.	181.	194.	210.	230.	242.	259.	269.
10	BAKERY	147.	140.	195.	206.	205.	207.	211.	222.	244.	259.
11	SUGAR	59.	71.	100.	101.	93.	87.	101.	109.	119.	126.
12	CANDY	66.	66.	77.	82.	63.	85.	84.	86.	90.	90.
13	BEVERAGES	327.	331.	395.	416.	424.	434.	459.	484.	499.	508.
14	MISC. FOOD PRODUCTS	254.	198.	230.	240.	249.	255.	267.	286.	310.	327.
15	TOBACCO	45.	59.	78.	83.	84.	82.	77.	88.	98.	107.
16	FABRICS AND YARNS	372.	486.	585.	567.	577.	557.	569.	578.	569.	570.
17	FLOOR COVERINGS	42.	69.	73.	72.	87.	79.	85.	90.	95.	100.
18	MISC. TEXTILES	58.	79.	78.	81.	87.	92.	95.	97.	96.	98.
19	KNIT FABRIC AND APPAREL	226.	173.	178.	216.	243.	255.	235.	258.	270.	283.
20	APPAREL	172.	182.	204.	205.	220.	225.	240.	238.	240.	241.
21	HSHLD TEXTILES + UPHOLST.	85.	113.	119.	194.	130.	143.	162.	165.	181.	189.
22	LOGGING AND LUMBER	341.	366.	494.	464.	414.	447.	457.	479.	502.	505.
23	PLYWOOD, MILLWORK, ETC.	229.	223.	290.	304.	347.	357.	349.	400.	453.	474.
24	WOODEN CONTAINERS	5.	9.	12.	12.	12.	13.	12.	11.	11.	12.
25	FURNITURE	124.	136.	169.	204.	208.	199.	202.	211.	216.	220.
26	PAPER+PROD. EX.CONTAINERS	871.	952.	1319.	1428.	1539.	1656.	1719.	1818.	1923.	2324.
27	PAPER CONTAINERS	142.	203.	254.	287.	298.	295.	295.	319.	342.	357.
28	NEWSPAPERS	186.	147.	224.	254.	261.	252.	271.	292.	311.	323.
29	PRINTING AND PUBLISHING	487.	466.	558.	585.	628.	677.	707.	739.	783.	815.
30	INDUSTRIAL CHEMICALS	1100.	1364.	1766.	1922.	2045.	2127.	2208.	2338.	2506.	2625.
31	AGRICULTURAL CHEMICALS	117.	131.	131.	144.	162.	167.	160.	178.	196.	210.
32	GLUE, INK, A.D FATTY ACID	111.	141.	129.	146.	150.	144.	146.	150.	154.	155.
33	PLASTICS AND SYNTHETICS	665.	741.	1029.	1248.	1242.	1213.	1336.	1432.	1566.	1645.
34	DRUGS	175.	192.	220.	234.	242.	255.	262.	283.	301.	311.
35	CLEANING AND TOILET ITEMS	140.	147.	143.	148.	162.	184.	184.	199.	214.	224.
36	PAINTS + ALLIED PRODUCTS	44.	58.	55.	60.	68.	75.	75.	73.	75.	78.
37	PETROLEUM REFINING	553.	476.	569.	655.	706.	736.	754.	815.	889.	954.
38	TIRE AND TUBES	87.	257.	279.	281.	333.	341.	369.	405.	440.	468.
39	RUBBER PROD. EX. TIRES	306.	121.	121.	143.	165.	186.	169.	173.	175.	179.
40	PLASTIC PRODUCTS	15.	345.	584.	659.	683.	711.	816.	933.	1094.	1185.
41	LEATHER+IND. LTHR. PROD.	38.	14.	16.	17.	18.	19.	16.	17.	17.	17.
42	FOOTWEAR AND OTHER LEATHER	192.	47.	54.	55.	57.	56.	56.	57.	57.	58.
43	GLASS AND GLASS PRODUCTS	529.	232.	291.	336.	338.	335.	364.	390.	426.	451.
44	STONE AND CLAY PRODUCTS	528.	559.	921.	874.	856.	935.	892.	931.	990.	1026.
45	IRON AND STEEL PRODUCTS	131.	1970.	2190.	2687.	2809.	2852.	2275.	2434.	2582.	2642.
46	NON-FERROUS METALS	36.	157.	895.	914.	964.	1047.	1043.	1008.	1073.	1109.
47	METAL CONTAINERS	180.	34.	39.	173.	181.	184.	198.	212.	227.	236.
48	PLUMBING AND HEATING	194.	227.	259.	270.	251.	292.	248.	46.	45.	46.
49	STRUCTURAL METAL PRODUCTS	267.	353.	342.	378.	412.	425.	385.	299.	322.	334.
50	STAMPINGS	143.	392.	363.	444.	464.	525.	499.	534.	583.	435.
51	HARDWARE,+PLATING+WIRE PRO	77.	153.	234.	264.	257.	268.	274.	290.	330.	349.
52	ENGINE AND TURBINES	185.	83.	105.	123.	123.	124.	123.	106.	114.	116.
53	FARM MACHINERY	141.	185.	255.	311.	348.	398.	343.	356.	415.	442.
54	CONST.+MINE.+MATRL HANDL EQ	97.	175.	365.	427.	406.	419.	392.	382.	441.	481.
55	METALWORKING MACHINERY		149.	149.	186.	108.	204.	204.	174.	185.	196.
56	SPECIAL INDUSTRIAL MACH.										

NOVEMBER 1973 FORECAST

PRODUCERS' DURABLE EQUIPMENT INVESTMENT

MILLIONS OF 1971$

		1971	1972	1973	1974	1975	1976	1978	1980	1983	1985	
58	GENERAL INDUSTRIAL MACH.	187.	202.	319.	373.	372.	407.	391.	364.	412.	443.	58
59	MISC. MACHINERY AND SHOPS	98.	126.	145.	145.	139.	149.	147.	150.	162.	169.	59
60	OFFICE AND COMPUTING MACH	232.	230.	315.	370.	435.	551.	398.	451.	476.	473.	60
61	SERVICE INDUSTRY MACH.	132.	80.	119.	138.	151.	178.	175.	178.	196.	215.	61
62	TRANSFORMRS,SWTHGR,EL MSR	71.	102.	124.	137.	137.	154.	151.	154.	169.	174.	62
63	ELECTRIC APP. + MOTORS	129.	159.	181.	253.	232.	256.	265.	258.	287.	307.	63
64	HOUSEHOLD APPLIANCES	97.	116.	156.	145.	154.	160.	147.	161.	165.	170.	64
65	ELEC. LIGHTING + WIRING	94.	107.	119.	140.	165.	169.	160.	187.	196.	204.	65
66	RADIO-, TV-SETS AND PHONO	40.	61.	97.	92.	93.	88.	100.	109.	119.	125.	66
67	COMMUNICATION EQUIPMENT	333.	399.	453.	480.	514.	564.	498.	530.	570.	591.	67
68	ELECTRONIC COMPONENTS	246.	396.	528.	532.	529.	557.	587.	641.	692.	722.	68
69	BATTERIES,X-RAY EQ.,ETC.	71.	83.	86.	86.	94.	113.	134.	122.	129.	133.	69
70	MOTOR VEHICLES	620.	948.	1278.	1354.	1344.	1360.	1448.	1537.	1656.	1741.	70
71	AIRCRAFT	198.	174.	451.	559.	525.	538.	543.	618.	700.	745.	71
72	SHIPS AND BOATS	48.	60.	64.	77.	86.	96.	106.	96.	121.	126.	72
73	RAILROAD EQUIPMENT	39.	33.	70.	78.	75.	81.	71.	62.	67.	69.	73
74	TRAILERS, CYCLES	36.	47.	47.	43.	39.	42.	44.	45.	51.	53.	74
75	ENGR. + SCIENTIFIC INSTR.	18.	19.	28.	28.	29.	29.	30.	31.	34.	35.	75
76	MECH. MEASURING DEVICES	45.	64.	68.	73.	73.	77.	81.	82.	87.	90.	76
77	SURGICAL + MEDICAL INSTR.	49.	51.	58.	68.	72.	83.	81.	88.	99.	103.	77
78	OPTICAL AND PHOTOGRAPHIC	146.	218.	216.	249.	314.	356.	337.	364.	413.	437.	78
79	MISC. MANUFACTURING	188.	262.	281.	285.	306.	338.	352.	371.	387.	393.	79
80	RAILROADS	1379.	1445.	2330.	2251.	2136.	2137.	2203.	2302.	2405.	2432.	80
81	TRUCKING	672.	494.	861.	910.	923.	971.	1078.	1193.	1361.	1460.	81
82	OTHER TRANSPORT	363.	303.	721.	934.	796.	570.	563.	526.	512.	483.	82
83	AIRLINES	1880.	1738.	3066.	3290.	3450.	3907.	3996.	4340.	4824.	5101.	83
84	WHOLESALE + RETAIL TRADE	8527.	9325.	10808.	12240.	12068.	12865.	13899.	15236.	16851.	17846.	84
85	COMMUNICATION	7765.	9510.	12092.	12280.	12431.	12907.	14271.	16100.	18007.	19200.	85
86	FINANCE AND SERVICES	6635.	6636.	10021.	10468.	11029.	10960.	11521.	12446.	12970.	13198.	86
87	ELECTRIC UTILITIES	6135.	6636.	8299.	8484.	8681.	9080.	10050.	11124.	12464.	13221.	87
88	NAT. GAS, WATER AND SEWER	1105.	755.	803.	872.	936.	943.	1002.	1060.	1156.	1209.	88
89	PERS., AUTO/FED. ENTERPRIS	4359.	4297.	4584.	4749.	4986.	5125.	5560.	5978.	6571.	6945.	89
90	COMPUTER RENTAL/S&L ENTER	1998.	2900.	3393.	3290.	3499.	3648.	4083.	4588.	5050.	5326.	90

NOVEMBER 1973 FORECAST

PRODUCERS' DURABLE EQUIPMENT INVESTMENT

ANNUAL GROWTH RATES

#	Industry	71-85	71-75	75-80	80-85	71-73	73-83	73-75	73-78	75-78	78-83
1	AGRICULTURE	1.74	4.13	.54	1.04	4.42	1.29	3.83	1.70	.28	.88
2	MINING	4.11	8.64	2.69	1.92	14.90	2.40	2.37	2.73	2.96	2.08
3	PETROLEUM AND GAS	4.94	8.51	4.07	2.96	12.83	3.85	4.18	3.86	3.64	3.83
4	CONSTRUCTION(NEW AND OLD)	5.26	12.54	2.38	2.30	18.16	3.32	6.93	3.70	1.55	2.93
5	ORDNANCE	-5.56	-2.08	-5.96	-7.95	15.62	-9.07	-19.79	-11.12	-5.35	-7.02
6	MEAT	2.82	3.19	2.99	2.35	.24	3.41	6.14	4.18	2.88	2.64
7	DAIRY	4.44	10.42	2.38	1.72	17.91	2.29	2.93	2.67	2.50	1.91
8	CANNED AND FROZEN FOODS	2.79	5.32	1.12	2.44	4.55	2.38	6.10	2.20	-.40	2.55
9	GRAIN MILL PRODUCTS	2.15	-.69	4.42	2.17	-4.57	3.51	3.19	1.56	5.73	2.32
10	BAKERY	4.05	8.34	1.55	3.42	14.16	2.23	2.52	.92	.92	2.91
11	SUGAR	5.02	11.22	3.36	2.94	26.11	1.78	-3.67	.10	2.61	3.46
12	CANDY	2.25	1.76	2.64	.87	8.06	1.42	3.46	1.71	.85	1.12
13	BEVERAGES	1.80	-.51	2.75	.97	-5.08	2.32	3.34	1.97	2.59	1.68
14	MISC. FOOD PRODUCTS	3.05	10.98	.03	2.69	9.04	3.00	4.07	3.01	2.30	2.99
15	TOBACCO	6.16	15.33	.91	4.07	27.20	2.24	3.47	-.20	-2.65	4.69
16	FABRICS AND YARNS	6.19	10.98	2.64	-.27	22.64	-.28	-.69	-.54	-.45	-1.01
17	FLOOR COVERINGS	1.54	14.26	3.84	2.10	27.72	2.58	.80	2.85	4.23	2.30
18	MISC. TEXTILES	3.78	2.12	2.12	.31	14.94	2.11	5.43	3.92	2.90	.30
19	KNIT FABRIC AND APPAREL	2.42	6.12	1.63	1.86	-7.22	3.12	10.44	3.45	-1.22	2.79
20	APPAREL	5.70	1.61	1.17	.25	8.55	1.61	.80	3.24	2.93	-.01
21	HSHLD TEXTILES + UPHOLST.	2.81	10.47	4.87	2.70	16.61	4.21	4.34	6.18	7.41	2.23
22	LOGGING AND LUMBER	5.20	6.73	1.42	1.06	17.43	.37	-3.98	-1.12	.79	1.87
23	PLYWOOD, MILLWORK, ETC.	5.42	10.31	2.94	5.38	11.81	4.46	8.81	3.72	.32	5.21
24	WOODEN CONTAINERS	4.09	20.41	-2.59	1.45	39.16	-.60	1.64	-.85	-.85	-1.35
25	FURNITURE	6.60	12.83	-.31	.88	15.39	2.47	10.28	3.82	-.48	1.12
26	PAPER+PROD, EX.CONTAINERS	6.60	14.22	3.34	2.15	20.72	3.77	7.72	5.30	3.69	2.25
27	PAPER CONTAINERS	6.02	12.83	3.26	2.02	29.15	2.99	8.09	3.01	-.37	2.97
28	NEWSPAPERS	3.95	8.62	2.25	1.97	9.31	3.39	7.65	3.79	1.91	2.00
29	PRINTING AND PUBLISHING	3.60	8.51	3.24	2.02	6.77	3.29	5.83	3.72	3.91	2.06
30	INDUSTRIAL CHEMICALS	6.21	6.35	2.68	2.32	23.69	3.50	7.31	4.47	2.57	2.53
31	AGRICULTURAL CHEMICALS	7.19	15.50	1.92	3.35	26.83	3.99	10.35	3.87	-.46	4.11
32	GLUE, INK, AND FATTY ACID	2.13	16.59	.05	.58	5.95	1.76	7.39	2.43	-.87	1.10
33	PLASTICS AND SYNTHETICS	6.52	6.67	2.67	2.78	22.95	4.04	9.05	4.91	2.16	3.17
34	DRUGS	4.12	16.00	3.13	1.89	11.64	3.11	4.67	3.46	2.65	2.77
35	CLEANING AND TOILET ITEMS	3.33	8.15	4.11	2.41	.77	4.06	6.25	5.11	4.35	3.01
36	PAINTS + ALLIED PRODUCTS	3.98	3.51	1.65	1.13	10.42	3.17	10.52	6.22	3.36	.12
37	PETROLEUM REFINING	3.90	10.47	2.89	3.15	1.43	4.46	10.79	5.65	2.22	3.28
38	TIRE AND TUBES	7.13	6.11	3.75	3.06	23.95	4.56	8.96	5.60	3.36	3.53
39	RUBBER PROD. EX. TIRES	5.15	16.46	.86	.77	16.44	3.64	15.51	6.62	.68	.67
40	PLASTIC PRODUCTS	9.68	15.98	6.24	4.78	32.37	6.28	7.81	6.70	5.96	5.86
41	LEATHER+IND.LTHR.PROD.	.79	20.09	-1.44	.30	3.99	.21	4.37	-.09	-3.07	.52
42	FOOTWEAR, EX. RUBBER LEATHER	2.74	4.18	-.14	.26	17.36	.54	2.89	.72	.72	.35
43	GLASS AND GLASS PRODUCTS	6.10	10.15	2.84	2.91	20.82	3.81	7.49	4.47	2.46	3.16
44	STONE AND CLAY PRODUCTS	6.10	12.04	1.67	1.95	27.82	.72	-3.64	.44	1.03	2.08
45	IRON AND STEEL	5.70	21.48	-2.87	1.65	30.51	1.65	12.45	.76	-1.03	2.54
46	NON-FERROUS METALS	5.30	15.05	.89	1.91	20.99	2.90	9.11	5.25	2.64	2.77
47	METAL CONTAINERS	4.21	8.08	3.20	2.12	15.00	2.51	1.15	4.21	2.99	-1.36
48	PLUMBING AND HEATING	1.82	8.84	-2.03	.07	18.12	1.42	13.48	-1.98	-1.98	2.21
49	STRUCTURAL METAL PRODUCTS	4.40	10.04	2.10	2.19	28.26	2.17	1.97	2.12	2.23	2.00
50	STAMPINGS	5.75	18.78	-.16	1.24	15.30	2.11	9.30	2.22	-2.49	3.05
51	HARDWARE,PLATING+WIRE PRD	5.75	14.86	1.97	2.24	15.52	4.70	14.43	6.36	.98	3.71
52	ENGINE AND TURBINES	6.38	14.61	2.45	3.72	24.73	4.50	6.12	.98	2.19	-1.39
53	FARM MACHINERY	2.95	11.82	-3.00	1.79	15.52	.88	8.13	3.15	-.16	3.71
54	CONST.MINE,MATRL HANDL EQ	6.22	15.80	.45	4.32	16.05	4.86	5.54	5.89	-.54	3.82
55	METALWORKING MACHINERY	8.73	26.34	-1.21	4.59	47.37	1.89	5.31	1.42	-1.18	2.37
56	SPECIAL INDUSTRIAL MACH.	5.04	16.66	-1.51	2.31	21.58	2.20	11.74	6.28	2.63	-1.88

NOVEMBER 1973 FORECAST

	PRODUCERS' DURABLE EQUIPMENT INVESTMENT					ANNUAL GROWTH RATES					
	71-85	71-75	75-80	80-85	71-73	73-83	73-75	73-77	75-78	78-83	
GENERAL INDUSTRIAL MACH.	6.16	17.18	-.43	3.92	26.78	2.53	7.58	4.03	1.66	1.04	58
MISC. MACHINERY AND SHOPS	3.87	8.67	1.53	2.38	19.26	1.15	-1.91	.29	1.76	2.00	59
OFFICE AND COMPUTING MACH	5.08	15.69	.74	.95	-5.29	4.12	16.08	4.67	-2.94	3.57	60
SERVICE INDUSTRY MACH.	3.48	3.59	3.23	3.80	-5.21	4.98	11.99	7.74	4.90	2.22	61
TRANSFORMRS,SWTHGR,EL MSR	6.40	16.40	2.36	2.44	27.88	3.10	4.92	3.95	7.31	2.24	62
ELECTRIC APP. + MOTORS	6.20	14.72	2.09	3.50	16.96	4.63	12.48	7.61	4.36	1.65	63
HOUSEHOLD APPLIANCES	3.99	11.45	.96	1.03	23.75	.57	-.85	-1.26	-1.53	2.41	64
ELEC. LIGHTING + WIRING	5.53	14.10	2.43	1.78	11.89	4.99	16.31	5.91	-1.02	4.06	65
RADIO-, TV-SETS AND PHONO	8.07	20.83	3.28	2.66	43.94	2.01	-2.27	.51	2.36	3.50	66
COMMUNICATION EQUIPMENT	4.09	10.83	.61	2.19	15.36	2.29	6.30	1.90	-1.04	2.68	67
ELECTRONIC COMPONENTS	7.69	19.15	3.82	2.38	38.16	2.71	.14	2.13	3.45	3.29	68
BATTERIES,X-RAY EQ.,ETC.	4.55	7.17	5.13	1.86	9.61	4.08	4.73	9.03	11.90	-.88	69
MOTOR VEHICLES	7.37	19.32	2.69	2.49	36.12	2.60	2.53	2.50	2.49	2.69	70
AIRCRAFT	9.48	24.43	3.25	3.74	41.22	4.40	7.65	3.75	1.15	5.05	71
SHIPS AND BOATS	6.83	14.23	2.29	5.45	13.80	6.36	14.66	10.11	7.08	2.62	72
RAILROAD EQUIPMENT	4.15	16.71	-4.03	2.29	29.61	-.35	3.82	-.29	-2.05	-.99	73
TRAILERS, CYCLES	2.47	.89	2.84	3.46	19.40	-.86	-8.21	-.99	4.09	2.71	74
ENGR. + SCIENTIFIC INSTR.	4.58	10.85	1.58	1.75	14.88	3.01	7.02	3.89	1.80	2.13	75
MECH. MEASURING DEVICES	4.34	9.99	2.50	3.09	20.60	2.51	3.38	3.66	3.84	1.36	76
SURGICAL +MEDICAL INSTR.	5.33	9.67	4.11	3.65	8.63	5.30	10.71	6.62	3.89	3.98	77
SURGICAL AID PHOTOGRAPHIC	7.82	19.14	2.94	3.90	19.46	6.50	18.82	8.96	4.75	4.05	78
MISC. MANUFACTURING	5.29	12.21	3.90	1.13	20.23	3.20	4.18	4.52	1.03	1.87	79
RAILROADS	4.05	10.93	1.50	1.10	26.22	.32	-4.35	-1.12	5.18	1.76	80
TRUCKING	5.54	7.92	5.14	5.18	12.39	4.57	3.44	4.49		4.66	81
OTHER TRANSPORT	2.05	19.65	-8.28	-1.69	34.37	-3.43	4.93	-6.42	-13.98	-.45	82
AIRLINES	7.13	15.18	4.59	4.65	24.46	4.53	5.90	5.15	4.65	3.91	83
WHOLESALE + RETAIL TRADE	5.27	8.68	4.66	3.16	11.85	4.44	5.51	5.02	4.60	3.86	84
COMMUNICATION	6.47	11.76	5.17	3.52	22.15	3.58	4.38	1.38	1.45	4.65	85
FINANCE AND SERVICES	4.91	12.70	2.42	1.47	29.61	2.58	4.79	2.79	4.88	2.37	86
ELECTRIC UTILITIES	.64	8.69	4.96	2.64	15.94	4.07	2.25	3.83	2.26	4.31	87
NAT. GAS, WATER AND SEWER	3.33	-4.14	4.14	3.00	2.52	3.64	7.67	4.43	3.63	2.85	88
PERS. AUTO/FED. ENTERPRIS	7.00	7.36	3.63	2.98	26.48	3.60	4.20	3.86		3.34	89
COMPUTER RENTAL/S&L ENTER		14.01	5.42			3.98	1.54	3.71	5.15	4.25	90

NOVEMBER 1973 FORECAST

PURCHASES OF STRUCTURES BY TYPE

MILLIONS OF 1971$

		1971	1972	1973	1974	1975	1976	1978	1980	1983	1985
1	RESIDENTIAL CONSTRUCTION	33854.	41506.	41933.	30076.	33316.	36562.	34935.	37526.	39722.	40745.
2	ADDITIONS AND ALTERATIONS	6645.	6646.	6803.	6916.	7065.	7157.	7431.	7700.	8068.	8291.
3	HOTELS,MOTELS,DORMITORIES	1541.	2146.	2288.	2391.	2525.	2608.	2852.	3091.	3416.	3613.
4	INDUSTRIAL CONSTRUCTION	4995.	3907.	9923.	10155.	9446.	9932.	9285.	9374.	9084.	8892.
5	OFFICES	6705.	7120.	7360.	7474.	7840.	7790.	8214.	8521.	8868.	9036.
6	STORES,RESTAURANTS,GARAGES	5485.	5826.	6374.	6195.	6181.	6250.	6456.	6671.	6784.	6784.
7	RELIGIOUS BUILDINGS	772.	737.	725.	712.	700.	690.	670.	650.	620.	600.
8	EDUCATIONAL BUILDINGS	827.	781.	877.	951.	1017.	1065.	1150.	1216.	1288.	1325.
9	HOSPITALS	2851.	2903.	3108.	3257.	3449.	3572.	3928.	4272.	4743.	5027.
10	MISCELLANEOUS BUILDINGS	1480.	1643.	1857.	2006.	2152.	2247.	2454.	2633.	2858.	2988.
11	FARM CONSTRUCTION	820.	735.	759.	757.	743.	736.	716.	688.	645.	617.
12	OIL + GAS DRILLING	1844.	1837.	2091.	2346.	2600.	2680.	2840.	3000.	3240.	3400.
13	RAILROAD CONSTRUCTION	263.	326.	371.	389.	394.	409.	426.	429.	431.	432.
14	TELEPHONE AND TELEGRAPH	3005.	2983.	3511.	3451.	3341.	3392.	3501.	3644.	3740.	3768.
15	ELECTRIC UTILITIES	5042.	5654.	5845.	5860.	5938.	6116.	6523.	6960.	7624.	8048.
16	PIPELINES + GAS UTILITIES	1682.	1410.	1899.	1916.	1862.	1938.	1944.	1999.	2098.	2150.
17	MISCELLANEOUS NON-BUILDING	903.	880.	1007.	1046.	1046.	1153.	1247.	1332.	1460.	1545.
18	HIGHWAYS	10658.	9908.	9959.	9929.	9900.	9480.	9847.	9800.	9740.	9700.
19	MILITARY CONSTRUCTION	894.	984.	939.	895.	850.	830.	790.	750.	690.	650.
20	CONSERVATION & DEVELOPMENT	2095.	2065.	2177.	2288.	2400.	2520.	2760.	3000.	3360.	3600.
21	SEWER SYSTEMS	1829.	1615.	1920.	2043.	2109.	2158.	2243.	2325.	2448.	2529.
22	WATER SYSTEMS	996.	1015.	1217.	1375.	1501.	1602.	1759.	1877.	2020.	2104.
23	PUBLIC RESIDENTIAL	1136.	833.	992.	1086.	1143.	1181.	1231.	1267.	1315.	1347.
24	PUBLIC INDUSTRIAL	572.	408.	449.	399.	350.	340.	320.	300.	270.	250.
25	PUBLIC, EDUCATIONAL	5563.	5251.	5301.	5350.	5400.	5480.	5640.	5800.	6040.	6200.
26	PUBLIC HOSPITAL	981.	939.	939.	953.	967.	982.	1013.	1045.	1092.	1124.
27	OTHER PUBLIC STRUCTURES	3144.	3096.	3438.	3683.	3873.	4032.	4308.	4560.	4926.	5168.
28	MISCELLANEOUS PUBLIC	1995.	2092.	2298.	2478.	2637.	2781.	3036.	3261.	3567.	3761.

NOVEMBER 1973 FORECAST

	PURCHASES OF STRUCTURES BY TYPE						ANNUAL GROWTH RATES				
	71-85	71-75	75-80	80-85	71-73	73-83	73-75	73-78	75-78	78-83	
1 RESIDENTIAL CONSTRUCTION	1.32	-.40	2.38	1.65	10.70	-.54	-11.50	-3.65	1.58	2.57	1
2 ADDITIONS AND ALTERATIONS	1.80	2.30	1.72	1.48	2.70	1.71	1.89	1.77	1.68	1.65	2
3 HOTELS,MOTELS,DORMITORIES	6.09	12.35	4.04	3.12	19.76	4.01	4.93	4.41	4.06	3.61	3
4 INDUSTRIAL CONSTRUCTION	4.12	15.93	-.37	-.84	34.32	-.88	-2.46	-1.33	-.57	-.44	4
5 OFFICES	2.13	3.26	2.18	1.17	4.66	1.86	1.87	2.20	2.41	1.53	5
6 STORES,RESTAURANTS,GARAGES	1.52	2.99	1.53	.34	7.51	.62	-1.54	.25	1.45	.99	6
7 RELIGIOUS BUILDINGS	-1.80	-2.45	-1.48	-1.60	-3.16	-1.56	-1.73	-1.57	-1.46	-1.55	7
8 EDUCATIONAL BUILDINGS	3.37	5.16	3.58	1.73	2.93	3.84	7.39	5.43	4.13	2.26	8
9 HOSPITALS	4.05	4.76	4.28	3.25	4.32	4.23	5.21	4.68	4.33	3.77	9
10 MISCELLANEOUS BUILDINGS	5.02	9.35	4.04	2.53	11.34	4.31	7.37	5.58	4.39	3.04	10
11 FARM CONSTRUCTION	-2.03	-2.46	-1.55	-2.17	-3.85	-1.62	-1.06	-1.18	-1.25	-2.07	11
12 OIL + GAS DRILLING	4.37	8.59	2.86	2.50	6.29	4.38	10.89	6.12	2.94	2.64	12
13 RAILROAD CONSTRUCTION	3.54	10.10	1.72	.11	17.22	1.50	2.98	2.78	2.64	.22	13
14 TELEPHONE AND TELEGRAPH	1.62	2.65	1.74	.67	7.79	.63	-2.49	-.06	1.56	1.32	14
15 ELECTRIC UTILITIES	3.34	4.09	3.18	2.91	7.39	2.66	-.79	2.19	3.13	3.12	15
16 PIPELINES + GAS UTILITIES	1.75	2.81	1.21	1.95	6.06	1.00	-.43	.47	1.07	1.52	16
17 MISCELLANEOUS NON-BUILDING	3.16	2.64	3.77	2.97	.72	3.71	4.55	4.27	4.08	3.15	17
18 HIGHWAYS	-.67	-1.84	-.20	-.21	-3.39	-.22	-.30	-.24	-.20	-.20	18
19 MILITARY CONSTRUCTION	-2.28	-1.26	-2.50	-2.86	2.47	-3.08	-5.00	-3.46	-2.44	-2.71	19
20 CONSERVATION & DEVELOPMENT	3.87	4.40	4.46	3.65	1.91	4.34	4.88	4.75	4.66	3.93	20
21 SEWER SYSTEMS	2.34	3.56	1.95	1.69	2.44	2.43	4.69	3.11	2.05	1.75	21
22 WATER SYSTEMS	5.34	10.25	4.48	2.28	10.02	5.07	10.47	7.37	5.30	2.77	22
23 PUBLIC RESIDENTIAL	1.21	.15	2.06	1.22	-6.75	2.82	7.06	4.30	2.47	1.33	23
24 PUBLIC INDUSTRIAL	-5.91	-12.28	-3.03	-3.65	-12.14	-5.08	-12.42	-6.76	-2.99	-3.40	24
25 PUBLIC, EDUCATIONAL	.77	-.74	1.43	1.33	-2.42	1.31	.93	1.24	1.45	1.37	25
26 PUBLIC, HOSPITAL	.97	-.35	1.53	1.46	-2.19	1.51	1.50	1.52	1.54	1.50	26
27 OTHER PUBLIC STRUCTURES	3.55	5.21	3.27	2.50	4.47	3.60	5.95	4.51	3.55	2.68	27
28 MISCELLANEOUS PUBLIC	4.53	6.98	4.24	2.85	7.07	4.40	6.89	5.57	4.69	3.23	28

NOVEMBER 1973 FORECAST

PERSONS EMPLOYED — THOUSANDS OF JOBS

#		1971	1972	1973	1974	1975	1976	1978	1980	1983	1985
1	AGRICULTURE	3744.	3546.	3415.	3274.	3152.	3035.	2823.	2629.	2366.	2203.
2	MINING	367.	357.	372.	362.	361.	361.	358.	359.	360.	362.
3	PETROLEUM AND GAS	287.	298.	302.	299.	297.	296.	289.	283.	270.	261.
4	CONSTRUCTION(NEW AND OLD)	4305.	4342.	4385.	4432.	4481.	4533.	4640.	4751.	4925.	5044.
5	ORDNANCE	196.	193.	194.	193.	192.	192.	191.	190.	187.	184.
6	MEAT	343.	346.	348.	351.	353.	356.	361.	367.	375.	381.
7	DAIRY	232.	227.	222.	217.	211.	206.	195.	185.	171.	161.
8	CANNED AND FROZEN FOODS	273.	278.	283.	287.	292.	297.	307.	317.	334.	346.
9	GRAIN MILL PRODUCTS	134.	137.	141.	141.	142.	144.	146.	149.	153.	156.
10	BAKERY	268.	270.	270.	269.	268.	267.	264.	261.	257.	254.
11	SUGAR	32.	35.	37.	37.	38.	38.	38.	38.	38.	37.
12	CANDY	78.	79.	80.	81.	82.	84.	85.	87.	91.	96.
13	BEVERAGES	235.	239.	243.	246.	246.	246.	245.	249.	247.	245.
14	MISC.FOOD PRODUCTS	143.	143.	143.	143.	142.	142.	142.	142.	141.	141.
15	TOBACCO	73.	75.	74.	73.	72.	71.	69.	66.	63.	61.
16	FABRICS AND YARNS	585.	586.	617.	609.	619.	608.	608.	600.	578.	561.
17	FLOOR COVERINGS	55.	54.	57.	57.	56.	56.	54.	51.	47.	43.
18	MISC. TEXTILES	72.	70.	70.	74.	77.	77.	77.	76.	73.	71.
19	KNIT FABRIC AND APPAREL	246.	246.	253.	250.	252.	249.	248.	245.	238.	232.
20	APPAREL	1186.	1169.	1248.	1349.	1406.	1446.	1518.	1570.	1608.	1615.
21	HSHLD TEXTILES + UPHOLST.	162.	156.	163.	173.	179.	183.	188.	191.	192.	190.
22	LOGGING AND LUMBER	288.	306.	315.	306.	308.	311.	313.	317.	321.	322.
23	PLYWOOD, MILLWORK, ETC.	270.	287.	297.	283.	294.	303.	309.	322.	336.	343.
24	WOODEN CONTAINERS	23.	20.	20.	22.	22.	21.	20.	18.	16.	15.
25	FURNITURE	453.	492.	536.	525.	548.	547.	562.	577.	581.	579.
26	PAPER+PROC. EX.CONTAINERS	462.	476.	503.	517.	531.	543.	563.	577.	590.	593.
27	PAPER CONTAINERS	214.	226.	236.	238.	244.	247.	255.	262.	271.	275.
28	NEWSPAPERS	366.	374.	390.	399.	407.	420.	422.	431.	454.	440.
29	PRINTING AND PUBLISHING	700.	700.	736.	729.	742.	748.	753.	757.	754.	746.
30	INDUSTRIAL CHEMICALS	311.	309.	322.	329.	330.	331.	326.	326.	315.	306.
31	AGRICULTURAL CHEMICALS	55.	57.	58.	58.	59.	59.	60.	60.	61.	61.
32	GLUE, INK, AND FATTY ACID	99.	107.	115.	117.	122.	125.	131.	137.	144.	148.
33	PLASTICS AND SYNTHETICS	208.	218.	239.	252.	262.	269.	279.	283.	280.	273.
34	DRUGS	149.	149.	153.	157.	159.	160.	160.	161.	157.	153.
35	CLEANING AND TOILET ITEMS	123.	131.	138.	141.	147.	149.	158.	167.	179.	186.
36	PAINTS + ALLIED PRODUCTS	67.	69.	71.	72.	73.	74.	76.	78.	82.	84.
37	PETROLEUM REFINING	189.	176.	170.	164.	160.	157.	152.	148.	142.	138.
38	TIRE AND TUBES	119.	118.	124.	127.	132.	135.	141.	147.	155.	160.
39	RUBBER PROD. EX. TIRES	170.	176.	183.	185.	189.	190.	194.	197.	200.	201.
40	PLASTIC PRODUCTS	284.	332.	380.	398.	430.	453.	501.	547.	599.	622.
41	LEATHER+IND. LTHR. PROD.	28.	28.	30.	30.	29.	29.	28.	26.	23.	21.
42	FOOTWEAR + OTHER LEATHER	309.	322.	319.	316.	320.	320.	320.	313.	297.	280.
43	GLASS AND GLASS PRODUCTS	191.	183.	192.	195.	199.	201.	204.	206.	205.	202.
44	STONE AND CLAY PRODUCTS	483.	465.	496.	489.	483.	494.	494.	508.	508.	509.
45	IRON AND STEEL	837.	896.	958.	954.	962.	965.	961.	962.	953.	944.
46	NON-FERROUS METALS	356.	348.	387.	392.	401.	408.	418.	429.	441.	447.
47	METAL CONTAINERS	80.	82.	86.	87.	89.	90.	92.	94.	95.	96.
48	PLUMBING AND HEATING	80.	76.	84.	81.	83.	85.	85.	87.	89.	90.
49	STRUCTURAL METAL PRODUCTS	409.	423.	460.	459.	467.	477.	489.	505.	525.	537.
50	STAMPINGS	301.	325.	349.	365.	376.	386.	402.	415.	430.	436.
51	HARDWARE,PLATING+WIRE PRD	429.	463.	511.	518.	539.	550.	567.	587.	608.	619.
52	ENGINE AND TURBINES	115.	121.	134.	137.	138.	139.	142.	146.	149.	149.
53	FARM MACHINERY	122.	117.	136.	141.	139.	135.	133.	135.	131.	129.
54	CONST,MINE,MATRL HANDL EQ	267.	288.	332.	346.	355.	365.	366.	379.	396.	405.
55	METALWORKING MACHINERY	247.	281.	337.	355.	363.	373.	371.	383.	398.	405.
56	SPECIAL INDUSTRIAL MACH.	173.	165.	180.	200.	206.	207.	201.	197.	193.	188.

NOVEMBER 1973 FORECAST

		PERSONS EMPLOYED						THOUSANDS OF JOBS			
		1971	1972	1973	1974	1975	1976	1978	1980	1983	1985
58	GENERAL INDUSTRIAL MACH.	244.	257.	299.	326.	333.	335.	330.	332.	336.	335.
59	MISC. MACHINERY AND SHOPS	195.	198.	216.	228.	236.	243.	257.	271.	288.	297.
60	OFFICE AND COMPUTING MACH	243.	260.	307.	314.	308.	303.	299.	291.	265.	245.
61	SERVICE INDUSTRY MACH.	135.	144.	161.	164.	168.	173.	178.	185.	192.	196.
62	TRANSFORMRS+SWTHGR+EL MSR	192.	208.	241.	245.	248.	252.	260.	269.	277.	279.
63	ELECTRIC APP. + MOTORS	195.	208.	232.	238.	244.	248.	253.	262.	272.	277.
64	HOUSEHOLD APPLIANCES	183.	196.	201.	198.	204.	204.	208.	211.	213.	212.
65	ELEC. LIGHTING + WIRING	181.	208.	236.	232.	242.	249.	258.	266.	270.	269.
66	RADIO-TV-SETS AND PHONO	137.	156.	160.	159.	161.	160.	161.	160.	156.	152.
67	COMMUNICATION EQUIPMENT	435.	493.	540.	539.	539.	544.	544.	590.	616.	633.
68	ELECTRONIC COMPONENTS	332.	367.	400.	403.	404.	447.	396.	389.	364.	345.
69	BATTERIES+X-RAY EQ.+ETC.	118.	115.	130.	136.	143.	147.	156.	164.	175.	180.
70	MOTOR VEHICLES	866.	892.	917.	942.	962.	1010.	1071.	1131.	1213.	1265.
71	AIRCRAFT	530.	505.	567.	589.	589.	589.	581.	575.	560.	547.
72	SHIPS AND BOATS	161.	175.	198.	207.	206.	199.	205.	212.	217.	219.
73	RAILROAD EQUIPMENT	50.	59.	70.	67.	65.	64.	62.	61.	59.	58.
74	TRAILERS+ CYCLES	120.	117.	120.	124.	128.	132.	138.	142.	152.	157.
75	ENGR. + SCIENTIFIC INSTR.	61.	64.	69.	71.	73.	74.	75.	75.	76.	75.
76	MECH. MEASURING DEVICES	96.	93.	96.	102.	105.	106.	107.	107.	107.	106.
77	SURGICAL + MEDICAL INSTR.	86.	88.	99.	105.	110.	115.	119.	124.	128.	129.
78	OPTICAL AND PHOTOGRAPHIC	183.	201.	223.	232.	241.	244.	249.	252.	252.	250.
79	MISC. MANUFACTURING	410.	413.	434.	446.	453.	455.	452.	442.	416.	395.
80	RAILROADS	600.	582.	569.	544.	525.	505.	467.	433.	384.	354.
81	TRUCKING	1240.	1286.	1343.	1369.	1406.	1435.	1490.	1546.	1624.	1673.
82	OTHER TRANSPORT	647.	659.	657.	695.	711.	727.	756.	785.	820.	842.
83	AIRLINES	396.	365.	365.	386.	374.	377.	392.	385.	388.	399.
84	WHOLSALE + RETAIL TRADE	17768.	17897.	18560.	19268.	19648.	20144.	20972.	21934.	22930.	23478.
85	COMMUNICATION	1130.	1168.	1228.	1247.	1278.	1298.	1350.	1403.	1464.	1497.
86	FINANCE AND SERVICES	17718.	17922.	18966.	19949.	20565.	21248.	22551.	23843.	25513.	26399.
87	ELECTRIC UTILITIES	484.	493.	506.	513.	522.	530.	546.	562.	586.	601.
88	NAT. GAS, WATER AND SEWER	226.	219.	217.	214.	211.	209.	204.	201.	197.	195.
89	PERS. AUTO/FED. ENTERPRIS	892.	866.	883.	901.	919.	937.	975.	1015.	1077.	1120.
90	COMPUTER RENTAL/S&L ENTER	534.	519.	538.	558.	578.	596.	642.	690.	767.	823.
91	DOMESTIC SERVANTS	2116.	2129.	2104.	2078.	2053.	2033.	1993.	1953.	1893.	1854.
92	DEFENSE CIVILIAN	1131.	1088.	1027.	967.	906.	906.	907.	907.	907.	908.
93	FEDERAL NON-DEFENSE	888.	889.	913.	937.	960.	971.	991.	1012.	1027.	1038.
94	PUBLIC EDUCATION	5562.	5744.	6017.	6114.	6348.	6369.	6583.	6694.	6851.	7010.
95	MILITARY	2813.	3057.	2901.	2745.	2587.	2591.	2597.	2604.	2613.	2618.
96	S&L NON-SCHOOL	4516.	4657.	4845.	4950.	5127.	5200.	5501.	5778.	6137.	6347.

NOVEMBER 1973 FORECAST

		PERSONS EMPLOYED			ANNUAL GROWTH RATES						
		71-85	71-75	75-80	80-85	71-73	73-83	73-75	73-78	75-78	78-83
1	AGRICULTURE	-3.79	-4.30	-3.63	-3.54	-4.60	-3.67	-4.00	-3.81	-3.68	-3.53
2	MINING	-.68	-.38	-.04	-.16	.67	-.31	-1.43	-.78	-.99	-.15
3	PETROLEUM AND GAS	-.68	.89	-1.03	-1.60	2.56	-1.11	-1.78	-.90	-.99	-1.31
4	CONSTRUCTION(NEW AND OLD)	1.13	1.00	1.17	1.22	.92	1.13	1.08	1.13	1.16	1.19
5	ORDNANCE	-.44	-.55	-.22	-.58	-.37	-.42	-.72	-.34	-.09	-.49
6	MEAT	-.75	-.72	-.76	-.76	-.76	-.75	-.73	-.74	-.74	-.76
7	DAIRY	-2.60	-2.38	-2.65	-2.74	-2.28	-2.64	-2.47	-2.56	-2.62	-2.72
8	CANNED AND FROZEN FOODS	1.68	1.69	1.65	1.71	1.74	1.66	1.63	1.63	1.63	1.69
9	GRAIN MILL PRODUCTS	1.09	1.55	.88	.93	1.95	.95	1.14	.99	.88	.91
10	BAKERY	-.37	.06	-.52	-.56	.43	-.49	-.31	-.43	-.50	-.55
11	SUGAR	1.10	4.08	.13	-.31	7.50	.14	.66	.34	.12	-.06
12	CANDY	1.28	1.02	1.34	1.42	.87	1.33	1.17	1.24	1.29	1.42
13	BEVERAGES	.27	1.08	-.17	-.27	1.48	.17	.68	.39	.20	-.06
14	MISC. FOOD PRODUCTS	-.10	-.04	-.12	-.14	.04	-.12	-.11	-.12	-.12	-.13
15	TOBACCO	-1.33	-.32	-1.72	-1.76	.99	-1.71	-1.62	-1.66	-1.69	-1.76
16	FABRIC AND YARNS	-1.30	-1.43	-1.64	-1.33	2.70	-1.66	-1.16	-1.32	-1.63	-1.00
17	FLOOR COVERINGS	-.06	1.54	-1.16	-3.33	1.69	-2.00	-1.42	-1.25	-1.07	-2.74
18	MISC. TEXTILES	-.42	1.77	-.16	-1.43	2.04	-.16	1.50	.64	-.55	-.96
19	KNIT FABRIC AND APPAREL	-.75	.64	-.56	-1.13	1.33	-.60	-.05	-.35	-.57	-.85
20	APPAREL	2.20	4.26	2.20	.56	2.54	1.66	5.98	3.92	2.55	1.16
21	HSHLD TEXTILES + UPHOLST.	1.14	2.49	1.32	-.12	.19	2.54	4.79	2.85	1.56	.47
22	LOGGING AND LUMBER	.80	1.63	.58	-.35	4.44	.18	-1.19	-.13	-.58	.48
23	PLYWOOD, MILLWORK, ETC.	1.72	2.14	1.80	1.30	4.86	1.21	-.58	.80	1.71	1.62
24	WOODEN CONTAINERS	-3.11	-.91	-3.59	-4.38	-6.51	-2.15	4.68	-.09	-3.28	-4.20
25	FURNITURE	1.75	1.05	.08	.55	8.31	.81	1.11	.97	.88	.64
26	PAPER+PROD., EX.CONTAINERS	1.78	3.47	1.67	-.08	4.21	1.60	2.74	2.26	1.94	.93
27	PAPER CONTAINERS	1.78	3.24	1.42	.98	4.78	1.37	1.71	1.54	1.42	1.21
28	NEWSPAPERS	1.30	2.60	1.18	.38	3.13	1.17	2.07	1.57	1.24	.78
29	PRINTING AND PUBLISHING	-.37	1.14	-.41	-.29	.49	-.52	1.78	.48	.51	.02
30	INDUSTRIAL CHEMICALS	-.17	1.45	-.52	-1.41	1.72	-.22	1.18	.48	.02	-.93
31	AGRICULTURAL CHEMICALS	1.90	1.90	2.52	.12	2.80	2.25	1.00	.76	.40	.27
32	PLASTIC,INK, AND FATTY ACID	2.90	5.28	2.50	1.71	7.64	1.56	2.92	2.57	2.34	1.93
33	PLASTICS AND SYNTHETICS	1.95	5.81	1.53	-.70	7.12	.25	4.50	3.05	2.08	.07
34	DRUGS	1.24	1.68	1.24	-.98	1.61	.25	1.75	.89	-.33	-.39
35	CLEANING AND TOILET ITEMS	2.91	4.28	2.65	2.08	5.40	2.61	3.16	2.83	2.61	2.40
36	PAINTS + ALLIED PRODUCTS	-1.57	2.02	1.46	1.33	2.70	1.40	1.34	1.40	1.44	1.41
37	PETROLEUM REFINING	-2.27	-4.16	-1.54	-1.50	-5.47	-1.77	-2.84	-2.14	-1.68	-1.40
38	TIRE AND TUBES	2.08	2.47	2.19	1.67	1.83	2.24	3.11	2.60	2.26	1.89
39	RUBBER PROD. EX. TIRES	1.20	2.62	.85	.41	3.70	.87	1.55	1.16	.90	.58
40	PLASTIC PRODUCTS	5.61	10.39	4.84	2.54	14.64	4.54	6.14	5.54	5.13	3.55
41	LEATHER+IND. LTHR. PROD.	-2.10	1.49	-2.33	-4.74	3.33	-2.50	-.36	-1.23	-1.80	-3.78
42	FOOTWEAR + OTHER LEATHER	-.71	.87	-.42	-2.25	1.55	-.73	.18	.05	-.03	-1.51
43	GLASS AND GLASS PRODUCTS	.79	2.31	.70	-.32	2.92	.65	1.71	1.22	.89	.08
44	STONE AND CLAY PRODUCTS	1.00	2.18	.79	-.26	5.72	.23	-1.36	-.11	.73	.57
45	IRON AND STEEL	.86	3.49	-.01	-.37	6.77	-.05	.06	.06	-.04	-.16
46	NON-FERROUS METALS	1.63	3.00	1.37	.79	4.28	1.30	1.72	1.50	1.35	1.09
47	METAL CONTAINERS	1.27	2.58	1.09	.41	3.39	1.30	1.78	1.50	1.18	.72
48	PLUMBING AND HEATING	1.81	.75	1.04	-.23	5.88	.57	-.84	-.22	.93	.91
49	STRUCTURAL METAL PRODUCTS	1.95	3.30	1.59	1.23	5.88	1.33	-.72	1.22	1.56	1.44
50	STAMPINGS	2.64	5.54	1.96	.99	7.37	2.07	3.72	2.78	2.16	1.36
51	HARDWARE,PLATING+WIRE PROD	2.61	5.67	1.74	1.05	8.72	1.74	2.62	2.09	1.74	1.40
52	ENGINE AND TURBINES	1.88	4.62	1.13	.45	7.66	1.07	1.59	1.26	1.04	.87
53	FARM MACHINERY	-.38	3.08	-.82	-.59	5.18	-.40	.98	-.37	-1.27	-.43
54	CONST,MINE,MATRL HANDL EQ	1.63	7.06	1.35	1.32	10.75	1.78	3.36	1.96	1.03	1.59
55	METALWORKING MACHINERY	2.97	9.63	1.07	1.11	15.49	1.67	3.36	1.95	.74	1.40
56	SPECIAL INDUSTRIAL MACH.	.61	4.47	-.94	-.92	2.22	.66	6.71	2.19	-.82	-.87

NOVEMBER 1973 FORECAST

	PERSONS EMPLOYED						ANNUAL GROWTH RATES			
	71-85	71-75	75-80	80-85	71-73	73-83	73-75	73-78	75-78	78-83
58 GENERAL INDUSTRIAL MACH.	2.24	7.71	-.04	.15	10.01	1.18	5.42	2.02	-.25	.34
59 MISC. MACHINERY AND SHOPS	3.00	4.84	2.75	1.78	5.21	2.88	4.47	3.45	2.77	2.30
60 OFFICE AND COMPUTING MACH	2.05	5.90	-.15	-3.44	1.66	-1.47	2.14	-.54	-.99	-2.41
61 SERVICE INDUSTRY MACH.	2.66	5.50	1.83	1.22	8.61	1.81	2.39	2.02	1.77	1.60
62 TRANSFORMRS,SWTHGEAR, MSR	2.66	6.31	1.66	.73	11.30	1.38	2.55	1.48	1.58	1.28
63 ELECTRIC APP.+ MOTORS	2.52	5.61	1.41	1.14	8.67	1.59	2.55	1.81	1.31	1.38
64 HOUSEHOLD APPLIANCES	1.05	2.65	.74	-.08	4.50	.59	.79	.73	.69	.45
65 ELEC. LIGHTING + WIRING	2.82	7.23	1.85	.26	13.19	1.33	1.27	1.76	2.08	.90
66 RADIO-, TV-SETS AND PHONO	.73	4.05	-.23	-.96	7.71	-.29	.40	.09	-.12	-.67
67 COMMUNICATION EQUIPMENT	2.68	5.36	1.80	1.41	10.81	1.32	-.08	.89	1.54	1.75
68 ELECTRONIC COMPONENTS	.27	4.92	-.77	-2.40	9.30	-.93	.55	-.11	-.54	-1.76
69 BATTERIES,X-RAY EQ.+ETC.	3.04	4.85	2.80	1.84	4.93	2.97	4.78	3.62	2.85	2.31
70 MOTOR VEHICLES	2.71	3.14	2.83	2.25	2.86	2.80	3.42	3.12	2.92	2.48
71 AIRCRAFT	.22	2.60	-.47	-.98	3.35	-.12	1.85	.49	-.42	-.74
72 SHIPS AND BOATS	2.19	6.14	.60	.62	10.24	.95	2.04	.73	-.15	1.18
73 RAILROAD EQUIPMENT	1.06	6.45	-1.16	-1.04	16.74	-1.63	-3.85	-2.43	-1.49	-.82
74 TRAILERS, CYCLES	1.92	1.25	2.09	2.05	.07	2.31	3.03	2.68	2.45	1.94
75 LNGR.+ SCIENTIF,AC INSTR.	1.45	4.27	.68	-.04	5.58	-.95	2.06	1.69	.85	.21
76 MECH.+ MEASURING DEVICES	.70	2.13	.43	-.18	-.27	1.14	4.53	2.20	.64	.08
77 SURGICAL + MEDICAL INSTR.	2.83	6.21	2.43	-.53	6.96	2.58	5.46	3.76	2.62	1.41
78 OPTICAL AND PHOTOGRAPHIC	2.23	6.90	.96	-.23	9.92	1.25	3.87	2.22	1.12	.27
79 MISC. MANUFACTURING	-.26	2.50	-.49	-2.25	2.92	-.43	2.09	.79	-1.07	-1.64
80 RAILROADS	-3.77	-3.34	-3.87	-4.03	-2.64	-3.94	-4.04	-3.95	-3.89	-3.92
81 TRUCKING	2.14	3.14	1.90	1.58	3.99	1.90	2.29	2.20	1.94	1.72
82 OTHER TRA;SPORT	1.88	2.36	1.91	1.46	2.28	1.91	2.45	2.20	2.03	1.62
83 AIRLINES	.84	1.94	.61	.19	2.65	.63	1.22	.92	.73	.33
84 WHOLESALE + RETAIL TRADE	1.99	2.51	2.12	1.45	2.20	2.11	2.83	2.44	2.19	1.79
85 COMMUNICATION	2.01	3.07	1.87	1.30	4.14	1.76	2.00	1.90	1.83	1.63
86 FINANCE AND SERVICES	2.85	3.73	2.96	2.04	3.40	2.97	4.05	3.44	3.04	2.49
87 ELECTRIC UTILITIES	1.56	1.90	1.49	1.34	2.24	1.48	1.56	1.52	1.48	1.44
88 NAT. GAS, WATER AND SEWER	-1.06	-1.77	-.97	-1.59	-2.11	-.95	-1.43	-1.21	-1.06	-.69
89 PERS, AUTO/FED, ENTERPRIS	1.63	1.97	1.98	1.98	-.49	1.98	1.98	1.98	1.98	1.98
90 COMPUTER RENTAL/S&L ENTER	3.09	1.95	3.54	3.94	-.39	3.54	3.04	3.54	3.54	3.54
91 DOMESTIC SERVANTS	-.95	-.76	-.99	-1.05	-4.82	-1.24	-1.23	-1.08	-.98	-1.03
92 DEFENSE CIVILIAN	-1.57	-5.54	-.01	.51	-.01	-1.24	-6.27	-2.50	-.01	.01
93 FEDERAL NON-DEFENSE	1.11	1.95	1.04	.92	1.35	1.18	2.55	1.65	1.05	.71
94 PUBLIC EDUCATION	1.65	3.30	1.06	.92	3.93	1.30	2.67	1.80	1.21	.80
95 MILITARY	-.51	-2.09	.13	.11	1.55	-1.05	-5.72	-2.21	.12	.80
96 S&L NON-SCHOOL	2.43	3.17	2.39	1.88	3.51	2.36	2.83	2.54	2.35	2.19

NOVEMBER 1973 FORECAST

OUTPUT (PRODUCT SHIPMENTS) — MILLIONS OF 1971$

#	Industry	1971	1972	1973	1974	1975	1976	1978	1980	1983	1985
1	DAIRY FARM PRODUCTS	6879	6218	6458	6540	6614	6690	6772	6848	6938	6993
2	POULTRY AND EGGS	4261	4136	4241	4289	4366	4412	4551	4642	4796	4887
3	MEAT ANIMALS, OTH LIVESTK	25936	23964	26199	27360	28542	29396	31059	32699	35217	36887
4	COTTON	1428	1417	1520	1523	1587	1591	1670	1730	1791	1825
5	GRAINS	13581	13581	14098	14755	15399	15916	16914	16930	17723	18294
6	TOBACCO	1499	1555	1619	1526	1530	1516	1546	1578	1638	1678
7	FRUIT, VEGETABLES, OTH CROPS	11389	12231	12748	12759	13219	13467	14075	14706	15569	16091
8	FORESTRY + FISHERY PROD.	2133	2439	2644	2529	2644	2674	2762	2827	2862	2859
9	AGR, FORESTRY+FISH SERVICES	3305	3343	3460	3483	3589	3646	3781	3914	4093	4200
10	IRON ORES	1310	1655	1786	1794	1780	1812	1857	1916	1972	1996
11	COPPER ORE	1400	930	1373	1351	1419	1460	1483	1540	1568	1575
12	OTHER NON-FERROUS ORES	984	1000	1158	1177	1219	1244	1284	1331	1376	1396
13	COAL MINING	4846	4799	5026	5027	5114	5212	5396	5600	5864	6016
14	CRUDE PETROLEUM, NAT, GAS	16705	18155	19308	20011	20835	21680	23145	24746	27013	28432
15	STONE AND CLAY MINING	2309	2429	2643	2611	2705	2803	2907	3053	3231	3333
16	CHEMICAL FERTILIZER MINING	949	646	702	727	762	788	839	884	943	977
17	NEW CONSTRUCTION	38883	42181	45444	41360	43422	45664	46625	49446	52745	54659
18	MAINTENANCE CONSTRUCTION	33121	35068	37395	38661	40565	41711	44844	47902	52143	54762
19	COMPLETE GUIDED MISSILES	3552	3323	3345	3329	3289	3351	3463	3572	3737	3848
20	AMMUNITION	1760	1736	1807	1836	2074	2079	2327	2375	2173	2242
21	OTHER ORDNANCE	1736	1735	1837	1838	2042	2053	2433	2505	2833	2933
22	MEAT PRODUCTS	28260	28838	29793	30640	31572	32467	34224	36050	38808	40645
23	DAIRY PRODUCTS	13936	13915	14279	14555	14817	15056	15448	15828	16355	16694
24	CANNED AND FROZEN FOODS	11107	11843	12516	12986	13557	13977	15015	16021	17565	18593
25	GRAIN MILL PRODUCTS	11398	11463	11942	12274	12670	12964	13645	14318	15305	15940
26	BAKERY PRODUCTS	7535	7860	8076	8234	8347	8477	8698	8934	9321	9563
27	SUGAR	3123	3337	3360	3395	3457	3513	3652	3795	3987	4096
28	CONFECTIONERY PRODUCTS	3362	3479	3703	3890	4016	4162	4388	4627	4910	5042
29	ALCOHOLIC BEVERAGES	11993	12035	12705	13110	13711	14018	14993	15756	16731	17194
30	SOFT DRINKS AND FLAVORINGS	5766	5946	6294	6568	6860	7095	7635	8176	8902	9329
31	FATS AND OILS	6308	6506	6825	7035	7296	7506	7961	8427	9115	9555
32	MISC FOOD PRODUCTS	9535	10086	10138	9939	9921	9965	10100	10251	10537	10732
33	TOBACCO PRODUCTS	5975	6068	6194	6230	6324	6443	6664	6903	7311	7594
34	BROAD AND NARROW FABRICS	16027	16457	18172	18280	19232	19247	20285	21024	21627	21891
35	FLOOR COVERINGS	2489	2711	3102	3140	3426	3326	3902	4305	4796	5103
36	MISC TEXTILES	2672	2659	2724	2982	3168	3239	3421	3581	3696	3811
37	KNITTING	6902	6954	7724	7982	8768	8929	10156	11178	12628	13374
38	APPAREL	18565	18400	21325	22060	23540	23826	25529	26953	28215	28439
39	HOUSEHOLD TEXTILES	4516	4295	4784	5087	5394	5594	6045	6481	7034	7350
40	LUMBER AND WOOD PRODUCTS	8735	10119	11045	10346	10593	10986	11212	11564	11883	11965
41	VENEER AND PLYWOOD	2251	2675	2896	2666	2905	3094	3240	3493	3790	3959
42	MILLWORK AND WOOD PRODUCTS	5081	5729	6160	5631	6124	6583	7004	7743	8743	9386
43	WOODEN CONTAINERS	380	281	361	375	389	389	386	384	377	371
44	HOUSEHOLD FURNITURE	6515	7180	7737	7622	8135	8140	8699	9167	9632	9905
45	OTHER FURNITURE	2964	3253	3820	3932	4128	4305	4512	4825	5144	5327
46	PULP MILLS	1092	1123	1218	1287	1373	1441	1568	1673	1805	1881
47	PAPER AND PAPERBOARD MILLS	9383	10098	10769	11034	11571	11916	12660	13306	14091	14525
48	PAPER PRODUCTS, NEC	6953	7321	7923	8226	8673	9007	9740	10468	11503	12163
49	WALL AND BUILDING PAPER	482	602	602	565	580	600	614	640	690	690
50	PAPERBOARD CONTAINERS	6981	7849	8062	8051	8449	8567	9494	9911	10997	11320
51	NEWSPAPERS	7065	7462	7918	8051	8449	8567	9054	9511	10058	10355
52	PERIODICALS	2953	3283	3386	3429	3558	3636	3860	4073	4337	4483
53	BOOKS	3860	3475	4036	4365	4667	4846	5234	5565	6034	6334
54	INDUSTRIAL CHEMICALS	16974	18609	20830	21891	23449	24619	27096	29484	32683	34609
55	BUSINESS FORMS, BLANK BOOK	1602	1757	1871	1932	2031	2099	2271	2447	2687	2835
56	COMMERCIAL PRINTING	4711	5115	5374	5512	5767	5938	6364	6779	7322	7666

NOVEMBER 1973 FORECAST

OUTPUT (PRODUCT SHIPMENTS)   MILLIONS OF 1971$

#		1971	1972	1973	1974	1975	1976	1978	1980	1983	1985	#
58	OTHER PRINTING, PUBLISHING	2045.	2153.	2309.	2391.	2499.	2572.	2750.	2927.	3175.	3329.	58
59	FERTILIZERS	1460.	1663.	1759.	1826.	1928.	2092.	2165.	2330.	2572.	2740.	59
60	PESTICIDES + AGRIC. CHEM.	981.	1004.	1259.	1211.	1349.	1409.	1505.	1632.	1632.	1705.	60
61	MISC. CHEMICAL PRODUCTS	3771.	3905.	4163.	4211.	4360.	4457.	4557.	4865.	5124.	5271.	61
62	PLASTIC MAT'LS. + RESINS	4745.	5410.	6228.	6697.	7372.	7983.	9241.	10543.	12443.	13660.	62
63	SYNTHETIC RUBBER	1168.	1219.	1339.	1390.	1481.	1537.	1665.	1786.	1948.	2047.	63
64	CELLULOSIC FIBERS	697.	685.	751.	753.	785.	781.	813.	833.	845.	848.	64
65	NON-CELLULOSIC FIBERS	2892.	3229.	3912.	4053.	4508.	4737.	5429.	6042.	6767.	7174.	65
66	DRUGS	6893.	7330.	7880.	8303.	8807.	9155.	10082.	10994.	12223.	12962.	66
67	CLEANING + TOILET PROD.	8437.	9501.	10327.	10735.	11425.	11728.	12854.	13906.	15249.	16066.	67
68	PAINTS	3163.	3382.	3759.	3728.	3856.	3944.	4097.	4285.	4496.	4611.	68
69	PETROLEUM REFINING	29341.	30401.	32632.	33963.	35421.	36863.	39393.	42139.	45944.	48284.	69
70	FUEL OIL	4823.	5378.	5771.	6022.	6366.	6662.	7246.	7858.	8723.	9286.	70
71	PAVING AND ASPHALT	1616.	1763.	1978.	1972.	2092.	2211.	2405.	2649.	3001.	3233.	71
72	TIRES AND INNER TUBES	5243.	5174.	5612.	5880.	6234.	6483.	7033.	7577.	8337.	8815.	72
73	RUBBER PRODUCTS	3675.	4040.	4448.	4553.	4832.	4938.	5247.	5512.	5821.	6001.	73
74	MISC. PLASTIC PRODUCTS	8424.	9940.	11700.	12717.	14250.	15621.	18679.	22055.	27105.	30438.	74
75	LEATHER + IND. LTHR PROD	952.	1033.	1075.	1071.	1092.	1081.	1070.	1033.	948.	872.	75
76	FOOTWEAR(EXC. RUBBER)	3175.	3386.	3562.	3594.	3630.	3258.	3396.	3366.	3863.	3595.	76
77	OTHER LEATHER PRODUCTS	1069.	986.	1087.	1191.	1282.	1258.	1326.	1366.	1395.	1395.	77
78	GLASS	5069.	5402.	5886.	6066.	6440.	6669.	7245.	7803.	8554.	9026.	78
79	STRUCTURAL CLAY PRODUCTS	1052.	1106.	1361.	1245.	1269.	1324.	1309.	1339.	1352.	1351.	79
80	POTTERY	701.	761.	831.	819.	866.	903.	949.	993.	1039.	1061.	80
81	CEMENT, CONCRETE, GYPSUM	7489.	8165.	9026.	8368.	8819.	9313.	9637.	10315.	11140.	11638.	81
82	OTHER STONE + CLAY PROD.	3671.	3922.	4391.	4374.	4575.	4764.	5006.	5313.	5702.	5933.	82
83	STEEL	30761.	33400.	37014.	37048.	37795.	38232.	38436.	38907.	39048.	38933.	83
84	COPPER	6515.	5421.	6827.	6836.	7128.	7345.	7523.	7802.	7993.	8047.	84
85	LEAD	530.	502.	592.	599.	620.	632.	657.	689.	721.	738.	85
86	ZINC	410.	480.	544.	541.	557.	564.	575.	590.	602.	607.	86
87	ALUMINUM	6648.	6722.	8039.	8431.	8887.	9279.	9977.	10788.	11859.	12525.	87
88	OTH PRIM NON-FER METALS	1058.	1033.	1131.	1167.	1216.	1244.	1291.	1333.	1370.	1383.	88
89	OTH NON-FER ROLL + DRAW	952.	932.	1019.	1075.	1121.	1143.	1184.	1226.	1261.	1273.	89
90	NON-FERROUS WIRE DRAWING	3795.	3652.	4496.	4418.	4492.	4621.	4826.	5073.	5328.	5545.	90
91	NON-FER CASTING + FORGING	810.	850.	931.	1015.	1095.	1108.	1138.	1163.	1528.	1545.	91
92	METAL CANS	3871.	4164.	4387.	4509.	4666.	4803.	5104.	5394.	5785.	6020.	92
93	METAL BARRELS AND DRUMS	435.	478.	527.	540.	572.	595.	639.	683.	740.	774.	93
94	PLUMBING + HEATING EQUIP.	1937.	1727.	2106.	1945.	2060.	2176.	2202.	2323.	2448.	2514.	94
95	STRUCTURAL METAL PRODUCTS	12250.	12909.	15170.	15080.	15553.	16226.	17091.	18268.	19786.	20706.	95
96	SCREW MACHINE PRODUCTS	2675.	2570.	3229.	3302.	3406.	3467.	3556.	3663.	3751.	3781.	96
97	METAL STAMPINGS	6981.	7570.	8014.	8279.	8732.	9000.	9644.	10237.	10974.	11402.	97
98	CUTLERY,HAND TOOLS,HARDWR	4293.	4595.	5112.	5115.	5502.	5703.	6049.	6399.	6799.	7025.	98
99	MISC FABRICATED WIRE PRODU	1892.	2032.	2248.	2287.	2393.	2458.	2575.	2695.	2831.	2907.	99
100	PIPES, VALVES, FITTINGS	3286.	3563.	4270.	4439.	4638.	4814.	5038.	5424.	5918.	6220.	100
101	OTH FABRICATED METAL PROD.	3659.	4109.	4604.	4757.	5020.	5198.	5571.	5950.	6414.	6684.	101
102	ENGINES AND TURBINES	5167.	5843.	6917.	7367.	7696.	8029.	8705.	9478.	10538.	11191.	102
103	FARM MACHINERY	4131.	3953.	4877.	5218.	5245.	5169.	5335.	5518.	5714.	5870.	103
104	CONSTR+MINE,OILFIELD MACH	6585.	7062.	8328.	8884.	9242.	9667.	9720.	10294.	11044.	11474.	104
105	MATERIALS HANDLING MACH.	2695.	3007.	3060.	4095.	4234.	4427.	4571.	4900.	5348.	5528.	105
106	MACH. TOOLS, METAL CUTTING	1192.	1758.	2060.	2185.	2234.	2349.	2664.	2661.	3652.	2907.	106
107	MACH. TOOLS, METAL FORMING	618.	945.	945.	1034.	1043.	1143.	1090.	1100.	1652.	1153.	107
108	OTHER METAL WORKING MACH	4947.	5038.	5960.	6272.	6663.	6836.	7180.	7600.	7836.	7836.	108
109	SPECIAL INDUSTRIAL MACH	5146.	5148.	6379.	6967.	7324.	7513.	7624.	7885.	8186.	8366.	109
110	PUMPS,COMPRESSORS,BLOWERS	3042.	3383.	4205.	4510.	4602.	4812.	4905.	5163.	5523.	5722.	110
111	BALL AND ROLLER BEARINGS	1280.	1518.	1837.	1941.	2021.	2101.	2216.	2372.	2585.	2716.	111
112	POWER TRANSMISSION EQUIP	1392.	1505.	1845.	1992.	2042.	2058.	2065.	2112.	2160.	2177.	112
113	INDUSTRIAL PATTERNS	1602.	1736.	2189.	2324.	2350.	2455.	2453.	2567.	2701.	2770.	113

NOVEMBER 1973 FORECAST OUTPUT (PRODUCT SHIPMENTS) MILLIONS OF 1971$

#	Industry	1971	1972	1973	1974	1975	1976	1978	1980	1983	1985	#
114	COMPUTERS + RELATED MACH.	5895	8663	10091	10348	11126	11698	12953	14109	15101	15636	114
115	OTHER OFFICE MACHINERY	1181	1165	1432	1562	1671	1747	1821	1905	1984	2011	115
116	SERVICE INDUSTRY MACHINERY	6837	7683	9088	9664	10348	11049	12210	13634	15696	17030	116
117	MACHINE SHOP PRODUCTS	4157	4541	5268	5672	6090	6485	7347	8307	9764	10765	117
118	ELECTRICAL MEASURING INSTR	1205	1313	1570	1673	1706	1728	1779	1876	1977	2024	118
119	TRANSFORMERS + SWITCHGEAR	3369	3661	4419	4526	4685	4906	5357	5842	6448	6795	119
120	MOTORS AND GENERATORS	2560	2927	3522	3735	3943	4135	4400	4746	5229	5532	120
121	INDUSTRIAL CONTROLS	1244	1455	1844	1967	2058	2170	2306	2547	2884	3100	121
122	WELDING APP, GRAPHITE PROD	1375	1385	1648	1778	1897	1995	2137	2303	2554	2707	122
123	HOUSEHOLD APPLIANCES	6245	7100	7572	7645	8162	8361	9093	9807	10695	11215	123
124	ELEC LIGHTING + WIRING EQ.	4782	5282	5885	5897	6101	6460	6899	7336	7860	8155	124
125	RADIO AND TV RECEIVING	3810	4944	5557	5690	6501	6289	6642	6727	7537	8773	125
126	PHONOGRAPH RECORDS	1194	1249	1373	1413	1461	1503	1596	1700	1829	1903	126
127	COMMUNICATION EQUIPMENT	13188	15196	16962	18819	17721	16250	19556	21085	22910	24057	127
128	ELECTRONIC COMPONENTS	7356	9078	10325	10819	11536	12050	13312	14520	16013	16941	128
129	BATTERIES	1194	1438	1702	1844	1975	2058	2228	2385	2577	2681	129
130	ENGINE ELECTRICAL EQUIP.	578	649	736	775	819	842	863	889	901	895	130
131	X-RAY, ELEC EQUIP,NEC	1613	1570	2069	2227	2359	2480	2644	2881	3154	3328	131
132	TRUCK, BUS, TRAILER BODIES	1710	68498	68498	71411	75889	78892	85529	91579	99519	104318	132
133	MOTOR VEHICLES	62016	65877	9179	10278	10711	11126	11790	12583	13625	14219	133
134	AIRCRAFT	8131	6961	4122	1104	1233	1300	1457	1577	1707	1769	134
135	AIRCRAFT ENGINES	3947	3979	4122	2797	3032	3043	3301	3447	3532	3537	135
136	AIRCRAFT EQUIPMENT, NEC	4946	4302	4823	5120	5222	5354	5551	5743	5972	6085	136
137	SHIP AND BOAT BUILDING	3458	3778	4479	4855	4911	4808	5201	5659	6211	6531	137
138	RAILROAD EQUIPMENT	2335	3270	4635	4555	4466	4537	4552	4688	4812	4843	138
139	CYCLES, TRANS EQUIP NEC	1176	1407	1504	1617	1771	1869	2021	2110	2247	2313	139
140	TRAILER COACHES	3231	3284	3284	3376	3468	3599	3830	4034	4547	4873	140
141	ENGR. + SCIENTIFIC INSTR.	1175	1228	1410	1513	1581	1634	1707	1801	1931	2006	141
142	OPTICAL, MEASURING DEVICES	2870	2443	1047	1629	2322	2408	2495	2680	1708	1832	142
143	OPTHALMIC + PHOTO GOODS	2207	2586	2870	3080	3345	3493	3877	4294	4769	5050	143
144	MEDICAL + SURGICAL INSTR.	4624	5431	6307	6897	7585	8117	9248	10453	12165	13241	144
145	PHOTOGRAPHIC EQUIPMENT	823	809	994	1104	1233	1300	1457	1577	1707	1769	145
146	WATCHES AND CLOCKS	2161	2446	2719	2797	3032	3043	3301	3447	3532	3537	146
147	JEWELRY AND SILVERWARE	3332	3708	4028	4225	4515	4656	5002	5263	5564	5730	147
148	TOYS,SPORT,MUSICAL INSTR.	852	911	981	1020	1067	1104	1186	1272	1385	1451	148
149	OFFICE SUPPLIES	3402	3536	3935	4101	4362	4503	4634	5123	5432	5590	149
150	MISC MANUFACTURING NEC	14701	15552	16759	16954	17596	18098	18943	19859	20991	21611	150
151	RAILROADS	5518	5686	5875	5975	6070	6172	6282	6421	6529	6528	151
152	BUSSES AND LOCAL TRANSIT	26398	28359	31314	32555	34620	36262	39579	43156	48383	51789	152
153	TRUCKING	4230	4736	4853	4794	4805	4807	4798	4809	4800	4783	153
154	WATER TRANSPORTATION	11991	12991	14130	14838	15717	16452	17800	19039	20762	21763	154
155	AIRLINES	1546	1682	1829	1934	2052	2174	2405	2662	3055	3517	155
156	PIPELINES	6658	2693	2736	3448	3773	3311	3902	396	396	3016	156
157	FREIGHT FORWARDING	20280	27004	29096	31464	33333	35101	39079	43255	49342	53298	157
158	TELEPHONE AND TELEGRAPH	4303	4615	4754	4977	5111	5304	5863	5805	6246	6483	158
159	RADIO+TV BROADCASTING	28604	30299	32544	33934	35670	37203	40422	43823	48813	52002	159
160	ELECTRIC UTILITIES	18085	18731	19562	20082	20990	21439	22688	24133	26470	28075	160
161	NATURAL GAS	4869	4966	5090	5139	5216	5304	5453	5634	5931	6129	161
162	WATER AND SEWER SERVICES	89178	93020	100331	103236	108409	112376	121196	130823	144114	154999	162
163	WHOLESALE TRADE	134005	140078	148734	153275	160226	164893	176828	189063	205715	215929	163
164	RETAIL TRADE	31190	33495	36739	38698	41275	42954	47514	52119	58510	62507	164
165	BANKS+CREDIT AGEN.+BROKERS	35335	36793	38913	40100	41691	42801	45502	48366	51901	53960	165
166	INSURANCE	67016	69450	72508	74825	77840	80075	86097	92045	101663	108023	166
167	OWNER-OCCUPIED DWELLINGS	79988	83713	89941	93148	98263	101105	109435	117591	127787	1337759	167
168	REAL ESTATE	6865	7296	7895	8269	8745	9077	9899	10751	11808	12433	168
169	HOTEL AND LODGING PLACES											169

NOVEMBER 1973 FORECAST   OUTPUT(PRODUCT SHIPMENTS)   MILLIONS OF 1971$

	1971	1972	1973	1974	1975	1976	1978	1980	1983	1985	
170 PERSONAL + REPAIR SERVICES	17272.	17945.	18850.	19384.	20163.	20563.	21863.	23398.	24848.	25701.	170
171 BUSINESS SERVICES	48590.	51859.	56269.	57707.	60609.	62849.	67488.	72422.	79049.	83043.	171
172 ADVERTISING	19947.	20825.	22056.	22436.	23211.	23589.	24650.	25677.	26828.	27418.	172
173 AUTO REPAIR	18520.	18945.	19668.	20022.	20636.	21120.	22209.	23367.	24981.	25957.	173
174 MOVIES + AMUSEMENTS	12284.	12478.	12875.	12928.	13230.	13199.	13595.	13869.	14112.	14134.	174
175 MEDICAL SERVICES	45078.	46919.	49437.	51012.	53444.	54654.	58907.	62905.	68267.	71525.	175
176 PRIVATE SCHOOLS + NPO	27665.	30352.	32320.	34081.	35755.	36943.	39747.	42471.	46036.	47868.	176
177 POST OFFICE	8381.	8978.	9570.	10004.	10503.	10841.	11677.	12529.	13678.	14371.	177
178 FEDERAL GOV. ENTERPRISES	842.	889.	951.	989.	1041.	1076.	1170.	1265.	1401.	1488.	178
180 ST+LOC ELECTRIC UTILITIES	1946.	2071.	2209.	2302.	2417.	2495.	2663.	2834.	3107.	3284.	180
181 NON-COMPETITIVE IMPORTS	5417.	5699.	6005.	6136.	6352.	6496.	6832.	7158.	7597.	7859.	181
182 BUSINESS TRAVEL(DUMMY)	17792.	18881.	20571.	21138.	22173.	22927.	24552.	26287.	28575.	29956.	182
183 OFFICE SUPPLIES(DUMMY)	3046.	3226.	3473.	3592.	3770.	3886.	4178.	4476.	4871.	5110.	183
184 UNIMPORTANT IND.(DUMMY)	304.	323.	363.	371.	390.	404.	428.	455.	489.	509.	184
185 COMPUTER RENTAL(DUMMY)	4753.	5373.	6237.	6837.	7551.	8191.	9566.	11007.	13035.	14291.	185

NOVEMBER 1973 FORECAST

	OUTPUT (PRODUCT SHIPMENTS)						ANNUAL GROWTH RATES			
	71-85	71-75	75-80	80-85	71-73	73-83	73-75	73-78	75-78	78-83
1 DAIRY FARM PRODUCTS	.12	-.98	.69	.42	-3.15	.72	1.19	.95	.79	.49
2 POULTRY AND EGGS	.98	.61	1.22	1.03	-.24	1.23	1.46	1.33	1.23	1.14
3 MEAT ANIMALS, OTH LIVESTK	2.52	2.39	2.72	2.41	.41	2.98	4.38	3.44	2.82	2.51
4 COTTON	1.43	2.83	2.72	1.07	3.13	2.29	4.13	3.07	2.70	1.40
5 GRAINS	1.45	.78	1.88	1.50	-2.85	2.29	4.41	3.02	2.70	1.55
6 TOBACCO	.80	.17	.89	1.23	-3.85	-.11	-3.51	-.93	2.09	1.16
7 FRUIT,VEGETABLES,OTH CROPS	2.47	3.72	2.13	1.80	5.63	2.00	1.82	1.98	2.09	2.02
8 FORESTRY + FISHERY PROD.	2.09	5.37	1.34	.23	10.75	.79	-1.01	.87	1.74	.72
9 AGR.FORESTRY+FISH SERVICES	1.71	2.06	1.74	1.41	2.30	1.68	1.82	1.77	1.74	1.59
10 IRON ORES	3.01	7.68	1.46	.82	15.51	.99	-.16	.78	1.40	1.20
11 COPPER ORE	.84	.34	1.64	.44	-1.00	1.33	-.16	1.55	1.46	1.12
12 OTHER NON-FERROUS ORES	2.50	5.37	1.75	.96	8.16	1.72	-1.68	2.06	1.71	1.39
13 COAL MINING	1.54	1.35	1.82	1.43	1.85	1.54	2.57	1.41	1.79	1.66
14 CRUDE PETROLEUM, NAT. GAS	3.80	5.52	3.44	2.78	7.24	3.36	3.81	3.63	3.51	3.09
15 STONE AND CLAY MINING	2.62	3.96	2.42	1.75	7.13	1.93	.84	1.76	2.40	2.11
16 CHEMICAL,FERTILIZER MINING	4.12	8.21	2.96	2.00	12.33	2.95	.79	3.55	3.19	2.35
17 NEW CONSTRUCTION	2.43	2.76	2.60	2.00	7.80	1.49	4.10	.51	2.37	2.47
18 MAINTENANCE CONSTRUCTION	3.59	5.07	3.32	2.68	6.07	3.32	4.07	3.63	3.34	3.02
19 COMPLETE GUIDED MISSILES	-1.73	-1.92	1.03	1.59	-3.00	1.87	-2.28	.51	1.72	1.52
20 AMMUNITION	1.73	1.57	2.05	1.59	-3.00	1.87	-.85	.69	1.72	1.74
21 OTHER ORDNANCE	3.74	6.11	3.20	2.12	7.90	3.21	-.83	2.00	2.12	2.61
22 MEAT PRODUCTS	2.59	1.53	2.65	2.40	2.61	2.64	1.83	2.79	2.71	2.50
23 DAIRY PRODUCTS	2.59	2.76	1.32	1.07	1.22	2.91	2.91	1.57	1.39	1.14
24 CANNED AND FROZEN FOODS	3.68	4.98	3.34	2.98	5.97	3.39	1.85	3.64	3.40	3.14
25 GRAIN MILL PRODUCTS	2.40	2.64	2.45	2.15	2.33	2.48	4.00	2.67	2.47	2.30
26 BAKERY PRODUCTS	1.70	2.56	1.36	1.36	3.47	1.43	2.96	1.49	1.37	1.38
27 SUGAR	1.94	2.54	1.86	1.53	3.65	1.71	1.65	1.67	1.83	1.75
28 CONFECTIONERY PRODUCTS	2.89	4.44	2.83	1.72	4.82	2.82	1.43	3.40	2.95	2.25
29 ALCOHOLIC BEVERAGES	2.57	3.35	2.78	1.75	2.88	2.74	4.06	3.23	2.84	2.25
30 SOFT DRINKS AND FLAVORINGS	3.44	4.34	3.51	2.64	4.38	3.47	3.81	3.86	3.57	3.07
31 FATS AND OILS	2.97	3.64	2.88	2.51	3.94	2.89	4.31	3.08	2.91	2.71
32 MISC FOOD PRODUCTS	1.71	1.42	1.75	1.91	1.39	1.74	3.34	1.63	1.75	1.85
33 TOBACCO PRODUCTS	2.84	.99	.65	.92	3.07	1.59	1.44	-.08	.60	.85
34 BROAD AND NARROW FABRICS	2.23	4.56	1.78	.41	10.28	1.74	-1.08	2.20	1.78	1.28
35 FLOOR COVERINGS	5.13	7.99	4.57	3.40	14.52	4.36	2.84	4.59	4.34	4.13
36 MISC TEXTILES	2.43	4.26	2.34	1.50	9.24	2.34	4.97	3.14	2.57	1.54
37 KNITTING	5.18	7.60	4.83	3.59	6.93	4.74	4.97	5.29	4.85	4.20
38 APPAREL	3.15	5.94	2.71	1.35	12.77	2.80	5.95	3.68	2.83	1.92
39 HOUSEHOLD TEXTILES	3.48	4.38	3.72	2.52	2.89	3.86	4.94	4.68	3.89	3.03
40 LUMBER AND WOOD PRODUCTS	2.25	4.82	1.75	.68	11.73	-.73	5.87	.30	1.89	1.16
41 VENEER AND PLYWOOD	4.03	6.37	3.69	2.50	12.58	2.69	-2.09	2.25	3.64	3.13
42 MILLWORK AND WOOD PRODUCTS	4.38	4.67	4.69	3.85	9.63	3.50	.16	2.57	4.48	4.44
43 WOODEN CONTAINERS	-.18	.56	-.23	-.72	-2.54	.42	-.30	1.34	-.21	-.51
44 HOUSEHOLD FURNITURE	2.99	5.55	2.39	1.55	8.59	2.19	3.66	2.34	2.24	2.04
45 OTHER FURNITURE	4.19	8.28	3.12	1.98	12.77	2.96	2.51	3.30	2.96	2.62
46 PULP MILLS	3.89	5.72	3.95	2.35	5.46	3.93	3.80	5.05	4.44	2.82
47 PAPER AND PAPERBOARD MILLS	3.12	5.24	2.79	1.75	6.89	2.69	5.98	3.24	3.00	2.14
48 PAPER PRODUCTS, NEC	2.56	5.53	1.99	1.00	6.53	3.73	3.59	5.05	3.87	3.33
49 WALL AND BUILDING PAPER	2.73	5.63	1.49	1.48	11.15	3.01	4.53	4.13	1.89	1.82
50 PAPERBOARD CONTAINERS	2.73	5.34	3.09	1.70	5.70	3.01	-1.88	.38	2.43	2.11
51 NEWSPAPERS	2.98	4.38	2.45	1.92	6.85	2.39	3.48	3.64	2.71	2.33
52 PERIODICALS	3.54	4.66	2.70	1.92	2.23	2.47	3.05	2.62	2.71	2.33
53 BOOKS	2.98	4.75	3.52	2.59	6.23	4.02	7.26	5.20	3.82	2.85
54 INDUSTRIAL CHEMICALS	5.09	8.08	4.58	3.20	10.24	4.50	5.92	5.26	4.82	3.75
55 BUSINESS FORMS,BLANK BOOK	4.08	5.92	3.73	2.94	7.74	3.62	4.10	5.88	4.82	3.36
56 COMMERCIAL PRINTING	3.48	5.06	3.23	2.46	6.59	3.11	3.53	3.38	3.28	2.83

NOVEMBER 1973 FORECAST

	OUTPUT (PRODUCT SHIPMENTS)					ANNUAL GROWTH RATES					
	71-85	71-75	75-80	80-85	71-73	73-83	73-75	73-78	75-78	78-83	
58 OTHER PRINTING, PUBLISHING	3.48	5.02	3.16	2.57	6.09	3.18	3.95	3.50	3.19	2.87	58
59 FERTILIZERS	4.50	6.95	3.79	3.25	9.31	3.83	4.58	4.16	3.87	3.50	59
60 PESTICIDES + AGRIC. CHEM.	3.95	6.03	3.71	2.53	6.79	3.73	5.27	4.48	3.96	2.97	60
61 MISC CHEMICAL PRODUCTS	2.50	4.02	2.19	1.60	5.72	2.08	2.31	2.24	2.19	1.91	61
62 PLASTIC MAT'LS. + RESINS	7.55	11.01	7.15	5.18	13.60	0.92	8.43	7.89	7.53	5.95	62
63 SYNTHETIC RUBBER	4.01	5.93	3.75	2.72	6.83	3.75	5.03	4.35	3.90	3.14	63
64 CELLULOSIC FIBERS	1.40	2.97	1.17	.37	3.72	1.18	2.22	1.58	1.15	.78	64
65 NON-CELLULOSIC FIBERS	6.49	11.10	5.81	3.44	13.81	5.74	8.39	7.07	6.19	4.41	65
66 DRUGS	4.51	6.12	4.44	3.29	6.69	4.39	5.06	4.93	4.51	3.85	66
67 CLEANING + TOILET PROD.	4.60	7.58	3.93	2.89	10.11	3.90	5.05	4.38	3.93	3.42	67
68 PAINTS	3.56	4.95	3.15	1.46	6.11	1.79	5.29	1.72	2.02	1.86	68
69 PETROLEUM REFINING	3.56	4.71	3.47	2.72	5.32	3.42	4.10	3.77	3.54	3.08	69
70 FUEL OIL	3.68	4.94	3.47	2.34	8.98	4.13	4.90	4.55	4.32	3.71	70
71 PAVING AND ASPHALT	4.95	6.46	4.72	3.98	10.12	4.17	2.79	3.91	4.65	4.42	71
72 TIRES AND INNER TUBES	3.71	4.33	3.90	3.03	3.40	3.96	5.25	4.51	4.02	3.40	72
73 RUBBER PRODUCTS	3.50	6.84	2.63	1.70	9.54	2.69	4.14	5.30	2.74	2.08	73
74 MISC PLASTIC PRODUCTS	9.18	13.14	8.74	6.44	16.42	8.40	9.86	9.36	9.02	7.45	74
75 LEATHER + IND LTHR PROD	-.63	3.42	-1.10	-3.39	6.08	-1.26	1.60	-.09	-.66	-2.43	75
76 FOOTWEAR(EXC. RUBBER)	1.09	5.03	-.53	-1.50	8.45	.27	1.60	1.22	.96	-.67	76
77 OTHER LEATHER PRODUCTS	2.32	4.68	2.32	.43	3.75	2.50	5.62	3.98	2.89	1.02	77
78 GLASS	4.12	6.00	3.83	2.91	7.47	3.74	4.53	4.15	3.90	3.33	78
79 STRUCTURAL CLAY PRODUCTS	1.79	4.69	1.08	.18	12.91	-.07	-3.52	-.79	1.03	.64	79
80 POTTERY	2.95	5.28	2.73	1.31	8.47	2.23	-1.16	2.67	3.04	1.80	80
81 CEMENT, CONCRETE, GYPSUM	3.15	4.09	3.13	2.41	9.33	2.11	-2.10	1.31	2.96	2.90	81
82 OTHER STONE + CLAY PROD.	3.43	3.91	2.99	2.21	8.95	2.61	2.04	2.62	2.90	2.61	82
83 STEEL	1.68	5.15	.58	.01	9.25	.54	2.25	.75	.56	.32	83
84 COPPER	1.51	2.25	1.81	1.39	2.34	1.58	2.27	1.94	1.80	1.21	84
85 LEAD	2.37	3.91	1.17	.56	5.55	1.97	1.12	2.06	1.93	1.87	85
86 ZINC	2.80	7.63	1.17	1.59	14.14	1.01	1.08	1.08	1.05	.94	86
87 ALUMINUM	4.52	7.26	3.86	2.99	9.50	3.89	5.01	4.32	3.86	3.46	87
88 OTH PRIM NON-FER METALS	1.91	3.47	1.84	.74	3.32	1.92	3.62	2.66	2.01	1.18	88
89 OTH NON-FER ROLL + DRAW	2.08	4.09	1.81	.74	3.42	2.13	4.75	3.01	1.85	1.26	89
90 NON-FERROUS WIRE DRAWING	2.57	4.21	2.43	1.41	8.03	1.77	-.39	1.59	2.39	1.95	90
91 NON-FER CASTING + FORGING	4.42	7.34	3.66	2.84	9.70	3.72	4.97	4.16	3.63	3.28	91
92 METAL CANS	3.15	4.79	2.80	2.19	6.25	2.77	3.32	3.03	2.83	2.50	92
93 METAL BARRELS AND DRUMS	4.12	6.87	3.56	2.48	9.60	3.40	4.14	3.88	3.70	2.93	93
94 PLUMBING + HEATING EQUIP.	1.86	1.54	2.40	1.58	4.24	1.50	-1.16	.87	2.23	2.12	94
95 STRUCTURAL METAL PRODUCTS	3.75	5.97	3.22	2.51	10.69	2.66	2.66	2.39	3.14	2.93	95
96 SCREW MACHINE PRODUCTS	2.47	6.04	1.46	.63	9.42	1.50	1.25	1.92	1.43	1.07	96
97 METAL STAMPINGS	3.50	5.59	3.18	2.16	6.90	3.14	2.66	3.37	3.31	2.58	97
98 CUTLERY,HAND TOOLS,HARDWR	3.52	6.21	3.02	1.87	8.73	2.85	4.29	3.37	3.16	1.90	98
99 MISC FABRICATED WIRE PRODU	3.07	5.88	2.38	1.74	13.63	2.31	3.68	2.71	2.44	3.22	99
100 PIPES,VALVES, FITTINGS	4.56	8.62	3.40	2.34	13.41	3.26	4.13	3.31	2.76	2.82	100
101 OTH FABRICATED METAL PROD.	4.30	7.91	4.16	2.33	11.49	2.43	4.32	3.81	3.48	3.82	101
102 ENGINES AND TURBINES	5.52	9.96	4.11	1.24	14.58	3.31	5.34	4.26	4.11	2.55	102
103 FARM MACHINERY	2.51	5.97	1.01	2.17	8.30	4.21	3.64	1.79	.57	1.38	103
104 CONSTR,MINE,OILFIELD MACH	3.97	8.47	2.16	2.77	11.74	1.59	5.21	3.09	1.68	2.55	104
105 MATERIALS HANDLING MACH.	5.26	11.29	2.92	2.33	17.97	2.82	4.62	3.38	2.56	3.14	105
106 MACH. TOOLS, METAL CUTTING	6.00	15.70	1.91	.93	26.23	3.26	5.17	3.03	1.60	2.47	106
107 MACH TOOLS, METAL FORMING	4.47	14.21	.22	1.75	21.39	2.75	7.03	2.84	.04	.83	107
108 OTHER METAL WORKING MACH	3.73	8.35	2.02	1.18	12.44	1.83	4.26	2.74	1.73	2.12	108
109 SPECIAL INDUSTRIAL MACH	3.42	8.63	1.48	2.06	10.35	2.43	6.91	3.57	1.34	1.42	109
110 PUMPS,COMPRESSORS,BLOWERS	4.51	11.41	2.04	2.71	16.19	2.49	4.79	3.08	1.69	3.08	110
111 BALL AND ROLLER BEARINGS	5.37	9.58	.67	.60	18.04	2.73	5.16	3.75	3.06	.90	111
112 POWER TRANSMISSION EQUIP	5.37	9.89	1.51	1.52	15.01	1.57	5.07	2.27	1.01	1.92	112
113 INDUSTRIAL PATTERNS	3.91	9.89	1.51	1.52	15.01	2.10	4.18	2.27	1.01	1.92	113

NOVEMBER 1973 FORECAST

	OUTPUT (PRODUCT SHIPMENTS)				ANNUAL GROWTH RATES						
	71-85	71-75	75-80	80-85	71-73	73-83	73-75	73-78	75-78	78-83	
COMPUTERS + RELATED MACH.	6.97	15.88	4.75	2.06	26.88	4.03	4.88	4.99	5.07	3.07	114
OTHER OFFICE MACHINERY	3.80	8.69	2.62	1.08	9.65	3.26	7.72	4.81	2.87	1.71	115
SERVICE INDUSTRY MACHINERY	6.52	10.36	5.51	4.45	14.24	5.46	6.49	5.91	5.52	5.02	116
MACHINE SHOP PRODUCTS	6.80	9.55	6.21	5.18	11.84	6.17	7.25	6.65	6.26	5.69	117
ELECTRICAL MEASURING INSTR	3.70	8.69	1.91	1.51	13.25	2.30	4.14	2.49	1.40	2.11	118
TRANSFORMERS + SWITCHGEAR	5.01	8.25	4.41	3.02	13.57	3.78	2.93	3.85	4.46	3.71	119
MOTORS AND GENERATORS	5.50	10.80	3.71	3.06	15.95	3.95	5.65	4.45	3.65	3.45	120
INDUSTRIAL CONTROLS	6.52	12.59	4.26	3.93	19.69	4.47	5.49	4.48	3.80	4.47	121
WELDING APP. GRAPHITE PROD	4.84	8.04	3.88	3.23	9.04	4.38	7.04	5.20	3.97	3.57	122
HOUSEHOLD APPLIANCES	4.18	6.69	3.67	2.48	9.63	2.45	2.70	3.66	3.60	3.25	123
ELEC LIGHTING + WIRING EQ.	3.81	6.54	3.33	2.12	10.58	2.69	3.75	3.18	3.30	3.61	124
RADIO AND TV RECEIVING	6.04	11.77	3.23	2.99	17.96	3.72	2.58	4.81	4.30	3.24	125
PHONOGRAPH RECORDS	2.73	1.43	3.52	2.99	-1.92	3.72	4.77	4.19	3.81	3.13	126
COMMUNICATION EQUIPMENT	4.29	7.38	3.48	2.64	12.58	3.01	2.89	2.89	3.35	3.69	127
ELECTRONIC COMPONENTS	5.96	11.25	4.60	3.08	16.95	4.39	5.55	5.01	4.77	2.73	128
BATTERIES	3.53	5.04	3.04	2.25	6.99	2.67	5.33	3.01	2.95	2.92	129
ENGINE ELECTRICAL EQUIP.	3.63	5.06	3.77	2.34	4.97	4.15	7.44	5.38	4.00	.85	130
X-RAY, ELEC EQUIP. NEC	3.13	8.72	1.64	2.88	12.11	2.02	5.33	3.01	3.99	3.52	131
TRUCK, BUS, TRAILER BODIES	4.76	8.05	4.00	2.60	12.58	3.74	6.57	4.91	3.80	3.03	132
MOTOR VEHICLES	3.71	5.05	3.76	2.45	6.99	3.95	5.12	5.01	3.20	2.89	133
AIRCRAFT	3.99	6.89	3.22	1.98	6.06	2.09	7.72	2.01	2.50	2.17	134
AIRCRAFT ENGINES	2.07	1.73	2.43	2.45	2.68	2.17	1.28	2.81	2.04	1.46	135
AIRCRAFT EQUIPMENT, NEC	1.48	1.36	1.90	1.16	-1.26	3.27	3.97	2.99	.63	3.55	136
SHIP AND BOAT BUILDING	4.54	4.34	2.84	2.86	12.93	3.27	4.61	2.81	1.91	1.11	137
RAILROAD EQUIPMENT	5.21	10.21	.97	.65	34.27	.38	-1.85	-.36	4.40	3.43	138
CYCLES, TRANS EQUIP NEC	4.83	7.42	3.03	2.18	12.31	4.02	8.19	5.91	2.56	2.12	139
TRAILER COACHES	1.92	3.76	1.50	.87	9.13	3.25	2.72	3.07	3.31	2.46	140
ENGR. + SCIENTIFIC INSTR.	3.83	12.42	2.61	2.58	3.89	3.14	3.63	2.33	1.46	1.26	141
MECH. MEASURING DEVICES	5.77	10.40	3.64	3.24	14.28	1.79	10.56	6.41	3.65	3.09	142
OPTICAL + OPHTHALMIC GOODS	5.91	12.37	4.99	4.73	13.13	4.75	5.72	6.02	4.91	1.63	143
MEDICAL + SURGICAL INSTR.	7.51	10.11	6.42	2.30	15.51	5.08	3.63	6.91	6.61	5.48	144
PHOTOGRAPHIC EQUIPMENT	5.47	8.46	4.92	4.73	15.51	6.57	9.23	7.66	6.54	3.17	145
WATCHES AND CLOCKS	3.52	7.60	2.57	.51	9.44	5.41	10.78	7.64	5.17	1.36	146
JEWELRY AND SILVERWARE	3.87	5.64	3.07	1.70	11.48	2.62	5.44	3.88	2.83	2.13	147
TOYS, SPORT, MUSICAL INSTR.	3.81	6.22	3.51	2.64	9.49	3.23	5.70	4.33	3.42	3.09	148
OFFICE SUPPLIES	3.55	5.64	3.21	1.74	7.05	3.45	4.22	3.81	3.53	2.33	149
MISC MANUFACTURING, NEC	2.75	4.49	2.42	1.69	7.28	3.22	5.15	4.11	3.42	2.05	150
RAILROADS	1.20	2.39	1.12	.33	6.55	2.25	2.44	2.45	2.46	.77	151
BUSSES AND LOCAL TRANSIT	4.81	6.18	.97	3.65	6.54	1.06	1.64	1.34	1.14	.01	152
TRUCKING	4.26	6.77	3.03	3.11	8.54	4.35	5.02	4.68	4.46	3.08	153
WATER TRANSPORTATION	5.45	6.19	3.84	2.67	8.67	-.11	-.50	-.23	4.15	1.72	154
AIRLINES	2.38	7.07	5.20	4.40	8.41	-1.85	5.32	4.62	4.25	4.76	155
PIPELINES	5.33	4.05	2.00	1.42	5.62	3.85	5.32	5.27	5.29	2.65	156
FREIGHT FORWARDING	3.34	6.96	5.17	4.18	5.62	5.12	2.48	2.21	2.03	3.77	157
TELEPHONE AND TELEGRAPH	4.27	5.08	3.08	2.21	8.39	1.96	5.53	5.32	5.18	3.08	158
RADIO AND TV BROADCASTING	3.14	5.52	4.12	3.42	6.39	5.01	5.53	5.37	5.10	1.68	159
ELECTRIC UTILITIES	1.64	3.36	3.08	3.03	6.45	3.01	4.59	4.34	4.17	3.46	160
NATURAL GAS	3.83	1.72	1.54	1.68	3.93	4.05	1.23	1.38	1.48	4.16	161
WATER AND SEWER SERVICES	3.41	4.47	3.76	3.07	2.21	3.02	1.38	2.96	1.48	3.03	162
WHOLESALE TRADE	4.97	7.00	3.31	2.66	5.89	1.53	3.87	3.78	3.29	2.63	163
RETAIL TRADE	3.02	4.14	4.67	3.64	5.21	3.62	3.72	3.46	3.72	3.32	164
BANKS, CREDIT AGEN. BROKERS	3.40	4.14	2.97	2.19	8.19	3.24	5.82	5.14	4.59	3.10	165
INSURANCE	3.72	5.30	3.59	2.58	3.89	4.65	3.45	3.13	2.92	3.53	166
OWNER-OCCUPIED DWELLINGS	3.02	4.14	2.97	2.19	3.89	2.68	3.45	3.13	2.92	2.63	167
REAL ESTATE	3.40	5.30	3.35	2.58	6.18	3.38	4.42	3.92	3.59	3.32	168
HOTEL AND LODGING PLACES	4.24	6.05	4.13	2.91	6.99	4.03	5.11	4.53	4.13	3.53	169

NOVEMBER 1973 FORECAST

OUTPUT (PRODUCT SHIPMENTS)

ANNUAL GROWTH RATES

	71-85	71-75	75-80	80-85	71-73	73-83	73-75	73-78	75-78	78-83	
170 PERSONAL + REPAIR SERVICES	2.84	3.87	2.98	1.88	4.37	2.76	3.37	2.97	2.70	2.56	170
171 BUSINESS SERVICES	3.83	5.53	3.56	2.74	7.34	3.40	3.72	3.64	3.58	3.16	171
172 ADVERTISING	2.27	3.79	2.02	1.31	5.03	1.96	2.55	2.22	2.00	1.69	172
173 AUTO REPAIR	2.41	2.70	2.49	2.10	3.01	2.39	2.40	2.43	2.45	2.35	173
174 MOVIES + AMUSEMENTS	1.00	1.85	.94	.38	2.35	.92	1.36	1.09	.91	.75	174
175 MEDICAL SERVICES	3.30	4.26	3.26	2.57	4.62	3.23	3.90	3.51	3.24	2.95	175
176 PRIVATE SCHOOLS + NPO	3.91	6.41	3.44	2.38	8.08	3.48	4.74	3.77	3.53	2.94	176
177 POST OFFICE	3.85	5.64	3.53	2.74	7.16	3.47	4.13	3.51	3.53	3.16	177
178 FEDERAL GOV. ENTERPRISES	4.07	5.31	3.89	3.25	6.09	3.88	4.54	4.15	3.90	3.60	178
180 ST+LOC ELECTRIC UTILITIES	3.74	5.42	3.19	2.95	6.35	3.41	4.49	3.74	3.24	3.08	180
181 NON-COMPETITIVE IMPORTS	2.66	3.98	2.39	1.87	5.15	2.35	2.81	2.58	2.43	2.12	181
182 BUSINESS TRAVEL(DUMMY)	3.72	5.50	3.40	2.61	7.26	3.29	3.75	3.54	3.40	3.03	182
183 OFFICE SUPPLIES(DUMMY)	3.70	5.34	3.43	2.65	6.57	3.38	4.11	3.70	3.42	3.07	183
184 UNIMPORTANT IND.(DUMMY)	3.68	6.24	3.06	2.25	8.80	2.99	3.69	3.31	3.06	2.67	184
185 COMPUTER RENTAL(DUMMY)	7.86	11.57	7.54	5.22	13.59	7.37	9.56	8.55	7.88	6.19	185

NOVEMBER 1973 FORECAST

		PRODUCTIVITY (OUTPUT PER EMPLOYED PERSON)						THOUSANDS OF 1971$/EMPLOYEE				
		1971	1972	1973	1974	1975	1976	1978	1980	1983	1985	
1	AGRICULTURE	19.	20.	21.	23.	25.	26.	29.	33.	38.	43.	1
2	MINING	31.	32.	34.	35.	36.	37.	38.	40.	41.	42.	2
3	PETROLEUM AND GAS	58.	61.	64.	67.	70.	73.	80.	88.	100.	109.	3
4	CONSTRUCTION(NEW AND OLD)	9.	10.	10.	9.	10.	10.	10.	10.	11.	11.	4
5	ORDNANCE	35.	35.	36.	37.	37.	38.	40.	42.	45.	47.	5
6	MEAT	82.	83.	86.	87.	89.	91.	95.	98.	103.	107.	6
7	DAIRY	60.	61.	64.	67.	70.	73.	79.	86.	96.	103.	7
8	CANNED AND FROZEN FOODS	41.	43.	44.	45.	46.	47.	49.	50.	53.	54.	8
9	GRAIN MILL PRODUCTS	85.	84.	86.	87.	89.	90.	93.	96.	100.	102.	9
10	BAKERY	28.	29.	30.	31.	31.	32.	33.	34.	36.	38.	10
11	SUGAR	98.	95.	91.	91.	92.	93.	97.	100.	106.	110.	11
12	CANDY	43.	46.	46.	48.	49.	50.	52.	53.	54.	54.	12
13	BEVERAGES	75.	74.	78.	78.	83.	86.	91.	96.	104.	108.	13
14	MISC. FOOD PRODUCTS	86.	88.	91.	93.	96.	98.	103.	108.	116.	122.	14
15	TOBACCO	131.	139.	136.	136.	138.	141.	147.	155.	168.	177.	15
16	FABRICS AND YARNS	27.	28.	29.	30.	31.	32.	33.	35.	37.	39.	16
17	FLOOR COVERINGS	45.	50.	54.	55.	61.	63.	73.	84.	103.	118.	17
18	MISC. TEXTILES	37.	38.	39.	40.	41.	42.	44.	47.	50.	53.	18
19	KNIT FABRIC AND APPAREL	26.	28.	31.	32.	35.	36.	41.	46.	53.	58.	19
20	APPAREL	16.	16.	17.	16.	16.	16.	17.	17.	18.	18.	20
21	HSHLD TEXTILES + UPHOLST.	28.	28.	29.	29.	30.	31.	32.	34.	37.	39.	21
22	LOGGING AND LUMBER	30.	33.	35.	34.	34.	35.	36.	37.	37.	37.	22
23	PLYWOOD,MILLWORK, ETC.	27.	29.	30.	29.	31.	32.	33.	35.	37.	39.	23
24	WOODEN CONTAINERS	17.	14.	18.	17.	18.	16.	19.	21.	23.	26.	24
25	FURNITURE	21.	21.	22.	22.	22.	23.	23.	24.	25.	26.	25
26	PAPER+PROD, EX.CONTAINERS	39.	41.	41.	41.	42.	42.	44.	45.	48.	49.	26
27	PAPER CONTAINERS	33.	30.	35.	35.	35.	36.	37.	39.	40.	41.	27
28	NEWSPAPERS	19.	20.	20.	20.	21.	21.	21.	22.	23.	24.	28
29	PRINTING AND PUBLISHING	21.	23.	24.	24.	25.	26.	21.	23.	31.	33.	29
30	INDUSTRIAL CHEMICALS	55.	60.	65.	67.	71.	74.	82.	90.	114.	73.	30
31	AGRICULTURAL CHEMICALS	45.	47.	50.	51.	54.	55.	59.	63.	69.	73.	31
32	GLUE, INK, AND FATTY ACID	38.	37.	36.	36.	36.	36.	36.	36.	36.	36.	32
33	PLASTICS AND SYNTHETICS	46.	48.	51.	51.	54.	56.	61.	68.	79.	87.	33
34	DRUGS	46.	49.	51.	53.	55.	57.	63.	68.	78.	85.	34
35	CLEANING AND TOILET ITEMS	68.	73.	75.	76.	78.	79.	81.	83.	85.	87.	35
36	PAINTS + ALLIED PRODUCTS	47.	49.	53.	52.	53.	53.	54.	55.	55.	55.	36
37	PETROLEUM REFINING	164.	183.	204.	219.	234.	246.	274.	302.	344.	374.	37
38	TIRE AND TUBES	44.	44.	45.	46.	47.	48.	50.	52.	54.	55.	38
39	RUBBER PROD. EX. TIRES	22.	23.	24.	25.	26.	26.	27.	28.	29.	30.	39
40	PLASTIC PRODUCTS	30.	30.	31.	32.	33.	34.	37.	40.	45.	49.	40
41	LEATHER+IND. LTHR. PROD.	34.	37.	36.	36.	37.	37.	39.	40.	41.	42.	41
42	FOOTWEAR + OTHER LEATHER	14.	15.	15.	16.	16.	16.	17.	17.	18.	18.	42
43	GLASS AND GLASS PRODUCTS	28.	29.	31.	31.	32.	33.	36.	38.	42.	45.	43
44	STONE AND CLAY PRODUCTS	29.	30.	31.	39.	32.	30.	34.	36.	38.	39.	44
45	IRON AND STEEL	37.	37.	39.	39.	39.	40.	40.	41.	41.	41.	45
46	NON-FERROUS METALS	58.	57.	61.	61.	63.	64.	60.	67.	68.	71.	46
47	METAL CONTAINERS	54.	57.	57.	58.	59.	60.	62.	65.	68.	71.	47
48	PLUMBING AND HEATING	24.	25.	25.	24.	25.	26.	27.	27.	28.	28.	48
49	STRUCTURAL METAL PRODUCTS	30.	30.	33.	33.	33.	34.	35.	36.	38.	39.	49
50	STAMPINGS	32.	32.	32.	32.	32.	33.	33.	33.	34.	35.	50
51	HARDWARE,PLATING+WIRE PROD	31.	31.	32.	32.	33.	33.	34.	35.	36.	37.	51
52	ENGINE AND TURBINES	45.	48.	52.	54.	56.	58.	61.	65.	71.	75.	52
53	FARM MACHINERY	34.	34.	36.	37.	38.	38.	40.	41.	44.	45.	53
54	CONST+MINE+MATRL HANDL EQ	35.	35.	37.	37.	38.	39.	39.	40.	41.	42.	54
55	METALWORKING MACHINERY	26.	26.	26.	27.	27.	27.	28.	28.	29.	29.	55
56	SPECIAL INDUSTRIAL MACH.	30.	31.	35.	35.	35.	36.	38.	40.	42.	45.	57

NOVEMBER 1973 FORECAST

PRODUCTIVITY (OUTPUT PER EMPLOYED PERSON)   THOUSANDS OF 1971$/EMPLOYEE

		1971	1972	1973	1974	1975	1976	1978	1980	1983	1985	
58	GENERAL INDUSTRIAL MACH.	30.	32.	34.	33.	33.	34.	35.	37.	39.	40.	58
59	MISC. MACHINERY AND SHOPS	21.	23.	24.	25.	26.	27.	29.	31.	34.	36.	59
60	OFFICE AND COMPUTING MACH	29.	38.	38.	38.	42.	44.	49.	55.	64.	72.	60
61	SERVICE INDUSTRY MACH.	51.	53.	57.	59.	61.	64.	69.	74.	82.	87.	61
62	TRANSFORMRS,SWTHGR,EL MSR	24.	24.	25.	25.	26.	26.	27.	29.	30.	32.	62
63	ELECTRIC APP. + MOTORS	27.	28.	30.	31.	32.	33.	35.	37.	39.	41.	63
64	HOUSEHOLD APPLIANCES	34.	36.	38.	39.	40.	41.	44.	46.	50.	53.	64
65	ELEC. LIGHTING + WIRING	26.	25.	25.	25.	26.	26.	27.	28.	29.	30.	65
66	RADIO-, TV-SETS AND PHONO	32.	35.	37.	39.	41.	43.	47.	51.	58.	63.	66
67	COMMUNICATION EQUIPMENT	30.	31.	31.	32.	33.	34.	35.	36.	37.	38.	67
68	ELECTRONIC COMPONENTS	22.	25.	26.	27.	29.	30.	33.	37.	44.	49.	68
69	BATTERIES,X-RAY EQ.,ETC.	29.	29.	29.	30.	30.	30.	33.	30.	30.	30.	69
70	MOTOR VEHICLES	74.	76.	77.	78.	60.	81.	62.	84.	85.	85.	70
71	AIRCRAFT	32.	30.	32.	33.	34.	35.	38.	40.	44.	47.	71
72	SHIPS AND BOATS	21.	22.	23.	23.	24.	24.	25.	27.	29.	30.	72
73	RAILROAD EQUIPMENT	47.	56.	66.	68.	69.	71.	74.	77.	81.	84.	73
74	TRAILERS, CYCLES	37.	39.	40.	40.	41.	42.	42.	43.	45.	46.	74
75	ENGR. + SCIENTIFIC INSTR.	19.	19.	21.	21.	22.	22.	23.	24.	26.	27.	75
76	MECH. MEASURING DEVICES	23.	22.	24.	24.	24.	24.	25.	25.	26.	27.	76
77	SURGICAL + MEDICAL INSTR.	26.	29.	29.	29.	30.	30.	33.	34.	37.	40.	77
78	OPTICAL AND PHOTOGRAPHIC	34.	35.	38.	40.	42.	44.	49.	54.	62.	67.	78
79	MISC. MANUFACTURING	24.	26.	27.	27.	29.	29.	32.	34.	38.	41.	79
80	RAILROADS	25.	27.	29.	31.	34.	36.	41.	46.	55.	61.	80
81	TRUCKING	21.	22.	23.	24.	25.	25.	27.	28.	31.	31.	81
82	OTHER TRANSPORT	18.	19.	20.	21.	19.	19.	19.	19.	19.	18.	82
83	AIRLINES	35.	37.	40.	49.	42.	44.	47.	15.	53.	56.	83
84	WHOLESALE + RETAIL TRADE	13.	13.	13.	13.	14.	14.	14.	15.	15.	16.	84
85	COMMUNICATION	26.	27.	28.	29.	30.	31.	33.	35.	38.	40.	85
86	FINANCE AND SERVICES	19.	20.	20.	20.	20.	20.	20.	21.	21.	21.	86
87	ELECTRIC UTILITIES	59.	61.	64.	66.	68.	70.	74.	78.	83.	86.	87
88	NAT. GAS, WATER AND SEWER	101.	108.	114.	118.	123.	126.	138.	148.	164.	175.	88

NOVEMBER 1973 FORECAST

	PRODUCTIVITY (OUTPUT PER EMPLOYED PERSON)						ANNUAL GROWTH RATES				
	71-85	71-75	75-80	80-85	73-83	71-73	73-75	73-78	75-78	78-83	
1 AGRICULTURE	5.69	6.22	5.68	5.28	5.84	5.42	7.01	6.29	5.82	5.39	1
2 MINING	2.20	3.67	2.08	1.15	1.94	4.78	2.56	2.37	2.25	1.51	2
3 PETROLEUM AND GAS	4.48	4.63	4.47	4.38	4.47	4.68	4.58	4.53	4.49	4.41	3
4 CONSTRUCTION(NEW AND OLD)	1.30	1.76	1.43	.81	.33	6.87	-3.36	-.62	1.21	1.27	4
5 ORDNANCE	2.15	2.04	2.41	2.36	2.31	1.16	1.96	2.23	2.42	2.39	5
6 MEAT	1.85	1.90	1.90	1.64	1.89	1.90	2.18	2.05	1.96	1.74	6
7 DAIRY	3.89	3.91	3.97	3.80	4.00	3.50	4.32	4.14	4.01	3.86	7
8 CANNED AND FROZEN FOODS	2.00	3.29	1.69	1.27	1.73	4.23	2.36	2.01	1.78	1.44	8
9 GRAIN MILL PRODUCTS	1.31	1.10	1.56	1.88	1.54	.38	1.82	1.68	1.59	1.39	9
10 BAKERY	2.07	2.50	1.88	1.92	1.92	3.04	1.96	1.91	1.88	1.93	10
11 SUGAR	.84	-1.54	1.74	1.84	1.57	-3.85	.77	1.33	1.70	1.82	11
12 CANDY	1.62	3.42	1.50	.29	1.49	3.95	2.69	2.16	1.67	.82	12
13 BEVERAGES	2.59	2.59	2.86	2.33	2.82	1.89	3.30	3.05	2.89	2.59	13
14 MISC. FOOD PRODUCTS	2.49	2.62	2.49	2.38	2.49	2.68	2.56	2.52	2.50	2.45	14
15 TOBACCO	2.18	1.31	2.38	2.68	2.10	2.08	.54	1.58	2.28	2.61	15
16 FABRIC AND YARNS	2.52	3.13	2.42	2.14	2.40	3.58	2.68	2.52	2.41	2.28	16
17 FLOOR COVERINGS	6.86	7.45	6.51	6.73	6.36	9.31	5.59	5.84	6.01	6.87	17
18 MISC. TEXTILES	2.49	2.49	2.50	2.50	2.50	2.48	2.50	2.50	2.50	2.50	18
19 KNIT FABRIC AND APPAREL	5.60	6.96	5.38	4.72	5.34	7.91	6.00	5.64	5.39	5.05	19
20 APPAREL	.94	1.68	.90	.29	.26	4.39	-1.03	-.24	.29	.76	20
21 HSHLD TEXTILES + UPHOLST.	2.34	3.19	1.16	2.64	2.55	2.59	1.08	1.83	2.33	2.56	21
22 LOGGING AND LUMBER	1.45	3.06	1.18	.33	.55	7.29	-.90	.43	1.31	.68	22
23 PLYWOOD, MILLWORK, ETC.	2.56	1.47	2.56	3.66	2.04	5.69	.43	1.43	2.42	2.42	23
24 WOODEN CONTAINERS	2.93	1.73	3.37	3.66	2.57	3.97	-1.02	1.69	3.07	3.70	24
25 FURNITURE	1.72	1.89	1.56	1.62	1.64	1.63	1.21	1.43	1.60	1.60	25
26 PAPER+PROD., EX.CONTAINERS	1.72	1.78	1.67	1.75	1.63	2.58	1.21	1.36	1.46	1.72	26
27 PAPER CONTAINERS	1.43	2.09	1.67	1.43	1.63	2.42	1.77	1.71	1.67	1.56	27
28 NEWSPAPERS	3.10	1.78	1.27	1.32	1.22	2.58	.98	1.10	1.19	1.33	28
29 PRINTING AND PUBLISHING	1.12	3.86	2.84	2.75	2.76	5.13	2.58	2.73	2.84	2.79	29
30 INDUSTRIAL CHEMICALS	5.91	6.63	4.80	4.62	4.73	8.52	4.74	4.78	4.80	4.68	30
31 AGRICULTURAL CHEMICALS	1.63	4.69	3.84	2.85	3.27	5.52	3.86	3.52	3.30	3.02	31
32 GLUE, INK, AND FATTY ACID	2.30	-.26	-.10	-.01	-.18	-1.91	-.60	-.33	-.15	-.02	32
33 PLASTICS AND SYNTHETICS	3.57	1.73	1.56	1.75	1.64	5.09	3.19	3.87	4.33	4.24	33
34 PLASTICS AND SYNTHETICS	1.47	4.14	4.20	4.28	4.40	5.08	3.81	4.03	4.18	4.92	34
35 DRUGS	2.11	4.45	1.27	1.43	1.28	4.71	1.89	1.55	1.32	1.02	35
36 CLEANING AND TOILET ITEMS	1.69	3.30	1.28	.81	1.28	4.71	1.05	.32	.57	4.55	36
37 PAINTS + ALLIED PRODUCTS	1.12	2.93	.65	.13	.39	5.92	-1.05	.32	1.57	1.51	37
38 PETROLEUM REFINING	5.91	8.96	5.08	4.30	5.24	11.05	6.87	5.92	5.28	1.49	38
39 TIRE AND TUBES	1.63	1.86	1.72	1.36	1.71	1.58	2.14	1.92	1.77	3.90	39
40 RUBBER PROD. EX. TIRES	2.30	4.22	1.78	1.29	1.82	5.84	2.59	2.14	1.84	1.35	40
41 PLASTIC PRODUCTS	3.57	2.75	3.89	3.90	3.86	1.79	3.72	3.82	3.89	1.27	41
42 LEATHER+I.D. LTHR. PROD.	1.47	1.93	1.23	1.35	1.24	2.75	1.12	1.13	1.14	3.25	42
43 FOOTWEAR + OTHER LEATHER	2.11	4.08	1.39	1.26	1.54	5.80	2.35	1.82	1.46	2.02	43
44 GLASS AND GLASS PRODUCTS	3.33	3.69	3.13	3.24	3.09	4.56	2.82	2.93	3.01	.48	44
45 STONE AND CLAY PRODUCTS	2.12	2.43	2.12	1.87	1.86	3.76	1.10	1.70	2.09	1.20	45
46 IRON AND STEEL	1.37	1.66	1.59	.38	.59	2.48	.84	.70	.60	1.83	46
47 NON-FERROUS METALS	1.98	1.80	1.38	1.81	1.77	2.21	1.39	1.38	1.37	1.21	47
48 METAL CONTAINERS	1.06	2.42	1.79	1.61	1.79	3.21	1.63	1.70	1.75	1.49	48
49 PLUMBING AND HEATING	1.80	.79	1.37	.95	.93	1.91	.32	.65	1.30	.82	49
50 STRUCTURAL METAL PRODUCTS	.60	.17	1.63	1.27	1.32	4.81	-.53	1.16	1.58	1.26	50
51 STAMPINGS	1.34	1.59	.75	.78	.62	.24	.11	.43	.64	2.95	51
52 HARDWARE+PLATING+WIRE PRD	3.64	1.33	3.04	1.14	1.90	1.90	1.28	1.30	1.31	1.81	52
53 ENGINE AND TURBINES	2.13	5.34	1.83	2.88	3.15	6.92	3.75	3.34	3.07	1.15	53
54 FARM MACHINERY	1.40	2.89	1.05	1.82	1.99	3.12	2.66	1.82	1.83	.67	54
55 CONST+MINE+MATRL HANDL EQ	.75	2.27	1.05	.69	1.19	2.88	1.66	1.27	.93	2.29	55
56 METALWORKING MACHINERY	.84	.84	.69	1.05	.77	.68	.99	.82	.78		56
57 SPECIAL INDUSTRIAL MACH.	2.81	4.16	2.42	2.11	1.84	8.13	.19	1.38	2.16		57

NOVEMBER 1973 FORECAST

		PRODUCTIVITY (OUTPUT PER EMPLOYED PERSON)						ANNUAL GROWTH RATES				
		71-85	71-75	75-80	80-85	71-73	73-83	73-75	73-78	75-78	78-83	
58	GENERAL INDUSTRIAL MACH.	2.07	2.72	1.94	1.68	5.99	1.35	-.55	.87	1.81	1.83	58
59	MISC. MACHINERY AND SHOPS	3.79	4.70	3.46	3.40	6.63	3.30	2.78	3.20	3.49	3.39	59
60	OFFICE AND COMPUTING MACH	6.48	8.91	5.64	5.38	12.72	5.41	5.10	5.51	5.78	5.32	60
61	SERVICE INDUSTRY MACH.	3.86	4.86	3.69	3.22	5.63	3.66	4.10	3.89	3.75	3.42	61
62	TRANSFORMRS,SWTHGR,EL MSR	2.03	2.05	2.11	1.93	2.18	2.03	1.92	2.02	2.09	2.04	62
63	ELECTRIC APP. + MOTORS	3.08	4.94	2.48	2.20	6.50	2.60	3.38	2.83	2.46	2.37	63
64	HOUSEHOLD APPLIANCES	3.13	4.05	2.93	2.60	5.13	2.86	2.96	2.93	2.91	2.79	64
65	ELEC. LIGHTING + WIRING	.99	-.69	1.48	1.86	-2.81	1.57	1.42	1.42	1.42	1.71	65
66	RADIO-, TV-SETS AND PHONO	4.97	6.66	4.40	4.20	8.21	4.50	5.12	4.67	4.38	4.32	66
67	COMMUNICATION EQUIPMENT	1.61	2.02	1.68	1.23	1.77	1.68	2.27	1.99	1.81	1.37	67
68	ELECTRONIC COMPONENTS	5.69	6.33	5.37	5.49	7.65	5.32	5.00	5.19	5.31	5.45	68
69	BATTERIES,X-RAY EQ.,ETC.	.40	.87	.32	.10	1.01	.35	.73	.51	.37	.18	69
70	MOTOR VEHICLES	1.03	1.99	.94	.36	2.24	.95	1.74	1.34	1.06	.56	70
71	AIRCRAFT	2.68	1.63	3.19	3.02	-.22	3.21	3.47	3.30	3.18	3.13	71
72	SHIPS AND BOATS	2.35	2.63	2.24	2.24	2.70	2.32	2.57	2.26	2.06	2.37	72
73	RAILROAD EQUIPMENT	4.15	9.76	2.13	1.70	17.53	2.00	1.99	2.13	2.13	1.93	73
74	TRAILERS,CYCLES	1.57	2.78	1.10	1.08	4.08	1.19	1.47	1.33	1.23	1.04	74
75	ENGR. + SCIENTIFIC INSTR.	2.38	3.16	1.92	2.22	3.56	2.19	2.76	2.13	1.71	2.25	75
76	MECH. MEASURING DEVICES	1.22	1.63	1.07	1.05	4.16	.66	-.91	.13	.82	1.18	76
77	SURGICAL + MEDICAL INSTR.	3.08	4.19	2.57	2.71	6.17	2.50	2.20	2.26	2.29	2.73	77
78	OPTICAL AND PHOTOGRAPHIC	4.83	5.20	4.93	4.45	4.68	4.97	5.72	5.28	4.98	4.66	78
79	MISC. MANUFACTURING	3.94	4.65	3.53	3.78	6.06	3.53	3.25	3.32	3.36	3.75	79
80	RAILROADS	6.53	7.84	6.29	5.72	9.19	6.19	6.48	6.40	6.35	5.98	80
81	TRUCKING	2.67	3.64	2.51	2.07	4.55	2.45	2.73	2.61	2.52	2.29	81
82	OTHER TRANSPORT	-.00	1.05	-.44	-.40	3.04	.52	-.94	-.31	.58	-.31	82
83	AIRLINES	3.42	4.83	3.23	2.39	5.05	3.22	4.11	3.70	3.42	2.75	83
84	WHOLESALE + RETAIL TRADE	1.59	2.12	1.37	1.28	3.29	1.28	.96	1.15	1.27	1.42	84
85	COMMUNICATION	3.08	3.24	3.39	2.66	3.98	3.00	3.29	3.17	3.09	2.83	85
86	FINANCE AND SERVICES	2.65	1.22	2.62	2.45	2.51	.30	1.28	.14	.29	.47	86
87	ELECTRIC UTILITIES	2.71	3.62	2.62	2.08	4.21	2.58	-.07	3.17	2.82	2.33	87
88	NAT. GAS, WATER AND SEWER	3.91	4.79	3.75	3.37	5.68	3.68	3.02	3.86	3.82	3.51	88

7 FRUIT,VEGETABLES,OTH CROPS

NOVEMBER 1973 FORECAST

```
OUTPUT(+)      ———
CONSUMPTION(*) -----
IMPORTS(0)     ———
EXPORTS(X)     ·······
```

	1955	1956	1957	1958	1959	1960	1961	1962	1963	1964	1965	1966
OUTPUT(+)	7274.	7821.	7478.	7137.	8325.	8148.	9106.	9151.	9805.	9815.	10325.	10968.
CONSUMPTION(*)	3990.	4089.	3864.	4014.	3933.	4201.	4070.	4069.	4190.	4046.	4188.	4089.
IMPORTS(0)	0.	0.	0.	-323.	-368.	-354.	-354.	-359.	-404.	-445.	-503.	-560.
EXPORTS(X)	0.	0.	0.	195.	234.	221.	235.	233.	267.	269.	310.	322.

	1967	1968	1969	1970	1971	1972	1973	1974	1975	1976	1977	1978
OUTPUT(+)	11321.	11128.	11020.	11204.	11389.	12231.	12748.	12759.	13219.	13467.	13815.	14073.
CONSUMPTION(*)	4240.	4226.	4228.	4294.	4265.	4305.	4382.	4388.	4460.	4447.	4521.	4555.
IMPORTS(0)	-557.	-610.	-619.	-696.	-630.	-676.	-716.	-712.	-745.	-761.	-788.	-809.
EXPORTS(X)	331.	291.	330.	352.	367.	351.	380.	399.	402.	420.	429.	440.

	1979	1980	1981	1982	1983	1984	1985
OUTPUT(+)	14406.	14706.	14987.	15303.	15569.	15827.	16091.
CONSUMPTION(*)	4602.	4636.	4668.	4712.	4735.	4758.	4781.
IMPORTS(0)	-839.	-865.	-891.	-919.	-944.	-968.	-992.
EXPORTS(X)	448.	458.	467.	475.	485.	493.	500.

```
0.   20.   40.   60.   80.   100.   120.   140.   160.   180.   200.   220.   240.
```

```
1955
1956
1957
1958
1959
1960
1961
1962
1963
1964
1965
1966
1967
1968
1969
1970
1971
1972
1973
1974
1975
1976
1977
1978
1979
1980
1981
1982
1983
1984
1985
```

1 AGRICULTURE   NOVEMBER 1973 FORECAST

OUTPUT69$(+) ———
EMPLOYMENT(*) -·-·-
INVESTMENT(O) -----
PRODUCTIVITY(X) ········

Year	OUTPUT69$(+)	EMPLOYMENT(*)	INVESTMENT(O)	PRODUCTIVITY(X)
1955	51319.	6768.	4147.	8.
1956	53358.	6663.	3463.	8.
1957	51052.	6264.	3477.	8.
1958	52760.	5890.	4245.	9.
1959	55555.	5866.	4204.	9.
1960	56211.	5763.	3556.	10.
1961	56369.	5510.	3792.	11.
1962	58793.	5259.	3924.	11.
1963	62205.	5005.	4590.	12.
1964	62110.	4839.	4640.	13.
1965	63805.	4686.	5227.	14.
1966	64572.	4430.	5739.	15.
1967	66432.	4174.	6077.	16.
1968	68668.	4151.	5338.	17.
1969	69442.	3951.	5090.	18.
1970	70245.	3816.	5131.	18.
1971	71755.	3744.	5368.	19.
1972	69183.	3546.	4839.	20.
1973	72937.	3415.	5864.	21.
1974	74763.	3274.	6315.	23.
1975	74466.	3152.	6332.	25.
1976	79205.	3035.	6285.	26.
1977	81050.	2927.	6256.	28.
1978	82590.	2825.	6385.	29.
1979	84232.	2725.	6386.	31.
1980	85853.	2629.	6506.	33.
1981	87399.	2538.	6491.	34.
1982	89080.	2451.	6595.	36.
1983	90627.	2366.	6673.	38.
1984	92129.	2283.	6790.	40.
1985	93655.	2203.	6853.	43.

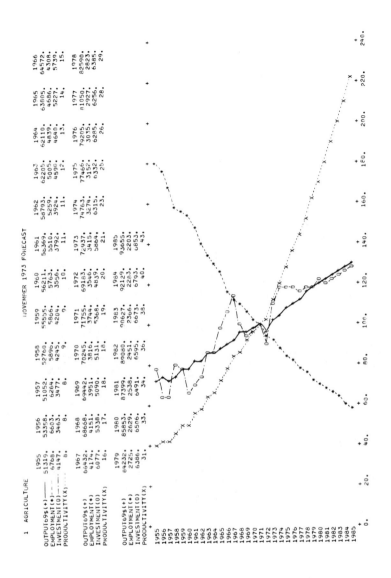

NOVEMBER 1973 FORECAST
SELLER 110 PUMPS, COMPRESSORS, BLOWERS

	1971	1973	1975	1980	1965	71-85	73-85	75-80	80-85	73-85
BUYER										
110 PUMPS,COMPRESSORS,BLOWERS	181.3	250.7	277.9	307.8	341.1	4.5	5.2	2.0	2.1	2.6
15 CRUDE PETROLEUM, NAT. GAS	37.8	44.3	48.4	59.5	70.6	4.5	4.5	4.1	3.4	3.9
19 MAINTENANCE CONSTRUCTION	75.9	86.9	95.6	116.7	137.8	4.3	4.6	4.0	3.3	3.8
48 PAPER AND PAPERBOARD MILLS	37.5	43.7	47.6	56.6	63.8	3.8	4.3	3.5	2.4	3.2
83 STEEL	22.6	27.6	28.6	30.4	31.4	2.3	1.7	1.2	.7	1.1
94 PLUMBING + HEATING EQUIP.	26.5	29.0	28.8	33.5	35.8	2.5	1.9	3.1	2.2	2.1
95 STRUCTURAL METAL PRODUCTS	29.5	37.1	38.5	46.8	54.8	4.5	3.9	2.7	2.9	3.3
102 ENGINES AND TURBINES	40.2	54.6	61.6	78.4	95.6	6.2	6.0	4.8	4.1	4.7
103 FARM MACHINERY	30.0	35.9	39.1	42.5	46.7	3.2	1.7	2.8	1.9	2.2
104 CONSTR,MINE,OILFIELD MACH	73.0	93.5	105.3	121.2	139.5	4.6	5.9	2.6	2.8	2.2
106 MACH. TOOLS, METAL CUTTING	27.1	46.5	52.2	59.4	68.9	6.7	5.9	2.6	3.0	3.3
108 OTHER METAL WORKING MACH	17.6	23.0	25.3	29.0	32.7	4.4	4.9	2.7	2.4	2.9
109 SPECIAL INDUSTRIAL MACH	22.0	27.5	32.0	35.6	39.0	4.4	7.6	2.1	1.8	2.9
116 SERVICE INDUSTRY MACHINERY	38.9	52.5	60.6	82.5	106.4	7.2	7.2	6.2	5.1	5.9
137 SHIP AND BOAT BUILDING	92.5	121.5	135.1	161.0	191.8	5.2	5.3	6.5	3.5	3.3
SUM OF INTERMEDIATE FLOWS	932.3	1206.0	1329.3	1560.2	1601.1	4.7	4.9	3.2	2.9	3.3
SALES TO CAPITAL EQUIPMENT BUYERS										
1 AGRICULTURE	16.7	17.6	18.3	17.2	16.8	.0	2.0	-1.2	-.5	-.4
3 MINING	80.2	105.1	106.8	114.0	158.1	2.7	.8	1.3	.7	1.0
5 PETROLEUM AND GAS	36.2	45.4	47.8	54.5	59.2	3.5	2.6	2.6	1.6	2.2
27 PAPER+PROD., EX.CONTAINERS	63.5	94.8	109.1	124.8	134.6	5.4	7.0	2.7	1.5	2.2
31 INDUSTRIAL CHEMICALS	92.2	145.6	165.8	182.3	197.3	5.6	6.5	1.9	1.6	2.5
34 PLASTICS AND SYNTHETICS	130.4	205.4	244.8	275.7	311.6	6.0	8.6	2.4	2.5	3.4
38 PETROLEUM REFINING	44.3	44.6	54.3	60.0	67.4	3.0	9.6	2.0	2.3	3.4
41 PLASTIC PRODUCTS	17.5	33.3	34.7	52.1	65.1	9.4	7.5	5.9	4.5	5.6
45 STONE AND CLAY PRODUCTS	38.5	65.2	58.9	60.2	62.7	3.2	-5.0	.4	-.0	-.3
46 IRON AND STEEL	98.4	177.9	224.2	186.3	194.5	4.8	11.6	-3.7	1.4	.7
47 NON-FERROUS METALS	87.4	131.6	156.3	159.0	170.3	4.8	8.6	.3	.9	2.1
70 MOTOR VEHICLES	53.0	107.3	111.1	122.3	133.6	6.6	1.7	1.9	1.8	1.8
86 FINANCE AND SERVICES	27.1	39.4	41.5	41.9	40.1	2.7	2.5	-.2	-.9	-.1
87 ELECTRIC UTILITIES	249.5	335.0	347.6	436.5	508.5	5.1	1.8	4.6	3.1	3.5
88 NAT. GAS, WATER AND SEWER	111.9	80.0	91.6	99.1	108.5	-.2	6.8	1.6	1.8	2.4
SUM OF SALES TO EQUIPMENT	1410.6	1992.3	2231.7	2429.0	2672.1	4.6	5.7	1.7	1.9	2.4
SALES TO CONSTRUCTION ACTIVITIES										
1 RESIDENTIAL CONSTRUCTION	97.3	121.0	99.5	114.7	128.5	2.0	-10.3	3.0	2.3	.5
2 ADDITIONS AND ALTERATIONS	15.9	17.0	17.2	20.0	22.5	2.5	-2.6	2.4	2.1	2.3
4 INDUSTRIAL CONSTRUCTION	42.7	80.6	77.2	72.0	72.5	4.2	-2.6	-.2	-.3	-.4
5 OFFICES	58.7	65.4	68.8	79.3	86.9	2.8	2.9	2.9	1.8	2.4
6 STORES,RESTAURANTS,GARAGES	47.9	56.4	55.5	61.9	65.0	2.2	-2.9	2.2	1.0	1.2
8 EDUCATIONAL BUILDINGS	32.9	32.2	34.0	38.4	42.5	1.8	2.6	2.5	2.0	2.3
10 MISCELLANEOUS BUILDINGS	33.1	38.4	44.3	54.7	64.1	4.7	7.1	4.2	3.2	4.3
15 ELECTRIC UTILITIES	55.7	65.4	67.4	81.7	97.5	4.0	1.5	3.8	3.5	3.3
SUM OF SALES TO CONSTRUCTION	421.4	518.2	507.9	589.8	642.8	3.0	-1.0	2.7	2.0	1.8
SALES TO FINAL DEMAND										
187 DEFENSE EXPENDITURES	49.3	49.3	49.3	54.2	59.2	1.3	.0	1.9	1.7	1.5
193 CHANGE IN INVENTORIES	-50.7	181.5	90.6	47.8	38.2	.0	-30.5	-14.5	-4.5	-13.0
194 EXPORTS	377.7	401.3	597.8	670.4	733.2	4.7	19.9	2.3	1.8	5.0
195 IMPORTS	-112.0	-158.4	-169.1	-199.3	-247.4	5.7	3.3	3.3	4.3	3.7
SUM OF SALES TO FINAL DEMAND	277.3	498.2	593.0	592.8	606.2	5.6	9.7	-.0	.4	1.8
TOTAL	3041.6	4204.7	4662.0	5162.8	5722.1	4.5	5.2	2.0	2.1	2.6

Index

Index

About the Authors

Clopper Almon, Jr. is professor of economics at the University of Maryland and director of the Interindustry Forecasting Project. He received the B.A. from Vanderbilt University and the M.A. and the Ph.D. from Harvard University. He is the author of two previous books, *The American Economy to 1975* (New York: Harper and Row, 1966) and *Matrix Methods in Economics* (Reading, Mass.: Addison-Wesley, 1967).

Margaret B. Buckler is a faculty research assistant for the Interindustry Forecasting Project, the University of Maryland. She received the B.A. and the M.A. from the University of Maryland.

Lawrence M. Horwitz received the A.B. from the University of Michigan and the M.A. from the University of Maryland, where he is a candidate for the Ph.D. He is a member of the National Association of Business Economists and the American Economic Association.

Thomas C. Reimbold received the B.S. in mechanical and industrial engineering from Polytechnikum (Friedberg, Hessen, Germany), the M.B.A. in marketing from the University of Akron, and the M.A. in economics from the University of Maryland where he is a candidate for the Ph.D. He is a member of the American Economic Association and Verein Deutscher Engenieure, Frankfurt, Germany.